ANNUAL EDITIONS

Violence and Terrorism 10/11
Twelfth Edition

EDITOR

Thomas J. Badey
Randolph-Macon College

Thomas J. Badey is a professor of Political Science and the director of the International Studies Program at Randolph-Macon College in Ashland, Virginia. He received a BS in Sociology from the University of Maryland (University College) in 1986 and an MA in political science from the University of South Florida in 1987. In 1993 he received a PhD in political science from the *Institut für Politische Wissenschaft* of the *Ruprecht-Karls Universität* in Heidelberg, Germany. He served as a security policeman in the United States Air Force from 1979 to 1988 and was stationed in the United States, Asia, and the Middle East. Dr. Badey regularly teaches courses on international terrorism and Homeland Security and has written a number of articles on the subject. He is also the editor of the McGraw-Hill Contemporary Learning Series *Annual Editions: Homeland Security.*

 **Higher Education**

Boston   Burr Ridge, IL   Dubuque, IA   New York   San Francisco   St. Louis
Bangkok   Bogotá   Caracas   Kuala Lumpur   Lisbon   London   Madrid   Mexico City
Milan   Montreal   New Delhi   Santiago   Seoul   Singapore   Sydney   Taipei   Toronto

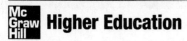

The McGraw·Hill Companies

Mc Graw Hill Higher Education

ANNUAL EDITIONS: VIOLENCE AND TERRORISM, TWELFTH EDITION

Published by McGraw-Hill, a business unit of The McGraw-Hill Companies, Inc., 1221 Avenue of the Americas, New York, NY 10020.

Some ancillaries, including electronic and print components, may not be available to customers outside the United States.

Annual Editions® is a registered trademark of the McGraw-Hill Companies, Inc.
Annual Editions is published by the **Contemporary Learning Series** group within the McGraw-Hill Higher Education division.

1 2 3 4 5 6 7 8 9 0 QWD/QWD 0 9

ISBN 978–0–07–812761–8
MHID 0–07–812761–0
ISSN 1096–4274

Managing Editor: *Larry Loeppke*
Managing Editor: *Faye Schilling*
Developmental Editor: *Dave Welsh*
Editorial Assistant: *Cindy Hedley*
Production Service Assistant: *Rita Hingtgen*
Permissions Coordinator: *DeAnna Dausener*
Senior Marketing Manager: *Julie Keck*
Marketing Communications Specialist: *Mary Klein*
Marketing Coordinator: *Alice Link*
Project Manager: *Joyce Watters*
Design Specialist: *Tara McDermott*
Senior Administrative Assistant: *Mary Foust*
Senior Production Supervisor: *Laura Fuller*
Cover Design: *Kristine Jubeck*

Compositor: Laserwords Private Limited
Cover Images: AE Violence and Terrorism—Department of Defense (inset); © Corbis/RF (background)

Library in Congress Cataloging-in-Publication Data
Main entry under title: Annual Editions: Violence and Terrorism. 2010/2011.
   1. Violence and Terrorism—Periodicals. I. Badey, Thomas J., *comp.* II. Title: Violence and Terrorism.
658'.05

www.mhhe.com

Editors/Academic Advisory Board

Members of the Academic Advisory Board are instrumental in the final selection of articles for each edition of ANNUAL EDITIONS. Their review of articles for content, level, and appropriateness provides critical direction to the editors and staff. We think that you will find their careful consideration well reflected in this volume.

ANNUAL EDITIONS: Violence and Terrorism 10/11
12th Edition

EDITOR

Thomas J. Badey
Randolph-Macon College

ACADEMIC ADVISORY BOARD MEMBERS

Preface

The election of President Obama signals a possible change in U.S. counterterrorism policy. The closing of the military prison at Guantanamo Bay indicates a potential shift from a military approach to counterterrorism, dominant during the Bush administration, back to a law enforcement approach advocated in the early years of the Clinton administration. Recent bombings in Iraq, a surge in violence in Afghanistan, and new violence in Asia and Africa remind us that the global war on terrorism is far from over. Violence and terrorism affect our lives and will continue to affect our lives well into this century. Political, economic, social, ethnic, and religious strife, fueled by the availability of weapons, advances in technology, and an ever-present international media, set the stage for the future of violence and terrorism. The only real defense against terrorism is to try to understand terrorism. Thus, *Annual Editions: Violence and Terrorism 10/11* continues to address some basic questions: Who are the terrorists? Why does terrorism occur? What tactics do they use? How can or should governments respond?

The selections for this edition of *Annual Editions: Violence and Terrorism* were chosen to reflect a diversity of issues, actors, and points of view. This revision incorporates many new articles that reflect the changes that have occurred since the previous edition was published. While, as always, influenced by recent events, this volume endeavors to maintain sufficient regional and topical coverage to provide students with a broad perspective as a basis for understanding contemporary political violence. Articles for this introductory reader were chosen from a variety of sources and reflect diverse writing styles. It is our hope that this broad selection will provide easy accessibility at various levels and will thus stimulate interest and discussion. In addition to the aforementioned considerations, elements such as timeliness and readability of the articles were important criteria used in their selection.

This anthology is organized into ten units. Unit 1 attempts to address the complex task of conceptualizing terrorism. It underlines the difficulty of finding a commonly accepted definition of the problem. Unit 2 examines the methods employed by terrorists. It focuses on tactics used by terrorist organizations. Unit 3 examines the role of state sponsors in international terrorism. Focusing primarily on so called "rogue states," this unit sheds light on the complex and changing relationship between sponsor states and terrorist organizations. Unit 4 provides an overview of some of the major actors in contemporary international terrorism. Shifting the focus to the domestic front, Unit 5 examines terrorism in America. In addition to articles on domestic terrorism, it highlights the potential impact of policies to combat terrorism on personal freedom and civil liberties. Unit 6 focuses on the role that the media plays in terrorism and points to potential consequences of increased terrorist exploitation of the media. Unit 7 examines the complex relationship between terrorism and religion and focuses on how religion is used by some to justify contemporary political violence. Unit 8 looks at the role of women, who continue to play an important and increasingly active role in contemporary political violence. Unit 9 examines how governments respond to terrorism, and finally, Unit 10 explores the future of international terrorism.

This anthology provides a broad overview of the major issues associated with political violence and terrorism. It is our hope that *Annual Editions: Violence and Terrorism* will introduce students to the study of terrorism and serve as a stimulus for further exploration of this vital topic.

I would like to thank the many scholars who provided feedback and submitted suggestions for articles to be included in this volume. I am also particularly grateful to a group of undergraduate students who worked as my research assistants on this project. Jessica Armstrong, Shafer Busch, Brittney Cox, Heather Lennon, and Jessee Perry helped review the numerous articles that were submitted for consideration. They provided valuable insights, and above all a critical students' perspective, which made the job of selecting articles for this edition much easier. I am also grateful to Colleen Hutchison, my administrative assistant for her work on this project. I hope that you, the reader, will take the time to fill out the article rating form in the back of this anthology so we can continue to improve future editions.

Thomas J. Badey
Editor

Contents

UNIT 1
The Concept of Terrorism

UNIT 2
Tactics of Terrorism

The concepts in bold italics are developed in the article. For further expansion, please refer to the Topic Guide.

UNIT 3
State-Sponsored Terrorism

The concepts in bold italics are developed in the article. For further expansion, please refer to the Topic Guide.

UNIT 4
International Terrorism

UNIT 5
Terrorism in America

The concepts in bold italics are developed in the article. For further expansion, please refer to the Topic Guide.

UNIT 6
Terrorism and the Media

The concepts in bold italics are developed in the article. For further expansion, please refer to the Topic Guide.

UNIT 7
Terrorism and Religion

UNIT 8
Women and Terrorism

The concepts in bold italics are developed in the article. For further expansion, please refer to the Topic Guide.

UNIT 9
Government Response

UNIT 10
Future Threats

The concepts in bold italics are developed in the article. For further expansion, please refer to the Topic Guide.

The concepts in bold italics are developed in the article. For further expansion, please refer to the Topic Guide.

Topic Guide

This topic guide suggests how the selections in this book relate to the subjects covered in your course. You may want to use the topics listed on these pages to search the web more easily.

On the following pages a number of websites have been gathered specifically for this book. They are arranged to reflect the units of this Annual Edition. You can link to these sites by going to *http://www.mhcls.com.*

All the articles that relate to each topic are listed below the bold-faced term.

Internet References

The following Internet sites have been selected to support the articles found in this reader. These sites were available at the time of publication. However, because websites often change their structure and content, the information listed may no longer be available. We invite you to visit http://www.mhcls.com for easy access to these sites.

Annual Editions: Violence and Terrorism 10/11

General Sources

Arab.Net Contents
http://www.arab.net/sections/contents.html

Web links to 22 Arab countries ranging from Algeria through Yemen. It includes a search engine.

DefenseLINK (U.S. government)
http://www.defenselink.mil

The Department of Defense's public affairs online service provides DoD news releases and other public affairs documents. This is a gateway to other DoD agencies (e.g., Secretary of Defense, Army, Navy, Air Force, Marine Corps).

FACSNET: "Understanding Faith and Terrorism"
http://www.facsnet.org/issues/faith/terrorism.php3#

This site is guided by the most current research from the nation's top institutions. FACS translates their knowledge and tailors it specifically for the educational needs of journalists.

Foreign Policy Association—Terrorism
http://www.fpa.org/newsletter_info2478/newsletter_info.htm

This page is a comprehensive source of information about terrorism and a gateway to the vast amount of information on the subject.

International Network Information Center at University of Texas
http://inic.utexas.edu

This gateway has many pointers to international sites, organized into African, Asian, Latin American, Middle East, Russian, and East European subsections.

ISN International Relations and Security Network
http://www.isn.ethz.ch

This is a one-stop information network for security and defense studies.

Israel Ministry of Foreign Affairs—The Exploitation of Palestinian Women for Terrorism
http://www.mfa.gov.il/mfa/go.asp?MFA0//10

This official website of the Israeli government chronicles the use of women by Arab terrorists as agents of terror.

U.S. Central Intelligence Agency Home Page
http://www.cia.gov

This site includes publications of the CIA, such as the *1996 World Fact Book; 1995 Fact Book on Intelligence; Handbook of International Economic Statistics, 1996;* and *CIA Maps.*

U.S. White House
http://www.whitehouse.gov

This official Web page for the White House includes information on the President and Vice President and what's new. See especially The Virtual Library and Briefing Room (today's releases) for hot topics and latest federal statistics.

UNIT 1: The Concept of Terrorism

Political Science Resources/International Relations
http://www.lib.umich.edu/govdocs/psintl.html

The Documents Center of the University of Michigan contains material relating to violence and terrorism under several headings, including Peace and Conflict and Human Rights. This site includes simulations.

Terrorism: Background and Threat Assessment Links
http://www.fas.org/irp/threat/terror.htm

This site provides documents covering a broad range of topics on terrorism.

The Terrorism Research Center
http://www.terrorism.com

The Terrorism Research Center is dedicated to informing the public of the phenomena of terrorism and information warfare. This site features essays and thought pieces on current issues, as well as links to other terrorism documents, research, and resources. Navigate the site by clicking on the area of interest.

UNIT 2: Tactics of Terrorism

Evolving Tactics of Terrorism
http://www.iiss.org/conferences/counter-terrorism-series/evolving-tactics-of-terrorism/

The International Institute for Strategic Studies provides a detailed look at how terrorism tactics are evolving.

The Al Qaeda Manual
http://www.usdoj.gov/ag/manualpart1_1.pdf

This website contains a copy of an Al Qaeda training manual which was found in Manchester, England by the Metropolitan Police during a search of an Al Qaeda member's home.

Centers for Disease Control
http://www.cdc.gov/mmwr/preview/mmwrhtml/rr4904a1.htm

This website outlines the CDC's strategic plan to address the deliberate dissemination of biological or chemical agents by terrorists.

UNIT 3: State-Sponsored Terrorism

Council on Foreign Relations
http://www.cfr.org/issue/458/state_sponsors_of_terrorism_html

This site provides a regional update on terrorist activities around the world. It provides an overview to a country's/region's ties to terrorism and more.

State Department's List of State Sponsors of Terrorism
http://www.state.gov/s/ct/rls/crt

This site contains the U.S. Department of State's list of State Sponsors of Terrorism.

Internet References

UNIT 4: International Terrorism

International Association for Counterterrorism and Security Professionals
http://www.iacsp.com/index.html

The International Association for Counterterrorism and Security Professionals was founded in 1992 to meet security challenges facing the world as it enters an era of globalization in the twenty-first century. The website includes a detailed overview of state-sponsored terrorism.

The International Policy Institute for Counter-Terrorism
http://www.ict.org.il

ICT is a research institute and think tank dedicated to developing innovative public policy solutions to international terrorism. The Policy Institute applies an integrated, solutions-oriented approach built on a foundation of real-world and practical experience.

International Rescue Committee
http://www.intrescom.org

Committed to human dignity, the IRC goes to work in the aftermath of state violence to help people all over the world. Click on Resettlement Problems, IRC Fact Sheet, Emergency Preparedness and Response, and links to other sites.

United Nations Website on Terrorism
http://www.un.org/terrorism

This site gives information on what the United Nations is doing to counter terrorism.

United States Institute of Peace
http://www.usip.org/library/topics/terrorism.html

This site contains links by topical categories to resources primarily in English providing information on terrorism/counter-terrorism.

UNIT 5: Terrorism in America

America's War Against Terrorism
http://www.lib.umich.edu/govdocs/usterror.html

This website by the University of Michigan provides a news chronicle of the September 11, 2001 attacks and the war against terrorism.

Department of Homeland Security
http://www.dhs.gov/dhspublic/index.jsp

The home page for the Department of Homeland Security includes up-to-date news and information.

FBI Home Page
http://www.fbi.gov

The home page for the Federal Bureau of Investigation includes up-to-date news and information and a section on terrorism.

UNIT 6: Terrorism and the Media

Institute for Media, Peace and Security
http://www.mediapeace.org

This web page from the University for Peace is dedicated to examining interactions between media, conflict, peace, and security.

Terrorism Files
http://www.terrorismfiles.org

This is an up-to-date web source for news and editorials covering terrorism and current events.

The Middle East Media Research Institute
http://www.memri.org

The Middle East Media Research Institute (MEMRI) explores the Middle East through the region's media. MEMRI bridges the language gap which exists between the West and the Middle East, providing timely translations of Arabic, Persian, and Turkish media, as well as original analysis of political, ideological, intellectual, social, cultural, and religious trends in the Middle East.

UNIT 7: Terrorism and Religion

Islam Denounces Terrorism
http://www.islamdenouncesterrorism.com

This website was launched to reveal that Islam does not endorse any kind of terror or barbarism and that Muslims share the sorrows of the victims of terrorism. It includes many references to the Koran that preaches tolerance and peace.

Religious Tolerance Organization
http://www.religioustolerance.org/curr_war.htm

This site provides some insight on civil unrest and warfare caused by religious belief.

UNIT 8: Women and Terrorism

Free Muslims Against Terrorism Jihad
http://www.freemuslims.org/news/articles.php?article=140

This site provides information and links such as Press Corner; Resources; and a Blog on the Muslim community.

UNIT 9: Government Response

Counter-Terrorism Page
http://counterterrorism.com

This site contains a summary of worldwide terrorism events, terrorist groups, and terrorism strategies and tactics, including articles from 1989 to the present of American and international origin, plus links to related websites, pictures, and histories of terrorist leaders.

ReliefWeb
http://www.reliefweb.int

This is the UN's Department of Humanitarian Affairs clearinghouse for international humanitarian emergencies. It has daily updates.

The South Asian Terrorism Portal
http://www.satp.org/

This site provides the current happenings of the intelligence community in South Asia.

UNIT 10: Future Threats

Centers for Disease Control and Prevention—Bioterrorism
http://www.bt.cdc.gov

The CDC website provides news, information, guidance, and facts regarding biochemical agents and threats.

UNIT 1

The Concept of Terrorism

Unit Selections

1. **How to Define Terrorism,** Joshua Sinai
2. **What Makes a Terrorist?,** Alan Krueger
3. **The Myth of the Invincible Terrorist,** Christopher C. Harmon

Key Points to Consider

- Why is developing a common definition of terrorism so difficult, yet necessary?

- Why do people become terrorists?

- Can terrorist organizations be defeated?

Student Website
www.mhcls.com

Internet References

Political Science Resources/International Relations
http://www.lib.umich.edu/govdocs/psintl.html
Terrorism: Background and Threat Assessment Links
http://www.fas.org/irp/threat/terror.htm
The Terrorism Research Center
http://www.terrorism.com

Defining and conceptualizing terrorism is an essential first step in understanding it. Despite volumes of literature on the subject, there is still no commonly agreed upon definition of terrorism. The application of former Supreme Court Justice Potter Steward's famous maxim, "I know it when I see it," has led to definitional anarchy. The U.S. government, in its efforts to fight a Global War on Terrorism, has further confounded the definitional problem by a myriad of confusing statements and policies.

Terrorists have also exacerbated this problem. They often portray themselves as victims of political, economic, social, religious, or psychological oppression. By virtue of their courage, their convictions, or their condition, terrorists see themselves as the chosen few, representing a larger population, in the struggle against the perceived oppressors. The actions of the oppressor, real or imagined, against the population they claim to represent, serve as motivation and moral justification for their use of violence. Existing institutional mechanisms for change are deemed either illegitimate or are in the hands of the oppressors. Hence, the terrorists portray themselves as freedom-fighters, as violence becomes the primary means of asserting their interests and the interests of the people they claim to represent.

While arguments among academics and policymakers about how terrorism should be defined continue, most would agree that terrorism involves three basic components: the perpetrator, the victim, and the target of the violence. The perpetrator commits violence against the victim. The victim is used to communicate with or send a message to the intended target. The target is expected to respond to perpetrator. Fear is used as a catalyst to enhance the communication and elicit the desired response.

Defining the problem is an essential first step in the accumulation of statistical data. Definitions impact not only the collection and collation of data, but also its analysis and interpretation. Ultimately, definitions have a profound effect on threat perceptions and policies developed to counter terrorist activities.

The articles in this section provide some insights into terrorists' motivations and the potential causes of violence. The first article in this section attempts to tackle the definitional problem. Joshua Sinai, as many others before him, attempts to address existing ambiguities in definitions of terrorism by offering a 'new definition.' In article two Alan Krueger, a Princeton economist, claims that neither poverty nor lack of education drive people to become terrorists. He argues that participation in terrorism is "a special application of the economics of choice." Finally, in the last article of this section, Christopher C. Harmon highlights some of the potential vulnerabilities of terrorist organizations and challenges the notion that terrorists are invincible.

How to Define Terrorism

JOSHUA SINAI

Terrorist insurgencies, in all their configurations and local conflicts, constitute the primary warfare threat facing the international community. This is especially the case following September 2001, when al Qaida demonstrated that it had world class ambitions to inflict catastrophic damages on its adversaries. In other conflicts, such as the Palestinian-Israeli arena, terrorist rebellions are primarily localized. Because of the world-wide reach of al Qaida and its affiliates, including the spontaneous emergence of al Qaida-inspired groupings and cells in Western Europe, North America, and elsewhere, many nations have been upgrading their homeland security defenses and calling on their academic communities to provide analytical understanding of the nature and magnitude of the threat and how to counteract and resolve it. As a result, terrorism courses, research institutes and certificate programs have been proliferating at universities and other academic institutions around the world. Despite the great attention being devoted to terrorism studies; however, there is no consensus about the most fundamental starting point in terrorism studies: how to define terrorism.

Defining terrorism is the most ambiguous component in terrorism studies, with no universally accepted definition that differentiates attacks against civilian noncombatants or armed military or takes into account the latest trends in terrorist objectives and warfare. In 1983, the U.S. Department of State (DOS) formulated one of the most widely used definitions of terrorism. According to this definition, terrorism is "premeditated, politically motivated violence perpetrated against noncombatant targets by subnational groups or clandestine agents, usually intended to influence an audience."[1] As part of this definition, the term "noncombatant" includes civilians and military personnel who are unarmed or not on duty.[2] The term 'international terrorism' refers to terrorism "involving citizens or the territory of more than one country,"[3] while the term 'terrorist group' refers to "any group practicing, or that has significant subgroups that practice, international terrorism."[4]

The DOS's definition is operationally useful for legal reasons because it provides a legal basis to arrest and indict the perpetrators of such acts. However, at the analytical level, as mentioned above, there are no consensual definitions on what constitutes terrorism. Literature survey by a National Research Council (NRC) panel found there are no "precise general definitions of terrorism", but rather "a multiplicity of overlapping efforts, some more satisfactory than others, but none

analytically sufficient."[5] Experts consider the term an "'essentially contested concept,' debatable at its core, indistinct around its edges, and simultaneously descriptive and pejorative."[6] To remedy this deficiency, the NRC formulated its own working definition, which includes the components of "(a) illegal use or threatened use of force or violence (b) with an intent to coerce societies or governments by inducing fear in their populations (c) typically with political and/or ideological motives and justifications and (d) an 'extra-societal' element, either 'outside' society in the case of domestic terrorism or 'foreign' in the case of international terrorism".[7] This definition has limited utility because other critical variables must be included. For example, in its February 2005 report on *Combating Terrorism* the National Science and Technology Council (NSTC) Subcommittee on the Social, Behavioral and Economic Sciences argues that using the term 'terrorism' "may over-simplify different types of actors, warfare and motivations, encapsulating them in a single group or act so that critical variables are overlooked."[8] Here, the 'overlooked critical variables' include activities that fall below the threshold of violence, such as mobilizing support among a group's radical subculture, providing social welfare services, and even maintaining internet-based websites.

Definitions of terrorism also vary as to whether terrorism includes attacks against only "noncombatant" targets (see DOS definition); or whether terrorism is also a tactic of warfare used by subnational groups against all citizens of a state, whether civilian or military, including attacks against an "armed" military. This has analytical, statistical, and legal implications that need to be addressed and resolved. If terrorism is defined as attacks against only noncombatant targets, then attacks by groups that engage in terrorism against "armed" military targets should not be included, as they are in many cases, in terrorist incident chronology databases.[9] These attacks are military operations, and the perpetrators should be tried in military courts as guerrillas or armed combatants. Alternatively, terrorist attacks against armed targets might be counted separately as "guerrilla" incidents, as they are in the International Policy Institute for Counter-Terrorism's (ICT) terrorist incident chronology database.[10]

In general, guerrilla organizations employ "a combination of military and political methods intended to overthrow the government of a state"[11] while terrorist groups aim to provoke a harsh governmental response in response to their operations, which generally—but not always—take place "off battlefield."

However, distinguishing these insurgent groups is not easy. For example, guerrilla organizations, such as the FARC in Colombia, also engage in terrorist tactics; and terrorist groups such as the Lebanese Hizballah and the Sri Lankan LTTE also consider themselves guerrilla forces that control territory. Nevertheless, both terrorist groups and guerrilla forces engage in continuous warfare that characterizes their operations as a form of insurgency.

Two solutions have been offered to remedy the problem of counting as terrorism either attacks against noncombatant or combatant targets (which would characterize them as guerrilla forces). The first, by Alex Schmid, advocates using as a point of departure the consensus of what constitutes a "war crime",[12] Thus, "[i]f the core of war crimes—deliberate attacks on civilians, hostage taking and the killing of prisoners—is extended to peacetime, we could simply define acts of terrorism as 'peacetime equivalents of war crimes.'"[13] The second solution, by Boaz Ganor, defines terrorism as "a form of violent struggle in which violence is deliberately used against civilians in order to achieve political goals (nationalistic, socioeconomic, ideological, religious, etc.)."[14] He asserts that the use of 'deliberate' targeting of civilians in order to achieve political objectives is what distinguishes a terrorist act from guerrilla warfare, where military units are targeted.[15]

Ganor's formulation is important because it facilitates the outlawing of terrorism by the international community because all nations can agree that the deliberate targeting of civilians is unlawful and should be universally legislated as a crime, whereas attacks against military personnel would be considered part of regular warfare, including the right to militarily retaliate against those perpetrators. Ganor concludes that if acts of terrorism were universally outlawed as a form of warfare by the international community, then terrorist groups would have no choice but to "abandon terrorism and focus on guerrilla activity to achieve their political aims."[16] However, because terrorists are not "guerrilla" warriors, but seek "soft" targets which are easier to attack; they are unlikely to abandon such a tactic against civilians even if it provoked international condemnation.

Second, most definitions of terrorism used in the analytical community focus on the use of terrorism to "influence" or "coerce" the targeted audience by spreading fear beyond the localized incident throughout the wider society.[17] However, as demonstrated by the attacks of 9/11 in New York and Washington and 3/11 in Madrid, groups such as al Qaeda (and its affiliates) also intend to cause their adversaries massive human casualties and physical destruction. Thus, a new component in the definition might include the mass destruction component of terrorism, which is a manifestation of the latest trends in terrorist warfare.

Third, it is necessary not only to define terrorism, but state who may be a "terrorist." According to U.S. statutes, a terrorist group consists of two or more individuals that directly engage in terrorist-related violence (i.e., a combat unit), as well as:

- Belonging to a supporting infrastructure whose activities contribute to violence in terms of:
  - Training
  - Planning
  - Fund raising (soliciting funds)
  - Logistics
  - Individuals who receive military training from terrorist groups
  - Individuals who "aspire" to commit violence in Internet chat rooms
  - Individuals who belong to political, social, or other groups that endorse or espouse terrorist activity
  - Individuals who endorse terrorist activity or persuade others to espouse such activity
    - Engage in incitement to violence (e.g., religious preachers)
  - Individuals who possess knowledge of an imminent operation by others but do not inform the authorities
- Belonging to a terrorist group (or "loosely" affiliated); or
- Being a "self-recruited" individual ("lone wolf") who engages in terrorist activities.

Finally, another definitional problem concerns counter-terrorism and homeland security. These terms are usually placed under the overall umbrella of combating terrorism, with anti-terrorism considered as largely defensive and "homeland security" oriented (e.g., involving law enforcement and judicial measures, as well as critical infrastructure protection), while counter-terrorism is viewed as the offensive (e.g, involving military and other "foreign" measures). However, the transnational nature of contemporary terrorism is leading to the blurring of the distinctions between defending national interests overseas and the "homeland," thereby necessitating a new conceptualization of counter-terrorism and homeland security.

To remedy these problem areas, a new definition of terrorism is hereby proposed: ["Terrorism is a tactic of warfare involving premeditated, politically motivated violence perpetrated by subnational groups or clandestine agents against *any* citizen of a state, whether civilian or military, to influence, coerce, and, if possible, cause mass casualties and physical destruction upon their targets. Unlike guerrilla forces, terrorist groups are less capable of overthrowing their adversaries' governments than of inflicting discriminate or indiscriminate destruction that they hope will coerce them to change policy."]

Hopefully, the new definition proposed in this article will spur new thinking by the analytical, policy, and operational communities involved in countering terrorism. Such thinking will bring to light the issues that should be considered in defining terrorism by individuals and groups against civilian and military targets and allow people to anticipate emerging trends in terrorist warfare. Understanding these issues at the analytical and policy levels will help to upgrade our anticipatory and preemptive operational capabilities to defeat the terrorist threat in all its current and future manifestations.

Notes

1. United States Department of State, *Patterns of Global Terrorism 2003* (Washington, DC: Office of the Secretary of State, Office of the Coordinator for Counterterrorism, April 2004), p. xii.

2. Ibid.

3. Ibid.

4. Ibid.

5. Smelser and Mitchell, eds., *Terrorism: Perspectives from the Behavioral and Social Sciences,* p. 2.

6. Ibid.

7. Ibid.

8. NSTC, *Combating Terrorism: Research Priorities in the Social, Behavioral and Economic Sciences,* p. 7.

9. This argument is also made by the United Nations Office on Drugs and Crime: "If terrorism is defined strictly in terms of attacks on non-military targets, a number of attacks on military installations and soldiers' residences could not be included in the statistics" [http://www.unodc.org/unodc/terrorism_definitions.html]. Interestingly, the MIPT Knowledge Base includes in its statistical data terrorist incidents against military targets, whereas the incident database compiled by the International Policy Institute for Counterterrorism (ICT), in Herzliya, Israel, differentiates between attacks against civilians, which it considers as "terrorist incidents," and attacks by terrorists against military targets, which it considers as "guerrilla incidents."

10. See http://www.ict.org.il.

11. Ian F.W. Beckett, "Terrorism" in *Encyclopedia of Guerrilla Warfare* (New York: Checkmark Books, 2001), p. 231.

12. United Nations Office on Drugs and Crime, "Definitions of Terrorism," http://www.undocs.org/unodc/terrorism_definitions.html.

13. Ibid.

14. Boaz Ganor, *The Counter-Terrorism Puzzle: A Guide for Decision Makers* (New Brunswick, NJ: Transaction Publishers, 2005), p. 17.

15. Ibid., p. 20.

16. Ibid., p. 24.

17. Bruce Hoffman, "Terrorism," *Microsoft® Encarta® Online Encyclopedia* 2005 http://encarta.msn.com © 1997–2005.

Joshua Sinai is a Program Manager for Counterterrorism Studies at The Analysis Corporation, in McLean, VA.

From *Perspectives on Terrorism,* Vol. II, Issue. 4, April 2008, pp. 9–11. Copyright © 2008 by Terrorism Research Initiative. Reprinted by permission.

What Makes a Terrorist?

It's not poverty and lack of education, according to economic research by Princeton's Alan Krueger. Look elsewhere.

ALAN KRUEGER

In the wake of the terrorist attacks on September 11, 2001, policymakers, scholars, and ordinary citizens asked a key question: What would make people willing to give up their lives to wreak mass destruction in a foreign land? In short, what makes a terrorist?

A popular explanation was that economic deprivation and a lack of education caused people to adopt extreme views and turn to terrorism. For example, in July 2005, after the bombings of the London transit system, British Prime Minister Tony Blair said, "Ultimately what we now know, if we did not before, is that where there is extremism, fanaticism or acute and appalling forms of poverty in one continent, the consequences no longer stay fixed in that continent." The Archbishop of Canterbury, Bill Clinton, Al Gore, King Abdullah of Jordan, Elie Wiesel, and terrorism experts like Jessica Stern of Harvard's Kennedy School also argued that poverty or lack of education were significant causes of terrorism.

Even President George W. Bush, who was initially reluctant to associate terrorism with poverty after September 11, eventually argued, "We fight against poverty because hope is an answer to terror." Laura Bush added, "A lasting victory in the war against terror depends on educating the world's children."

Despite these pronouncements, however, the available evidence is nearly unanimous in rejecting either material deprivation or inadequate education as important causes of support for terrorism or participation in terrorist activities. Such explanations have been embraced almost entirely on faith, not scientific evidence.

Participation in terrorism is just a special application of the economics of occupational choice. Some people choose to become doctors or lawyers, and others pursue careers in terrorism. Economics can help us understand why.

Why is an economist studying terrorism? I have two answers. First, participation in terrorism is just a special application of the economics of occupational choice. Some people choose to become doctors or lawyers, and others pursue careers in terrorism. Economics can help us understand why.

The second answer is that, together with Jörn-Steffen Pischke, now at the London School of Economics, I studied the outbreak of hate crimes against foreigners in Germany in the early 1990s. Through this work, I concluded that poor economic conditions do not seem to motivate people to participate in hate crimes.

The modern literature on hate crimes began with a remarkable 1933 book by Arthur Raper titled *The Tragedy of Lynching*. Raper assembled data on the number of lynchings each year in the South and on the price of an acre's yield of cotton. He calculated the correlation coefficient between the two series at -0.532. In other words, when the economy was doing well, the number of lynchings was lower. A pair of psychologists at Yale, Carl Hovland and Robert Sears, cited Raper's work in 1940 to argue that deprivation leads to aggression. People take out their frustrations on others, the researchers hypothesized, when economic conditions are poor.

In the 1930s, Raper assembled data on the number of lynchings each year in the South and on the price of an acre's yield of cotton. He found an inverse relationship: when the economy was doing well, the number of lynchings was lower. Raper's work was influential, but it turned out to be flawed.

While this view seems intuitively plausible, the problem is that it lacks a strong empirical basis. In 2001, Donald Green, Laurence McFalls, and Jennifer Smith published a paper that demolished the alleged connection between economic conditions and lynchings in Raper's data.

Raper had the misfortune of stopping his analysis in 1929. After the Great Depression hit, the price of cotton plummeted and economic conditions deteriorated, yet lynchings continued to fall. The correlation disappeared altogether when more years of data were added.

In 1997, Pischke and I, writing in the *Journal of Human Resources,* studied the incidence of crimes against foreigners across the 543 counties in Germany in 1992 and 1993. We found that the unemployment rate, the level of wages, wage growth, and average education were all unrelated to the incidence of crimes against foreigners.

With evidence from hate crimes as a background, next turn to terrorism. Terrorism does not occur in a vacuum. So to start, I considered evidence from public opinion polls, which can help identify the values and views of those in communities from which terrorism arises.

The Pew Research Center's Global Attitudes Project conducted public opinion surveys in February 2004 in Jordan, Morocco, Pakistan, and Turkey, involving about 1,000 respondents in each country. One of the questions asked was, "What about suicide bombing carried out against Americans and other Westerners in Iraq? Do you personally believe that this is justifiable or not justifiable?" Pew kindly provided me with tabulations of these data by respondents' personal characteristics.

The clear finding was that people with a higher level of education are in general *more* likely to say that suicide attacks against Westerners in Iraq are justified. I have also broken this pattern down by income level. There is no indication that people with higher incomes are less likely to say that suicide-bombing attacks are justified.

Another source of opinion data is the Palestinian Center for Policy and Survey Research, headquartered in Ramallah. The center collects data in the West Bank and Gaza Strip. One question, asked in December 2001 of 1,300 adults, addressed attitudes toward armed attacks on Israeli targets. Options were "strongly support," "support," "oppose," "strongly oppose," or "no opinion."

Support turned out to be stronger among those with a higher level of education. For example, while 26 percent of illiterates and 18 percent of those with only an elementary education opposed or strongly opposed armed attacks, the figure for those with a high school education was just 12 percent. The least supportive group turned out to be the unemployed, 74 percent of whom said they support or strongly back armed attacks. By comparison, the support level for merchants and professionals was 87 percent.

Related findings have been around for a long time. Daniel Lerner, a professor at MIT at the time, published a book in 1958 called *The Passing of Traditional Society* in which he collected and analyzed data on extremism in six Middle Eastern countries. He concluded that "the data obviate the conventional assumption that the extremists are simply the have-nots. Poverty prevails only among the apolitical masses."

> **Daniel Lerner published a book in 1958 that looked at extremism in six Middle Eastern countries. He concluded that 'the data obviate the conventional assumption that the extremists are simply the have-nots. Poverty prevails only among the apolitical masses.'**

Finally, the Palestinian survey included questions about whether people were optimistic for the future. Responses suggested that, just before the outbreak of the second *intifada,* the Palestinian people believed that the economic situation was improving—a judgment consistent with the falling unemployment rate at the time. The *intifada,* then, did not appear to be following dashed expectations for future economic conditions.

Public opinion is one thing; actual participation in terrorism is another. There is striking anecdotal evidence from Nasra Hassan, a United Nations relief worker in the West Bank and Gaza Strip who described interviews with 250 militants and their associates who were involved in the Palestinian cause in the late 1990s. Hassan concluded that "none of them were uneducated, desperately poor, simple-minded, or depressed. Many were middle class and, unless they were fugitives, held paying jobs. Two were the sons of millionaires."

Claude Berrebi, now of the RAND Corporation's Institute for Civil Justice, wrote his dissertation at Princeton on the characteristics of Palestinians from the West Bank and Gaza Strip who were involved in terrorist activities. For example, he compared suicide bombers to the whole male population aged 16 to 50 and found that the suicide bombers were less than half as likely to come from families that were below the poverty line. In addition, almost 60 percent of the suicide bombers had more than a high school education, compared with less than 15 percent of the general population.

> **Among Palestinians, almost 60 percent of the suicide bombers had more than a high school education, compared with less than 15 percent of the general population.**

Jitka Malecková and I performed a similar study of militant members of Hezbollah, a multifaceted organization in Lebanon that has been labeled a terrorist organization by the U.S. State Department. We were able to obtain information on the biographies of 129 deceased *shahids* (martyrs) who had been honored in the group's newsletter, "Al-Ahd." We turned translations by Eli Hurvitz at Tel Aviv University into a dataset and then combined it with information on the Lebanese population from the 1996 Lebanese Ministry of Social Affairs Housing Survey of 120,000 people aged 15 to 38.

These deceased members of Hezbollah had a lower poverty rate than the Lebanese population: 28 percent versus 33 percent.

And Hezbollah members were better educated: 47 percent had a secondary or higher education versus 38 percent of adult Lebanese.

This is also the case, apparently, with al-Qaeda. Marc Sageman, a forensic psychiatrist and former Central Intelligence Agency (CIA) case officer, has written a book titled *Understanding Terror Networks*. He found that a high proportion of members of al-Qaeda were college educated (close to 35 percent) and drawn from skilled professions (almost 45 percent). Research on members of the Israeli extremist group, Gush Emunim, that Maleckóva and I conducted, also pointed in the same direction. Perhaps most definitively, the Library of Congress produced a summary report for an advisory group to the CIA titled, "The Sociology and Psychology of Terrorism: Who Becomes a Terrorist and Why?" which also reached this conclusion—two years before 9/11.

> **Marc Sageman, a forensic psychiatrist and former CIA officer, found that a high proportion of members of al-Qaeda were college educated (close to 35 percent) and drawn from skilled professions (almost 45 percent).**

Why are better educated, more advantaged individuals more likely than others to join terrorist groups? I think of terrorism as a market, with a supply side and a demand side. Individuals, either in small groups or on their own, supply their services to terrorist organizations.

On the supply side, the economics of crime suggests that people with low opportunity costs will become involved in terrorism. Their costs of involvement are lower—that is, they sacrifice less because their prospects of living a rich life are less. In other domains of life, it is those with few opportunities who are more likely to commit property crime and resort to suicide.

However, in the case of the supply of terrorists, while consideration of opportunity cost is not irrelevant, it is outweighed by other factors, such as a commitment to the goals of the terrorist organization and a desire to make a statement. Political involvement requires some understanding of the issues, and learning about those issues is a less costly endeavor for those who are better educated. I argue that better analogies than crime are voting and political protest. Indeed, better educated, employed people are more likely to vote.

On the demand side, terrorist organizations want to succeed. The costs of failure are high. So the organizations select more able participants—which again points to those who are better educated and better off economically.

One of the conclusions from the work of Laurence Iannaccone—whose paper, "The Market for Martyrs," is supported by my own research—is that it is very difficult to effect change on the supply side. People who are willing to sacrifice themselves for a cause have diverse motivations. Some are motivated by nationalism, some by religious fanaticism, some by historical grievances, and so on. If we address one motivation and thus reduce one source on the supply side, there remain other motivations that will incite other people to terror.

That suggests to me that it makes sense to focus on the demand side, such as by degrading terrorist organizations' financial and technical capabilities, and by vigorously protecting and promoting peaceful means of protest, so there is less demand for pursuing grievances through violent means. Policies intended to dampen the flow of people willing to join terrorist organizations, by contrast, strike me as less likely to succeed.

The evidence we have seen thus far does not foreclose the possibility that members of the elite become terrorists because they are outraged by the economic conditions of their countrymen. This is a more difficult hypothesis to test, but, it turns out, there is little empirical support for it.

To investigate the role of societal factors, I assembled data on the country of origin and target of hundreds of significant international terrorist attacks from 1997 to 2003, using information from the State Department. I found that many socioeconomic indicators—including illiteracy, infant mortality, and GDP per capita—are unrelated to whether people from one country become involved in terrorism. Indeed, if anything, measures of economic deprivation, at a country level, have the *opposite* effect from what the popular stereotype would predict, international terrorists are more likely to come from moderate-income countries than poor ones.

One set of factors that I examined did consistently raise the likelihood that people from a given country will participate in terrorism—namely, the suppression of civil liberties and political rights, including freedom of the press, the freedom to assemble, and democratic rights. Using data from the Freedom House Index, for example, I found that countries with low levels of civil liberties are more likely to be the countries of origin of the perpetrators of terrorist attacks. In addition, terrorists tend to attack nearby targets. Even international terrorism tends to be motivated by local concerns.

Additional support for these conclusions comes from research I conducted on the nationalities of foreign insurgents in Iraq. Specifically, I studied 311 combatants, representing 27 countries, who were captured in Iraq. Although the vast majority of insurgents are native Iraqis, motivated by domestic issues, foreigners are alleged to have been involved in several significant attacks. I looked at the characteristics of the countries insurgents came from, and, importantly, of the countries with no citizens captured in Iraq. It turned out that countries with a higher GDP per capita were actually more likely to have their citizens involved in the insurgency than were poorer countries.

Consistent with the work on international terrorist incidents, countries with fewer civil liberties and political rights were more likely to be the birthplaces of foreign insurgents. Distance also mattered, with most foreign insurgents coming from nearby nations. The model predicted that the largest number of insurgents—44 percent—would have emanated from

Saudi Arabia, a nation not known for its protection of civil liberties but with a high GDP per capita.

The evidence suggests that terrorists care about influencing political outcomes. They are often motivated by geopolitical grievances. To understand who joins terrorist organizations, instead of asking who has a low salary and few opportunities, we should ask: Who holds strong political views and is confident enough to try to impose an extremist vision by violent means? Most terrorists are not so desperately poor that they have nothing to live for. Instead, they are people who care so fervently about a cause that they are willing to die for it.

ALAN KRUEGER is the Bendheim Professor of Economics and Public Policy at Princeton and has been an adviser to the National Counterterrorism Center. This article is adapted from his new book, "What Makes a Terrorist: Economics and the Roots of Terrorism," which is based on the Lionel Robbins Memorial Lectures he gave at the London School of Economics in 2006. Copyright © 2007 by Princeton University Press. All rights reserved.

From *The American* Magazine, November/December 2007, pp. 16–24. Copyright © 2007 by American Enterprise Institute. Reprinted by permission. www.american.com

The Myth of the Invincible Terrorist

CHRISTOPHER C. HARMON

We are in a hard march in rough country. The "Global War on Terrorism" requires patience and perseverance, and yet notes of pessimism have become audible among our ranks as citizen-soldiers. This is not surprising. After five years we still have not caught up with fugitive Osama bin Laden. Hard-working military officers wonder aloud if the polity back home will keep supporting its military services. Politicians sound more and more partisan. Academics are no better: A professor at Harvard declares that the president's war on terror has been a "disaster," while at a conference in Washington in September two well-known national security analysts say we are "losing" the war on terror.

In fact, there are good reasons to judge that we are winning this global war against terrorists. And not only because we have arrested or killed two-thirds of the middle- and lower-level leaders, as well as some of their superiors and commanders. It is because terror groups all have vulnerabilities. They are human organizations with human problems; al Qaeda is no exception. For all the talk of the new "flatter" al Qaeda organization, rarely does anyone ever mentions that a *flatter* organization means *less* organization, and that in global war, that cannot help Osama bin Laden.

The history of counterterrorism and counterinsurgency is rich, and the last four or five decades offer good lessons in terrorism's vulnerabilities and counsel on how to exploit them. What follows here is a review of some of those.

Human Factors and Personnel

Terror group leaders have large egos, as they must to order the deaths of multitudes who are innocent and whom they have never met. The more famous and successful terrorist leaders become, the more these egos are likely to swell. The Kurdistan Worker's Party's Abdullah Ocalan, Shining Path's Abimael Guzman, Abu Nidal—these are example of outsized and ferocious egos. But that fact of character has disadvantages, of which one can be fatal. Ego may prevent such leaders from mentoring successors. And, struggle being as it is, when the leader and his cult of personality succumb to arrest or death, the entire organization may collapse.

In September 1992 this came to pass with the arrest of Sendero Luminoso's leader, Dr. Guzman, who called himself "The Fourth Sword of Marxism." His organization had been winning control of immense swaths of the Peruvian countryside. His capture doomed this progress and began a swift regression. Soon the group could boast only a few thousand fighters, and today it is down to a few hundred. Guzman had surrounded himself with female lieutenants but readied none to command in his absence. Only one likely male successor appeared, a field commander, soon caught by the army. Now the group manages an occasional terrorist attack, but its profile has shrunk beyond belief.

Something similar took place with the Kurdistan Worker's Party. Abdullah Ocalan built it from the ground up over a quarter century. He controlled both the military and political wings and made all key decisions. His successes against the Republic of Turkey and its armed forces were impressive and advanced the dream of an independent Kurdistan. But he was caught in early 1999, and the buoyant balloon of his nationalist and Marxist hopes hissed to near-empty. PKK congressed, deciding initially they would not appoint a successor. They then renamed themselves and promised pacific politics. Later, terrorism was renewed; some goes on in southern Turkey now. But PKK/Kongra Gel is not what it once was. It commanded some 30,000 guerrillas but now can muster less than a sixth as many.

These cases support "decapitation" strategies by opponents of terrorism. Former Defense Secretary Caspar Weinberger posed a question in an article a few years back: "Can We Assassinate the Leaders?" His answer was that we can and should assassinate some terror leaders. Whether death by martial or judicial means is necessary, and whether rendering death is even as prudent as capturing a terror group leader, are other questions. What is clear is that decapitation strategies might indeed work. In some cases, they have. The approach uses the terrorist group's most apparent strength against it; if "the great leader" is the center of gravity, then when he is imprisoned, so is the movement.

In the case of the guerrilla and terrorist supergroup "Tamil Tigers," LTTE of Sri Lanka, it is evident that founder and leader, Velupillai Prabhakaran, is the center of gravity, or "the hub of all power and movement," as Clausewitz wrote. A formidable organization under his control, with elaborate finance and logistical networks, a fierce army, a navy, capable suicide bombers, etc.—yet it could all dissipate without Prabhakaran. Members swear loyalty to him, not to LTTE, or the concept of a free land of the Tamils. The clan of the Tigers could dissolve were he killed, or jailed and publishing a plea for peace (as Guzman and Ocalan both did from jail). The master of LTTE apparently has no designated successor. Tamil nationalism is not so strong that it could be certain of holding its militant and terrorist form in his absence.

Decapitating al Qaeda by removing bin Laden and al Zawahiri isn't impossible, but it's likely to be difficult.

Unfortunately, al Qaeda is better structured. It was a stroke of brilliance, shortly before the 9/11 assaults, to merge the Afghans and others at "The Base" controlled by Osama bin Laden with the Egyptians of Ayman al Zawahiri, himself already a practiced terrorist leader. If today one or the other of these two men were to be taken, his counterpart would carry on ably. In this they enjoy some of the strength of an authentic Communist Party, instead of the weakness of a caricature of one, such as Romania's Nico-lae Ceausescu ran before his destruction in 1989. Decapitation of al Qaeda by removing both bin Laden and al Zawahiri is not impossible, but it is likely to remain difficult. And if it were achieved, possibly their old friend, the Taliban chief and favored mullah, Mohammad Omar, would cobble together some of the old organization and take command. Efforts to capture or kill the top leaders should continue, but al Qaeda is most likely to be defeated by other means.

A second problem in terror group personnel management goes through all the levels of an organization and is most intense at the lowest. Underground life has unattractive qualities, and some brutish ones. Terrorism means years on the run, eating poor food, and enduing primitive medical care, with all the stresses of campaigning and doubts about one's family back home. There is, as well, for at least some, the problem of conscience over the horrific things the group is doing to innocent people. It adds up to immense stress and strain. I once had an opportunity to ask Oxford historian Michael Howard how it is that terrorist groups end. "Fatigue," he replied.

Terrorists' memoirs recur to these strains of underground life. Red Brigades depositions published by RAND are one example of how continuous and complex are the pressures of secrecy and attention to details of self-protection. Marc Sage-man, a psychologist and analyst of Muslim terrorists, writes of how personal attitudes may change, too, as the years slip by. Once-powerful motives to join do not always translate into certainty about staying.

The German neo-Nazi Ingo Hasselbach was a rising star in the underground after 1988. He had charisma when the sputtering movement needed it, fighting spirit, and organizational skills. But he gradually became sickened. He felt the total absence of normal friendships, and he disapproved of a lethal 1992 fire-bombing of an immigrants' hostel in Molln. Hasselbach simply dropped out. On the far left, in Germany's underground, the once-formidable Baader-Meinhof crowd experienced its own fatigue. The threat of jail and the patient press of German police operations wore down some outside; jail in Stanheim prison had its own effects on leaders inside the justice system. The "Red

Army Faction"—the last generation of these violent radicals—did not formally quit until 1992, but by then their East German aid and their operational abilities had waned, along with their zeal for the mission and any sense they were making progress with the German public.

I once had an opportunity to ask historian Michael Howard how it is that terrorist groups end. "Fatigue," he replied.

This means that counterterrorists must have well-evolved methods for encouraging defections. Dropouts like Hasselbach are absolutely perfect for the public cause of counterterrorism. They mean a confession of some sort, which itself is a media spectacle. They mean a certain amount of public healing; a defector does not just reject something, he affirms something. They are a body blow to the particular political cause the terrorist once represented. And for intelligence officers, a defector—especially when he or she talks before the illegal organization is able to react defensively—can be priceless.

Against rebellions in the Philippines, captives and defectors have had great public value. The U.S. war of a century ago was not won by butchery on Samar so much as by the ruse of an American general who captured nationalist leader Emilio Agui-naldo. Caught in 1901, he wrote extensively and toured the U.S., a picture of defeat which discredited the notion of resisting the U.S. authorities. A half century later came the Hukbalahap—Marxist-Leninists who emerged within the Philippines after World War II under the command of Luis Taruc. Taruc became worn down and worn out, later writing two books that reveal much about the rebels' problems and inadvertently affirm much about Filipino democracy. Today we see a third kind of example: the Philippines' military intelligence organization has a new top officer, Victor Corpus, a defector from the New People's Army. After coming over to the government side, he became an invaluable asset to the military for all that he knows, and to the public for all that his defection represents. Now he commands a size-able structure dealing with guerrilla and terrorist opponents of the republic. Meanwhile, the NPA is intact, but largely inactive militarily.

Some assume, perhaps encouraged by TV shows and dashes of history, that captives from terror movements might be mined for information by torture. But that practice is foolish, as well as immoral. Skilled commanders think that stress, or cleverness, or understanding the person's greatest psychological needs, are better sources of information. Even kindness may elicit information from certain prisoners. A Nepalese brigadier general told me he has been surprised at how sometimes sitting down to tea with a prisoner could elicit cooperation. Perhaps this is because the Maoist cadres have been briefed to expect barbari-ties or death if they are captured; perhaps it is because others in Nepal's army who first acquired the captive were less kind than the general; perhaps there are always complex motives affecting each prisoner. The point is that counterterrorist forces need strategies for encouraging defections. Then they need a good system for questioning or interrogation. It must be done promptly and thoroughly, by experts. Then the intelligence must be disseminated quickly to those who can act on it before the terrorist group morphs to accommodate its loss. Defectors, when well-managed, can be gems, whether or not their conversions are full. At the very least, they cause the deepest kinds of doubts within their old clandestine organization.

Internal strife is an important factor of undergrounds, but it has largely been ignored, even by analysts of terrorism.

Internal strife is another human factor of undergrounds—though it has largely been ignored, even by terrorism analysts. The grounds for terror group strife may be political, financial, personal, or other. Bloody and sometimes large-scale battles and purges have sometimes gripped the guts of a terrorist organization or larger insurgency. These episodes should give hope to legitimate states fighting to protect sovereignty and citizens.

Before he was mysteriously and repeatedly shot in Iraq four years ago, Sabri al Banna (a.k.a. Abu Nidal) ran a tight ship called "Black June" or Fatah—The Revolutionary Council. Abu Nidal captained a tight ship in part because he was an effective organizer and in part because he was a demented paranoid. In 1987, however, concerns over defectors or leaks swept through the Abu Nidal Organization (ANO)—or swept through the head of Sabri al Banna. In Lebanon and in Libya, ANO murdered its own, most of them young Palestinian men. This formidable organization, "credited" with some 900 external victims throughout the world, was already small; it can only have been wrecked internally by this self-destruction of 600 personnel—more than a third of its strength. Even surviving cadres could be crippled psychologically or operationally by such "discipline," in the way Stalin's army was wrecked by the crazed purges of the mid-1930s. There are several reasons why ANO became almost inoperative in its last years, and surely one of them is the climate of terror *inside*. Counterterrorist psychological operations should further such obsessions.

Other groups making frequent use of terrorism as a strategy have undergone large purges or defections. Even the disciplined, highly-successful LTTE Tigers have been battling a defecting commander named Karuna since April 2004. The dissidents killed four dozen LTTE personnel in 2005. Could it be that Sri Lankan intelligence helped engineer or aggravate this split? Past cases of insurgencies wracked by internal pangs in the 1980s include such communist groups as FARC, or Revolutionary Armed Forces, in Colombia, and the Filipino New People's Army. This September, police uncovered yet another mass grave from the NPA's self-inflicted wounds of the 80s, this time in southern Leyte. The Japanese Red Army staged a self-indulgent bloodbath in December 1971 called the "Snow Murders." It unfolded in (and under) a safe house in the mountains during a Japanese winter when both human isolation and police pressure were afflicting the group. The members were mostly university students with a penchant for fierce debate and Maoist self-criticism. One session of this became particularly nasty. After confessing, or declining to do so sufficiently, loyal members were beaten to death or left outside, bound, to freeze from exposure. The group's founder, a woman named Fusako Shigenobu, had shown fire and charisma, and certainly the Japanese left was well-stocked with Marxist-Leninists ready to fight capitalist success. But imagine how recruiting efforts might go after this kind of news seeped out. The Japanese Red "Army" remained platoon-sized, and today it does not operate.

Terror is ugly, terrorists are morally ugly; this ugliness is weakness in the struggle for public opinion.

Relativists do not understand the depths of their error when they pronounce that "terrorism is just a word for violence we don't like," or "terrorism is a Westerners' epithet." Terrorists are living, breathing men and women using vile but calculated means to make political gains, and it is vital that politicians and academics and police chiefs continue pointing that out. Terror is ugly, making terrorists morally ugly; this ugliness is weakness in the struggle for public opinion. More must be made of that, in the service of truth and of counterterrorism. Another lesson flows from the facts above: Groups and their leaders may well be vulnerable to psychological operations. As circumstances allow, counterterrorism can play up rivals around the leaders, or create fissures between working partners, or throw doubt over loyalties of old comrades.

Violent organizations have pressure points; our challenge is to find and use them. Against the Huks, there were clever psy-ops by Defense Secretary Ramon Magsaysay and American advisor Edward Lansdale of the new CIA, and some of these fueled internal divisions among the communist militants. An example was their handling of "bounties," which states often proffer for bringing in a wanted man "dead or alive." The Philippines published many such offers. But they added with care a few sums which were deliberately lower than the monetary level the targeted terrorists could find honorable. In lowballing rewards for certain fugitives, the government counted on provoking and angering and embarrassing them. Such movements may seem too subtle for war, but Sun Tzu advised that the essence of war is not destroying the enemy but throwing him off balance.

At least one further weakness haunts terror organizations: personal foibles and corruption.

Today, the Abu Sayyaf Group in the Philippines is a rattled outfit. Its founding leader A.A. Janjalani was killed in a government shootout in December 1998. Filipino army pursuit has been relentless, and ASG has lost two more leaders. Almost comically, 19 defections were induced in an April 2002 incident in which the armed forces promised good treatment and air-delivered cheeseburgers to a starving Abu Sayyaf section. Ransom monies, once a source of ASG's power, have become something over which members have had fights, at least once with guns. ASG is no longer a regional apple of Osama's eye; the Saudi benefactor became disillusioned with the organization. He has turned to courting another veiled Filipina, MILF, or Moro Islamic Liberation Front.

At least one further weakness in personnel matters haunts terror organizations: personal foibles and corruption. These can be pointed to, and attacked, whether publicly or covertly, to destroy terrorists' reputations, enhance illusions, spread dissension, create rivalries, and the like.

Michael J. Waller of the Institute of World Politics has rightly called for further use of ridicule in our political warfare. Several cases in counterterrorism come to mind which might support Waller's approach. Apparently that mysterious and terrifying man Abimael Guzman was somewhat demystified in Peruvian eyes after the release of a single videotape: the great man was caught looking silly, dancing drunkenly, at the wrong kind of "party gathering." The prospect for undermining a cocky terrorist in Iraq arose in June 2006 with the surfacing of outtakes of footage for an Abu Musab al Zarqawi video. The cutting-room material showed the insurgent fumbling ignorantly with a weapon he was using as a prop in his hagiographical video. Both examples show that limited release of personal details, or description of a particular unsavory episode in the media, or magnification of these through private channels, may damage a leader's credibility. Quite possibly, ridicule or bad publicity could prod an arrogant terrorist into reckless action, the sort that would blow his cover or reveal something new about his organization.

Cowardice is an underused but potent charge. "Commanders" of terror groups often stash themselves in safety for years in comfortable villas in states such as Syria and Iran, while their troops get fired upon or die in distant operations. What could goad a terrorist leader more easily than a charge of cowardice? And one must not forget sex. Sexual misconduct was one of the firing points that nearly immolated the Japanese Red Army in 1971. Sex is a vulnerable point for certain terror group leaders. A senior officer may be an abuser; a mid-level commander of an insurgency may be one of those who takes virtual sex slaves. Such practices, especially by organizations posturing as religious or ideologically pure, can harm the group if revealed. There are dozens of other kinds of corruption or personal lapses which might be publicly or secretly used against terror group leaders. Yet our media and government often do little to publicize such facts.

Iraq is a regime that was on the U.S. list of state sponsors of terrorists for decades. Yet, I remember exactly where I was when learning for the first time that Saddam Hussein's two sons controlled their own apparatus of personal terrorism. They abducted women, had opponents shot, ordered the torture of Olympic athletes who disappointed Iraq's audiences, etc. Such information profoundly affects one's view of a regime; the information

sticks hard. Before war came in March 2003, why did we not do more to publicize such facts as these for Iraqi audiences? The same holds for Abu Musab al Zarqawi, the recently-deceased insurgent. He did jail time in Jordan for pimping and other acts of petty crime. Such a case history is not unusual. Ali La Pointe, a famed terrorist for the FLN during the Battle of Algiers, had exactly that same profile—pimp and petty criminal—before time and choices remade him as a "nationalist" and "fedayeen." Criminals are in fact commonplace in political undergrounds; Mao wrote of how to understand and use them; we should use their pasts to discredit them.

Tactics and Technology

A second area in which the vulnerabilities of terrorists are evident, and may be exploited, is the tactical and the technical. Terror group leaders are often well-educated, but this does not mean they are good military planners or adept handlers of technology. Even the very good may be deceived by someone more clever.

One top commander of the Algerian FLN forces of the 1950s lusted after a modern radio to control his battles and his men. Learning this, French counterinsurgents obliged him, "mistakenly" leaving behind such a device during their own army operations in the target's sector. The treasured radio was immediately brought to the FLN commander in his cave. Many loyalists died when the French bomb inside detonated. In a second case, French intelligence made skilled use of a defector who called himself Safy-le-Pur. This defector maintained his top-level FLN communications, and coaxed one group of leaders to a "conference"—at which they were all arrested by the French. The tactic had strategic effects: Amirouche, the guerrilla leader most affected by the disaster, began an infuriated hunt for informers that left many dead loyalists in his own region. The purges extended into the adjoining guerrilla region, and hundreds of insurgents killed hundreds of other insurgents. It was all most economical for the French—and disastrous for the FLN. Terrorists are prone to such manipulation.

Sometimes, the terrorists fool themselves. The Irish Republican Army is a deep reservoir of martial skill and lethality. Yet these same "Provos" have had many failures with technology and tactics. Indeed, they have had so many bitter experiences with their own bombs detonating during manufacture, or prematurely during transit, that there is an expression for the disaster—"own goals." The metaphor is taken from the soccer mistake of accidentally knocking the ball into your own net. Sean O'Callaghan, the best-known defector from the IRA, describes a day on which he nearly blew himself up in his bomb-making shop. Three Weathermen once did exactly that, burning down a New York City townhouse.

Terrorist "commanders" often stash themselves in villas while their troops die in distant operations.

12

In war, counterinsurgents sometimes sabotage arms and arrange to get them into terrorist hands. France did this systematically to the FLN by influencing arms factories in Spain and Switzerland where they knew the FLN was buying weapons. The results on insurgent morale can be profound. In the Philippines, during the Huk rebellion, observers of the location of a rebel ammo dump sometimes put sabotaged shells into the collection, knowing the rebels would recover and use the stuff, wounding themselves. Such tricks also cast doubts on all ammo caches, even those untouched by state agents. This is insidious and effective. One can imagine Afghans using such tricks in their war with al Qaeda and the Taliban in remote border regions.

Under calmer circumstances, or in peacetime efforts against a small terrorist group, such actions might be illegal or inappropriate. What can always be tried, however, within bounds in a democratic society, is *neutralization* of weapons, rather than their sabotage. Technical failing in arms and shells is not at all unusual, and so it need not arouse a conviction among the terrorists that their stores have been tampered with. And yet technical failings can wreck tactical attacks, embarrass the users, lead to the exposure and capture of the gunmen, or provoke internal dissent about the "idiots down in logistics."

It appears that the FBI may have done this to snuff one Libyan ploy of the 1980s. Tripoli was paying a black Chicago street gang called El Rukns to make trouble within the United States, and at some point the group tried to use a shoulder-launched weapon against an airplane at O'Hare Airport. The missile was inert. A series of later cases has come to light as varied groups pursue ground-to-air weapons to destroy airliners. In the U.S. and Britain, for example, individual buyers or technicians for the IRA have repeatedly been foiled as they've sought to acquire means of shooting down British helicopters. Stings by undercover G-men have often been the reason.

Terrorist failings may easily disable a good plan. A timely leak from inside a terror cell can wreck a tactical plan months or years in preparation. It is stunning to consider what could have occurred had we properly questioned and jailed even two of the foreign hijackers "sleeping" here before 9/11 but stopped by police on driving charges or for other petty infractions. With luck, we might have had a red-hot warning, or at least "connected some dots." Instead, al Qaeda's plotting continued.

Stings by undercover G-men have kept the IRA from acquiring the means to shoot down British helicopters.

It is clear that having an agent inside a terror organization can foil operations. Once Sean O'Callaghan weakened in his IRA convictions, he did not try to poison others' morale, or shoot his comrades, but he did make sure important plots failed. He disabled a 1983 attempt on the lives of the Charles and Diana. In the next year, O'Callaghan betrayed the arriving arms ship *Valhalla* carrying $2 million worth of arms to the IRA from Boston. He did this without blowing uncovered as an informer

for the Irish police. American examples of such penetrations and disruptions include the work of Larry Grathwohl, who got inside the Weathermen, neutralized several of their operations, and walked away to write memoirs (*Bringing Down America*, Arlington House, 1976). Not many have such coolness and skill. But this is skill that can be developed by intelligence agencies that demand results and have political support to attain results.

A very different sort of tactical vulnerability attends the management of guerrilla armies. Insurgents frequently use terrorism but also irregular combat forces. When they do, they must master the difficult problem of when to risk forces in positional fighting against better-prepared and better-armed government forces. Some always decline. Others accept battle and pay a huge price. The challenge always lies before such modern groups as the Taliban, al Qaeda, the LTTE, and FARC. They may prefer murder of soft targets one day but choose battle against a company of soldiers or police the next. A venerated teacher of strategy, Harold W. Rood (*Kingdoms of the Blind*, Carolina Academic Press, 1980), likes to say that the greatest problem in counterinsurgency is bringing the guerrilla to battle, but that once you do, you may well have your way with him. This was true in Vietnam, where General Giap's army (as against Ho Chi Minh's terrorists) too early brought about pitched battles with the French, in the Red River Valley, and were beaten. It was true again at Tet, in 1968, when Viet Cong guerrillas were ordered into positional fighting throughout Vietnam, and were worse than decimated by the contact. These dangers help explain why many aspiring guerrillas can never transition into a real national army.

Bin Laden, normally self-controlled, crowed visibly on videotape over the extent of damage he did to the Twin Towers, saying that as an engineer he could not have hoped for both to tumble down after the planes hit. But he did no crowing on camera about the arrival of American forces in Afghanistan in October and November of 2001. It had been his prized sanctuary. He clearly believed in the myths of guerrillaism. He was wrong. The White House was determined to oust the regime in Afghanistan, a country that has always been a candidate for the most remote and unappealing in the world. No fear, no legacy of Red Army defeat, no terror of further suicide bombings, kept President Bush from ordering the action. The U.S. worked well with Afghan allies, central to the larger coalition. Bin Laden, vaunted "guerrilla" leader, must have aged notably seeing his men and Taliban troopers dying in masses in static trenches while unseen American guerrillas with radios directed the fall of aerial bombs. Instead of extending the Afghans' legacy of victory over conventional force, the Arabs of al Qaeda and the Pakistanis and Afghans of the Taliban were smashed and driven from Afghanistan in one of modern history's fastest campaigns. It took years, and foreign refuge and Pakistani help, for the Taliban to recover. Al Qaeda has not recovered; it is running on half-power.

No fear, no legacy of Red Army defeat, no terror of further suicide bombs, kept President Bush from ordering action.

Far smaller groups than the Taliban risk the same fate when they take a stand against trained and established forces with mechanisms for command and control. Self-described guerrillas and Castroites of Peru, MRTA/Tupac Amaru, had quite a profile and many small successes with "hit and run" actions and terrorism. Then they seized the Japanese ambassador's residence in Lima in 1996. Their Latin teledrama was good press for MRTA/Tupac Amaru for many months. But President Fujimori was a tough man, and his brother was a captive in the residence. He did not yield. MRTA found that staking 14 terrorists' lives on holding this building was harder than, say, shooting unsuspecting citizens in a public marketplace. Once Peru's commandos were ordered in, in April 1997, all the terrorists quickly got shot. MRTA has gone dead quiet since.

The new technical requirements for contemporary terrorism bring many challenges and problems for the groups. For example, reconnaissance on targets used to entail surveillance as well as quiet work in libraries and clipping newspapers. Today terrorists videotape a great deal. This has the disadvantage of placing them on the attack site more often. Terrorists may be observed when they are observing, as have several Muslims in the U.S. since 9/11. Even if the resultant questioning does not led to arrest, or if the arrest does not lead to conviction, they can be inhibited and obstructed by police attention and perhaps public exposure. A security expert for the contractor Blackwater advises me after years in Iraq that many times, terrorists and insurgents were shot or captured while trying to videotape their next target. Yet they press on: to operational and tactical requirements for such tape there is added a new custom in the Middle East of making propaganda pictures of their own attacks for later release. And while that videotape is good publicity for the terrorists, it also reveals things about the operation: the time of year and day on which the reconnaissance was made; the place from which the attack was made; details about the camera and its crew, etc. Videotape might also be captured before it is edited, revealing far more.

Prominent groups now brief cadres on how to resist police tricks and torture, because they assume they will be caught.

The same principle applies to other terrorist intelligence operations and record-keeping. It can produce a counterintelligence nightmare for them. Consider what authorities learned from the personal computer of Ramzi Youssef, caught in the Philippines with plans for terrorizing air operations over the Pacific. Consider what they might have learned from the same computer had they been smarter and shared intelligence better. The machine on which the terrorist worked up and preserved his plans became a terrible vulnerability. Some of the most exciting material ever seen about the inner workings of al Qaeda was captured in Afghanistan by a reporter, Alan Cullison, who bought two al Qaeda PCs from a thief in Kabul just days after looters sacked a headquarters. Recall the undisguised

enthusiasm of U.S. forces discovering documents in the rubble of al Zarqawi's rural safehouse in July 2006.

Finances are now computerized by such groups as Colombia's National Liberation Army, or ELN. There were advantages of going from ledgers—which can erode or mold in that climate or be burned in fires—to diskettes, copies of which can be dispersed and better protected. But police found a stash of diskettes on one occasion, and it bore the entire record of ongoing ELN collections from peasants, cattle farmers, oil companies meeting ELN extortion demands, and kidnapping. The catch detailed the wealth of the group. More important, it revealed the workings of the organization and the range of its operations. In counterintelligence it was a body blow to ELN.

With sufficient trained manpower, it is practical to use even everyday policing and police technologies to obstruct and pursue undergrounders. Terrorists must engage in criminal practices, such as document fraud and robbery, and thus may expose themselves to alert police. Today the "GWOT" is more about policing than it is about armies. Adept policing yields more arrests and causes other operational problems for terrorists. Several prominent groups now thoroughly brief their cadres on how to resist police tricks and torture, because they assume their members will be caught. The IRA published a *Green Book* which displays the dangers members face under interrogation and coaches them in responding to British inquisitors. The al Qaeda manual *Military Studies in the Jihad Against the Tyrants* has detailed pages on such matters for the "Brothers." The Greek terrorists of "Revolutionary Organization November 17th" were invisible to police eyes for a quarter-century. But in 2002 when a member suffered an "own goal" and ended up in a hospital, he talked to authorities. Now, all are caught and jailed. November 17th is gone. It is a fact of the underground that secrecy is hard to maintain and easy to lose.

Strategies

Terrorism is a sword with two cutting edges. While it frightens, it may frighten the wrong people. When it frightens, it risks cutting into the group's popular support. Terrorist acts may prove political potency, or they can appear nihilistic. This is another reason that successfully leading a terrorist group is harder than it appears.

One reads in histories of the Malayan Emergency that "Communist Terrorists" fighting British rule after 1948 overused terrorism and alienated the people they sought to win over. In our day, Algerians of the Armed Islamic Group (GIA) may have done the same in their country. They are famous, but they have not won over most of the population, and they have certainly not defeated the Algerian government. Indeed, when the other prominent Algerian Muslim terrorist group, the Front for Islamic Salvation, made a pact with Algiers, GIA became isolated politically.

Abu Musab al Zarqawi, a Jordanian, was enormously successful with terrorism while in Iraq. There he was a hero, capitalizing on Iraqi troubles and divisions, fears for the future, and the unwelcome coalition presence. If Jordanians next door were troubled by his massacres, they did not loudly say so. But then

Zarqawi dared to strike his native Jordan. He blew up tourist hotels, killing many Muslims and creating horrors and problems for the authorities. His "poll numbers" dropped dramatically. He angered Jordan. Jordanian intelligence agents reportedly did the work that allowed the precision air strike that killed Zarqawi in June 2006.

Zarqawi made a strategic mistake and made himself appear shameful. The terrorism weapon always comes with such risks, and governments may often exploit them publicly through well-aimed rhetoric. By definition, terrorists' horrific actions open them to charges of murdering the innocent. Varied and good arguments present themselves, even if Washington has usually had a tin ear for them, or failed to marshal them well. U.S. strategy for public diplomacy should combat the strategy of terrorism by throwing light (and statistics) on the realities of terrorism: (1) Muslim terrorists have usually killed more Muslims than Jews or Christians. (2) The prime reason for Shiite deaths in Iraq today is terrorism by Sunni minorities, not the U.S. occupation. (3) When al Qaeda "struck at America" in 1998, its two embassy bombs killed and wounded thousands of East Africans while killing exactly 12 Americans. Such "targeting" is morally sick; it can only damage al Qaeda's image in Africa—if the truth is well-told and the good arguments are well-marshaled by skilled officers of public affairs and public diplomacy.

Terrorists themselves, being calculating, recognize this danger, and do hold debates about strategy. *Inside Al Qaeda* (Diane Publishing, 2004) by Algerian journalist and infiltrator Mohamed Sifaoui is the latest book to show how some members of even the most hardened terrorist organization will dissent, or argue, or otherwise oppose killing the innocent and civilians. There are often advocates for alternative approaches, violent or nonviolent. Sean O'Callaghan developed a bad conscience over a particular murder the IRA performed, and began to turn. Marc Sageman's book *Understanding Terror Networks* (University of Pennsylvania Press, 2004) shows how a debate on strategy split up the Egyptians of "Jihad" or al Jihad, which had murdered Anwar Sadat.

Sean O'Callaghan developed a bad conscience over a particular murder committed by the IRA, and began to turn.

Public pressures by adept political figures may create or enhance such internal disputes, increasing fissures. Skilled penetrators—if we have them—can begin internal debates where they do not yet exist. There are ways to advance internal confusion and dissension, and they should be used when the stakes are so high and the essential activity of the terror group is by nature repugnant and dangerous. It sounds odd to suggest promoting debate within terrorist organizations. But even terrorists can have, or develop, conscience. And terrorists also are well-attuned to self-interest. No one should forget the damage done to the Italian Red Brigades by once-loyal insiders

when authorities offered "repentants" good deals with prosecutors. Many terrorists talked, and it tore out the guts of the once-clandestine networks in Italian cities.

Terrorists' morale has also been beaten by brilliant counterterror operations. This is denied by the errant who speak endlessly and only of the "root causes" of terrorism. We have already seen how MRTA in Peru saw its star fall from the skies in a few minutes, shot down by the guns of Peruvian commandos retaking the Japanese residence in Lima. Similar violence was done to the hopes of the Baader-Meinhof chiefs counting time in jail in Germany in 1977. They planned on a Lufthansa hijacking to free them, in a bargain with authorities. But German authorities had recovered from the indulgence and incompetence shown at Munich in 1972. The new GSG-9 counterterror force flew after the plane to Mogadishu, broke into it on the ground, killed the terrorists, and rescued the hostages. The moral effect was strategic: four of the Baader-Meinhof leaders attempted suicide, three succeeding. While all red dreams did not die with them in Germany, neither did this group recover. War is an interactive process, as Clausewitz taught. Governments can break terrorists' will; governments need not themselves always be the ones broken.

State support for terrorism is another problem at the strategic level, and it, too, can be countered. State support to transnational "substate" killers is intolerable under international law, both traditional and modern. That means it can be exposed and then politically opposed—by capitals and their allies. Military pressure may also stop state sponsors. Turkey endured years of Kurdish PKK training in Syrian safe havens, but when it finally mobilized troops within Turkey over the matter, Abdullah Ocalan was sent packing—and could then be caught in Kenya by the Turks. The effect on PKK capabilities as a guerrilla force was dramatic.

Political Ideologies

Hannah Arendt and other experts on totalitarian regimes felt they look as invulnerable as sheet steel from the outside, but that once cracked slightly, they could fall apart like broken glass. We later watched this happen to the Soviet bloc. Terror groups may be vulnerable to political complexities and errant decisions. Certainly they are vulnerable to what communists criticize as "splittism"—the terrifying risk of ideological division, sometimes over rather minor matters. Small groups can be vulnerable to frustration in political obscurity as the minority of all minorities. The "White Power" movement within the U.S. showed at least two signs of division in the past year or so. One was open and ideological—over the question of whether "Jews are *the* enemy," or whether all minorities are the enemy. The second case was physical, at a "Nordic Fest" in Kentucky, when the National Socialist Movement found its members bloodily assaulted by another faction of neo-Nazis—over personal insults at a speech.

By contrast, moderation and democracy have many natural human allies and natural international appeal. It is a simple truth—not a simplistic one—that in most matters of terrorism, U.S. counterterrorists are far more on the side of virtue than of vice. Set aside Abu Ghraib for a moment and the several military scandals in Iraq. In the overall global war on terrorism, during the past five years, and in far larger matters of political philosophy and our role in the world, democracy does not have much to apologize for. Terrorism does. So if we use the right arguments abroad we will have some political effect. Instead, as all of Washington knows, our public diplomacy has seemed absent for years at a time, or has been ham-handed when it should be a firm, communicative handshake. And even when public diplomacy can be good, as in sending American speakers and nongovernmental experts abroad as citizens representing our country, such efforts are so inadequately funded that they cannot reach very many hearts and minds.

Who is the enemy in Iraq? The otherwise powerful insurgency in Iraq is totally open to charges of incoherence and aimlessness and contradictory positions. Yet when did we last see U.S. diplomats, or the Iraqi government, forcefully point this out? The Achilles heel of the Iraqi insurgency is that its elements have no unified platform of the sort the Algerian FLN published when starting its war in November 1954. That document guided the FLN's work over the years to complete victory in 1962. It created some consensus where there had been none and committed a mix of interests and parties to submit to discipline in ways once foreign. It was an essential political instrument. The Iraqi terrorists today have no counterpart. This is an opening through which we should be driving a truck.

President Bush is right to decry Muslim militancy that spills innocent blood as a repudiation of true religion.

Or consider religion and the global war on terrorism. Religion is by definition idealistic. It is a different form of ideology from, say, political realism. Therefore if the actions of "religious" terrorists can be shown to be base, or self-serving, or contrary to the religion, the terrorists can be discredited.

For that reason, President Bush and others are right to decry Muslim militancy that spills innocent blood as a repudiation of true religion. But their point demands expansion and elaboration. Bin Laden should be ridiculed for his self-assumption of clerical authorities; the man never studied at a seminary. There is every reason to point to the shocking arrogance of published fatwas which cast legitimate imams into the shadows while dictating who should be killed. And when moderate Muslims condemn terrorism, as they have in Spain, Britain, and the United States, their judgments deserve respect—and much better press and official attention.

Specific vulnerabilities also lie within the heart of each terrorist ideology. Classical fascism, for example, lacked the advantages of internationalism—in appeal, and in operations. Japan's self-centered world view left her with almost no partners during World War II, while democracies in the "The Atlantic Charter" could hold hands naturally, no matter how wide the seas between them. Neofascism today is hobbled by the thorough discrediting of its doctrine in the eyes of most of the world by or before 1945. Becoming a fascist in 1927 was dramatic, revolutionary, interesting—it even showed optimism of an odd sort. Becoming a fascist in 2007 is to be a pariah in most social or political sitting rooms. It means no coalitions or weak coalitions with other parties, less money, and regular ill treatment by the press. Today a convinced southern Austrian neo-Nazi might say encouraging things about Danish storm troopers, but that does not mean he'll tender a third of his party treasury to them to watch them start up more cells. Actual cooperation, let alone joint planning, between neofascists from different nations is very unusual. There is as well the discredit of one's intellectual heroes, for example David Irving, who lost in a court opportunity to prove his case. The most important neo-Nazi group in recent times, at Hayden Lake, Idaho, has been broken by a lawsuit; its "church" and compound are plowed under. The lawyer who did it, Morris Dees, is a national hero, which points to another problem for American neofascists: public resistance. In America it has been true for several decades that the Ku Klux Klan or the neo-Nazis can usually get a permit to march; but then they are met by five or ten times as many counterdemonstrators. A neofascist march in the United States is a tiny parody of the demonstrations of power once seen in downtown Munich or Nuremberg.

Bin Laden should be ridiculed for his self-assumption of clerical authorities; he never studied at a seminary.

Consider an opposite case. Al Qaeda's internationalism is its most important characteristic, after its lethality. Internationalism is a source of power—ideologically, operationally, and for recruiting. Do opportunities for us lie within that center of gravity? Might there be exploitable grievances? There might. About where the new caliphate would be sited, and what territories it could cover—and exclude. About whether Asian al Qaeda members get the same credit and respect as Arabs with bin Laden's organization. About what geographical theaters get emphasis from the logistical comptrollers at "The Base" while others might go relatively hungry, or even starve. About whether large cash contributions from known donors are being well spent by management, or whether some are wasted, or hiding in foreign banks for individuals planning to depart the revolution. About the places al Qaeda chooses to fight: surely some of al Zawahiri's Egyptians must resent these protracted efforts across the globe which—let's face it—have created *no change* at home in Egypt.

Today's Islamofascism, as Mohamed Sifaoui and Francis Fukuyama call it, has another specific failing: It leaves out most Muslims. Our world is home to more than a billion Muslims, but only 100,000 to 200,000 may really believe that the murder, maiming, and menacing of the innocent to inspire fear and create a new political force will actually strengthen Islam. Still fewer count on a new caliphate. The willpower and current enthusiasm of the minuscule minority seem important to us, and they are; but they can wane, as surely as Baader-Meinhof/Red Army faction pretensions to popularity gave way over time to the sober views and desires of tens of millions of Germans. Isolating the terrorists may take years, but it can and must be done.

Another vulnerability that must keep terrorism's planners up at night is the difference between Shiite and Sunni. Zarqawi enjoyed exploiting those deep divisions in Iraq, up to the point of his death, but for many terror group leaders, inter-Islamic warfare would be a horrid prospect and a dangerous weapon. Using terror to start internal war can be akin to using a grenade made in a back street shop—it is just as likely to hurt you as whomever you throw it at. The strategists of internecine Muslim warfare expect to defeat the infidels first and then deal later with their closer Muslim enemies. But there are political disadvantages to such an approach, and most terror leaders lack the skill of an Osama bin Laden, long known for building alliances.

Other ideologies have their own inherent vulnerabilities that weaken political militancy and beg for exploitation. Anarchism was potent a century ago, yet it suffers from the ineradicable problem that anarchists do not want to organize! And in their diversity, defeat awaits. Contemporary anarchism has some political muscle but no instinct for the kill, and no well-developed doctrine of militancy. Anarchists today illuminate certain causes, such as antiglobalism and the environment. They are little threat to government. When anarchist gunmen appear, they may succeed in firing an opening scatter of shots, but the movement is most unlikely in our day to be able to mount a pitched battle.

Tamil Tigers in Sri Lanka and the FARC in Colombia have only totalitarian communism to offer to populations well accustomed to democracy. Since democracy works well in most parts of both those very different countries, democracy has a natural credibility with voters and citizens. Communism's promise to overthrow it in favor of a now-discredited system of economics and politics is not the strongest suit of these contemporary terrorists. Their appeal is limited. Colombia is the second oldest democracy in this hemisphere. The alternative is an offshoot of Castroite communism in a year when Fidel is 80. That cannot much impress sober Colombians.

We are indeed in a hard march through rough country. No one is quite sure how long it will take to defeat al Qaeda. But as a determined Englishman said when his people were on a "stony road" during 1942, some things are not to be doubted. "We have reached a period in the war when it would be premature to say that we have topped the ridge, but now we see the ridge ahead. . . . We shall go forward together." If anything is clear, it is that his war was far harder than our own.

CHRISTOPHER C. HARMON holds the Kim T. Adamson Chair of Insurgency and Terrorism at Marine Corps University. He is author of *Terrorism Today* (Taylor & Francis). He writes in his personal capacity and is not a representative of the U.S. government.

UNIT 2

Tactics of Terrorism

Unit Selections

Key Points to Consider

- How has political violence changed?

- Has Al Qaeda's ability to produce biological weapons been underestimated?

- To what extent do terrorists use extortion as a tactic?

- Why are youths in conflict zones particularly susceptible to terrorist recruitment?

Student Website

www.mhcls.com

Internet References

Evolving Tactics of Terrorism
   http://www.iiss.org/conferences/counter-terrorism-series/evolving-tactics-of-terrorism/
The Al Qaeda Manual
   http://www.usdoj.gov/ag/manualpart1_1.pdf
Centers for Disease Control
   http://www.cdc.gov/mmwr/preview/mmwrhtml/rr4904a1.htm

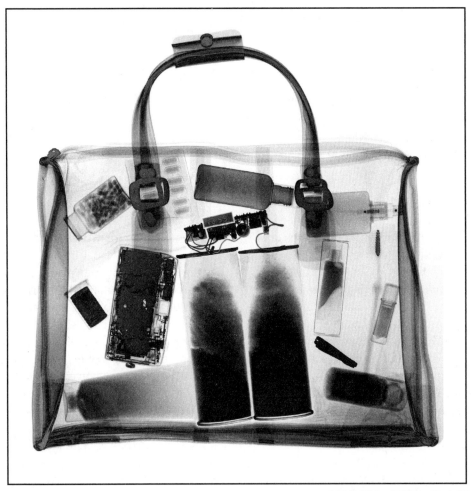

The tactics of terrorism appear to be universal. While ideologies and motivations vary, terrorist organizations in different parts of the world often use similar methods to instill fear and wreak havoc. It's unclear whether this is the consequence of increased communications among terrorist organizations, or the result of greater access to information in this age of global media. Some argue that terrorists simply tend to be conservative in their selection of tactics, relying on tactics that have proven successful for others rather than risking failure by attempting to use new methods. Regardless of the underlying reasons, the tactics used by terrorist organizations have remained remarkably consistent. While bombs have increased in size and sophistication, they are still the primary tool employed by terrorist organizations. On average, bombs are used in over two-thirds of all terrorist attacks around the world. In addition to bombings, kidnapping, hostage taking, hijacking, armed attacks, and arson are tactics commonly employed by terrorist organizations. To finance these activities terrorists are increasingly resorting to organized crime and drug trafficking.

The articles in this unit highlight some contemporary terrorist tactics. André Glucksmann provides an historical overview of terrorism. He argues that we have left "the era of the H-bomb" and entered the era of "the human bomb." Ed Blanche provides an overview of Al Qaeda's efforts to produce weapons of mass destruction. Blanche argues that Al Qaeda's ability to produce these weapons has been largely underestimated. Dean C. Alexander examines the impact of extortion by terrorist groups on transnational companies. Finally, Cheryl Benard argues that demographic changes in the Middle East have led to the increased recruitment of youths by terrorist organizations. She believes that immature brain development, thrill-seeking behavior, and misperceptions of reality make this group particularly vulnerable.

From the H-Bomb to the Human Bomb

Modern terrorism seeks to combine the annihilating power of Hiroshima with the nihilistic gospel of Auschwitz.

Andrè Glucksmann

With what measureless naivety has the twenty-first-century democratic citizen managed to be surprised when hate breaks down his door? He has—along with his father and his father's father—witnessed, directly or indirectly, wars, murderous revolutions, and the genocides that were the last century's specialty. How could he believe himself immune? "Not here, not me," he told himself. But then, on September 11, 2001, Americans saw several thousand of their own assassinated, for no reason. There they were, unsuspecting, in their usual places, at work or at a café, white, black, and yellow, housewife and banker, when they suddenly realized that they were targets of an indiscriminate, merciless will to kill.

On 9/11, Americans suddenly realized that they were targets of an indiscriminate, merciless will to kill.

A pitiless new day is dawning. The powers of the inhuman and the efficacy of hatreds mutate dangerously. A generation that worked diligently to tame the threat of nuclear war finds itself driven toward a horizon more frightening to contemplate than the one it dreamed of avoiding. Now it must try again to think the unthinkable, to leave the era of the H-bomb and enter the time of the human bomb.

Barely two generations separate us from the shock of Hiroshima, whose terrifying force we have tried over the decades to neutralize. At the time, overcome by the unprecedented event, Jean-Paul Sartre, along with many others, described a fundamental break in history: "The community that has made itself the custodian of the atomic bomb is above the natural realm, since it is responsible for life

and death: it will now be necessary that each day, each minute, it consent to live." Irreversibly endowed with the power to blow up the world, mankind became defined by its capacity for universal homicide, and thus for suicide. The previously unimaginable capacity to put an end to the human adventure remained the privilege first of a single nuclear power, then of two, and then of seven.

But soon, people grew used to the new condition. Coexistence on the edge of the cliff, a balance of terror, seemed more and more reasonable. The prospect of mutual annihilation for the rival powers chilled bellicose passions. Five billion vaguely concerned men and women attended to their affairs and delegated—democratically or not—the ultimate care for their survival to a small number of political leaders. For half a century, we fashioned our peace, both external and internal, according to Sartre's fragile axiom: "The atomic bomb is not available to just anyone; the crazy person [who unleashed Armageddon] would have to be a Hitler."

Great confusion understandably resulted when this certainty disintegrated before our eyes, exploded by human bombs in Manhattan. An annihilating power is available today, or will soon be available, to just about anyone; the destructive will of an enemy without borders, equivalent to Nazi dreams, targets civilians: this combination amounts to a do-it-yourself Hitler kit. How can one make sense of, how can one neutralize, a human bomb?

The history of our last 100 years consists of a number of unexpected ruptures, of which September 11 is the most recent. Revelations so powerful as to rob us of breath have confronted us with the scorched face of a human condition too troubling, too overwhelming, to perceive during ordinary times. Rare but decisive moments of truth have short-circuited current opinions. Respected traditions have yielded to the greater strength of a searing realization. The events broke out like lightning in a calm sky, like the storm before the shipwreck.

These poor metaphors inadequately represent the irresistible enthusiasm of August 1914, which plunged Belle Époque Europe—enlightened, unaware, and tranquil—into the abyss. The declaration of war, the unexpected zeal, the joyful mobilization on all sides—in the end, these overturned the material, economic, and social foundations of the old continent, wounding civilians in their flesh and in their spirit, shaking their convictions and their faith. But this amazing reversal of values came to light only after the fact, little by little. In 1915, Freud, among the first to describe it, unveiled the prodigious "disappointment" or "disillusion" of the war, a war that rejected "all the restrictions pledged in times of peace." The "blind rage" that our civilizations unknowingly harbored "hurls down . . . whatever bars its way, as though there were to be no future and no peace after it is over." The inventor of psychoanalysis detected at the heart of the human condition a "death wish," burrowing silently beneath the pleasure principle, the musical and deceptive call of Eros.

Four years later, the peace treaties were signed but nothing was settled. Those who insisted on worshiping at the altar of soporific right thinking—those who thought that conflict had become obsolete—were swept away in less than 20 years. "The asses!" whispered France's prime minister, Édouard Daladier, after winning a plebiscite for saving the "peace" by backing down from Nazi Germany; he had expected—wanted—to lose. The upheaval of World War I had produced only partial truths; history would repeat its tragic warnings more harshly still.

World War II was hardly over when the need to think through its horrors—Auschwitz, the atom bomb, millions dead—became pressing. *Les Temps Modernes,* the journal for European intellectuals after the war, set the tone for a whole generation, at least until disagreements between its founding editors, Sartre and Maurice Merleau-Ponty, tore it apart. Even in its first issue, in 1945, Merleau-Ponty showed scant respect for the sleepwalking intellectual elders who had guided his studies: "We knew that the concentration camps existed, that the Jews were persecuted, but these certainties belonged to the universe of thought. We did not yet live in the presence of the cruelty of death; we had never confronted the alternative of submitting to them or confronting them." Sartre, a few pages removed, was no more sanguine: "We believed without proof that peace was the natural state and the substance of the universe,

that war was only a temporary agitation on its surface. Today, we recognize our error: the end of war was merely the end of *this* war."

It is doubtful whether these authors' writings and commitments after 1945 truly addressed the radicality of the existential problem that they raised here. Indeed, twice in one century, unprecedented conflicts drove a kind of questioning that turned out to be more important, more profound than the answers that intellectual elites dispensed to prove their innocence and to comfort fragile souls. The answers camouflaged the truth. The questioning, by contrast, reflected the true image—scrambled and torn—of man reduced to nothing.

Western universities had for two centuries taken pride in responding in Enlightened terms to critical questions: What can one know? What must one do? For what may one hope? There were, according to Immanuel Kant, three different ways—learned, moral, and religious—to formulate the question of questions: What is man? After 1918, and still more after 1945, the idea of man became equivocal. In the dark light of mass graves that assumed an increasingly planetary scale, other questions took priority: What about the *in*humanity of man? About what is it necessary to despair?

The European conflict offered not just the truth of the man in uniform but that of man stripped naked—the truth of man purged of the illusions of guaranteed peace, whether a Roman or a modern peace, an internal or an external one. Terrible ordeals tear individuals from their false shelters and rose-colored dreams, summoning society to face the hardness of reality. In the best case, Aeschylus teaches, the lesson enables one to move from passion to reason, or, more precisely, from the experience of suffering to the knowledge of that experience. This tragic understanding consists of awareness of the human condition and of its limits.

More often, though, one runs up against the limits of awareness. The worst of the storm has barely passed, and one is busy "moving on"—renovating dead-end roads, regilding the clocks of Cloud-Cuckoo-Land. We turn away from reality and its truths, which are neither easy to live with nor pleasant to talk about. Before long, repression is complete.

Will repression overtake us again as we get further from the revelation of 9/11? "Who is a terrorist?" we increasingly hear. The despot or invader says: Terrorists are all those who take part in irregular warfare, led by nonuniformed combatants against those in uniform. This was Napoleon's definition as he engaged Spanish and Russian guerrillas; and the Nazis' as they hunted down resistance movements.

Terrorism is aggression against unarmed civilians like these Chechnyan villagers, survivors of a 1995 massacre by Russian soldiers.

A better definition of terrorism is a deliberate attack by armed men on unarmed civilians. Terrorism is aggression against civilians *as* civilians, inevitably taken by surprise and defenseless. Whether the hostage-takers and killers of innocents are in uniform or not, or what kind of weapons they use—whether bombs or blades—does not change anything; neither does the fact that they may appeal to sublime ideals. The only thing that counts is the intention to wipe out random victims. The systematic resort to the car bomb, to suicide attacks, randomly killing as many passersby as possible, defines a specific style of engagement. When, after Saddam Hussein's fall, terrorist attacks multiplied in Iraq, they spared no one, especially not Iraqis: schoolchildren in buses or on sidewalks, men and women at the market, the faithful at prayer.

When the naive, the falsely naive, and the downright evil blur categories in support of their ideological prejudices and christen the killer of innocents a "resistance fighter," more lucid minds disclose a different landscape. Consider an editorial published in a Lebanese paper on August 20, 2003, the day after a bomb-laden cement truck destroyed the United Nations' center of operations in Baghdad: "Yesterday's operation against the Baghdad headquarters of the United Nations exemplifies this mentality of destruction. Expel all mediators. Banish every international organization. Let things collapse. Let electricity and water be cut off, and the pumping of oil cease. Let theft prevail. Let universities and schools close. Let businesses fail. Let civic life cease. And at the end of the day the occupation will fail. 'No!' protests Joseph Samara, 'at the end of the road, there will be a catastrophe for Iraq. . . . The attack against the United Nations' headquarters in Baghdad belongs to another world: it is a form of nihilism, of absurdity, and of chaos hiding behind fallacious slogans, which proves the convergence among those responsible for this action, their intellectual limitation and their criminal behavior.'"

We have entered another world. The threat of a new Ground Zero, small or great, advances behind a mask. The human bomb claims the power to strike anywhere, by any means, at any time, spreading his nocturnal threat over the globe, invisible and thus unpredictable, clandestine and thus untraceable. The terrorist without borders makes us think about him always, everywhere. Without an accidental delay on the tracks—just a few minutes—the pulverization of two trains in Madrid, at the Atocha station, would have claimed 10,000 victims, three times more than in Manhattan. Then there was London. Whose turn is next? Each of us waits for the next explosion.

The business of terrorists, after all, is to terrorize—so said Lenin, an uncontested master in the field. The ultimate refinement lies in the inversion of responsibility. Operating instructions: I take hostages, I cut off their heads, I show them on video; those who beg for mercy must address themselves to their governments, who alone are to blame for my crimes: my hubris is their problem. The less the terrorist's restraint, the more he causes fear and the sooner you will yield in tears, or so he believes.

Recall the cries of hostage Nick Berg, agonizing as his torturers persisted laboriously over his bent body. "You know, when we behead someone, we enjoy it," one of them informs us. "We did not kidnap to frighten those we hold," another corrects him, "but to put pressure on the countries that help or might help the Americans. . . . It is not a good thing to decapitate, but it is a method that works. In a fight, Americans tremble. . . . Besides, I tried to negotiate an exchange of prisoners for Nick Berg. It was the Americans who refused. They are the ones truly responsible for his death." Terrorist hubris bases its arguments on uncontrollable drives: I can't help myself—give up! A similar strategy shows up on playgrounds: Stop me or I'll do something terrible! The terrorist refines this rationale; he draws out his pleasure, prolongs death, cuts the throat slowly, goes beyond physical torture.

To resurrect the dead, if only by video, in order to execute them a second time: this compulsion prolongs war infinitely from the other side of life. It is pure hatred. A traditional war, however savage, comes to an end. Terrorist war, given over to limitless fury, knows no cease-fire. For the demonstration of force it substitutes the demonstration of hatred, which, nourished by its own atrocities, becomes inextinguishable.

Nowhere is this demonstration more visible than in Iraq. For a long time, the mental sin of Western armies was to dive into a new conflict as if they were fighting the previous war. This weakness now affects pundits and politicians, who reproach the U.S. for getting bogged down in "another Vietnam." But Zarqawi was not Ho Chi Minh. No geopolitical fact permits us to impose the framework of the last great hot war or the cold war on the current situation in Iraq. Every month, thousands of Iraqis fall, indiscriminate victims of terror—over 500 peaceful Iraqi Yezidis on August 14 of this year, in the deadliest terrorist attack since September 11—while the total number of American soldiers killed in four years is approximately 3,600. In Iraq, then, what rages is a war of terror against civilians, not a war of independence against an occupying foreign army and its indigenous military supporters. Vietnam is far away; those who miss Woodstock forget that the world has changed in 40 years.

What threatens Iraqi society is not Vietnamization but Somalization. Recall Operation Restore Hope, in which an international force, led by Americans, disembarked in Mogadishu in 1993, seeking to ensure the survival of a population that was starving and being massacred by rival clans. After losing 19 in a horrific trap, the GIs left. The rest is well known. An angry President Clinton swore "never again," and a year later refused to intervene in Rwanda, where 5,000 blue helmets would have been enough to interrupt the genocide that wiped out as many as 1 million Tutsi in three months.

The Somalian model has spread across the planet, from the Congo to chaotic East Timor to Afghanistan, where the Taliban have violently resurfaced, to Iraq. Populations are taken hostage, terrorized, and sacrificed, the spoils of wars by local gangsters. Under various pretexts—religion, ethnicity, makeshift racist or nationalist ideology— commandos contend for power at the point of AK-47s. They fight against unarmed populations; most of their victims are women and children. Terrorism is not the prerogative of Islamists alone: the targeting of civilians has been used by a regular army and by militias under the command of the Kremlin in Chechnya, where the capital city of Grozny was razed to the ground. Where the killers appeal to the Koran, it is still primarily Muslim passersby who suffer. Algeria, Somalia, and Darfur (at least 200,000 dead and millions of refugees in just a few years, with the Sudanese government, protected by China and Russia, acting with impunity) are live laboratories of the abomination of abominations: war against civilians.

Between 1945 and 1989, the war between Eastern and Western blocs was a cold one, in Europe as in North America. Everywhere else, however, there were outbreaks of revolution and counter-revolution, coups d'états and massacres. Never before were human societies so shaken as during that brief half-century, in which colonial empires crumbled, but in which, all too often, the uprisings, insurrections, and wars of liberation gave birth to new despotisms. Centuries-old regimes, customs, and bonds were destroyed. As a result of this world-historical earthquake, two-thirds of the globe's population lost its bearings. These people can no longer live as before. Nor can they—yet, says the optimist—exist as tranquil citizens of Western-style liberal democracies.

Across the world, breeding grounds have as a consequence formed for young and not-so-young warriors, who—uniformed or not—prove equally eager to conquer homes, women, and wealth, equally ready to use machine guns or mortars to take control of the countryside or to use car bombs or human bombs to dominate urban slums. Ambitious and unscrupulous forces readily exploit these breeding grounds, sponsoring diverse terrorist groups to gain power.

The war unleashed this process in Iraq. Would it have been better, therefore, not to have overthrown Saddam Hussein and to have allowed him another decade to complete his horrible record of tortures, mutilations, and corpses—1 or 2 million victims in a quarter-century? The Iraqis, despite the threat of murder, have gone to the polls three times, en masse; they do not seem to regret the dictator's fall. Should the GIs and their allies now withdraw, as in Somalia? Even some anti-American governments must cross their fingers against the possibility of abandoning the terrain to the beheaders.

The fight to avoid the Somalization of the planet is just beginning, and it will probably dominate the twenty-first century. If they resist the sirens of isolationism, Americans will learn from their mistakes. Europe will either resolve to help them or abandon itself to the care of the petro-czar Vladimir Putin, who stands ready to police the old continent, while preaching antiterrorist terrorism, with his devastation of Chechnya as a case in point. The borderless challenge of emancipated warriors allows us little leisure for procrastination.

Astrophysicists have found, wandering in the starry expanse, certain black holes. When far-away stars come into contact with them, the stars disappear, along with their planets, swallowed by bottomless darkness. From the beginning, human civilizations have existed alongside analogous moral abysses, which foreshadow an end of all things. According to tradition, such annihilation suggests a jealous and vengeful divinity, or malevolent demons.

In their endeavor to understand the black holes that threaten societies, the inventors of Western philosophy, comparing them to natural cataclysms, earthquakes, volcanoes, and epidemics, refused to see in them a supernatural sanction or to deny the responsibility of mortals. If God is not a cause, the darkness that threatens to overtake humanity is human, irreducible to an impersonal fate. The destructive principle inheres in us, whether we know it or not—this is the persistent message of the tragedians. Hate moves like Thucydides's plague, not a purely physiological condition but an essentially mental disorder, which takes over bodies, minds, and society. The idea of a contagion of hatred must be taken literally: hatred spreads hatred, an outbreak that inoculates itself against all who oppose it.

Maybe one day, we will view the last century with nostalgia, even if it was dealt Auschwitz and Hiroshima. For today's terrorism strives to mix these two ingredients into new cocktails of horror. During the cold war, the threat to man was dual: one, between two blocs, involved reciprocal annihilation; the other, terrorist, confined the savage extermination of civilian populations to the interior of each camp. Today, global terrorism eliminates geostrategic borders and traditional taboos. The last seconds of the condemned of Manhattan, of Atocha, and of the London Underground sent us two messages: "Here abandon all hope," the Dantesque injunction carried by a bomb that wipes the slate clean; and "Here there is no reason why," the nihilist gospel of SS officers. Hiroshima signified the technical possibility of a desert that approaches closer and closer to the absolute; Auschwitz represented the deliberate and lucid pursuit of total annihilation. The conjunction of these two forms of the will to nothingness looms in the black holes of modern hatred.

Imre Kertész was twice a survivor, once from the death camps and then again from Communism; saved by literature, he was Hungary's first Nobel Prize winner. He writes: "Some day we should analyze the mass of resentments that bring the contemporary mind to scorn reason; we should undertake an intellectual history of the hatred of the intellect." The various forms of racism, chauvinism, fanaticism, and the apparent rebirth of an aggression that was thought to be a thing of the past surprise us. Should we not be surprised at our surprise? The understandable but wrongheaded choice to sleep peacefully, whatever the price, puts us all in jeopardy.

The Al Qaeda Weapons Race Continues

Ed Blanche

The Egyptian known as Midhat Mursi Al Sayyid Umar was supposed to be dead, killed in a US missile strike on suspected terrorists in Pakistan's turbulent northwestern tribal belt on 13 January, 2006. Pakistani generals claimed he was one of several senior Al Qaeda figures slain by Hellfire missiles fired from a Central Intelligence Agency Predator at a clandestine gathering in the village of Damadola near the Afghan border.

But it seems that Mursi, a chemical engineer known as Osama bin Laden's "sorcerer", with a $5m US bounty on his head, is still alive and, the Americans believe, working in secret laboratories across the badlands of the tribal zone to develop chemical, biological and radiological weapons—and maybe even nuclear weapons—for Al Qaeda.

US intelligence officials were never convinced that Mursi, alias Abu Khabab Al Masri, died in Damadola and now even Pakistani intelligence chiefs concede that he's alive and kicking. The Americans say that electronic surveillance of known and suspected Al Qaeda figures in recent months has turned up conversations in which Mursi is mentioned in the present tense.

However, they have not been able to pinpoint his whereabouts because he has gone deep underground and is believed to communicate only by courier. But from what they have been able to piece together, they believe the 45-year-old Mursi has revived the chemical and biological warfare (CBW) programme Al Qaeda had in Afghanistan before the US-led invasion in October 2001. At that time, the Egyptian headed a programme codenamed Project Al Zabadi (Arabic for 'curdled milk') at Al Qaeda's Darunta training complex in the Tora Bora region of Afghanistan. According to the evidence the Americans have put together from electronic intercepts, informants, the interrogation of captured militants and tracking Al Qaeda's financial networks, Mursi is concentrating on manufacturing cyanide, chlorine and other lethal poisons.

Chris Quillen, a former CIA analyst who until he left the agency in 2006 specialised in Al Qaeda's efforts to produce weapons of mass destruction (WMD), said earlier this year that Mursi and his people may have made major advances in their Pakistani hideouts. "I'm not saying the programmes are great and ready for an attack tomorrow," he said. "But whatever they lost in the 2001 invasion, they're back at that level at this point."

Mursi is believed to have served with the Egyptian Army as an ordnance expert before he became involved in Bin Laden's Project Al Zabadi at the Darunta complex about 120km east of Kabul. He was considered one of Al Qaeda's master bombmakers and was highly regarded despite his oversized ego and argumentative disposition.

Computer files on Project Zabadi uncovered by the coalition in Afghanistan in 2002 showed that Bin Laden gave Mursi a startup budget in May 1999 to get the project off the ground. Because he had to account for the money, he videotaped his experiments that included using what seemed to be hydrogen cyanide on dogs. The tapes were captured by US forces.

Mursi also worked on developing a pathogen identified as Agent X, which terrorism experts believe is almost certainly anthrax, although US officials have long warned that Al Qaeda was seeking to produce botulinum toxin, smallpox, plague or ebola.

At that time, according to US and western European intelligence agencies, Mursi headed a nine-member Al Qaeda committee that oversaw CBW development and possibly planning for any attacks using its deadly products. This group included some of Bin Laden's top people, underlining the commitment of Al Qaeda Central to developing weapons of mass destruction. That commitment, US and European officials believe, has not diminished and it is likely that the committee has been reconstituted in Pakistan.

The original committee included such people as Assadallah Abdul Rahman, a son of the blind Egyptian cleric Sheikh Omar Abdul Rahman, the iconic radical convicted of the 1993 World Trade Centre bombing in New York. The younger Rahman, who was in charge of procuring material for the programme, was captured in February 2003.

Another member was Mustafa Setmariam Nassar, alias Abu Musab Al Suri, a veteran Al Qaeda figure with a $5m US bounty on his head. He was one of the network's top strategists and ideologues who espoused global jihad and encouraged chemical warfare against the enemies of Islam.

He worked closely with Mursi and was described by one counter-terrorism analyst as "the most dangerous terrorist you've never heard of". The red-bearded Nassar, a dual citizen of Syria and Spain, was captured in Pakistan on 31 October, 2005. He was handed over to US agents several months later, a prize catch with intimate knowledge of Al Qaeda's WMD programme.

According to western CBW experts who examined Mursi's Darunta operation following the dispersal of Al Qaeda by the

US-led invasion of Afghanistan in October 2001, he appeared to be experimenting rather than actually producing weapons-grade stocks at that time. The presumption is that he continued his efforts elsewhere when Al Qaeda was forced to flee.

Mursi went to the Pankisi Gorge region of Georgia with other Al Qaeda luminaries to find refuge with Chechen jihadis and began planning bioweapons attacks, largely employing North African personnel, according to US officials. The Russians have reported attempts by Islamist Chechen rebels to use chemical weapons.

US officials say that these days Mursi is suspected of training special operatives in his lethal alchemy to carry out attacks in Europe. Western intelligence agencies have long believed Bin Laden hoped to unleash CBW attacks on the cities of the US and Europe to inflict the kind of mass casualties caused by the 9/11 suicide attacks.

The US presidential commission that investigated the failure of US intelligence services to prevent 9/11, reported in March 2005 that these agencies had badly underestimated Al Qaeda's efforts to develop chemical and biological weapons and still did not have a full understanding of the organisation's capabilities.

But if the reports of Mursi's activities are anything to go by, that threat clearly remains. Europe's intelligence services have warned that the likelihood of chemical or biological attacks is growing as Islamist extremists extend their cell network, increasingly comprised of veterans of the Iraq war, across the continent.

There have been at least six Al Qaeda operations involving chemical weapons that have all been thwarted, including one reported plot to attack the New York subway system with cyanide that was supposedly scrapped by Al Qaeda itself. Jordanian authorities say they foiled a major chemical attack on Amman in 2004. Although there is some scepticism that the plot was as ambitious as the Jordanians claimed it was, it illustrated the kind of mass-casualty attack Al Qaeda sought to mount in the West.

The plot to attack the New York subway with cyanide was supposedly scheduled for the spring of 2003, about the time the US-led invasion of Iraq took place. Whether there was any correlation between the two remains unclear.

The plot was first reported in June 2006 in a book, *The One Percent Doctrine* by journalist Ron Suskind. He claimed Al Qaeda had successfully developed a portable device to disperse cyanide gas, which kills when it is inhaled. US security officials confirmed that a plot had been foiled, but gave no details.

It was presumably modelled on the 20 March, 1995, attack on Tokyo's subway by a little-known doomsday cult known as Aum Shinrikyo (Supreme Truth) with sarin, a lethal nerve gas developed by the Nazis in World War II. Twelve people were killed and more than 5,000 were injured, some permanently.

Ayman Al Zawahiri, Bin Laden's deputy and eminence grise who was apparently in charge of the plot, called off the attack 45 days before it was scheduled to be launched, possibly because it was not deemed apocalyptic enough to surpass the 9/11 carnage.

Michael Scheuer, a former senior CIA officer who headed the unit tasked with tracking Bin Laden, wrote after the book was published: "This judgment seems to be on solid ground.

Since declaring war on the United States in 1996, Osama bin Laden has repeatedly underscored his preferred method of operation . . . incrementally increase the pain that (Al Qaeda's) attacks cause the United States until it forces Washington to change its politics toward Israel and the Muslim world."

Scheuer questioned that if thousands of people killed in the New York subway did not satisfy Bin Laden, what would? The answer, he surmised, "may well be the detonation of a nuclear weapon of some sort. While there is no definitive evidence that Al Qaeda has such a device, the group has a specialised unit—staffed by hard scientists and engineers—that has sought one since at least 1992, and events . . . suggest that such a possibility remains current."

In April 2004, Jordanian authorities claimed to have thwarted a major chemical attack in Amman masterminded by Abu Musab Al Zarqawi, then leader of Al Qaeda in Iraq. The Jordanian-born Zarqawi, a fierce opponent of the Hashemite monarchy, was killed in a US air strike near Baghdad on 7 June, 2006.

According to confessions made by several of the suspects on television—a practice used by Arab governments in which the prisoners' statements are generally seen as carefully stage-managed—the group planned to use three trucks packed with explosives and 20 tons of toxic chemicals to attack the Dairat Al Mukhabarat, the hilltop headquarters of the General Intelligence Department (GID), on the outskirts of Amman; the prime minister's office; and the US Embassy.

According to King Abdullah II, the militants planned to decapitate the Jordanian government. Had the attack actually taken place it would have been the first terrorist CBW operation on that scale.

Zarqawi was something of a maverick who did not always coordinate with Al Qaeda Central, so it is not known whether the Amman plot had been sanctioned by Bin Laden and his cohorts, or whether Mursi was involved. But it was the kind of spectacular that Bin Laden sought as a follow-up to 9/11.

The Jordanians claimed that Zarqawi's plot could have killed up to 80,000 people, mostly from a poisonous toxic cloud created by the bomb explosions. That projected death toll, nearly 30 times greater than the 9/11 carnage, was considered in many quarters to have been highly inflated for propaganda purposes by the Jordanian authorities.

On 7 November, 2006, Dhiren Barot, an Indian-born Hindu who converted to Islam, was sentenced to life imprisonment at Woolwich Crown Court in London for plotting unprecedented carnage on both sides of the Atlantic, including detonating a "dirty bomb" laced with radioactive material to cause massive contamination in heavily populated urban centres. State prosecutor Edmund Lawson said Barot planned "to strike at the very heart of both America and Britain, and to cause the loss of human life on a massive scale".

Barot, who was arrested on 3 August, 2004, while having a haircut at his local barber in London, was considered Al Qaeda's top operative in the United Kingdom. According to British intelligence, he was controlled by senior Al Qaeda figures in Pakistan's tribal belt, including the alleged 9/11 mastermind Khaled Sheikh Mohammed before he was captured in Pakistan in March 2003.

Barot, a former airline ticket clerk who contacted Al Qaeda in 1995, was convicted of planning to blow up major London hotels such as the Dorchester and the Savoy, and railway terminals such as Waterloo and King's Cross.

The most developed plot was one he called the "Gas Limos Project" which involved packing three limousines with explosives and gas cylinders and blowing them up in the basement car parks of the target buildings. He also planned to bomb iconic US buildings such as the New York Stock Exchange, The World Bank in Washington and the Prudential building in Newark, New Jersey.

But Barot was also obsessed with constructing "dirty bombs", known as radio-logical dispersal devices (RDDs). He and his seven-man cell planned to use one in London. The range and sophistication of his planning chilled British police when they decoded his meticulous computer files, which included research on "dirty bombs" hidden in files entitled "Brad Pitt" and "radio-active children".

In October 2004, the CIA said in a voluminous report that another Iraqi group, Jaish Al Mohammed (Mohammed's Army), largely made up of former military and intelligence personnel from Saddam Hussein's regime, hired two chemists to develop crude chemical or biological weapons. But in the seven months before the group, known as the Al Abud network, was uncovered in June 2004 it failed to produce even a rudimentary weapon.

The exhaustive 960-page report was the work of Charles Duelfer, the CIA's chief weapons investigator in Iraq and a former deputy chairman of the United Nations Special Commission that hunted down Saddam Hussein's weapons of mass destruction in 1992–98.

Duelfer's report said the Iraq Survey Group, the largely CIA unit tasked with tracking down Saddam's WMD programmes following the 2003 invasion, stumbled across the insurgent chemical and biological warfare operation in March 2004 after US troops raided a laboratory in Baghdad. They discovered an Iraqi chemist who had produced small quantities of ricin, made from castor beans and one of the deadliest known toxins.

Duelfer said Jaish Al Mohammed had begun working on CBW in December 2003 in Fallujah, a city that became an insurgent stronghold, when it recruited "an inexperienced Baghdad chemist" to help them produce tabun, a lethal nerve agent. The CIA report said captured Jaish operatives told interrogators from Duelfer's group that they planned to fill mortar shells and other munitions to use against the occupation forces.

The chemist was not able to produce tabun, but the rebels filled nine mortar rounds with another poisonous mixture he concocted. Duelfer's team deemed those shells useless as CBW weapons because the explosions on impact would incinerate the poison.

The Al Abud network switched to working on mustard gas in early 2004, but again failed to produce a deployable weapon. However the scientists were able to produce ricin cake, which can be converted into ricin poison. Duelfer's team concluded that the chemists could produce ricin in small quantities, but were "not capable of facilitating a mass-casualty ricin attack". Still, ricin was involved in jihadist plots in London, Paris and Rome soon after. All were thwarted before they could be carried out.

Duelfer noted that the insurgents' efforts to produce rudimentary CBW capabilities caused great alarm in the US-led coalition because the group had been able to recruit scientists from Saddam's secret weapons programmes and to fund their efforts. If the Al Abud network had not been rolled up, he maintained, "the consequences . . . could have been devastating to coalition forces". The leaders and financiers of the network "remain at large and alleged chemical munitions remain unaccounted for".

The report concluded that Al Abud "was not the only group planning or attempting to produce CBW agents" and cautioned that the "availability of chemicals and materials dispersed throughout the country, and intellectual capital from the former WMD programmes increases the future threat to coalition forces."

Terrorism and Extortion

Dean C. Alexander

A sinister threat to global business is worth highlighting. In particular, an under-appreciated form of terrorism continues to have far-reaching implications for business, particularly transnational companies (TNCs). A tactic used by terror groups is extortion, whereby a group obtains money through threats or actual violence against corporate personnel and other assets.

Increasingly companies are facing the reality and risks of doing business in an unstable world. Any company in energy, mining, agriculture or manufacturing will likely come up against the threat of terror and subsequent extortion payments.

To give an idea of just how big this problem is for TNCs, consider Nigeria. For several years, the eighth largest oil exporter has suffered bombings against oil rigs and compounds as well as kidnappings and other extortive acts by the Nigerian terror group MEND. In September 2007, Mexico, another top oil exporter, experienced bomb blasts against state-owned Pemex oil and natural gas pipelines, perpetrated by the terror group EPR. Recent cases of terror extortion tactics include the ETA in Spain, Abu Sayef in the Philippines, Hizballah in South America's tri-border area and narco-terror groups in Colombia.

Terror group extortion, such as revolutionary payments or protection money, is an ongoing issue for TNCs. Giving in and paying the terrorists off may initially afford a TNC peace and quiet. Yet ultimately, employing such defensive measures, which are akin to bribery payments, can result in far-reaching negative operational, financial and legal consequences.

Chiquita and Colombian Terror Groups

Recently, Chiquita revealed to the U.S. Justice Department that it had been illegally paying extortion fees to known terrorist groups for several years. Chiquita stated that its management felt it had no choice but to ensure the safety of the company's employees.

Chiquita voluntarily alerted Justice that it paid $1.7 million between 1997 and 2004 to AUC, a terror group responsible for some of the worst massacres in Colombia's civil conflict and for a sizable percentage of the country's cocaine exports. Additionally, Chiquita made payments to the terror groups ELN

and FARC, as control of the company's banana-growing area shifted.

Ultimately, Chiquita agreed to a $25 million criminal fine, the requirement to implement and maintain an effective compliance and ethics program, and five years probation. Also, Chiquita executives narrowly avoided U.S. criminal charges in this regard.

In the face of extortion, Chiquita had to decide between several unappealing options: Pay terrorists the extortion; refuse to pay them and possibly suffer attacks on employees and facilities; stop operations temporarily; or sell operations, most likely at a loss. While making payments may seem like the lesser of many evils, a TNC's decision to make protection payments undermines its status at home and with host countries. Even worse, extortion payments encourage similar conduct by terrorists against business worldwide.

Additional Ramifications

Aside from the obvious disadvantage of dealing with terrorists, terror group extortion payment pressures can have negative operational effects such as declining production, often with poorer quality deliverables; higher costs of production due to heightened labor, security and transportation costs; lower efficiencies; underutilization of assets; production stoppages and threats to business continuity; adjustments to and pressures on supply chains; and corporate governance complexities.

There are also significant financial implications from giving in to terror extortion such as: higher costs for labor, security, capital, inputs and insurance; reduced profitability; loss of goodwill and declining stock price; financial penalties; and/or liabilities arising from host and home country litigation initiated by the government, private sector or even employees.

Reducing the Terror Risk

There are steps that transnational companies and their chief security officers can undertake to reduce the risks of terror extortion.

Prior to following such a path, the TNC must analyze whether the benefits outweigh the risk of doing business in the host country. If the TNC decides to proceed, it can reduce risks by exploring whether land grants or subsidized loans are available from the

Buy Insurance?

Many enterprises, and especially transnational companies, purchase kidnap and ransom insurance for their employees and certain contractors.

Such coverage may also provide access to a crisis response organization. These response teams offer advisory assistance to the VIP's family or chief security officer of the business specific to independent investigations, negotiations, arrangement and delivery of funds and numerous other services.

Sometimes enterprises have security connections in other countries. At other times, companies purchase insurance when their executives, who don't usually travel outside the United States, go on a trip to a country that has a history of risk.

Most kidnap and ransom insurance includes common benefits and services, with some of the menu for an optional fee:

- Ransom money
- Informant money
- Crisis management services
- Accidental death
- Legal liabilities
- Rehabilitation
- Personal security consultation
- Reward money
- Negotiation services
- Family counseling
- Loss of ransom in transit
- Medical services and emergency evacuation
- Interpretive and forensic services
- Business security consultation

host country or a development agency (e.g., the World Bank or a regional development bank). The TNC can also invest in political risk insurance covering war and civil disturbance/terrorism,

expropriation, breach of contract and inconvertibility of currency offered by commercial, government (e.g., U.S. Government's Overseas Private Investment Corporation) and non-governmental organization (e.g., the World Bank's Multilateral Investment Guarantee Agency).

In cases of terror extortion, the kidnapping of TNC personnel is a very real threat. Kidnapping and ransom insurance, along with other insurance products (e.g., property and casualty, business interruption, life, disability and health insurance), should be seriously considered. It is also critical to apply disparate security products, services and methodologies—ranging from risk and vulnerability assessments to business and risk intelligence data reports—that can aid in lessening the likelihood, frequency and severity of terrorism, in general, and terror extortion, in particular.

Other preventative measures TNCs can pursue include developing alliances and gathering support from host country government, business, civic and labor entities, along with home country representatives (e.g., U.S. embassy) and non-governmental institutions (e.g., World Bank). Likewise, engendering support for bilateral economic and political relations between host and home countries (e.g., trade and investment agreements) will aid TNC efforts abroad.

This discussion demonstrates that while terror group extortion can have substantial pernicious operational, financial, and legal effects on TNCs, a variety of alternatives and instruments are available to lessen such threats. In doing so, TNCs can help enhance global trade, investment and business while contributing to the reduction of terrorism internationally by eliminating a considerable source of terror funding.

Professor **DEAN C. ALEXANDER,** a member of the Advisory Council of Marsh's Center for Risk Insight and author of *Business Confronts Terrorism* (Wisconsin, 2004), is Director, Homeland Security Research Program at Western Illinois University. He is a frequent contributor to *Security* Magazine. Link to securitymagazine.com for other articles by Prof. Alexander.

Toy Soldiers

The Youth Factor in the War on Terror

"Membership in a clandestine terrorist cell; online linkages with glamorous, dangerous individuals; the opportunity to belong to a feared and seemingly heroic movement complete with martyrs—all of this is inherently appealing to young people."

CHERYL BENARD

"About the time of Easter . . . , many thousands of boys, ranging in age from six years to full maturity, left the plows or carts which they were driving, the flocks which they were pasturing, and anything else which they were doing . . . [and] put up banners and began to journey to Jerusalem. . . . They [said] that they were equal to the Divine will in this matter and that, whatever God might wish to do with them, they would accept it willingly and with humble spirit. Some were turned back at Metz, others at Piacenza, and others even at Rome. Still others got to Marseilles, but whether they crossed to the Holy Land or what their end was is uncertain. One thing is sure: that of the many thousands who rose up, only very few returned."

—*From a description of the so-called
Children's Crusade in* Chronica Regiae Coloniensis
Continuatio prima, *translated by James Brundage*

Much has been made of an ominous demographic reality prevalent in the Middle East. Although the exact number varies from country to country, any speaker who mentions the proportion of the population below age 20, or below age 16, can count on receiving gasps of surprise from Western audiences. Fifty percent of the population below age 19! Sixty-five percent below age 25! And no functioning economy to absorb them. It is clear even to a layperson that this spells trouble.

Experts will point out that it could also spell prosperity—in theory. In theory, a young population has the potential to be productive and to bless its society with a low dependency ratio: that is, with a larger segment of productive workers supporting a smaller segment of the elderly, the very young, the incapacitated, and otherwise nonproductive individuals who must count on tapping into the income of others. In reality, though,

cultural, political, and economic factors can—and throughout much of the Islamic world do—stand in the way of productivity and prosperity. The youth overhang, instead of constituting a motor for growth, becomes what Isobel Coleman of the Council on Foreign Relations has called a potential "youthquake" and a "massive demographic tsunami."

Many young people in the Middle East, especially the famously more volatile young males, are deprived of sensible activities, bereft of real hope for a happy and independent future, unschooled in practical modes of thinking, and sexually frustrated in their strict and puritanical societies. Many are hammered with the rousing appeals of radical preachers and ideologues. Others are simply bored and purposeless. Clearly this is not a promising recipe for stable social advancement.

All of these social conditions and their implications in the region are being discussed and fretted over, and with good cause. But another variable in the situation has received less attention: the underlying mindset and mental development of young adults generally. I would argue that, beneath many of the conflicts tearing at the Middle East today, including the "war on terror," the Palestinian intifada against Israel, and the insurgency in Iraq—as indeed underneath probably most instances of major violence throughout history—there lies an unspoken, disturbing social contract in which older people pursue agendas by deploying the volatile weapon of mentally not-yet-mature younger men.

The Immature Brain

While this issue has important ethical dimensions, the question is raised more neutrally by recent neurological and developmental findings that in turn are the product of improved medical technology. Increasingly sophisticated Magnetic Resonance Imaging (MRI) of brains, in combination with research in experimental psychology, indicates that maturation may take place more gradually and conclude later than formerly presumed. A number of studies suggest that mental and behavioral development continues to be in considerable flux until somewhere between the ages of 22 and 24; that before this time, young people and particularly young men are inclined to show particular responses, behaviors, and mind-sets; and that these are of high relevance to their own personal safety and well-being and to those of others around them.

The findings can be summed up as follows: young men are strongly inclined to seek out situations of risk, excitement, and danger; and they also are likely to make fallacious judgments about their own abilities, overestimating their capacities and underestimating objective obstacles and dangers. In a variety of important interactive contexts, as a result, their reactions predictably veer toward the impulsive taking of unwise risks. All of this affects their ability not so much to understand, but to process and "believe in" the potential for negative outcomes and even catastrophic consequences of their decisions.

Not much of this, of course, really comes as a surprise. That young people are impulsive and that young men like to test themselves in situations of high risk is well known. Recent research, however, provides a much more specific window into the mechanics of youthful responses and decisions, as well as the situations that represent a particular risk for reactions that can be harmful to the individual or to others. It also reveals the inherence of some of these behaviors, which are not individual failings or errors but flow from a natural developmental process to which all individuals are subject—and which others might exploit.

The first conclusion that suggests itself from current research in neurological development is that adolescence and young adulthood conclude later than formerly assumed. Brain development is of course an ongoing process. Adolescence, however, is a time of particularly high change. Longitudinal studies following changes in the prefrontal cortex indicate that the changes do not wind down until age 22 or even later. The prefrontal cortex is jovially referred to by experts in this field as the "area of sober second thought." This is the part of the mind that carefully considers the consequences of a decision, weighs the pros and cons, reflects, and, depending on the evidence, may come to reconsider. In the absence of a fully developed prefrontal cortex, an individual will be more inclined to follow through on a spontaneous, impulsive decision.

In a 2004 study titled "Adolescent Brain Development and Drug Abuse," Ken Winters of the University of Minnesota noted that three brain structures that undergo maturation during youth— the nucleus accumbens, amygdale, and prefrontal cortex—have important implications for understanding adolescent behavior. "An immature nucleus accumbens is believed to result in preferences for activities that require low effort yet produce high excitement. . . . The amygdale is the structure responsible for integrating emotional reactions to pleasurable and aversive experiences. It is believed that a developing amygdale contributes to two behavioral effects: the tendency for adolescents to react explosively to situations rather than with more controlled responses, and the propensity for youth to misread neutral or inquisitive facial expressions of others as a sign of anger. And one of the last areas to mature is the prefrontal cortex . . . responsible for the complex processing of information, ranging from making judgments to controlling impulses, foreseeing consequences, and setting goals and plans. An immature prefrontal cortex is thought to be the neurobiological explanation for why teenagers show poor judgment and too often act before they think."

Better-adjusted male teenagers satisfy their craving for excitement with video games; those who belong to a disaffected minority may be drawn to the real thing.

Recent MRI and brain mapping research has also focused on the cerebellum, a part of the brain formerly thought to relate primarily to physical movement, but now found to coordinate a variety of cognitive processes and to enable individuals to "navigate" social life. As Jay Giedd of the National Institute of Mental Health, among others, has pointed out, this portion of the brain is not fully developed until well into the early twenties.

Besides magnetic resonance imaging, a second strand of research employs experiments to measure the responses and the decision making of individuals in relation to an assortment of variables, among them, age and gender. These include tests that place an individual in simulated decision-making scenarios, such as a driving situation in which he or she must make a split-second decision on whether or not to proceed through an intersection; tests that require the individual to override a physical reflex, for example by deliberately not looking in the direction of a suddenly bright light; gambling tasks that measure risk aversion; and many more. Young men perform very poorly on all of these tasks.

Thrill Seekers

In turn, outcomes suggested by the findings of both of these research methods are reflected in broader social data. Changes that begin with adolescence and conclude at the end of young adulthood incline young people, and young men in particular, to seek excitement, to misjudge situations, and to dismiss danger. These inclinations are clearly readable in morbidity rates, which increase by a dramatic 200 to 300 percent between childhood and full adulthood.

Roadside accidents, for example, are one arena in which this plays itself out. In a 2005 study commissioned by the Allstate Foundation, accident fatalities and car-related injuries to young drivers were studied in collaboration with Temple University, which brought neuropsychiatric and experimental findings to bear in an analysis of accident causation. The study noted that "key parts of the brain's decision-making circuitry do not fully develop until the mid-20s. So, in actual driving situations, teens may weigh the consequences of unsafe driving quite differently than adults do. This, combined with the increased appetite for novelty and sensation that most teens experience at the onset of puberty, makes teens more disposed to risk-taking behind the wheel—often with deadly results."

Males below the age of 24 have nearly three times as many accidents as their older counterparts; their accidents are significantly more likely to be fatal; and accident analysis reveals that the young men are almost always at fault. This is not attributable, as some might suppose, to a lack of experience or technical skill. Rather, the problem lies in the propensity of young men to take risks, to misjudge or ignore danger, and to make erroneous split-second decisions on the basis of factually unwarranted optimism and overconfidence. Young people are also substantially more likely to make the decision to drive while under the influence of alcohol or drugs.

The Allstate study found that conventional drivers' education programs are not effective in countering these dangerous youthful inclinations. They can enhance skill levels and convey information, including warnings about dangers and advice about safer decisions, but they do not affect the underlying impulses and motivators. Interestingly, the expedient of placing a female passenger in the vehicle with the young male driver effects more improvement in safe driving than a lecture or a class. Having him joined by another young male, on the other hand, will increase the likelihood of reckless driving.

Another example of how young adulthood differs from both childhood and full adulthood can be found in recent research on Post Traumatic Stress Disorder—in particular, a study published in the October 2006 issue of the *American Journal of Psychiatry*. Research conducted at Walter Reed Army Medical Hospital on veterans of combat in Afghanistan and Iraq found that soldiers below age 25 are 3.4 times more likely to experience Post Traumatic Stress Disorder than older soldiers. This is in accordance with other research showing that adolescence and young adulthood are a time of particular vulnerability to stress, and an age at which grief and loss are felt with enhanced severity.

A few caveats are in order before speculating on the political significance of these insights into young people's mentality. First, this research is fairly young and we may come, at some future point, to challenge or even reverse its findings. Second, the determinism of responses and behaviors varies. The mere fact that inclinations or reflexes push an individual in a certain direction does not mean that he or she is unable to override them; it just means that this may be more difficult.

Finally, the point being made by the research is that maturation is a process. The findings do not mean that individuals are irresponsible and volatile until, at some arbitrary point, be it 18 or 21 or 22 or 24, they suddenly emerge as mature and sober adults. Maturation unfolds at different rates and to different degrees; it seems reasonable to presume, though this has not yet been studied, that much will also depend on the surrounding societal circumstances, on education, and on other variables affecting the life circumstances and influences operating on the individual young adult.

It remains nonetheless a telling fact that, within the Middle East and Muslim communities worldwide, young males constitute the most numerous participants in violent behavior and pose the greatest security threat to Western societies. Indeed, Western European security agencies report that radicalization among European Muslim minority communities is manifesting itself at ever-younger ages, with 14 and 15 now the typical age at which young people are drawn into extremism. (The most effective recruiting tool today is the Internet.)

It is not difficult to see that propensities inherent in this age group, and effective until age 24 or so, make this subpopulation an ideal audience for radical recruitment. Membership in a clandestine terrorist cell; online linkages with glamorous, dangerous individuals; the opportunity to belong to a feared and seemingly heroic movement complete with martyrs—all of this is inherently appealing to young people. And membership comes with flaming speeches, weapons, face-masks, and all the accoutrements of a forbidden armed struggle. Better-adjusted male teenagers satisfy their craving for excitement with video games; those who belong to a disaffected minority may be drawn, at least in some instances, to the real thing.

How Real Is Real?

After all, when you are an adolescent, how real is real? The question cannot yet be scientifically measured, but we can glimpse an answer in some of the Muslim suicide bomber videos circulating on the Internet. Do not look, for the moment, at the chanting group of celebrants surrounding the prospective bomber. Ignore the splendid, resolute text he is reading from his notes. Look instead at his face, and take note of the momentary expression of surprise, even shock. Did this young man, when he signed up to become a suicide bomber, truly understand that this moment would come, that it would feel like this, that it would be real and irreversible? His expression suggests otherwise, but there is no turning back, not with the video camera rolling and his cheering comrades ready to pack him into the truck—where in many cases, to strengthen his resolve, he will be handcuffed to the steering wheel.

Similarly, the teenagers who place improvised explosive devices (IEDS) on the streets of Baghdad may not have thought very far beyond the money, or the approbation of their clique, with which this act is rewarded. US intelligence officers report seeing children, including a 14-year-old girl, placing roadside IEDS. Iraqi officials report capturing near the Syrian border a 10-year-old boy who had "come to wage jihad."

This is not to dismiss the more elaborate, complex approaches that are being put forward to explain and respond to the threat of Islamist radicalism, global terrorism, and the insurgency in Iraq. Certainly, political and ideological and cultural and ethnic and economic and perhaps religious reasons play a part. But with all of that, it would be a mistake to forget that most of the minds involved are very young and acting on impulses and a logic that any proposed solutions should take into account.

It is necessary to mention, as well, that the same is true on the other side of this conflict. If America's adversaries in Iraq, for example, are primarily young, then so are the soldiers that the United States is sending forward to confront them. There is some difficulty in criticizing Islamist recruitment videos aimed at teenage viewers, when the online game "America's Army" similarly seeks to rope in 14-year-olds for subsequent service. This multi-player interactive online game is a recruiting tool created by the us military. It is popular because of its excellent graphics and because it is free. Research conducted by the US military shows that the game is instrumental in the decision of numerous young people to join the actual armed services.

The point here obviously is not to equate the goal of these two "recruiting agencies." The point is that 14-year-old males are largely vulnerable to the promise of thrills and danger and largely oblivious to risk, and that—if the research cited above is correct—they will not have changed enough by 17 or 18 years of age to assure that their decision to join a war and risk death and dismemberment has been judicious, thoughtful, and taken in full understanding of what it can entail. Research on young people's brain development also implies that militaries ought, at a minimum, to consider some of the revealed inclinations and predispositions of young adults in their training and deployment of younger soldiers. Thus, a propensity to interpret facial expressions as reflecting hostility can clearly be detrimental in interactions with civilian populations, for example in house searches.

More generally, developmental research raises provocative questions for a US intervention in Iraq in which the largest proportion of casualties is borne by troops aged 21 and below. Do optimistic risk assessments and split-second decisions in favor of the more dangerous path play a role? Does the United States really have a "volunteer army" if very young adults have an impaired ability to judge the consequences of their decisions? And perhaps most intriguingly of all: What would the "war on terror" look like if neither side could deploy large numbers of young men with high affect, operating on hair-trigger responses, and low on "sober second thought"?

CHERYL BENARD is a senior political scientist with the RAND Corporation and director of RAND's Initiative on Middle East Youth. She is the author of *Civil Democratic Islam* (Rand, 2004).

UNIT 3

State-Sponsored Terrorism

Unit Selections

Key Points to Consider

- How has the relationship between terrorist organizations and their state sponsors changed?

- How has the creation of suicide brigades affected Iran's neighbors?

- Should the U.S negotiate with states that sponsor terrorism?

- Do democratically elected regimes in Latin/America pose a threat to the United States?

Student Website
www.mhcls.com

Internet References

Council on Foreign Relations
   http://www.cfr.org/issue/458/state_sponsors_of_terrorism.html

State Department's List of State Sponsors of Terrorism
   http://www.state.gov/s/ct/rls/crt

The role of states in international terrorism has long been the subject of debate. It is clear that states often support foreign groups with similar interests. This support can take a number of forms. States may provide political support, financial assistance, safe havens, logistical support, training, or in some cases even weapons and equipment to groups that advocate the use of political violence. State support for terrorist organizations, however, does not necessarily translate into state *control* over terrorism. As Martha Crenshaw has noted, "while terrorists exclude no donors on principle . . . the acceptance of support does not, however, bind clients to the wishes of their patrons."

Nevertheless, since the passage of the Export Administration Act of 1979, the U.S. government has sought to hold some states responsible for the actions of groups they support. Section 6 (j) of the Export Administration Act requires the publication of an annual list of state sponsors of terrorism and thus provides the basis for contemporary U.S. anti-terrorism and sanctions policy. This list currently includes Cuba, Iran, Libya, North Korea, Sudan, and Syria. Not surprisingly, this list includes only states perceived to be, for a wide variety of reasons, a threat to U.S. interests. States in which the United States has significant political or economic interests, such as Saudi Arabia and Pakistan, are, regardless of their record on terrorism, deliberately excluded.

In the first article in this unit, Daniel Byman examines the changing dynamics of state-sponsored terrorism. He concludes that the biggest challenge the United States faces is preventing "passive sponsorship" of terrorist organizations by states like Saudi Arabia, Iran, Pakistan, and Lebanon. In the second article, Ali Alfoneh examines Iran's use of "martyrdom-seekers" against internal and external threats. He describes the training and command of these units, their role in internal power struggles, and their potential impact on Iran's relationship with its neighbors. Next, Lee Kass discusses the difficulty in dealing with Syria's investment in weapons of mass destruction since the nation's ties with terror groups has been established. Finally, William Ratliff examines the volatile relationship between Colombia, and Venezuela and Ecuador. He warns that democratically elected

'chavista' leaders may provide new safe havens for terrorist organizations in Latin America.

Rogue Operators

Daniel Byman

We live in a world where the greatest terrorist threats to the United States can hardly even be given a label. The actors are neither traditional terrorist groups nor the classic state sponsors. In the murkiest of undergrounds, weaknesses within states and their governments' desires to bolster their security often result in an inability to rein in societies' darkest undercurrents. In this netherworld, Saudi Arabia funded the kind of networking that ultimately led to 9/11. Pakistan becomes in part responsible for the Talibanization of its own country as sectarian strife explodes and members of its intelligence service abet radicals. Even Iran, a classic state sponsor, finds itself hedging its bets, funding all kinds of radical groups in Iraq, even ones that are fighting its favored proxies. These states create serious problems for the United States, deadly problems for their regions and at times catastrophic problems for themselves.

For all the talk of "nonstate actors" or "networked organizations," states remain at the core of the war on terror. Some are willing to fight al-Qaeda and become invaluable allies; others ignore the danger or even tacitly support it. Yet these states' motivations and activities are far different than the types of sponsorship seen during the cold war. Then, terrorists were funded to act as deniable proxies for states; now, many terrorist groups are as much "playing" their sponsors as vice versa. Indeed, states are often more anxious to support terrorism not to cause trouble for others but to keep it out of their own backyards.

A closer look at states like Pakistan and Saudi Arabia and many other countries linked to terrorism reveals that the primary problem today is government passivity rather than active support. It is what states are not doing that poses the greatest danger—especially when such states deliberately turn a blind eye as terrorists recruit, raise money and otherwise build their organizations on their territory.

One way that states try to deal with terrorism is to pawn the problem off on someone else: they give suspected militants the choice of staying and being arrested if they target locals or leaving for another country, where these same radicals often commit or plan acts of terror. Yemen, on paper a strong U.S. ally, is the poster child for this method. On the one hand, Sanaa's security forces have made dramatic arrests of leading al-Qaeda figures. Yet terror detainees have repeatedly escaped from the country's jails and many Yemeni jihadists who went through the government's "reeducation" program later went to Iraq to fight against U.S. forces.

Yemeni political-analyst Murad Abdul Wahed Zafir has compared his country to a bus station: some terrorists are stopped, but others are permitted to go on their merry way. "We appease our partners in the West," he says, "but we are not really helping" to destroy transnational terrorist networks. And this phenomenon is not limited to Yemen. It can be observed in several other North African and Middle Eastern states—local radicals shipped off to the jihad battlefields of Iraq as a way of passing the buck.

We are also observing a fundamental shift in the power relationship, as many terrorist groups are better thought of as partners of governments rather than merely state proxies. But judging these changes can be difficult. The idea of sponsorship itself is clouded: governments are at times divided or do not control their own intelligence services or regional branches. In some cases, terrorist groups have "captured" at least part of the state apparatus for their own ends. Complicating the picture is "blowback": state sponsors regularly become infected with the terrorism virus they seek to spread to others. What's happening in Pakistan and Saudi Arabia—two key U.S. allies—underscores these dangers.

Pakistan's Passive Aggression

Pakistan's ties to terrorism are hardly new. In its fight with India, the Pakistani government worked with groups such as Lashkar-e-Taiba, Jaish-e-Mohammad and Harakat ul-Mujahedeen to train jihadists to fight in Kashmir. Islamabad both armed and trained groups directly and encouraged various Islamist movements in Pakistan to raise money and support recruitment efforts. Many of these groups were temporarily banned or forced to change their names in response to U.S. pressure after 9/11, but they or their successors remain active.

Pakistan long tried to maintain the fiction of deniability, claiming these groups operated without its support. But the size of the training camps, the scale of the recruitment effort, and the repeated reports of direct army and intelligence-service coordination all suggest an extensive relationship. If Islamabad does not exercise full control over the groups fighting in Kashmir, this is because it has chosen to remain unaware of all their activities.

Although support for Kashmiri groups remains roughly constant, Pakistan's evolving relationship with terrorism is apparent when considering its relationship with the Taliban. Before 9/11, Pakistan's ties to the Taliban were extensive and well documented; despite Islamabad's claims to the contrary, there was at best a short hiatus in the relationship after 9/11. But Pakistan has shifted its emphasis away from funding and working with the Taliban directly. It no longer sends Pakistani troops to fight alongside the Taliban, as it did during the 1990s, but it now allows this group to operate inside Pakistan with little interference. The Taliban's leadership today is based in Pashtun areas of Pakistan, and the government does not arrest or kill them; moreover, they are in a position to plan and direct attacks in Afghanistan from their Pakistani safe havens. NATO commanders in Afghanistan complain that Pakistani efforts to prevent these attacks and to close down the border have been halfhearted at best.

Some of what used to be "official" Pakistani support for terrorism has now been "outsourced" from the government to other nonstate actors, particularly political parties. For example, the Jamiat Ulema-e-Islam of Fazlur Rehman (JUI-F), a political and religious group that calls for religious government and endorses many militant Islamist positions, openly backs the Taliban. In addition, the JUI-F has extensive ties to an array of jihadists who are involved not only in fighting in Afghanistan and Kashmir, but also in various struggles throughout the Muslim world. JUI-F-linked individuals provide training, networking, financing and other services for various jihadists writ large. It is difficult to believe that all of this can be occurring without the tacit approval—or studied ignorance—of the Pakistani government.

But this raises the question: to what extent is the government of Pakistan still able to control the situation? In other words, when are military officers or agents of the Inter-Services Intelligence (ISI) acting on behalf of the Pakistani state, or in defiance of it?

Pakistan's traditional strategic ambitions in Kashmir and Afghanistan—to frustrate Indian ambitions in the former and to gain strategic depth for Pakistan in the latter—were a major motivation in the past for Islamabad to work with radical groups with ties to terrorism. But in the Pervez Musharraf era, domestic politics grew as a vital factor too. The general, who had little backing from the traditional "secular" parties for his regime, reached out to Islamist parties such as the Muttahida Majlis-e-Amal for support. These parties tended to be much more sympathetic to the cause of the radicals in Kashmir as well as to the Taliban—and this caused the government to turn somewhat of a blind eye to their support of the radicals. Moreover, such causes are supported by many segments of the Pakistani population, while, as polling data suggest, anything that indicates Pakistan is performing Washington's bidding in the "war on terror" is unpopular. These sentiments may prove to be even more constraining for democratically elected politicians in being able to accommodate America's requests than for Musharraf.

Pakistan, as a government, seems to have tried to walk a fine line: cooperating with the West against al-Qaeda but being less willing to crack down on the Taliban and those engaged in jihad in Kashmir. After prolonged clashes, particularly in the tribal areas, leading to hundreds of deaths of soldiers and civilian officials, there seems to be more willingness to tolerate radical activity, particularly if it's directed away from Pakistan. This trend has been reflected in cease-fire attempts in Waziristan, from which the government may gain a measure of domestic peace but at the price of greater local freedom of action to support Taliban fighters in Afghanistan and foreign jihadists.

And whether any Pakistani government is in firm control of its intelligence services is open to question. The ISI is reported to channel resources to various Islamist groups, tip them off about government counterterrorism actions, and look the other way as they recruit and raise money. Whether this has been official policy or not is difficult to assess. On the one hand, former-U.S. Ambassador to Pakistan William Milam claims that the ISI has been firmly under Musharraf's control. Musharraf also cleaned house at the ISI after 9/11, replacing many of its senior leaders with loyalists. Some have concluded that Musharraf tried to play both sides: depicting the ISI as a "rogue elephant" to gain goodwill in the West, while at the same time maintaining Pakistani ties to the Taliban and Kashmiri jihadists. But others maintain that loyalties are quite difficult to ascertain, particularly at the lower levels of the ISI and the military.

Whether the government was covering its tracks or not, one major cost of "outsourcing terrorism" has been a decline in government control. Organizations like the JUI-F, for example, did not draw a distinction between those engaged in jihad abroad and those who also violently oppose the government of Pakistan itself. The dozens of small foreign jihadist groups, as well as the large cadre of Taliban, have cross-fertilized with various Islamist groups in Pakistan, producing a dangerous mix of organization, political ambition and violence. Militants in Pakistan openly raise money and issue propaganda in support of jihadist causes. From the ranks of such groups have come those who have not been content to fight the Indians in Kashmir or the Americans in Afghanistan, but who have wanted to take power in Pakistan itself. Since 1999, Musharraf suffered at least seven assassination attempts, several of which came quite close to success—plots that were incubated in the bosom of the groups also supporting the Taliban and fighters in Kashmir. Particularly troubling was the revelation that several members of the Karachi-based al-Almi terrorist organization, which had split off from the Kashmir-focused (and thus government-supported) Harakat ul-Mujahedeen, tried to kill Musharraf in 2002. Another stunning example of blowback was last year's assassination of former—Prime Minister Benazir Bhutto. During the 1990s, her government originally sought to use the Taliban to advance Pakistani strategic interests in Afghanistan. But once the Pakistani state lost control of the forces she helped unleash, Bhutto paid with her life.

Redefining Saudi Sponsorship

Whatever lingering doubts the Saudi government might have had about al-Qaeda post-9/11, after May 2003—when jihadists targeted the kingdom itself and heavy fighting broke out between these homegrown jihadists and the security services—any official toleration for fund-raising and recruitment for jihadist organizations came to a close. Today the Saudi regime regularly arrests or kills radicals who are plotting attacks from its soil.

Despite this aggressive stance, the kingdom remains a problem for counterterrorism—but not because of what the government in Riyadh does. Wealthy Saudis continue to contribute large sums of money for the support of jihadists seeking to fight in Iraq. (A recent estimate is that 41 percent of the "foreign fighters" in Iraq are Saudi nationals.) Private Saudi support remains essential for many other jihadist causes, ranging from insurgent groups tied to al-Qaeda to radical religious schools both in the West and in the Muslim world.

So far, the Saudi government has been loath to altogether forbid Saudi citizens from using their personal fortunes to support popular causes. The self-styled "Guardian of the Two Mosques" does not want to be accused of abandoning Muslims in Palestine, Kashmir or elsewhere. In addition, long-standing Arab-Sunni prejudices against the Shia and the pervasive fear that Iraq is on the verge of being taken over by the "Persians" make it quite difficult to stem the flow of funds and recruits to various Sunni insurgent groups in Iraq.

Because the House of Saud relies upon the endorsement of the Sunni religious establishment to bolster its legitimacy and right to rule, it can take action against al-Qaeda for its attacks on fellow Muslims but risks drawing the opprobrium of leading clerics and the public if it were to curtail altogether the ability of Saudis to support jihadist-linked causes elsewhere in the world. There is also little stomach in the kingdom to censor the large amounts of anti-Shia and anti-Western propaganda generated by the religious establishment, even though this material provides the justification for violence and terrorism. As in Pakistan, Riyadh often finds it easier to redirect terrorists' energies away from Saudi soil rather than control or stop them.

But, over time, this strategy could backfire. Many of the Saudi foreign fighters in Iraq also virulently oppose the royal family—and their return could lead to the emergence of a large group of "Iraq alumni" who might then take the skills honed in battle against the United States and employ them against the Saudi regime. And the continual stoking of the Sunni-Shia rift threatens to inflame tensions in the kingdom's oil-rich Eastern Province.

From Proxies to Partners

These two examples challenge the traditional view of state sponsorship, which puts the state in the driver's seat, with the terrorist group meekly carrying out the regime's instructions. This shift is visible today in the Hezbollah-Iran connection—one of the oldest and deepest relationships between a state and a terrorist group. Iran has long provided Hezbollah with military training, financial support and weapons, as well as ideological guidance. In the 1980s, Hezbollah proudly saw itself as Iran's proxy, and its leaders swore allegiance to Ayatollah Khomeini, Iran's supreme leader. Hezbollah not only attacked its own enemies in Lebanon, but also struck Iran's in the Middle East and Europe. Today, Iran and Hezbollah remain exceptionally close, but Iran's day-to-day control of Hezbollah in Lebanon is more limited than it once was. Tehran appears not to have initiated or orchestrated the kidnapping incident that sparked the July 2006 war between Hezbollah and Israel. Hezbollah also has its own funding sources and training capabilities that would enable it to weather a decrease in backing from its longtime benefactor.

Hezbollah can also be more of a partner with Iran than in the past because Hezbollah has now successfully captured at least part of the Lebanese state. This goes beyond those pieces of real estate it controls, particularly in south Lebanon, in the Bekaa Valley and in several poor Shia suburbs of Beirut. After months of protest, the Party of God now wields veto power over all cabinet

decisions. And the Lebanese Army could not defeat Hezbollah if it confronted it, in part because many of its members would disobey orders if asked to fight the group.

Moreover, Hezbollah itself is now a sponsor of other terrorist organizations. Both Iran and Hezbollah view the peace process as illegitimate and support the goals of Palestinian rejectionist movements. Since the outbreak of the latest intifada in September 2000, Hezbollah has stepped up its support for Hamas, the Palestine Islamic Jihad and other anti-Israel groups. This support includes guerrilla training, bomb-building expertise and tactical tips such as how to use mines against Israeli armor. Hezbollah has even placed its own extensive media holdings—including radio and satellite television stations—at the disposal of these Palestinian organizations. Again, the relationship is of a partner rather than a proxy. Tehran and Hezbollah appear to even have broken down Hamas training, with the bulk of it occurring under joint Iranian and Hezbollah tutelage in Lebanon while a smaller, more-select group of Palestinians goes to Iran for advanced training.

Iran's relationship with its so-called proxies in Iraq also demonstrates these changing dynamics. During the 1980s, Iran utilized the Supreme Council for the Islamic Revolution in Iraq (SCIRI) as an auxiliary in its struggle with Saddam Hussein's Iraq. Iran even organized part of SCIRI into the Badr Corps to fight against Iraqi forces on Iran's behalf. Today, SCIRI is the "Islamic Supreme Council of Iraq" (ISCI) and an integral part of the U.S.-backed Iraqi government.

Although ISCI may be Iran's closest ally in Iraq, Tehran has sought out many other relationships, even at the price of weakening ISCI. Traditionally, Moktada al-Sadr and his Mahdi Army had sought to keep distance between themselves and Iran, blasting ISCI as an Iranian puppet. But as ISCI moved into the U.S. orbit, Tehran reached out to al-Sadr. Tehran has also worked with elements of the Mahdi Army to form lethal "special groups" that U.S. commanders blame for deadly attacks on coalition and Iraqi forces. Iran has also bolstered its ties to the Patriotic Union of Kurdistan and a variety of local Kurdish leaders. Finally, there are consistent reports that Tehran has even made contact with various Sunni jihadist groups, though the level of cooperation is difficult to discern from unclassified sources. All of this suggests that Iran wants to hedge its bets in Iraq—and that Kurds and Sunnis and less-than-pro-Iranian Shia have found it beneficial to accept funds, arms and training from Iran no less than Iran's immediate proxies. Iran definitely has its fingers in many pies in Iraq—but many of these groups are not part and parcel of an Iranian Wurlitzer and have their own agendas.

Should violence among various Shia groups grow in Iraq, Tehran would try to tamp it down and foster a degree of unity. However, it is not clear that Iran could control the chaos it has brewed. Even its closer allies like ISCI have a strong independent streak and respond first and foremost to events in Iraq, while the Mahdi Army, as much as it is unified, is very much its own master. Iraqi Shia groups would pause and listen to Iran, but they would then decide on their own whether or not to escalate.

Ironically, Iran's support for Hezbollah and especially Shia groups has worked against one of Iran's primary foreign-policy goals: to overcome the Sunni-Shia split and emerge as the leader of the Islamic world. The clerical regime in Iran has long seen itself as an "Islamic" and "revolutionary" government rather than a Shia one and has sought to work with groups like Hamas that share its anti-status quo agenda. The rise of sectarian tension in Iraq and Lebanon—in part due to Iran's support for Shia groups there and the fear this has engendered—is making it harder for Tehran to bridge this gulf.

An Inadequate U.S. Response

Fighting state sponsorship is an exceptionally difficult task even with perfect policies, but the U.S. approach remains stuck in the 1980s, when Iran, Libya, Syria, the Soviet bloc and other states provided the bulk of support for terrorists and exercised a good deal of control over their activities. Back then, the threat of sanctions or military force could be more easily employed to stop or at least curtail terrorist activities.

But what does it mean to be a state sponsor today?

Is Lebanon a sponsor—because of Hezbollah, which is part of the government? What about Pakistan? And, in the case of a country like Saudi Arabia, if part of the country's elite is willing to put its personal blood and treasure at the service of terror, how do we square that with the al-Sauds' recent determination to fight terrorists? And we aren't going to be attacking Riyadh, Beirut or Islamabad anytime soon.

The emerging challenge today is to end passive sponsorship. From a U.S. point of view, passive sponsorship is particularly problematic because many of the regimes in question are close U.S. allies in the war on terror. Getting states to sever their active links to terrorist groups is only half the battle. Encouraging more countries to combat a permissive environment in which terrorists can flourish will be far more difficult.

The United States will have to do a better job of convincing its allies that the "bus station" strategy will not work in the long run. Jihadists returning from Kashmir or Iraq will pose a threat to governments in Islamabad and Riyadh—not all of them are going to fall in battle with the Indian or U.S. armies.

In addition, as we have seen in Jordan in the aftermath of the Amman attacks, when terrorism ceases to be a problem for "someone else" and strikes close to home, public support for jihadists and their ideologies drops. Efforts to play up terrorist missteps and atrocities should be done at the popular level as well as at the governmental level. The United States and its allies need to place more focus on the stories of victims of terrorism: it is usually easier (and more important) for other publics—especially in the Islamic world—to hate the terrorists than to love the United States. What the United States should seek is for citizens to support their own government in a crackdown, not back a U.S. campaign directly.

A constant challenge is government capacity. If regimes do seek to turn the corner on fighting terrorism, U.S. assistance in training and equipping local military and security forces can be exceptionally useful. At times, when local allies are too weak, U.S. forces may even fight alongside, helping them locate, capture or kill terrorists, as is happening now in Afghanistan. Washington should also expand efforts to train allied police and intelligence services and help them with tasks like tracking terrorist financing that require advanced skills.

Finally, the United States needs to accept that "state sponsorship" can often be something that occurs at the substate level and to respond accordingly. Where the government is exceptionally weak and capacity cannot be realistically developed in the medium term, U.S. policy must engage local actors or bureaucracies directly. In Iraq, for example, in the Kurdish north, the Iraqi central government is exceptionally weak and "cannot mobilize a single soldier," as an article in *Al-Quds al-Arabi* contended. The Kurdish regional authorities, however, are able to counter terrorism, as they have shown in their efforts to go after Arab jihadists who try to operate in Kurdish areas. The challenge for the United States is finding a way to work with the Kurdish regional government to stem the actions of Kurdish terrorist groups operating in Turkey-which would require Washington to bypass Baghdad and directly engage Erbil. A similar strategy might need to be employed in places like Yemen, where central authority is weak, or in Somalia, where it is nonexistent altogether.

The challenge of sponsorship today is tougher than in the past. Rather than put a state on a list in order to compel it to change its behavior, ending support often requires truly fundamental changes in the regime and society. The primary drivers of state support, particularly with regard to what states choose not to do, have little to do with Washington. Some states seek to appease domestic critics, while others want to divert them. Saudi Arabia only got serious with regard to al-Qaeda and its allies after the kingdom was attacked in May 2003. Even the 9/11 attacks did not push the kingdom from its passivity into the war footing it is now on. For Pakistan, easily the biggest counterterrorism headache for the United States today, the primary drivers are the regime's ambitions for Afghanistan and Pakistan, desire to court Islamists at home, and limited capacity.

When these regimes consider whether to support terrorists, Washington's policies enter into the equation, but they are not the deciding factor. Even if all the above recommendations are implemented, the United States will not solve the problem of state sponsorship. Washington is trying to get these regimes not to stop doing something but to stop doing nothing—a much-tougher task. So even as we try to fight and limit state sponsorship, we must also recognize that we will have to manage and guard against it for years to come.

DANIEL BYMAN is the director of the Center for Peace and Security Studies at the Edmund A. Walsh School of Foreign Service at Georgetown University and a senior fellow at the Saban Center for Middle East Policy at the Brookings Institution. This article draws on his longer study *The Changing Nature of State Sponsorship of Terrorism* for the Saban Center for Middle East Policy at the Brookings Institution, which is available at http://www.brookings.edu/saban.aspx.

From *The National Interest*, July/August 2008, pp. 52–59. Copyright © 2008 by National Interest. Reprinted by permission.

Iran's Suicide Brigades
Terrorism Resurgent

ALI ALFONEH

More than five years after President George W. Bush's declaration of a global war against terrorism, the Iranian regime continues to embrace suicide terrorism as an important component of its military doctrine. In order to promote suicide bombing and other terrorism, the regime's theoreticians have utilized religion both to recruit suicide bombers and to justify their actions. But as some factions within the Islamic Republic support the development of these so-called martyrdom brigades, their structure and activities suggest their purpose is not only to serve as a strategic asset in either deterring or striking at the West, but also to derail domestic attempts to dilute the Islamic Republic's revolutionary legacy.

Such strategy is apparent in the work of the Doctrinal Analysis Center for Security without Borders (*Markaz-e barresiha-ye doktrinyal-e amniyat bedun marz*), an Islamic Revolutionary Guard Corps think tank.[1] Its director, Hassan Abbasi, has embraced the utility of suicide terrorism. On February 19, 2006, he keynoted a Khajeh-Nasir University seminar celebrating the anniversary of Ayatollah Ruhollah Khomeini's *fatwa* (religious edict) calling for the murder of British author Salman Rushdie. As Khomeini often did, Abbasi began his lecture with literary criticism. He analyzed a U.S. publication from 2004 that, according to Abbasi, "depicts the prophet of Islam as the prophet of blood and violence." Rhetorically, he asked, "Will the Western man be able to understand martyrdom with such prejudice? [Can he] interpret Islam as anything but terrorism?" The West sees suicide bombings as terrorism but, to Abbasi, they are a noble expression of Islam.

So what is terrorism if not suicide bombing? To Abbasi, terrorism includes any speech and expression he deems insulting to Islam. According to press coverage of his lecture, Abbasi noted that "[German chancellor] Merkel and [U.S. president] Bush's support of the Danish newspaper, which insults Islam's prophet, has damaged their reputation in the Islamic world and has raised the question of whether Christianity, rather than Islam, is of terrorist nature."[2] From the Iranian leadership's perspective, therefore, *Jyllands-Posten*'s cartoons are evidence of Christian terrorism.

By Abbasi's definition, Iran may not sponsor terrorism, but it does not hesitate to promote suicide attacks. He announced that approximately 40,000 Iranian *estesh-hadiyun* (martyrdom-seekers) were ready to carry out suicide operations against "twenty-nine identified Western targets" should the U.S. military strike Iranian nuclear installations.[3]

Such threats are not new. According to an interview with Iran's Fars News Agency released on Abbasi's weblog, he has propagated *haras-e moghaddas* (sacred terror) at least since 2004. "The front of unbelief," Abbasi wrote, "is the front of the enemies of God and Muslims. Any deed which might instigate terror and horror among them is sacred and honorable."[4] On June 5, 2004, he spoke of how suicide operations could overcome superior military force: "In 'deo-centric' thought, there is no need for military parity to face the enemy . . . Deo-centric man prepares himself for martyrdom while humanist man struggles to kill."[5]

Abbasi's rise to prominence in the state-controlled Iranian media coincides with the growth of a number of organizations that have constrained those prone to moderation within the Islamic Republic. Take, for example, the Headquarters Commemorating the Martyrs of the Global Islamic Movement (*Setad-e Pasdasht-e Shohada-ye Nehzat-e Eslami*), an organization founded in 2004 as a protest against President Mohammad Khatami's attempts at improving Iran's relations with Egypt.[6]

The organization's prominence continued to grow throughout the year. On June 5, 2004, the reformist daily *Shargh* granted Mohammad-Ali Samadi, Headquarters' spokesman, a front page interview.[7] Samadi has a pedigree of hard-line revolutionary credentials. He is a member of the editorial boards of *Shalamche* and *Bahar* magazines, affiliated with the hard-line Ansar-e Hezbollah (Followers of the Party of God) vigilante group, as well as the newspaper *Jomhouri-ye Eslami,* considered the voice of the intelligence ministry.[8] Samadi said he had registered 2,000 volunteers for suicide operations at a seminar the previous day.[9] Copies of the registration forms show that the "martyrdom-seekers" could volunteer for suicide operations against three targets: operations against U.S. forces in the Shi'ite holy cities in Iraq; against Israelis in Jerusalem; and against Rushdie. The registration forms also quote Khomeini's declaration that "[I]f the enemy assaults the lands of the Muslims and its frontiers, it is mandatory for all Muslims to defend it by all means possible [be it by] offering life or property,"[10] and current supreme leader Ali Khamene'i's remarks that "[m]artyrdom-seeking operations mark the highest point of the greatness of a nation and the peak of [its] epic. A man, a youth, a boy, and a girl who are prepared to sacrifice their lives for the sake of the interests of the nation and their religion is the [symbol of the] greatest pride, courage, and bravery."[11] According to press reports, a number of senior regime officials have attended the Headquarters' seminars.[12]

Suicide Units

The Iranian officials appeared true to their word. During a September 2004 speech in Bushehr, home of Iran's declared nuclear reactor, Samadi announced the formation of a "martyrdom-seeking" unit from Bushehr while Hossein Shariatmadari, editor of the official daily *Keyhan,* called the United States military "our hostage in Iraq," and bragged that "martyrdom-operations constitute a tactical capability in the world of Islam."[13]

Then, on November 23, 2004, in response to the U.S. campaign against Iraqi insurgents in Fallujah,[14] Samadi announced the formation of the first suicide unit. Named after the chief bomb-maker of Hamas, Yahya Ayyash, also known as Al-Muhandis (The Engineer) assassinated on January 5, 1996, it consisted of three teams of unknown size: the Rim Saleh ar-Riyashi team, named after Hamas's first female suicide bomber; the Mustafa Mahmud Mazeh team, named after a 21-year-old Lebanese who met his death in a Paddington hotel room on August 3, 1989, priming a book bomb likely aimed at Salman Rushdie; and the Ahmad Qasir team, named after a 15-year-old Lebanese Hezbollah suicide bomber whose operation demolished an eight-story building housing Israeli forces in Tyre, southern Lebanon, on November 11, 1982.[15] Samadi said there would be an additional call for volunteers at Tehran's largest Iran-Iraq war cemetery, the Behesht-e Zahra, the following week,[16] and even promised to consider establishing special elementary schools to train for suicide operations.[17]

He kept his word. On December 2, 2004, the Headquarters gathered a crowd in the Martyr's Section of Behesht-e Zahra,[18] where those who conducted suicide operations are honored. According to the Iranian Mehr News Agency, the organization unveiled a memorial stone commemorating the "martyrs" killed in the 1983 Hezbollah attacks on the U.S. Marine and French peacekeepers' barracks in Beirut. They set the stone next to one commemorating Anwar Sadat's assassin. Samadi concluded the ceremony with a raging speech, declaring, "The operation against the Marines was a hard blow in the mouth of the Americans and demonstrated that despite their hollow prestige and imagined strength . . . they [have] many vulnerable points and weaknesses. We consider this operation a good model. The cemeteries in which their dead are buried provide an interesting view and cool the hearts of those Muslims who have been stepped upon under the boots of the Yankees while they were ignored by the international community."[19]

The suicide corps continued to expand even though there is no evidence that their patrons have made them operational. In April 2005, the semi-official daily *Iran* announced convocation of a unit of female suicide bombers nicknamed the Olive Daughters.[20] The *Baztab* news website, which is associated with Mohsen Rezai, head of the Islamic Revolutionary Guard Corps from 1981 to 1997 and since secretary of the Expediency Council, cited one Firouz Rajai-Far, who said, "The martyrdom-seeking Iranian

women and girls . . . are ready to walk in the footsteps of the holy female Palestinian warriors, realizing the most terrifying nightmares of Zionists."[21] Rajai-Far, a former hostage taker at the U.S. Embassy in Tehran, holds the license for *Do-Kouhe* (*Two Mountains,* referring to one of the fiercest battlegrounds of the Iran-Iraq war) magazine, which is affiliated with the vigilante organization Ansar-e Hezbollah.[22]

Ayatollah Hossein Nouri Hamedani bestowed theological legitimacy upon such suicide terror operations in a written message to the gathering.[23] Attendance at the rally indicates some endorsement and a support network for suicide operations. Attending the rally were Palestinian Hamas representative Abu Osama al-Muata; Muhammad Hasan Rahimian, the supreme leader's personal representative to the powerful Bonyad-e Shahid (The Martyr Foundation); Mehdi Kuchakzadeh, an Iranian parliamentarian; Mustafa Rahmandust, general secretary of the Association for Support to the People of Palestine; and model female fighter Marziyeh Hadideh Dabbagh.[24]

More vocal expressions of solidarity are limited, however. The Mehr News Agency reports only a single declaration of solidarity from the spokesman of the University Basij at the Tehran branch of Islamic Azad University, who compared contemporary suicide operations with the "revolutionary deeds" of Mirza-Reza Kermani, the assassin of Nasser al-Din Shah, a nineteenth-century king vilified by the Islamic Republic, and with Navvab Safavi, founder of the Fadaiyan-e Islam and famous for assassinating the liberal nationalist author and historian Ahmad Kasravi.[25] Still, that a group at the Islamic Azad University endorsed the organization is significant. Founded to broaden the reach of education after the Islamic Revolution, the university has several dozen satellite campuses across the country and today is the largest higher education system in Iran.

On May 13, 2005, officials declared the second suicide terror unit, the so-called "Martyr Shahada unit," consisting of 300 martyrdom-seekers, to be ready.[26] Some months later, there was a gathering of the "martyrdom-seekers" at Shahrud University. While the invited Hamas representative did not attend, they watched Mahmoud Ahmadinejad's speech from the "World without Zionism" conference on screen.[27] While the status of the third and fourth suicide brigades remains unclear, new suicide units continue to declare their readiness. In May 2006, a fifth "martyrdom-seeking" unit, named after Commander Nader Mahdavi, who died in a 1988 suicide mission against the U.S. Navy in the Persian Gulf, declared itself ready to defend Iran. The Headquarters even claims to have recruited "thirty-five foreign Jews" for suicide attacks.[28]

Lebanese Hezbollah's abduction of two Israeli soldiers on July 12, 2006, provided another press opportunity for Iranian suicide brigades. On July 17, 2006, Arya News Agency reported an expedition of two "martyrdom-units," one consisting of eighteen and the second consisting of nine "martyrdom-seekers," to Lebanon.[29] At demonstrations in Tehran and Tabriz ten days later, sixty Iranian volunteers declared their readiness for holy war.[30] There was also a rally in Rasht, capital of the Caspian province of Gilan, on July 29.[31] But despite the bravado, Iranian police stopped a caravan of self-described "martyrdom-seekers" at the Turkish border. A leftist weblog quoted the governor of the West Azerbaijan province in which the border crossings with Turkey lie as saying he received a telephone call from Ahmadinejad asking him to stop the suicide units.[32]

Training and Command

While the Iranian government seeks propaganda value out of announcements of new suicide units, it remains in doubt just how committed recruits are. When an Iranian youth magazine interviewed Rajai-Far, an organizer of the Olive Daughters, she remained elusive about how serious her recruits were about suicide.[33]

Despite its rhetoric and the occasional rally, there is little evidence that the Iranian government has established camps to train suicide terrorists. While the Revolutionary Guards operate a network of bases inside Iran, there is little coverage—at least in open source newspapers and Iranian media—of actual training of those recruited by the Headquarters. There have been two mentions of a military exercise for the suicide brigades around the Karaj Dam. Muhammad-Reza Ja'afari, commander of the Gharar-gah-e Asheghan-e Shahadat (Congregation of the Lovers of Martyrdom) training camp, referred to one exercise as the "Labeik Ya Khamene'i" (We are responding to your call, Khamene'i).[34] With the exception of the representation of Hamas in the early development of the Iranian "martyrdom-seekers," there is little proof of organizational links to external terrorist organizations.

Nor does the training of any unit mean that the Iranian government is prepared to deploy such forces. In June 2004, Samadi explained that the "activities of the Headquarters will remain theoretical as long as there is no official authorization, and martyrdom-seeking operations will not commence unless the leader [Khamene'i] orders them to do so."[35]

But command and control remain vague. Hussein Allah Karam, a well-known figure from Ansar-e Hezbollah without formal ties to the "martyrdom-seekers," stresses that Khamene'i need not grant permission for any exercises since the trainees are not armed. Evading the question of what need there is to create "martyrdom-seeking" units parallel with the Basij, Karam responded, "Martyrdom-seeking groups are nongovernmental organizations,"[36] not part of Iranian officialdom.

The Basij, a paramilitary militia of irregulars loosely charged with defending the revolution, has not been happy with the competition. Basij Commander Mohammad Hejazi condemned the Headquarters' declaration that it sought to dispatch suicide units to Lebanon. "Such actions have absolutely no link to [Iran's] official apparatus and only serve propaganda aims," he declared. In an indirect critique of the suicide units' leadership, he added: "Some seemingly independent groups are trying to attract . . . the youth with no coordination with official institutions and without the approval of the command structure for propaganda purposes. Their goals might be noble, but their means are not correct."[37] Government spokesman Gholam-Hussein Elham underlined this argument.[38]

The nongovernmental status of the Headquarters and the "martyrdom-seekers" was reinforced in comments of an anonymous Revolutionary Guards commander to *Shargh*. He explained, "Since the Headquarters . . . is a nongovernmental organization, the organization does not look for orders from the military in case they should take action. Their operations are to be compared with the martyrdom-operations of the Palestinians which are not related to the government of Iran."[39] The foreign ministry, which under Khatami was more reformist than the hard-line Revolutionary Guards, referred to the Headquarters members as "irresponsible elements" who did "not reflect the line of government,"[40] and, on August 3, 2006, Iranian parliamentarian Mehdi Kuchekzadeh called the Headquarters an NGO during a rally at Behesht-e Zahra.[41]

Baztab reacted angrily to the publication of advertisements for "martyrdom operations" in *Partov*, the hard-line monthly of the Imam Khomeini Research Institute in Qom, accusing the publication, the Headquarters, and the director of the institute, Ayatollah Mohammad Taghi Mesbah Yazdi—perhaps the most radical of the Islamic Republic's religious theoreticians—of enabling outsiders more easily to label Iran as a terror sponsor.[42] Vice President Mohammad Ali Abtahi expressed similar sentiments. "Martyrdom-operations against the interests of other states must remain secret . . . The public exposure of such gatherings is the very proof that they are not going to do anything," he wrote. Abtahi accuses Yazdi of harming the national interests of Iran, and more seriously, of attempting to create parallel institutions in the Islamic Republic in order to eliminate internal opposition to his political interests.[43] Such attacks called member of the parliament Shokrollah Attarzadeh to the defense of Mesbah Yazdi. Attarzadeh said that volunteers without connection to the ayatollah organized the "martyrdom operations," which he claimed, at any rate, to be purely defensive.[44]

An Instrument for Power Struggles

Baztab's hostility toward Mesbah Yazdi is significant. The Islamic Republic of Iran has long sanctioned widespread use of terror and vigilante justice to keep its citizens in line. Perhaps the most prominent example was the 1997–99 serial killings in which the Iranian secret services systematically liquidated Iranian intellectuals with the aim of intimidating dissidents. This case has been subject to extensive debate, causing a considerable uproar among the Iranian public. The Iranian Ministry of Intelligence and National Security claims that the murders were committed by rogue cells in the ministry. However, Iran's most famous journalist and political dissident, Akbar Ganji, accuses the former minister of intelligence, Ali Fallahian, and Khamene'i of responsibility for the killings.[45]

During the 2005 presidential campaign, the reformist daily *Rooz* warned of the formation of a new Forghan,[46] a radical Islamist group from the early days of the Islamic Revolution.[47] Ali Yunesi, minister of intelligence, and Abtahi both seconded such concerns.[48] Baqir Nobakht, spokesman for Ali Akbar Hashemi Rafsanjani's election campaign, criticized Yazdi by suggesting that he sought to use the "army of martyrdom-seekers" for operations against his political enemies inside Iran.[49]

For more than a century, hard-line officials have turned to vigilante groups during periods of political upheaval.[50] Their political influence is noticeable.[51] The 1979 Islamic revolution only strengthened such tendencies, and there is no doubt that the patrons of the "martyrdom-seekers" have used the Headquarters as a tool to maintain revolutionary values against those that might ameliorate them.

Here, the crisis regarding the change in Iran's policy towards Egypt is instructive. From almost the start of the Islamic Republic, there has been considerable tension between Tehran and Cairo. Ayatollah Khomeini objected to Egyptian president Anwar Sadat's recognition of and peace treaty with Israel. After Sadat's assassination, Iranian authorities named a street after his assassin, Khaled Islambouli. For years after, this action has been an irritant in Egyptian-Iranian relations.[52] But in January 2004, toward the end of Muhammad Khatami's presidency, the Mehr News Agency reported that the Iranian government had asked Tehran's city council to change the street name.[53] The city council acquiesced, renaming it "*Intifada* Street." Foreign Ministry spokesman Hamid-Reza Asefi attributed the decision to improving Egyptian-Iranian relations.[54]

The Headquarters protested, sending a letter to then-mayor Mahmoud Ahmadinejad.[55] Ahmadinejad defended the decision in the name of promoting unity among Muslim countries "in order to face the global Zionist front."[56] The Headquarters responded with a press release,[57] and a demonstration against the decision.[58] Mehdi Chamran, the Tehran city council chairman and brother of the late commander of the Revolutionary Guard, Mostafa Chamran, said that the foreign ministry had imposed the decision but that he preferred to honor Islambouli.[59] In an Iranian-style compromise, the street was finally called Mohammad al-Durrah Street after a 12-year old boy who was caught in crossfire and killed in the opening days of the second *intifada*.[60] But the Headquarters was successful in scuttling rapprochement with the largest Arab state to make peace with Israel. On January 28, 2004, the London-based Arabic daily *Asharq al-Awsat* announced that Egyptian president Hosni Mubarak would not visit Iran due to the presence of a picture of Khaled Islambouli on public display in Tehran.[61]

Those associated with the Headquarters appear willing to use irregular forces against enemies not only foreign but also domestic. Groups connected to Mesbah Yazdi roughed up Rafsanjani on June 5, 2006, in Qom.[62] In the past, vigilantes directed such attacks against reformers or free thinkers, but now the first generation of the Iranian revolutionaries such as Rafsanjani receive the same treatment.

And as in the past, the violence is connected to the same groupings in Iranian politics: the *Keyhan* editor Shariatmadari, now close to the Headquarters, as the intellectual proponent of violence against liberal elements,[63] and Hussein Allah Karam of Ansar-e Hezbollah, now also linked to the "martyrdom-seekers"[64] and, more directly, with Ansar-e Hezbollah itself, which publishes advertisements for the Headquarters and interviews with their spokesmen.[65]

Conclusions

Since 9-11, the increased focus on international terror has amplified fear of terrorism. By forming suicide terrorists units, Tehran can, at a minimum, exploit such fear. Already, Western policymakers warn that any strike against Iran could spark a resurgence of Iranian-backed terror. That the Islamic Republic has already formed suicide bomber brigades underscores that point. But the fact that the Iranian leadership must embrace such nonconventional deterrents may suggest that Tehran recognizes that the Iranian military is weaker than Iranian figures admit.

However, the suicide units may serve a dual function. They are, in effect, the most radical factions' guns-for-hire, unquestioning loyalists who are willing to die to preserve revolutionary values. As such, Iranian hard-liners can use them to saber-rattle as well as to keep reformers and liberals at bay. This may pose the more immediate threat since the willingness of Iranian hard-liners to use violence against their internal political opponents, could pose an almost insurmountable impediment to those who might seek to liberalize the Islamic Republic from within.

Notes

1. Doctrinal Analysis Center for Security without Borders website, accessed Aug. 8, 2006.
2. *Shargh* (Tehran), Feb. 20, 2006.
3. *Shargh,* Feb. 20, 2006.
4. Hassan Abbasi weblog, June 5, 2004, accessed Aug. 6, 2006.
5. Abbasi weblog, June 5, 2004.
6. Mehr News Agency (Tehran), Jan. 5, 2004.
7. *Shargh,* June 5, 2004.
8. *Shargh,* June 5, 2004.
9. *Shargh,* June 5, 2004.
10. Ruhollah Khomeini, *Tawzih al-Masa'il,* 9th ed. (Tehran: Entesharat-e Iran, 1999), pp. 454–5.
11. Ali Khamene'i, May 1, 2002 speech.
12. Mehr, Oct. 16, 2004.
13. *Iran* (Tehran), Sept. 11, 2004.
14. *Iran,* Nov. 20, 2004.
15. Mehr, Nov. 29, 2004.
16. Mehr, Nov. 23, 2004.
17. *Iran,* Sept. 11, 2004.
18. For a pictorial report, see Mehr, Dec. 2, 2004.
19. Mehr, Dec. 3, 2004.
20. *Iran,* Apr. 19, 2005.
21. *Baztab* (Tehran), Apr. 21, 2005.
22. *Shargh,* June 5, 2004.
23. *Baztab,* Apr. 21, 2005.
24. *Baztab,* Apr. 21, 2005; *Shargh,* Apr. 23, 2005.
25. Mehr, Dec. 5, 2004.
26. Mehr, May 13, 2005.
27. *Rooz* (Tehran), Nov. 18, 2005.

28. *Shargh,* May 27, 2006.

29. Arya News Agency, July 17, 2006.

30. CNN, July 27, 2006.

31. *Shargh,* July 30, 2006.

32. *Peik Net* (Tehran), Aug. 3, 2006.

33. *Javan* (Tehran), July 9, 2005.

34. *Javan,* Aug. 16, 2005.

35. *Shargh,* June 5, 2004.

36. *Iran,* Sept. 5, 2005.

37. *Shargh,* July 22, 2006.

38. *Jahan-e Eghtesad* (Tehran), July 25, 2006.

39. *Shargh,* June 5, 2004.

40. *Shargh,* Aug. 17, 2004.

41. *E'temad* (Tehran), Aug. 3, 2006.

42. *Baztab,* July 24, 2005.

43. See Mohammad Ali Abtahi, *Webnevesht* website, July 27, 2005.

44. *Shargh,* July 31, 2005.

45. Akbar Ganji, *Tarik-khaneh-ye ashbah. Asibshenasi-ye gozar be dowlat-e democratic-e tosé-gara* (Tehran: Tarh-e No, 1999), pp. 408–10; idem, *Alijenab-e sorkhpoush va alijenaban-e khakestari: Asibshenasi-ye gozar be dowlat-e demokratik-e tose'e-gara* (Tehran: Tarh-e No, 2000), pp. 210–8.

46. *Rooz,* June 21, 2005.

47. For more information, see Rasoul Ja'farian, ed., *Jaryan-ha va sazeman-ha-ye mazhabi-siyasi. Sal-ha-ye 1320–1357* (Tehran: Markaz-e Asnad-e Enghelab-e Eslami, 2004), pp. 568–82; Michael Rubin, *Into the Shadows. Radical Vigilantes in Khatami's Iran* (Washington, D.C.: The Washington Institute for Near East Policy, 2001), pp. 21–2.

48. Iranian Students' News Agency (ISNA), July 16, 2005 ; Abtahi, *Webnevesht,* July 27, 2005.

49. *Iran,* June 22, 2005.

50. Richard Cottam, *Nationalism in Iran* (Pittsburgh: University of Pittsburgh Press, 1964), pp. 37–8; Marvin Zonis, *The Political Elite of Iran* (Princeton: Princeton University Press, 1971), p. 348.

51. Rubin, *Into the Shadows,* p. xviii.

52. Shahrough Akhavi, "Egypt: Political and Religious Relations in the Modern Period," *Encyclopaedia Iranica Online,* accessed Aug. 23, 2006; William Millward, "Egypt and Iran: Regional Rivals at Diplomatic Odds," *Commentary,* May 1992; *Neshat Daily* (Tehran), June 6, 1999, in *BBC Summary of World Broadcasts,* June 8, 1999; *Al-Hayat* (London), June 7, 1999, in *BBC Summary of World Broadcasts,* June 9, 1999.

53. Mehr, Jan. 5, 2004.

54. Mehr, Jan. 6, 2004.

55. Mehr, Jan. 7, 2004.

56. Mehr, Jan. 7, 2004.

57. Mehr, Jan. 9, 2004.

58. Mehr, Jan. 9, 2004.

59. Mehr, Jan. 9, 2004.

60. *BBC News,* Jan. 5, 2004.

61. Mehr, Jan. 28, 2004.

62. For a pictorial account of the attack against Rafsanjani, see ISNA, June 5, 2006.

63. *Iran,* Sept. 11, 2004.

64. *Iran,* Sept. 5, 2005.

65. Firouz Rajai-Far, interview, *Ya Lesarat al-Hossein* (Ansar-e Hezbollah, Tehran), May 10 and 17, 2006; see advertisements for "martyrdom operations," *Ya Lesarat al-Hossein,* Apr. 12, 2006.

ALI ALFONEH is a PhD fellow in the department of political science, University of Copenhagen, and a research fellow at the Royal Danish Defense College. He thanks Henrik Joergensen and Thomas Emil Jensen, both from the Institute for Strategy at the Royal Danish Defense College, for their input.

The Growing Syrian Missile Threat: Syria after Lebanon

Lee Kass

Even though international pressure succeeded in forcing Damascus to withdraw its troops from Lebanon, the Syrian regime remains in the cross hairs of U.S. defense and intelligence concern about four other Syrian activities. First, the Syrian regime has continued its attempts to acquire sophisticated surface-to-surface missiles. Second, U.S. intelligence officials remain concerned that the Syrian government has become custodian to Iraq's biological and chemical weapons. Third, questions remain about whether Damascus benefited from the network of Abdul Qadir Khan, the Pakistani nuclear scientist who sold nuclear secrets to a number of rogue regimes. Lastly, Bashar al-Assad continues to flirt with international terrorism. The young president shows no inclination to cease the behavior that has for more than a quarter century led the U.S. government to designate Syria a state-sponsor of terrorism.

Left unresolved, such questions about Syrian proliferation ambitions, coupled with the regime's demonstrated willingness to use terrorism to advance its goals, will make any rapprochement between Washington and Damascus impossible.

A Syrian Ballistic Missile?

Much of Syria's arsenal consists of Cold War remnants received from the Soviet Union. The Syrian military has already begun upgrading its tanks, acquiring the faster, tougher T-72s from a cash-starved Russian military industry.[1] Analysts believe that Damascus acquired the tanks for their speed—to maneuver and advance more effectively on the Golan Heights. The Syrian regime has also sought to upgrade its air force. While much of the fleet is old, the Syrian military still has enough planes to saturate Israeli air defenses and conduct a significant strike against the Jewish state. Still, the Israeli air force remains far superior, and because Syrian air defenses are old and lack complete interoperability,[2] Jerusalem still maintains a large advantage.

Perhaps to compensate for this weakness, the Syrian regime has sought to upgrade its weapons capability. When Israeli warplanes struck a Palestinian Islamic Jihad base ten miles northwest of Damascus in October 2003 following the terrorist group's suicide bomb attack in a Haifa restaurant, Iraqis who were in Damascus at the time said Syrian air defense did not react.

The Syrian regime's efforts to upgrade its missile capability threaten U.S., Israeli, and Turkish interests. With a stronger Syrian missile capability, the Assad regime could launch either a preemptive strike or, more likely, feel itself secure enough in its deterrent capability to encourage terrorism without fear of consequence.

Launched from Damascus, the Iskander-E could reach Tel Aviv in less than three minutes.

Syrian officials have sought to obtain the advanced SS-X-26 surface-to-surface missiles, also known as Iskander-Es, from Russia, but Russian president Vladimir Putin cancelled the deal after learning from his experts that Israel would not have a capability to intercept the missiles.[3] With a range of 174 miles (280 kilometers), the Iskander-E could have hit cities such as Tel Aviv, Jerusalem, and Haifa. While a significant threat due to the proximity of Israeli population centers, the missiles fall under the 186 mile (300 kilometer) range subject to the Missile Technology Control Regime to which Russia, the United States, and thirty-two other countries are subject. It is unclear from unclassified sources whether countries that obtain Iskander-Es can extend the missiles' range, but if so, they would pose an enhanced threat to Turkey, Jordan, and Iraq as well.[4] Regardless, the chance that the Syrian government might provide the missile to terrorists or other rogue states undermines both the spirit and the effectiveness of the Missile Technology Control Regime and other nonproliferation agreements.

The Iskander-E would be a particularly dangerous upgrade. Unlike Scuds, Iskander-Es have solid fuel propellants. Solid propellants are less complicated because the fuel and oxidizer do not need to travel through a labyrinth of pumps, pipes, valves, and turbo-pumps to ignite the engines. Instead, when a solid propellant is lit, it burns from the center outward, significantly reducing launch preparation time.

Immediately after launch, Iskander-Es perform maneuvers that prevent opponents from tracking and destroying the launchers. Once in flight, the Iskander-Es can deploy decoys and execute unpredictable flight paths to confuse missile defense systems.[5] Moreover, they are fast. According to Uzi Rubin, former head of Israel's Arrow-Homa missile defense program, the Iskander can fly at 1,500 meters per second, equivalent to 3,355 miles (5,370 kilometers) per hour,[6] Launched from Damascus, the Iskander-E could reach Tel Aviv in less than three minutes, sooner if the Iskanders' mobile launchers were moved closer to the border. This capability might prevent Israel's multi-tiered missile defense shield from adequately protecting the country.

Even though Iskander-Es lack the range to hit many strategic targets, their accuracy and varied warhead types make them an adaptable military system. The missile was intended to obliterate both stationary and mobile targets, particularly short-range missile launchers, ports, command and control facilities, factories, and hardened structures. Such flexibility would allow Syria to destroy an enemy's existing military capabilities and its ability to wage a future war.[7]

These concerns have led both the U.S. and Israeli governments to criticize the Syrian regime's attempts to acquire the new technology. One U.S. official stated, "We don't think that state sponsors of terrorism should be sold weapons of any kind.[8] Israel's government is focused on the possibility that Palestinian terrorists might obtain the equipment.[9] According to the State Department's *Patterns of Global Terrorism*, Syria supports or provides safe-haven to a number of terrorist groups, including Islamic Jiliad. Hamas, and the Popular Front for the Liberation of Palestine-General Command.[10]

Russian defense minister Sergey Ivanov acknowledged such concerns when he announced, at least temporarily, that Moscow would halt export of the missile to Syria.[11] At an April 2005 meeting with senior Israeli officials, Russian president Vladimir Putin confirmed that he cancelled the Syrian Iskander contract because Israel lacks the ability to intercept those missiles.[12]

Instead, Putin said that the Russian government would only authorize sale of Strelet surface-to-air systems that are unable to penetrate Israel.[13] While a nominal downgrade, even with a range of just three miles (five kilometers),[14] the system can pose a significant threat to Israel. These missiles can proliferate to Hezbollah and other terrorist organizations supported by the Syrian regime. In such hands, the Strelets could endanger passenger planes on descent to Ben Gurion International Airport, outside Tel Aviv and just four miles from the West Bank.[15] Russian officials say they will only sell Damascus the vehicle-mounted version and not the shoulder-held type, but Western defense officials say operators can easily dismantle Strelets to make them transportable.[16]

Augmenting concern was the Israeli disclosure of a Syrian launch of three Scud missiles on May 27, 2005.[17] The tests were the first since 2001 and represented a significant milestone in the country's missile program—the three carried airburst warheads. This capability reinforced Israeli concerns that Syria could use the Scuds to deliver chemical weapons. One of the missiles launched was an older Scud B, with a range of about 185 miles (300 kilometers), while the remaining two were newer Scud-Ds with a range of approximately 435 miles (700 kilometers).[18] The greater range not only gives Syria greater reach but also allows launches from deeper within Syrian territory, making it more difficult to undertake a preemptive aerial attack on the launchers.

Questions about a possible transfer of Iraqi weapons to Syria remain unanswered.

U.S., Israeli, and other Western governments' concerns over Russian missile sales to Syria will likely go unheeded. After all, international security concerns have not stopped Russian support for the Iranian nuclear program.[19] Sergey Kazannov, head of the Russian Academy of Sciences World Economics and International Relations Institutes' Geopolitics Division, said that in Soviet times, political reasons and the need to maintain the Soviet defense industry motivated Moscow's arms sales.[20] The post-Cold War climate undercut opportunities for the Russian defense industry. He elaborated, "Seventy percent of our defense complex's output goes for export. And depriving ourselves of that factor under our unenviable conditions is almost tantamount to death." He also added that the missile sales allow Moscow, Damascus, and other regional actors the independence to develop policies without regard to U.S. pressure.[21] As relations between Putin and the West worsen, such political calculations might re-enable the Iskander-E sale.

Iraqi Weapons in Syria?

White Western governments were able to pressure Moscow to alter its weapons shipments, Bashar al-Assad may not have limited himself to over-the-counter weapons purchases. The Syrian military's unconventional weapons arsenal already has a significant stockpile of sarin. The Syrian regime has also attempted to produce other toxic agents in order to advance its inventory of biological weapons.[22]

Several different intelligence sources raised red flags about suspicious truck convoys from Iraq to Syria in the days, weeks, and months prior to the March 2003 invasion of Iraq.[23]

These concerns first became public when, on December 23, 2002, Ariel Sharon stated on Israeli television, "Chemical and biological weapons which Saddam is endeavoring to conceal have been moved from Iraq to Syria."[24] About three weeks later, Israel's foreign minister repeated the accusation.[25] The U.S., British, and Australian governments issued similar statements.[26]

The Syrian foreign minister dismissed such charges as a U.S. attempt to divert attention from its problems in Iraq.[27] But even if the Syrian regime were sincere, Bashar al-Assad's previous statement—"I don't do everything in this country,"[28]—suggested that Iraqi chemical or biological weapons could cross the Syrian frontier without regime consent. Rather than exculpate the Syrian regime, such a scenario makes the presence of Iraqi weapons in Syria more worrisome, for it suggests that Assad might either eschew responsibility for their ultimate custody or may not actually be able to prevent their transfer to terrorist groups that enjoy close relations with officials in his regime.

Two former United Nations weapon inspectors in Iraq reinforced concerns about illicit transfer of weapon components into Syria in the wake of Saddam Hussein's fall. Richard Butler viewed overhead imagery and other intelligence suggesting that Iraqis transported some weapons components into Syria. Butler did not think "the Iraqis wanted to give them to Syria, but . . . just wanted to get them out of the territory, out of the range of our inspections. Syria was prepared to be the custodian of them."[29] Former Iraq Survey Group head David Kay obtained corroborating information from the interrogation of former Iraqi officials. He said that the missing components were small in quantity, but he, nevertheless, felt that U.S. intelligence officials needed to determine what reached Syria.[30]

Baghdad and Damascus may have long been rivals, but there was precedent for such Iraqi cooperation with regional competitors when faced with an outside threat. In the run-up to the 1991 Operation Desert Storm and the liberation of Kuwait, the Iraqi regime flew many of its jets to Iran, with which, just three years previous, it had been engaged in bitter trench warfare.[31]

Subsequent reports by the Iraq Survey Group at first glance threw cold water on some speculation about the fate of missing Iraqi weapons, but a closer read suggests that questions about a possible transfer to Syria remain open. The September 30, 2004 Duelfer report,[32] while inconclusive, left open such a possibility. While Duelfer dismissed reports of official transfer of weapons material from Iraq into Syria, the Iraq Survey Group was not able to discount the unofficial movement of limited material. Duelfer described weapons smuggling between both countries prior to Saddam's ouster.[33] In one incident detailed by a leading British newspaper, intelligence sources assigned to monitor Baghdad's air traffic raised suspicions that Iraqi authorities had smuggled centrifuge components out of Syria in June 2002. The parts were initially stored in the Syrian port of Tartus before being transported to Damascus International Airport. The transfer allegedly occurred when Iraqi authorities sent twenty-four planes with humanitarian assistance into Syria after a dam collapsed in June 2002, killing twenty people and leaving some 30,000 others homeless.[34] Intelligence officials do not believe these planes returned to Iraq empty. Regardless of the merits of this one particular episode, it is well documented that Syria became the main conduit in Saddam Hussein's attempt to rebuild his military under the 1990–2003 United Nations sanctions,[35] and so the necessary contacts between regimes and along the border would already have been in place. Indeed, according to U.S. Defense Department sources, the weapons smuggling held such importance for the Syrian regime that the trade included Assad's older sister and his brother-in-law. Assaf Shawqat, deputy chief of Syria's military intelligence organization. Numerous reports also implicate Shawqat's two brothers who participated in the Syrian-Iraqi trade during the two years before Saddam's ouster.[36]

While the Duelfer report was inconclusive, part of its failure to tie up all loose ends was due to declining security conditions in Iraq, which forced the Iraq Survey Group to curtail its operations.[37] The cloud of suspicion over the Syrian regime's role in smuggling Iraq's weapons—and speculation as to the nature of those weapons—will not dissipate until Damascus reveals the contents of truck convoys spotted entering Syria from Iraq in the run-up to the March 2003 U.S.-led invasion of Iraq.[38] U.S. intelligence officials and policymakers also will not be able to end speculation until Bashar al-Assad completely and unconditionally allows international inspectors to search suspected depots and interview key participants in the Syrian-Iraqi weapons trade. Four repositories in Syria remain under suspicion. Anonymous U.S. sources have suggested that some components may have been kept in an ammunition facility adjacent to a military base close to Khan Abu Shamat, 30 miles (50 kilometers) west of Damascus.[39] In addition, three sites in the western part of central Syria, an area where support for the Assad regime is strong, are reputed to house suspicious weapons components. These sites include an air force factory in the village of Tall as-Sinan; a mountainous tunnel near Al-Baydah, less than five miles from Al-Masyaf (Masyat); and another location near Shanshar.[40]

While the Western media often focus on the fate of Iraqi weapons components, just as important to Syrian proliferation efforts has been the influx of Iraqi weapons scientists. *The Daily Telegraph* reported prior to the 2003 Iraq war that Iraq's former special security organization and Shawqat arranged for the transfer into Syria of twelve mid-level Iraqi weapons specialists, along with their families and compact disks full of research material on their country's nuclear initiatives. According to unnamed Western intelligence officials cited in the report, Assad turned around and offered to relocate the scientists to Iran, on the condition that Tehran would share the fruits of their research with Damascus.[41]

The Weapons Proliferation Hydra

The Iraqi government may not have been Bashar al-Assad's only source of advanced weapons technology. Following his January 29, 2002, State of the Union speech. Bush launched the Proliferation Security Initiative.[42] Participation grew quickly to include over sixty countries. Participants seek to deter rogue states and non-state actors from obtaining material for weapons of mass destruction and ballistic missile initiatives through various activities—interdiction of suspicious shipments, streamlined procedures to analyze and disseminate information, and strengthened national and international laws and regulations. Liberia and Panama's participation marked a key development because vessels registered from both countries account for approximately 50 percent of the world's total shipping.[43]

The Syrian government remains convinced that U.S. efforts to isolate it will fail.

In 2003, cooperation between U.S. and British intelligence and coordination with their militaries led to the seizure of a Libya-bound ship that carried material for its nuclear weapons program. The capture partly led to Tripoli's agreement to dismantle and destroy its weapons of mass destruction capabilities.[44] Additionally, it was the seizure of this ship that unraveled Pakistani nuclear scientist Abdul Qadir Khan's clandestine nuclear proliferation network. While the exposure of the network drew international attention, the limelight did not eradicate the program. As one former aid of Khan's acknowledged, "The hardware is still available, and the network hasn't stopped."[45]

Khan visited various countries throughout Europe, Africa, and Asia. While no credible evidence yet links Khan's network to Damascus, Western diplomats said that he gave numerous lectures on nuclear issues in late 1997 and early 1998 in Damascus. According to sources, starting in 2001, meetings with the Syrians were held in Iran to avoid any possible linkages between Damascus and Khan's nuclear network. One senior U.S. official stated that an experimental electronic monitor recognized the unique patterns of operational centrifuges in Syria in early to mid-2004. The source reaffirmed Washington's suspicion that the technology originated from Khan's nexus.[46]

The Pakistani government has been unwilling to cooperate fully in the investigation of Khan's activities. As Pakistani president Pervez Musharraf explained, "This man is a hero for the Pakistanis, and there is a sensitivity that maybe the world wants to intervene in our nuclear program, which nobody wants . . . It is a pride of the nation."[47] In addition to safeguarding the nuclear weapons program, some analysts note that Islamabad fears Khan might disclose the extent of support he obtained from the Pakistani military. Further complicating efforts to determine what assistance, if any, the Khan network provided Syria. Pakistan's interior ministry denied exit visas to over a dozen technicians who worked in the country's nuclear weapons program. The officials were also barred from meeting or exchanging information with any foreigner.[48] Such unknowns about the extent of weapons know-how and material acquired from Iraq and Pakistan may not equate to proof, but they raise serious concerns about Syrian intentions, all the more so because Damascus has not been forthcoming with explanations and simultaneously has worked to acquire potential delivery systems from Russian firms.

Assad's Terrorist Game

U.S. concerns about Syrian weapons ambitions are magnified by the Syrian regime's flirtation with terrorism as a method to advance policy. According to the 2004 *Patterns of Global Terrorism* report, the Syrian regime provides Hezbollah, Hamas, Islamic Jihad, and other groups both logistical and financial assistance.[49]

Syrian willingness to encourage terrorism, not only against Israel but also against other neighbors, is well documented.

The Syrian government denies harboring terrorists although much of this denial is based on unwillingness to recognize terrorist groups as such. Damascus views many terrorists as soldiers in its war against Israel. Syrian-backed terrorists have attacked Israel, often from Syrian-occupied Bekaa Valley in neighboring Lebanon.[50] Even though the Syrian military has officially ended its occupation of Lebanon under terms of U.N. Security Council Resolution 1559,[51] the Syrian intelligence presence remains significant.[52]

Syrian willingness to encourage terrorism, not only against Israel but also against other neighbors, is well documented. Until 1999, the Syrian regime provided Kurdistan Workers Party (PKK) terrorists safe-haven from which to strike at Turkey.[53] Syrian intelligence or its proxies remain the chief suspect in the February 14, 2005 assassination of former Lebanese Prime Minister Rafik Hariri.[54]

The Syrian regime has also played a double game with regard to Iraq. General John Abizaid, the commander of U.S. forces in the Middle East, commented that although Damascus made some progress in the curtailment of insurgents entering Iraq, "I don't regard this effort as being good enough . . . I cannot tell you that the level of infiltration has decreased."[55] CIA director Peter Goss concurred. In March 2005, he told the U.S. Senate Armed Services Committee, "Despite a lot of very well-intentioned and persistent efforts to try and get more cooperation from the Syrian regime, we have not had the success I wish I could report."[56] Syrian support for terrorism combined with its lack of support for the new Iraqi government make more troubling the possibility that the Syrian regime became custodian to Iraq's chemical and biological weapons capability in the final days of Saddam Hussein's regime.

The confluence of weapons of mass destruction ambitions and Syrian willingness to sponsor terrorism make Syrian ambitions particularly dangerous. In April 2004, for example, Jordanian authorities intercepted, arrested, or killed several al-Qaeda-sponsored terrorists who planned to attack the U.S. embassy and Jordanian targets in Amman with chemical weapons. The terrorists gathered their materials in Syria and used that country as a base from which to infiltrate Jordan.[57] While the Syrian government denies any role, the implication that it participated in such a potentially catastrophic tragedy underlines Damascus's opposition to the war on terrorism.

The Syrian government may feel that it can ameliorate or outlast U.S. concerns about its flirtation with terrorist groups. In the aftermath of 9-11, Syrian officials detained some alleged al-Qaeda operatives, but they allowed U.S. officials only to submit questions in writing, not to interrogate the suspects directly.[58] Realists within the Bush administration did not sanction such a la carte for the war on terrorism. Deputy Secretary of State Richard Armitage, for example, remarked. "If you oppose terrorism, you oppose all terrorism."[59] Secretary of State Condoleezza Rice's new lineup at the State Department shows no sign of deviating from such positions.

The Syrian government may also believe that Washington is not able to back its rhetoric against Syria with action. With more than 100,000 U.S. troops committed in Iraq, looming crises over the Iranian and North Korean nuclear programs, and European Union cynicism, the Syrian government remains convinced that U.S. efforts to isolate Damascus will fail. As Assad recently told the Italian newspaper *La Repubblica,* "Sooner or later [the Americans] will realize that we are the key to the solution. We are essential for the peace process, for Iraq. Look, perhaps one day the Americans will come and knock on our door."[60]

But, Assad's belief that Washington needs his cooperation may be a significant misread of U.S. policy. Partly in response to Damascus's refusal to cooperate completely in the war on terrorism. President Bush signed the "Syria Accountability and Lebanese Sovereignty Restoration Act of 2003."[61] Under terms of the act, American firms cannot export any products to Syria beyond food and medicine. The president can wave this provision for an unspecified duration provided he determines that it would further U.S. national security and he submits justification for the waiver to the appropriate Congressional committees.[62] However, Bush increasingly shows little inclination to waive such provisions. In late February 2005, some U.S. government officials suggested that the Bush administration was exploring additional measures against Syria. Under the Syrian Accountability Act, Bush could cut off Syrian access to U.S. banks, limit the travel of Syrian diplomats within the United States, and freeze Syrian assets.[63] Other provisions call for the secretary of state to submit to Congress an annual report on provisions relating to the prevention of dual-use technologies that Damascus could use to advance its ballistic missiles and weapons of mass destruction projects; such reports will also prevent questions over Syrian compliance to fade from policymakers' attention.[64]

Future Policy

In a recent interview. Bashar al-Assad stated, "I am not Saddam Hussein. I want to cooperate."[65] Evidence indicates otherwise. Syrian attempts to obtain a sophisticated Russian ballistic missile undermine Washington's ability to prevent terrorist sponsors from advancing their military capabilities. Damascus's failure to come clean regarding prewar Iraqi convoys and immigration of Iraqi weapons personnel, as well as its flirtation with Abdul Qadir Khan, raise questions about Assad's sincerity.

The Syrian withdrawal from Lebanon has neither changed basic Syrian behavior nor altered its regional ambitions.

The unknowns regarding Syria's weapons programs are especially worrisome given Assad's continued rejection of international norms of behavior. Syrian obstructionism and attempts to augment its weapons of mass destruction stock make expansion and enforcement of the Proliferation Security Initiative imperative, a strategy supported by U.S. defense secretary Donald Rumsfeld.[66] Offering economic or political incentives to Yemen, Turkey, Egypt, and other countries which retain close relationships with Syria might help shut down avenues which the Syrian regime uses to advance its weapons projects although the damage to counter-proliferation efforts caused by Abdul Qadir Khan's network suggests that there should be a verification mechanism beyond simple diplomatic assurance.

Failure to counter Syrian weapons ambitions could undercut U.S. democracy and antiterror initiatives. The Syrian withdrawal from Lebanon has neither changed basic Syrian behavior nor altered its regional ambitions. The combination of a ballistic missile capability, chemical and biological weapons, and a willingness to arm or turn a blind-eye to terrorists—including those targeting the U.S. presence in Iraq—might lead to bolder terror initiatives, like the attempt in Amman in April 2004, as well as embolden rejectionism by a Syrian regime feeling its arsenal sufficient to deter a U.S. response. Only with sustained pressure can Washington prevent the Syrian regime from such a miscalculation.

Notes

1. *Yedi'ot Ahronot* (Tel Aviv), Sept. 16. 1994.
2. *Syria Primer,* Virtual Information Center, Apr. 24, 2003, p. 38, 47.
3. Associated Press, Apr. 28, 2005.
4. "The SS-26," The Claremont Institute, accessed June 8, 2005.
5. Ibid.
6. *Ha'aretz* (Tel Aviv), Jan. 13, 2005.
7. "The SS-26," The Claremont Institute.
8. Agence France-Presse, Feb. 16, 2005.
9. Radio Free Europe/Radio Liberty, Jan. 13, 2005.
10. "Overview of State-Sponsored Terrorism," *Patterns of Global Terrorism, 2004* (Washington, D.C.: U.S. Department of State, Apr. 2005).
11. *Agenlstvo Voyennykh Novostey* (Moscow), Mar. 25, 2005.
12. Associated Press, Apr. 28, 2005.
13. Associated Press, Apr. 21, 2005.
14. Associated Press, Apr. 26, 2005.
15. Yaakov Amidror, "Israel's Requirements for Defensible Borders," *Defensible Borders for a Lasting Peace* (Jerusalem: Jerusalem Center for Public Affairs), p. 33.
16. Reuters, Apr. 21, 2005.
17. *The Jerusalem Post,* June 5, 2005.
18. *The New York Times,* June 4, 2005.
19. *BBC News,* May 21, 2005.
20. *Potitkum.ru* (Moscow), Feb. 21, 2005.
21. Ibid.
22. "Unclassified Report to Congress on the Acquisition of Technology Relating to Weapons of Mass Destruction and Advanced Conventional Munitions, 1 July through 31 Dec. 2003," CIA, Nov. 2004, p. 6.
23. *The Washington Times,* Oct. 28, 2004.
24. Israel's Channel 2, Dec. 23, 2002.
25. *Petah Tiqva,* Yoman Shevu'i supplement (Tel Aviv), Feb. 21, 2003.
26. "Syria's Weapons of Mass Destruction and Missile Development Program," testimony of John R. Bolton. U.S. undersecretary of arms control and international security, before the House International Relations Committee, Subcommittee on the Middle East and Central Asia, Sept. 16. 2003; *BBC News,* Apr. 14, 2003; Alexander Downer, Australian minister of foreign affairs, news conference, Canberra, June 5, 2003.

27. Agence France-Presse, Apr. 17, 2003.

28. *Time,* Mar. 14, 2005.

29. Agence France-Presse, Apr. 15, 2003.

30. *Sunday Telegraph* (London), Jan. 25, 2005.

31. *Los Angeles Times,* Oct. 8, 1991.

32. Complied by Charles Duelfer, special advisor for strategy to the director of Central Intelligence.

33. *Comprehensive Report of the Special Advisori- to the DCI on Iraq's WMD,* vol. 1 (Washington, D.C.: CIA, Sept. 30, 2004), hereafter, Duelfer report, p. 104.

34. *The Times* (London), June 17, 2002.

35. Duelfer report, p. 239.

36. Dueller report, p. 104.

37. *Addendums to Comprehensive Report of the Special Advisor to the DCI on WMD,* Mar. 2005, accessed on June 8, 2005.

38. *The Washington Times,* Oct. 28. 2004.

39. *Petah Tiqva,* Yoman Shevu'i supplement, Feb. 21, 2003.

40. *De Telegraaf* (Amsterdam), Jan. 5, 2004.

41. *The Daily Telegraph* (London), Sept. 26, 2004.

42. State of the Union Address, Jan. 29, 2002.

43. "The Proliferation Security Initiative," U.S. Department of State, Bureau of Nonproliferation, July 28, 2004.

44. *The Washington Times,* Dec. 23, 2004.

45. *Time,* Feb. 14, 2005.

46. *Los Angeles Times,* June 25, 2004.

47. *Los Angeles Times,* Dec. 6, 2004.

48. *The News* (Islamabad), Jan. 5, 2005.

49. *Pattern of Global Terrorism,* 2004, p. 93.

50. *Patterns of Global Terrorism,* 2003 (Washington, D.C.: U.S. Department of State, Apr. 2004), p. 93.

51. U.N. Security Council Resolution 1559, S/RES/1559 (2004), Sept. 2, 2004.

52. Reuters, May 20, 2005.

53. Ben Thein, "Is Israel's Security Barrier Unique?" *Middle East Quarterly,* Fall 2004, p. 29.

54. Agence France-Presse, Mar. 25, 2005.

55. Associated Press, Mar. 1, 2005.

56. Reuters, Mar. 17, 2005.

57. *CNN News,* Apr. 26, 2004.

58. *The Washington Post,* June 19, 2002.

59. U.S. Embassy news release, Sept. 10, 2004.

60. *BBC NEWS,* Feb. 28, 2005.

61. "Fact Sheet: Implementing the Syria Accountability and Lebanese Sovereignty Restoration Act of 2003," White House news release, May 11, 2004.

62. Ibid.

63. *The Washington Post,* Feb. 17, 2005.

64. "Fact Sheet," May 11, 2004.

65. *Time,* Mar. 14, 2005.

66. *The Washington Times,* Dec. 23, 2004.

LEE KASS is an analyst in the research and analysis division of Science Applications International Corporation (SAIC). The views expressed in this article are his own.

Chávez Bides His Time

**A threat of war flared in Latin America, and just as quickly subsided.
Look closely, if you dare, at what Venezuela was up to.**

WILLIAM RATLIFF

South America's most serious threat of regional conflict in several decades erupted and receded during the first week of March, and most people in the United States didn't even notice. A shooting war between Colombia, on one side, and Venezuela and Ecuador, on the other, was averted—but there was no resolution of critical long-term regional disagreements. Indeed, these continue to grow more serious, not least because of information discovered in the computers of a dead Colombian guerrilla that may force Washington into a showdown with Venezuela.

What precipitated the crisis, and why should North Americans care? The trigger was simple enough, even though news reports and most Latin American leaders were quick to muddy the waters. A band of guerrillas of the Revolutionary Armed Forces of Colombia (FARC) from Colombia's Putumayo province retreated into what they considered a safe haven just two kilometers into northern Ecuador. Because the group included Raúl Reyes, the number-two leader of the FARC, the Colombian government decided it couldn't miss the opportunity to take him out, which it did, along with twenty-four others.

In the debris of the Ecuadorean guerrilla camp, Colombian forces found Reyes's body and his laptops, which reportedly were full of information about FARC that the world was not supposed to know, including evidence of secret support from Venezuela and Ecuador. (As of early April, Interpol was examining the laptops and messages to determine if they are authentic.) Ecuador's President Rafael Correa protested the Colombian incursion and traveled around the Americas lining up other presidents to stand behind him. Predictably, it was Venezuelan leader Hugo Chávez who led the charge against Colombian President Alvaro Uribe Vélez; Chávez mobilized troops on the border and threatened trade boycotts and war.

After a week of saber rattling and dire threats, the three presidents suddenly declared a truce March 7, and the Organization of American States (OAS) sent a commission to investigate the near clash. Uribe, whose incursion was supported by 83 percent of Colombians, apologized and said he would not repeat the action. Chávez and Correa reportedly agreed to fight threats to regional stability arising from irregular or criminal groups.

But although regional military conflict is probably no longer an immediate danger, popular frustration seethes and problems multiply in the Andes region. And Chávez and Correa have their own definitions of key terms of the agreement.

The U.S. Stake in the Conflict

Americans who support the development of functioning democracies and free markets should take a vital interest in what is happening in the northern Andean countries. Nowhere else in the Americas does a single region offer such clear and contrasting versions of domestic and international life, a virtual laboratory in which to test two contrary perspectives. Colombia has a democratic, pro-American government and for many years has had a reasonably productive market-oriented economy, despite decades of internal warfare against Marxist guerrillas, paramilitaries, and drug lords. Venezuela, on the other hand, has a militantly anti-American, increasingly authoritarian populist government, with an oil-rich but nonetheless grossly mismanaged and troubled economy. Venezuela in many ways apes all other failed populist regimes, though with a stronger international agenda.

Nowhere in the Americas does a single region offer such clear and contrasting versions of domestic and international life, a virtual laboratory in which to test two contrary perspectives.

Most of Latin America is full of frustrated people who are badly served or mistreated by their governments. Those people, who vote under conditions that often are only formally democratic, are courted by self-proclaimed Chavista messiahs like Correa in Ecuador and Evo Morales in Bolivia. Those two and other messiahs have turned to using democracy according to their own lights to consolidate personal power with the goal of remaining in office permanently. There are also democratically elected Chavista or Chavista-tilting leaders from Nicaragua to Argentina, and Chavistas have nearly won presidencies in places like Peru and Mexico.

Governments in Brazil, Uruguay, Chile, Peru, and Mexico are striving to develop and stave off Chavismo, though the results will depend on how successful they are in serving popular needs and aspirations. Always in the wings are demagogic leaders who play on and manipulate legitimate frustrations and offer the favorite cure-all of the day, now "twenty-first-century socialism," a Chávez concoction that carries the torch of Cuba's Fidel Castro, the recently retired anti-American icon of generations past.

Colombia is tangled up in the web of the disruptive—and destructive—war on drugs. For many years, Colombia has been the main recipient of U.S. aid in the Americas; since 2000, that support has totaled $5 billion, most of it military aid that has contributed much toward weakening FARC and improving national stability. FARC began decades ago as the military wing of the pro-Soviet Communist Party of Colombia, and it has been terrorizing, killing, and kidnapping Colombians ever since. After the collapse of the Soviet bloc and its financial and logistic support, FARC had to find another way to sustain itself; in Colombia that predictably meant drugs. FARC holds hundreds of prisoners in the jungles and mountains, who now serve above all as shields to discourage government attacks on top FARC leaders.

FARC membership (according to official Colombian estimates, about 6,000 fighters) has declined by two-thirds since Uribe became president. A week after Reyes's death, a second member of FARC's seven-member ruling body was killed by his own bodyguard. But FARC remains a dangerous force, and many governments, including those of the United States and the European Union, brand it a terrorist organization. Chávez and Correa, to the contrary, want FARC to be classified as a legitimate belligerent in Colombia; indeed, the Venezuelan president has called FARC a liberation movement and brands Uribe's government a "criminal . . . terrorist state."

The Venezuelan president has called FARC a liberation movement and brands Colombia's government a "criminal . . . terrorist state."

Chávez's hostility appears to go beyond bluster. If the files on the laptops found after Reyes's death prove authentic (Correa and Chávez have naturally called them fakes), the years of rumors of Chávez involvement with FARC will be shown to be true, with significant implications for the future. According to a *Washington Post* article by Jackson Diehl, the files included a plan to sanitize the FARC internationally and then have it put forward a Chavista presidential candidate in the next Colombian elections (not an entirely bad idea, although FARC has its own tragic history in Colombia). FARC needs sanctuaries

and supplies, and Chávez is eager to support any group that will fight America and its allies; he has spent billions of dollars arming Venezuela for what he warns is an almost inevitable confrontation with the United States. His key Andean goal is overthrowing the most unequivocal U.S. ally in South America, Colombia's Uribe.

But now a link between Chávez and terrorists, if proven, may force Washington either to deny the connection or to break ties with Venezuela and cut off purchases of its oil. The United States could adjust to such a cutoff with an effort, but the Venezuelan economy would be hit hard; its heavy oil is unusable for most purposes unless it is refined, and most of the refineries used by Venezuela are in the United States. Conspiracy theorists might even argue that the CIA planted the laptops to force the U.S. government to cut the oil bonds between Washington and Caracas and, in so doing, throw Venezuela into a crisis sufficient to topple Chávez or perhaps set him to attacking his neighbors.

Also among the laptop revelations, as reported by *Jane's Terrorism and Security Monitor* on April 4, were messages indicating Correa's knowledge of and support for guerrillas using border camps. Stored e-mail messages show that there were relatively fixed FARC camps in Ecuador, which were known to at least some of Ecuador's military commanders, and that Ecuador's president not only wanted the camps to remain well-stocked safe havens but was willing to remove military leaders who objected.

Hard Questions about Sovereignty

Uribe characterized Colombia's response to the guerrillas, and to regional criticism of the Ecuador incursion, as follows: "We are not warmongers, but we are not weak. We cannot allow terrorists who seek refuge in other countries to spill the blood of our countrymen."

Most Latin American leaders reacted predictably to the crisis of early March. As soon as the border crossing was reported, they repeatedly invoked the national sovereignty of Ecuador, as if by repetition they could treat a complicated problem as a simple matter of law. To be sure, it is desirable to defend national sovereignty, but the nature of this complex border case was left unexamined: principally, the possibility of state-sponsored terrorism. Tal Becker, an international lawyer and a legal adviser to Israel's Ministry of Foreign Affairs, wrestled with similar issues in his book *Terrorism and the State: Rethinking the Rules of State Responsibility*. Becker articulates "a causation-based system of state responsibility for terrorism." He acknowledges the difficulty of assigning that responsibility, but concludes that "to protect the foundations of the international system . . . it is necessary to see in state toleration of terrorist activity, or its failure to prevent it, a fundamental violation of the covenants made both between states and within them."

Using this as a guideline, and considering the messages on Reyes's computer, it is clear that Colombia's sovereignty was effectively violated by Ecuador's knowingly harboring the FARC terrorists.

Statements by the Organization of American States placed responsibility for the incursion on Colombia and reaffirmed its absolute defense of the "national sovereignty of Ecuador." One resolution presumably committed all member states "to combat threats to security caused by the actions of irregular groups or criminal organizations, especially those associated with drug trafficking." But the OAS did not acknowledge that the March 1 attack came precisely because Ecuador was failing to combat those threats inside its own borders. Nor did it clearly define its terms so that Chávez and Correa could be held to the OAS promise. Chávez's compliance will be very difficult to monitor, compared to Uribe's commitment not to invade again.

Colombia's strike rejected the idea that international law permits terrorists to attack and then to flee with impunity to a neighboring country that tolerates or even supports them. Just a week before the Colombian action, the Turkish military launched a multiday invasion into northern Iraq to wipe out Kurdistan Workers Party (PKK) forces that were attacking Turkey from sanctuaries there. If international law does not sanction self-defense in such cases, it ceases to be relevant in some of the most explosive areas of the world, where it is desperately needed.

WILLIAM RATLIFF is a research fellow at the Hoover Institution and the curator of the Americas Collection at the Hoover Archives.

UNIT 4

International Terrorism

Unit Selections

Key Points to Consider

- Do India and Pakistan share a common enemy?

- What factors contributed to violence in the Basque region? Will there be peace at last?

- Will a military victory against the Tamil Tigers bring an end to the conflict?

- What factors have contributed to the polarization of the Muslim population in Europe?

Student Website
www.mhcls.com

Internet References

International Association for Counterterrorism and Security Professionals
   http://www.iacsp.com/index.html
The International Policy Institute for Counter-Terrorism
   http://www.ict.org.il
United Nations Website on Terrorism
   http://www.un.org/terrorism
United States Institute of Peace
   http://www.usip.org/library/topics/terrorism.html
United Nations Office on Drugs and Crime
   http://www.unodc.org/unodc/en/terrorism/index.html
Terrorism Studies: Directory of Online Sources
   http://www.academicinfo.net/terrorism.html
Free Muslims Coalition
   http://www.freemuslims.org/

International terrorism has changed significantly over time. Simply said, it has become more complex. Increased organizational complexity, improved communications, and an increased willingness to cause mass casualties, pose new challenges for the international community.

Individuals and small groups dominated international terrorism in the 1970s. Larger groups and organizations played a critical role in international terrorism in the 1980s. More complex multinational terrorist networks emerged in the 1990s. More recently, small independent groups of individuals, of local origin, have emerged to carry out attacks in their home countries in support of broad global movements. Now, all four generations and levels of organizational structure appear to exist. Sometimes terrorists act locally or regionally to pursue independent agendas. At other times they take advantage of cross-national links to obtain greater access to weapons, training, or financial resources. On occasion, they may even temporarily set aside local interests and objectives to cooperate within loosely connected international networks to pursue broader ideological agendas. At a given point in time international terrorists can be engaged in activities at all levels, posing unique challenges to those engaged in the study of, and struggle against, international terrorism.

Modern communications technologies have changed the way international terrorists operate. The cellphone and the laptop computer have become as important as the bomb and the AK-47 in the terrorist arsenal. The Internet has provided terrorists with instant access to global communications, has enhanced their ability to exchange information, and provides them with an effective vehicle to rally their supporters. Almost all major international terrorist organizations operate their own websites and communicate via the Internet.

A particularly disturbing trend in contemporary international terrorism is the increasing willingness by some terrorists to cause mass casualties to innocent victims. While, the potential causes of this trend are subject to debate, this trend has elevated terrorism to the top of the international agenda. While, over the past several decades, the number of international terrorist incidents has declined, the casualties caused by international terrorism have steadily increased. More importantly, this trend has focused international attention on terrorist methods

© Royalty-Free/Corbis

deemed unlikely only a few years ago. Potential threats posed by biological, chemical, or radiological weapons are again at the forefront of international concern.

The selections in this unit reflect some of the diversity in international terrorism. The first article, examines the events leading to the Mumbai attacks through the eyes of Muhammad Ajmal Kasab, the only gunman captured. In the article, Michael Petrou argues that despite the perpetrators ties to Pakistan, recent attacks by Islamic terrorists in India and Pakistan indicate that they "share a common enemy." Next, Joshua Hammer explores the roots of the conflict in the Basque region of Spain. While skepticism remains high on both sides, there is some hope that the latest cease-fire will lead to a peace agreement ending decades of separatist violence. In the third article, Jason Motlagh claims that despite victories on the battlefield, a defeat of the Tamil Tigers by the Sri Lankan army will not end the conflict. He believes that a lasting peace can only be achieved through a political strategy that addresses the root causes of Tamil nationalism. Finally, Gary Younge argues that the attacks of 9/11 and the bombings in London and Madrid have polarized hard-right nationalist and anti-immigrant parties in Europe. He believes that violence and bigotry by neo-fascists may further alienate Europe's Muslim population.

Trail of Terror

Michael Petrou

It is unlikely that Muhammad Ajmal Kasab drew a second glance from onlookers when he walked into Mumbai's historic Chhatrapati Shivaji Terminus railway station a little after 9 P.M. on Nov. 26. The 21-year-old man's upper body was heavily muscled, but his clean-shaven face was broad and youthful, softened by the remnants of baby fat. He wore sneakers, a pink wristband, baggy cargo pants and a T-shirt with a Versace designer label across the chest. With a blue backpack slung across his shoulder, he looked like a typical college student enjoying a bit of carefree travel—perhaps on his way to Goa, a favourite destination a little further down the coast.

But in his backpack, in addition to dried fruit and a mobile phone, Kasab carried grenades and ammunition magazines for the AK-47 assault rifle he had managed to conceal as well. When he reached crowded platform 13, Kasab and his partner Ismail Khan began shooting indiscriminately at commuters and diners in the train station café. The crowd panicked and those who could, fled. One of two police at the station tried to return fire while hiding in an alcove, but he was armed with a Second World War-era rifle and was forced to scramble for shelter while Kasab and Khan blazed away from their hips with automatic weapons.

The pair left the station and ambushed a police van, spraying it with gunfire and dumping the bodies of the slain officers on the road, one of whom was the anti-terrorism squad chief Hemant Karkare. Unknown to them, two police, including Const. Arun Jadhav, were alive but wounded in the back seat. The van careened through the city, with one of the two terrorists driving and the other shooting out the window. When Jadhav's colleague's cellphone rang, one of the gunman turned around and shot him. The terrorists said little, joking at one point about a police officer they murdered who had been wearing a bulletproof vest. Jadhav, who had been shot three times, was unable to reach his weapon. "I wish I could have lifted my gun," he would later say from his hospital bed.

When one of the van's tires went flat, Kasab and Khan abandoned the vehicle and hijacked another car. Police intercepted the pair and shot Khan dead. An enraged crowd at the scene descended on Kasab, kicking and thrashing him with sticks before police intervened and saved him. Here, Kasab's perverted good fortune turned. He would later tell police that he had been trained to "kill to the last breath." Instead, Kasab was captured alive. While he initially begged medical staff to give

him saline to save his life, following interrogations by police he has reportedly said, "I don't want to live."

But Kasab is alive and talking. He is now telling Indian investigators about the attacks, how they were planned, and who the people were who sent him and his terrorist colleagues on their mission. The picture Kasab paints is blurry and is further confused by Indian officials—perhaps numbering as many as 15—who sat in on his interrogations and are furiously leaking often inconsistent reports of what they heard to local and international media. Throw in recollections from the odd hospital volunteer who might have overheard a snippet of conversation and the story that emerges is one that will change as further evidence is compiled, and rumours and hearsay are separated from facts. For the moment, though, Kasab's testimony—at least the version of it passed on by Indian officials crowded around his hospital bed—is the foundation for what is so far known about the atrocities in Mumbai and who was behind them.

Muhammad Ajmal Kasab's road to infamy began over a year ago at a mountain training camp near Muzaffarabad, in Pakistan-administered Kashmir. The camp was run by Lashkar-e-Taiba, a radical Islamist organization linked to international jihadist groups, including al-Qaeda, as well as to Pakistan's spy agency, Inter-Services Intelligence (ISI)—which has long sponsored Islamist insurgent groups, including the Taliban, in both Afghanistan and Indian-administered Kashmir.

Details about Kasab's life before arriving at the camp are vague. He is reportedly from Faridkot village in Pakistan's Punjab province. His rural village lies in an area that is a rich recruiting ground for jihadists. He grew up poor, the son of a snack vendor, and left the village about four years ago. According to some press reports, Kasab told interrogators that his father "sold" him to a leading member of Lashkar-e-Taiba, for about $4,500. One Faridkot villager told journalist Saeed Shah that Kasab would return home about once a year and talk about "freeing" Kashmir from Indian rule.

In Muzaffarabad, Kasab met other members of the eventual team of 10 who would assault Mumbai. Some reports have it that they were selected from a larger group of 24 trainees, and that not all were initially trained at the same camp. They were reportedly given false names and discouraged from talking with each other about topics other than their mission. They were trained in the use of explosives, urban warfare, and hand-to-hand combat. At another Kashmiri camp near the massive Mangla Dam, they practised beach landings. All became extremely muscular in the course of their training. An Indian official suggested that traces of steroids were found in the blood of the slain terrorists, along with cocaine and other stimulants that allowed the 10 men to battle hundreds of Indian police and soldiers for 60 hours, apparently without sleep.

Kasab and his colleagues travelled to Rawalpindi when their training was over. Here, they memorized their targets: the Chhatrapati Shivaji Terminus railway station, the Taj Mahal and Oberoi hotels, and the Chabad House Jewish Centre. A reconnaissance team had reportedly chosen the targets and the routes to reach them in advance. Extra ammunition and weapons were allegedly cached in at least one of the hotels, and explosives might also have been smuggled into the city—perhaps with the assistance of local collaborators. Indian police have arrested several native Indians on suspicion of a connection to the attacks.

Kasab's assault team then moved to the Pakistani port city of Karachi to begin their journey to Mumbai by ship. A wealthy gangster named Dawood Ibrahim makes his home there. He is originally from Mumbai, and his crime syndicate, "D-Company," still controls smuggling into the city. Although he has a taste for lavish parties, Bollywood movies, and women, Ibrahim began moving in Islamist circles in the 1990s and is believed to have financed the 1993 bombings in Mumbai that killed more than 250 people. Some have argued that, given his extensive connections in Mumbai's criminal underworld, he might have played a role in these attacks as well. He is thought to be living under the protection of the ISI. India has demanded that he be handed over; Pakistan denies knowledge of where he is.

When the terrorists left Karachi, the Indian navy was boarding and searching foreign ships in the Arabian Sea, and the team grew nervous. Abandoning their vessel and using motorized dinghies, they hijacked a local fishing boat, the *Kuber,* and killed everyone but the captain, whom they forced to steer for India. As they closed in on Mumbai, the terrorists slit the captain's throat, climbed back into their dinghies and slipped into Mumbai. They brushed aside questions from the harbourmaster, split into teams, and raced into the night. Within minutes, Mumbai was awash in carnage and mayhem that would last more than two days. Kasab and his fellow terrorists murdered almost 200 people. He is the only one of the 10 attackers still alive.

Amid the many horrific details that Kasab has disclosed, by far the most consequential, is his claim to have been trained and dispatched by Lashkar-e-Taiba. While unproven, it is a credible admission and is supported by intelligence agencies in both India and the United States. Pakistan initially said it had seen no evidence linking the attacks to any Pakistani groups. But earlier this week the Pakistani army raided a Lashkar-e-Taiba camp near Muzaffarabad and arrested the group's operational chief, Zakiur Rehman Lakhvi—an implicit acknowledgment that it, too, accepts Lashkar's possible responsibility for the Mumbai assault.

Lashkar-e-Taiba, whose name means "Army of the Pure," has its origins in the late 1980s and early 1990s as the military wing of the Pakistani Islamist organization Markaz al-Dawa wal-Irshad, which has since changed its name to Jamaat-ud-Dawah. It was created with the assistance of the ISI to wage an insurgency in Indian-controlled Kashmir and to train other Muslim extremists in India. According to Husain Haqqani, a former professor at Boston University and now Pakistan's ambassador to the U.S., the group, which promotes the ultra-conservative Wahhabi form of Islam, was supported with Saudi money. Bruce Riedel, a senior fellow at the Brookings Institution who spent three decades working for the CIA, says Osama bin Laden was also an early supporter.

Lashkar-e-Taiba was officially banned by Pakistan in 2002, following heavy pressure on Pakistan from the U.S. But it continues to operate behind its still-legal front organization, Jamaat-ud-Dawah, which claims to be a charity, and does help many poor Pakistanis. The Muzaffarabad camp, for example, officially functioned under the banner of Jamaat-ud-Dawah, rather than Lashkar-e-Taiba. Jamaat's leader, Hafiz Muhammad Saeed, denies any association with Lashkar-e-Taiba, but it is widely understood that he leads that group, too—given that he founded it.

Although liberating Kashmir is Lashkar's primary goal, it has adopted what Haqqani has described in a 2005 essay as "a maximalist agenda for global jihad." Haqqani cites a Markaz al-Dawa wal-Irshad publication titled "Why Are We Waging Jihad?" that describes the U.S., Israel, and India as enemies of Islam. The publication goes on to list several often-cited reasons for jihad, including facilitating the conversion to and practice of Islam, ensuring Islam's ascendancy, and liberating Muslim territories under non-Muslim occupation. On this last point, Lashkar's rhetoric echoes that of Osama bin Laden. Supposedly occupied Muslim lands include: Spain, India, Bulgaria, Hungary, Cyprus, Sicily, Ethiopia, Israel and Palestine, as well as parts of Russia, China, France and Switzerland. All these territories "were Muslim lands, and it is our duty to get them back from unbelievers."

To this end, Lashkar-e-Taiba co-operates with other jihadist groups. One Lashkar militant in Pakistan told a local researcher hired by *Maclean's* that some members of his organization regularly meet with al-Qaeda and the Taliban to discuss strategy. "Not everyone agrees with these meetings," he says. "Since the war in Afghanistan started, there have been disagreements about how to fight our enemies. We are surrounded by them now." He said some Lashkar members who have embraced the global jihad might have been involved in the Mumbai attacks, but he doesn't think the group as a whole was behind it.

Lashkar has sent its members to fight with the Taliban in Afghanistan and with Islamist insurgents in Iraq. At least seven Lashkar members were killed there in 2003. "The powerful Western world is terrorizing Muslims. We are being invaded, humiliated, manipulated and looted. How can we respond but through jihad?" Lashkar leader Hafiz Muhammad Saeed said in the weeks after the American-led invasion of Iraq. "We must fight against the evil trio, America, Israel, and India. Suicide missions are in accordance with Islam. In fact, a suicide attack is the best form of jihad."

Lashkar's co-operation with al-Qaeda appears to have solidified since the Sept. 11, 2001, terrorist attacks. Links between the two groups are "extensive," Bruce Hoffman, a professor of security studies at Georgetown University and a former scholar-in-residence for counterterrorism at the CIA, told *Maclean's*. "I would describe them as al-Qaeda's stalking horse in many respects. They have global ambitions, and they play very directly into the global jihad. They're much more than a Kashmiri separatist group."

Senior al-Qaeda member Abu Zubaydah was captured in a Lashkar safe house in Pakistan in 2002. Others have met the same fate. Gary Schroen, the CIA's former station chief in Islamabad who led the first CIA team into Afghanistan after 9/11, has noted that "since 2002, whenever a raid has been conducted in Pakistan against al-Qaeda, al-Qaeda members are found being hosted by militant Pakistanis, primarily from the LeT group." According to Riedel, Lashkar actively recruits among Pakistan's large diaspora in Britain.

What remains unclear is Lashkar's relationship with Pakistan's government and the ISI. Lashkar-e-Taiba is "a creation of the ISI and the Pakistani government," Hoffman says. But he notes that many of the connections that bound Lashkar to the ISI have "frayed or atrophied" as Lashkar expanded its reach beyond Kashmir, and the government was pressured to rein it in. "This historically is not unusual if a government supports terrorist organizations where there is a commonality of aims—in this case the liberation of Kashmir," Hoffman says. "But then very often the terrorist groups divert and pursue their own agenda. I don't think the ISI necessarily has the same interest in global jihad."

India's retort, quite naturally, would be that even if Pakistan has let slip its grip on Lashkar's leash, the dog still sleeps in Islamabad's backyard. Lashkar and its front organization Jamaat-ud-Dawah have hundreds of schools, mosques, medical clinics and offices, in addition to training camps. Until the raid on the Lashkar camp this week, these were rarely targeted. "It depends how you define complicity," Hoffman says, when asked about Pakistan's responsibility. "Are they complicit in the sense that the Pakistani government was involved in the attacks? That's one thing. But are they complicit in the sense that Lashkar-e-Taiba is allowed to operate almost unmolested in Pakistan? I mean, yeah."

Complicating the question of accountability is the fact that even the ISI does not have control over all of its agents—some of whom are more loyal to the Islamist militant groups they helped create than to their government. A senior member of the ISI told a *Maclean's* researcher that elements of the security services warn radical Islamist groups when government forces are sent to apprehend them. "Whatever intelligence we get," he says, requesting anonymity, "quickly becomes obsolete. We hear about a meeting of the senior leadership but before we can swoop in, they know. They shift and we come up empty-handed."

This ISI official's frustration with his rogue spies reflects a larger lesson Pakistan is learning about the dangers of sowing the wind. For years, Pakistan's army and spy agency quietly funded and trained Islamist terror groups, political parties, and even aspirant governments—such as Lashkar-e-Taiba, Jamiat-e-Islami, and the Taliban—as a means of projecting influence and, most often, of hitting India while retaining a semblance of plausible deniability. But now the whirlwind has come home. Islamist militias, including a Pakistani version of the Taliban, have launched an insurrection along the country's northwest frontier with Afghanistan, and Islamist terror attacks are increasingly frequent elsewhere across the country. One such attack last December killed former prime minister Benazir Bhutto, who had returned home to run for office and had promised to defeat the Islamist insurgents. Her husband, Asaf Ali Zardari, is now the nation's elected president.

Pakistan's civilian government is hitting back. It has sent the army into the country's Tribal Areas, where al-Qaeda, the Pakistani Taliban and affiliated Islamist groups have found refuge and planned several international terror attacks. But these offensives produce a backlash. Among the motivations for the attacks on Mumbai might have been a desire to relieve pressure on Islamists in the Tribal Areas by ratcheting up tensions with India in the east. "Our brothers in the Tribal Areas are suffering," says the Lashkar-e-Taiba member. "The people who carried out this attack probably want to damage Indian and Pakistani relations so that Pakistan is forced to send troops back to the Indian border." Zardari has also speculated that the Mumbai attacks were designed to "divert attention from the real war between the terrorists and the Pakistani army in the Tribal Areas."

It's a sensible strategy, and one with a precedent. The December 2001 terrorist attack on the Indian parliament brought India and Pakistan to the brink of war, as each nation mobilized one million men for nearly a year. As the Pakistani journalist Ahmed Rashid notes in his recent book, *Descent into Chaos*, Pakistan was forced to move its troops away from the Afghan border to face the Indian army in the east. This allowed the Taliban and al-Qaeda escaping from Afghanistan to slip into Pakistan and establish a safe haven there.

Today, as in late 2001, the Taliban, al-Qaeda, and other radical Islamists on the Afghan-Pakistan frontier risk being squeezed between the Pakistani army—now acting with more resolve—and NATO and U.S. forces in Afghanistan. American unmanned Predator drones send Hellfire missiles into militants' homes on the Pakistani side of the border, and Barack Obama's pledge to send thousands of additional soldiers to Afghanistan will only increase the pressure. But were India and Pakistan to move to a war footing, this pressure would dissipate—Pakistani troops would withdraw, the Pakistani Taliban would take more territory, and al-Qaeda would likely be emboldened by its greater freedom.

It may still come to this. India's moderate government, led by Prime Minister Manmohan Singh and his Congress party, is weak and will face demands for revenge—both from the general public and the opposition Hindu nationalist Bharatiya Janata Party, which may whip up anti-Muslim and anti-Pakistani rhetoric in an upcoming election. Already there has been heated public anger on both sides of the border.

And yet the governments of the two nuclear-armed nations, which have been creeping toward peace since 2004, have so far shown restraint. Pakistan has promised to co-operate with India in its investigation, and its Muzaffarabad raid suggests Islamabad is willing to back up its words with action. The

Pakistani government fears an Indian military strike. It is also facing enormous pressure from the U.S., which has provided Pakistan with more than US$10 billion in military and economic assistance since 2001. But with suspected Islamist terrorists attacking civilian targets in Pakistan, even in the aftermath of the assault on Mumbai, it is becoming unavoidably apparent that the two countries share a common enemy. It's too soon to know what all the ramifications of the assault on Mumbai will be. But if, as seems likely, the attacks were designed to push India and Pakistan toward a deeper conflict, it's not unrealistic to hope that they will backfire.

With Adnan R. Khan.

Peace at Last?

Home to glittering beaches, robust wines, piquant foods and Bilbao's sparkling new Guggenheim Museum, the Basque Country of northern Spain has been riven by separatist violence for decades. Though political tensions linger, terrorists agreed to a cease-fire this past March. Will it mean peace at last?

JOSHUA HAMMER

The first blast reverberated through the old quarter of San Sebastián at one o'clock in the afternoon. It rattled the windows of the ornate buildings around the 18th-century Santa Maria del Coro church and sent a flock of pigeons into the sky. We were standing in a cobblestone plaza outside one of the town's most famous *pintxos*—tapas—bars, La Cuchara de San Telmo, eating braised rabbit and sipping red Rioja wine when we heard it. A minute later came a second explosion, and then a third. "Let's go see what's happening," said my companion, Gabriella Ranelli de Aguirre, an American tour operator married to a San Sebastián native, who has been living there for nearly 20 years.

I didn't know what to think. This was Basque Country, after all, the homeland of Euskadi Ta Askatasuna, or ETA (Basque for "Basque Homeland and Freedom"), which has been waging a violent campaign for independence from Spain for nearly four decades. True, the group, which has killed some 800 people and maimed hundreds more, had not carried out a bombing or shooting for three years, and momentum appeared to be building toward a lasting peace.

This past March, in a communiqué that stunned Spain and the world, the group had even declared a "permanent cease-fire" and said it was committed to promoting "a democratic process." Batasuna, ETA's political arm—which had been banned by the Spanish supreme court in 2003—has engaged in quiet talks with the Basque Nationalist Party and other Basque political parties about establishing a road map to a permanent peace. And, in another sign of changing times, Gerry Adams, the head of Sinn Fein, the IRA's political wing, and Gerry Kelly, a convicted bomber turned Sinn Fein deputy, traveled to the Basque Country last spring to give Batasuna advice on peace negotiations. The Sinn Fein leaders, who once gave ETA counsel on bomb-making technology, have also been lobbying the Spanish government to drop charges against top Basque separatists, legalize Batasuna and move 700 ETA prisoners held in Spanish and French jails closer to their families. "We are approaching

the beginning of the end of ETA," Prime Minister José Luis Rodríguez Zapatero declared in February 2006.

But as Ranelli and I raced toward the harbor, I had to wonder if the group had returned to its old tactics. Then I saw the cause of the commotion: a white-haired man wearing a blue Napoleonic military uniform with epaulets and brandishing a musket was firing into the air. He belonged, he explained, to Olla Gora, one of San Sebastián's dozens of "eating societies," male-only clubs dedicated to the pursuit of socializing and gastronomic indulgence. "It's our [society's] centennial," he said, and its members were reenacting the Napoleonic battles that raged here in the 19th century As Ranelli and I made our way back down through the quaint alleys of the old quarter—rebuilt after 1813, when British and Portuguese troops burned down almost all of it—she said my reaction was all too common. "San Sebastián is a wonderful town," she went on, "but the violence has eclipsed everything else. A lot of my friends have had the impression that this is a scary place—another Beirut."

Comparisons to Lebanon may be exaggerated. But this rugged region in the shadow of the Pyrenees has long been an anomaly—an enclave marked by an ancient language, a tradition of fine food and wine, and a political culture soaked in blood. Feeding on Basque pride and decades of repression by Spanish dictator Francisco Franco, ETA's campaign of terror turned elegant cities such as San Sebastián and Bilbao into caldrons of fear and violence. At the height of its violent campaign for independence, in 1980, the separatists murdered 91 people, and countless business enterprises have fallen victim to ETA extortion over the past four decades. "Everybody in Basque Country has a cousin or an uncle who has either been a victim or a member of the group," one Basque journalist told me.

Now ETA is widely regarded as an anachronism, a hold-over from the days when radical groups such as Italy's Red Brigades and West Germany's Baader-Meinhof gang were recruiting European youth with their Marxist-Leninist rhetoric and desperado chic. In 1997, the United States government designated ETA a foreign terrorist organization. Since then, a number of developments—the Basque Country's growing prosperity; a post 9/11 crackdown on terrorist groups; widespread revulsion at violent tactics in the aftermath oral Qaeda's 2004 Madrid train bombing (for which ETA was initially blamed); arrests of ETA fugitives in both Spain and France; and a waning enthusiasm for ETA's aim of independence—have drained the movement of much of its vigor.

The peace process, however, is still fragile. In recent years, ETA has declared other cease-fires, all of which collapsed. The main Spanish opposition party, led by former prime minister José María Aznar, has urged the government not to negotiate. The peace initiative is being challenged by victims of ETA terror, and any deal is likely to leave unresolved the still contentious issue of Basque independence. Zapatero, in June 2006, warned that the process would be "long, tough and difficult," saying that the government would proceed with "prudence and discretion."

Then, a series of setbacks jolted the Spanish government and raised fears of a return to violence. First, in August, ETA publicly criticized the Spanish and French governments for "continuous attacks" against the Basques, apparently referring to the arrests and trials of ETA members that have gone on in spite of the cease-fire. Three hooded ETA members read a communiqué at a pro-independence rally in late September, confirming the group's "commitment to continue fighting, arms in hand, until independence and socialism is achieved in Euskal Herria [Basque Country]." A week later, a hiker in the woods in French Basque Country, near the Spanish border, stumbled across hidden weapons—including guns and chemicals for bomb-making—sealed in plastic bins, evidently intended for ETA. Later in October, some 350 guns disappeared from a gun store in Nîmes, France; it was suspected that ETA had engineered the theft. It was perhaps the starkest indication yet that the group could be preparing for the collapse of negotiations, and the resumption of attacks.

But despite all the obstacles, the mood is upbeat. Traveling around Basque Country, from the avenues of San Sebastian to mountain villages deep in the Basque heartland, I encountered a sense of optimism—a belief that the Basques have a real chance of a lasting peace for the first time in decades. "I still remember the day I heard the news [about the cease-fire]. It gave me goose pimples," says Alejandra Iturrioz, mayor of Ordizia; a mountain town where a dozen citizens have been killed by the group since 1968.

In Bilbao, Basque Country's biggest city and an emerging cultural capital (home to architect Frank Gehry's Guggenheim Museum), the change is already being felt. "More people came this summer than ever before," says Ana López de Munain, the communications director for the striking titanium-and-glass creation. "The mood has become more relaxed. We just hope it stays that way."

Nowhere are the benefits of waning tension more evident than in San Sebastián, a cosmopolitan seaside resort that comfortably straddles the Basque and Spanish worlds. Twelve miles west of the French border, along a rugged, horseshoe-shaped bay facing the Bay of Biscay, San Sebastian was a Basque fishing and trading town until the mid-19th century; in 1845 Spanish queen Isabel II, stricken with a skin ailment, came to bathe in the Bay of Concha on her doctor's orders. Aristocrats from Madrid and Barcelona followed, throwing up beachfront cabanas and Belle Epoque villas, wedding-cake structures adorned with turrets and spires. Along the Rio Urumea, a tidal river that empties into the Bay of Concha and divides the city in two, I strolled the Paseo de Francia—a faux stretch of the Ile St. Louis, with a Seine-like promenade.

San Sebastian itself has been the scene of political violence: in 1995, an ETA gunman walked into a downtown bar and shot dead one of the city's most popular politicians, Gregorio Ordoñez. Six years later, thousands marched silently through the streets to protest the murder of newspaper executive Santiago Oleaga Elejabarrieta. But there hasn't been a shooting or bombing here in years. Real estate is booming, with two-bedroom condominiums facing the sea fetching up to a million euros.

I went to lunch in the affluent Gros neighborhood with Gabriella Ranelli and her husband, Aitor Aguirre, a 39-year-old former professional player of pelota, similar to the sport better known in the United States as jai alai, the indoor game played with a hard rubber ball and gloves with basket-like extensions. (Pelota is the most popular sport in Basque Country) We stopped by Aloña Berri, a pintxos bar known for its exquisite food miniatures, and ordered plates of Chipiron en Equilibria, a tiny square of rice infused with squid broth, served with sugar crystals spun around a wooden stick that spears a baby squid. Sophisticated establishments like this one have transformed San Sebastian into one of the culinary centers of Western Europe. Aguirre told me that these days the city is dedicated far more to the pursuit of good times than political agitation. "The roots of the Basque problems are in the provinces, where Basque culture is strongest, the language is spoken all the time and people feel that their identity is more threatened," he added. "Here, on the coast, with the cosmopolitan influence, we don't feel it as much."

Still, San Sebastian remains distinctly Basque. About 40 percent of its population speaks Basque; identification with Spain is not strong. Here, separatist politics still stir emotions. Spanish director Julio Medem's documentary *La Pelota Vasca* (*The Basque Ball*), featuring interviews with 70 Basques about the conflict, created a furor at the 2003 San Sebastian film festival. And memories of Franco's brutalities are etched into the city's psyche. The palace, where Franco vacationed for 35 years, has been shuttered since his death in November 1975; the city still debates whether to turn it into a museum, a hotel or a memorial to his victims.

One rainy afternoon, after taking in an exhibition of Russian paintings at Bilbao's Guggenheim Museum, I made the 30-minute drive to Gernika, set in a narrow riverine valley in Vizcaya Province. Gernika is the spiritual capital of the Basques, whose ancient culture and language, some believe, date back several thousand years. From medieval times, Castilian monarchs met here, beneath a sacred oak, to guarantee the Basques their traditional rights, or fueros, including special tax status and exemption from serving in the Castilian army. But in 1876, at the end of the second Carlist War in Spain, these guarantees were finally abrogated, and the Basques' dreams of autonomy or independence from Spain were indefinitely deferred.

I parked my car at the edge of town and walked to the main square, the site of the Gernika Peace Museum, which commemorates the event that has come to define the town. When the Spanish Civil War broke out in 1936, the Basques allied themselves with the Republican government, or Loyalists, against the fascists, led by Franco. On April 26, 1937, the Italian and German Air Forces, on Franco's orders, carpet-bombed and strafed Gernika, killing at least 250 people, an event immortalized by Picasso's painting named for the town. (The artist used an alternate spelling.) "Gernika is seared into the heart of every Basque," I was told by Ana Teresa Núñez Monasterio, an archivist at the city's new Peace Museum, which features multimedia displays chronicling the bombing.

Franco's fascist forces defeated the Loyalists in 1939; from then on, the dictator waged a relentless campaign to erase Basque identity. He drove the leadership into exile, banned the Basque flag and traditional dancing, and made even speaking Basque punishable by a prison term. Some families reverted to speaking Spanish, even in the privacy of their homes; others taught the language to their children in secret, or sent them to clandestine schools, or ikastola. Children caught speaking Basque in regular schools were punished; teachers would pass a steel ring from one student caught speaking Basque to the next; the last one to hold the ring each day would be whipped. Margarita Otaegui Arizmendi, the director of the language center at the Deusto University in San Sebastian, recalls, "Franco was very successful in instilling fear. A lot of the children grew up without a knowledge of Basque—we call them "the generation of silence.""

After Franco's death, King Juan Carlos took power and legalized the Basque language; in 1979, he granted autonomy to the three Spanish Basque provinces, Alava, Guipúzcoa and Vizcaya. (Basque separatists also regard the Spanish province of Navarra as part of their homeland.) In 1980, a Basque parliament elected a president and established a capital at Vitoria-Gasteiz, beginning a new era. But ETA, founded by a small group of revolutionaries in 1959, has never given up its goal-full independence for the Spanish Basque provinces and unification with the three Basque-speaking provinces on the French side (where the nationalist movement is less fervent). For many Spanish Basques, the goal of independence has come to seem meaningless. "There's a whole generation of people under the age of 30 who have no memories of Franco," a Basque journalist told me. "We have prosperity, we have autonomy; we're pretty well off on all counts."

The journey from San Sebastián to Ordizia takes only 30 minutes by road through rugged hills cloaked in forests of oak, apple and pine, but it bridges a gap as wide as that between, say, Washington, D.C. and Appalachia. It had been raining nonstop for three days when I set out; the mist shrouding the slopes and red-tile-roofed villages conveyed a sense of a world cut off from Europe. Located in the highlands of Guipúzcoa, regarded as the most "Basque" of the three provinces, Ordizia is a town of 9,500 that was founded in the 13th century. When I arrived, crowds were flocking to the market in the town square, beneath an Athenian arcade-style roof supported by a dozen Corinthian columns. Elderly men wearing traditional wide, black berets, known as txapelas, browsed through piles of fresh produce, wheels of Idiazabal sheep cheese, olives and chorizo sausages. Outside rose green hills covered by concrete high-rises; Franco had ordered them built in the 1960s and packed them with workers from the rest of Spain—a strategy, many in Ordizia say, intended to weaken Basque identity.

With almost no unemployment and fertile highlands, Ordizia is one of the wealthiest corners of Spain. Yet almost everybody here has been touched by violence: there is the Basque policeman, posted out of town, who keeps his job secret from his neighbors for fear of being killed, the stationery store owner whose daughter, a convicted ETA bomb-maker, languishes in a Spanish prison hundreds of miles away in a seedy bar clubhouse in one of the high-rises on the outskirts of town, I met Iñaki Dubreuil Churruca, a Socialist town councilman: in 2001, he narrowly escaped a car bomb explosion that killed two bystanders. I asked him how many people from Ordizia had been murdered by ETA, and he and a friend began counting, rattling off a dozen or so names: "Isidro, Ima, Javier, Yoye. . . . We knew them all," he said.

Later I walked through the town center to a flagstone plaza, where a single rose painted on a tile marked Ordizia's most notorious killing: that of María Dolores González Catarain, known as Yoyes. An attractive, charismatic woman who joined ETA as a teenager, Yoyes tired of life in the group and, with her young son, fled into exile in Mexico. After several years she grew homesick and, reaching out to ETA's leaders, received assurances she would not be harmed if she came back. In 1986 she moved to San Sebastián and wrote a critical memoir about her life as a terrorist. That September, she returned to Ordizia for the first time since her exile to attend a fiesta and, in a crowded plaza, was shot dead in front of her son. David Bumstead, an English teacher who ran a language school in the town, later observed the scene. "I remember seeing her body, covered in a sheet, lying on the cobblestones," he says, recalling that "sadness enveloped the town."

Though Yoyes' murder caused widespread revulsion in Ordizia, enthusiasm for Basque independence has never flagged here. In 1991, Batasuna received 30 percent of the votes in municipal elections and came close to naming the town's mayor. (A coalition of other political parties formed a majority and blocked the appointment.) In a dank, smoke-filled bar beside the town's marketplace I met the man who nearly won the post, Ramon Amundarain, a grizzled former Batasuna politician. He told me that 35 percent of the highland population favored independence. "I didn't even speak Spanish until I was 10," he said. "I don't feel Spanish at all." He pulled an Euskal Herria ID card out of his wallet. "I carry it in protest," he told me. "I could be arrested for it." When I asked whether he believed violence was an acceptable way of achieving his goal, he answered, cautiously, "We did not reject it."

The next day I drove farther south into the province of Alava, part of the Rioja wine-producing region. Alava is considered the least Basque, and most Spanish, of the Basque Country's three provinces. Here, the weather cleared, and I found myself in an arid, sun-splashed valley framed by gray basalt mountains. Jagged mesas loomed over groves of cypress trees and a rolling sea of vineyards, and medieval walled villages climbed hillsides; the landscape, the climate, all seemed classically Spanish.

The 12th-century village of Laguardia was having one of its summer fiestas, this one celebrating San Juan, the town's patron saint. Then I heard a distant clattering of hoofs, and I leapt into a doorway just as half a dozen bulls roared down the main street. I had stumbled into one of the hundreds of "running of the bulls" festivals that take place every summer across Spain—this one, unlike Pamplona's a few dozen miles to the northeast, relatively unspoiled by tourists.

Later that morning, I made my way to Bodega El Fabulista, a wine cellar owned by Eusebio Santamaría, a third-generation winemaker. Santamaría has chosen to keep his operation small—he produces 40,000 bottles a year, entirely for local distribution—and he makes most of his money from the private tours of his cellar he conducts for tourists. Since the ETA cease-fire, he told me, the number of visitors had grown significantly "The atmosphere across the Basque Country has changed," he said. I asked him whether people felt their Basqueness strongly here, and he laughed. "It's a mixture of identities here, Rioja, Alava and Navarra," he said. "I say I belong to all of them. Wine does not understand or care about politics."

But people do, and everywhere I traveled in Basque Country, debates over Basque identity and independence still raged. In Vitoria-Gasteiz, a modern city on the arid plains of Alava Province and the Basque capital, María San Gil vented her contempt for the cease-fire declaration. San Gil, 41, a gaunt, intense woman, saw the separatists' brutality firsthand in 1995, when an ETA gunman walked into a bar in San Sebastian and shot to death her colleague Gregorio Ordoñez, a popular, conservative Basque politician. Soon after that, she entered politics as a candidate for San Sebastián's city council, and is now president of the Populist Party in the Basque Country San Gil has likened Batasuna's leader, Arnaldo Otegi, to Osama bin Laden and, despite ETA's truce, remains adamantly opposed to any negotiations. "These people are fanatics, and one cannot legitimize them at the political table," San Gil told me. She dismissed comparisons between ETA and the IRA, whose cease-fire call in 1997 was embraced by the British government. "Ours is not a war between two legitimate adversaries. It's a war between terrorists and democrats, so why do we have to sit down with them? It's like sitting down with Al Qaeda. We have to vanquish them."

Others, however, see such intransigence as self-defeating. Gorka Landaburu, the son of a leading Basque politician who fled into exile in France in 1939, also knows the extremists' brutality firsthand. Landaburu, 55, grew up in Paris and moved to San Sebastián in his 20s. There he began writing for French and Spanish newspapers and became a leading voice of ETA opposition. "My parents were Basque nationalists, but I've never been," he told me as we sat in a café in front of San Sebastián's Hotel Londres, a whitewashed, early-20th-century landmark with filigreed iron balconies and French windows, overlooking the seafront promenade. "We have our own taxation, our own laws, our own government. What do we need independence for? Money? We have the euro. Frontiers? The borders are open. Army? It's unnecessary."

Landaburu's critiques made him an enemy of the separatists. "I got my first warning in 1986—an anonymous letter, with the ETA seal"—a serpent coiled around an ax—"warning me to 'keep quiet,'" he said. "I ignored it." In the spring of 2001, a parcel bearing his newspaper's return address arrived at his home. While heading out the door to work the next morning, he opened the letter; five ounces of dynamite blew up, mangling his hands, destroying the vision in his left eye and lacerating his face. "I remember every second—the explosion, the burst of fire," he told me. He staggered out the door covered in blood; a neighbor took him to a hospital. "Every time I pick up a drink, button my shirt, I think about the attack, but I can't let it dominate me or I'd go insane," Landaburu said.

In the months after I spoke to Landaburu, increasingly belligerent pronouncements by ETA, increased incidents of street violence and the theft of the handguns in Nîmes seemed to strengthen the arguments of hard-liners such as Maria San Gil. But it was difficult to know whether ETA's vows to carry on the struggle were rhetorical or whether they foreshadowed another campaign of terror. Nor was it out of the question that a radical splinter group sought to sabotage the peace process—the Basque equivalent of the Real IRA, which killed 29 people in a car bombing in Omagh, Ireland, in August 1998 in reaction to the IRA's cease-fire the previous year.

Landaburu told me that he expected setbacks: the bitterness and hatred caused by decades of violence were too deeply engrained in Basque society to be overcome easily Even so, he was willing to give peace a chance. "I'm not going to forgive, I'm not going to forget, but I'm not going to oppose the process," he told me. He took a sip of *orujo blanco,* a strong liquor distilled from white grapes, and gazed upon the Bay of Concha—the crescent of beach, the azure waters framed by forested cliffs, the hundreds of people strolling the promenade at sunset. "After 40 years of Franco's dictatorship, and 40 years of a dictatorship of terror, we want to live in a world without threats, without violence," Landaburu said. "I want peace for my kids, for my grandkids. And for the first time, I think we are going to get it."

Writer **JOSHUA HAMMER** lives in Berlin.

From *Smithsonian,* January 2007, pp. 43–50. Copyright © 2007 by Joshua Hammer. Reprinted by permission of the author.

Tamil Tiger Trap

JASON MOTLAGH

Not even the United Nations can stand in the way of the Sri Lankan army now. Looking to finish off the Tamil Tigers, the government has ordered the few aid agencies still in the northern war zone to leave, saying it can't guarantee their safety.

Asia's longest-running civil war has left many claims of imminent victory in its wake, along with an estimated 70,000 dead. The difference today is that Tiger losses on the battlefield are compounded by high-level defections, and a stranglehold on the fundraising and smuggling operations that have sustained them.

In January, the government abandoned a truce and pledged to defeat the Tigers by the year's end. It has poured $1.5bn (£840m) into a multi-front offensive. The Mannar peninsula was reclaimed in July; forces are driving up east and west coasts to cut off a vital sea supply line from India, spearheaded by "deep penetration" units—armed plain-clothes agents—tasked with spying and sabotage. President Mahinda Rajapaksa, riding a swell of Sinhalese nationalism, insists his forces will not turn back "until every inch of land is recaptured and every terrorist is killed or captured".

The Tigers have lost more than 6,300 fighters and three-quarters of their territory, according to the country's ministry of defence. Claims and counterclaims are a staple of the propaganda war, but even the Tigers admit they have lost ground. Generals say they are within artillery range of the political capital, Kilinochchi, where the guerrilla leader Prabhakaran is believed to be holed up.

This is bad news for the 145,000 displaced native Tamils, now without help from the aid agencies, and the UN has warned that their number could surge above 200,000. For all its aggression, the government wants to avoid being accused of killing relief workers, as happened after the August 2006 massacre of 17 employees of a French aid agency.

At the same time, rights groups charge the Tigers with once again forcibly recruiting women and children to boost their ranks. They also allege that civilians will be used as a human shield at Kilinochchi. "The rebel military installations and civilian areas are mixed," says D B S Jeyaraj, a defence analyst. "If the army advances and confines the rebels into a smaller region, then civilian vulnerability will increase."

Kilinochchi has been in government hands before, only to be reclaimed by the Tigers in 1999 when they reversed army gains in just days. This time, however, they are without the former eastern commander Colonel Karuna Amman. He split from the rebels in March 2004 and took 6,000 cadres with him, cutting the Tigers' ranks by as much as 60 percent. Last July the Tigers were ousted from the east, a long-time bastion.

Another former Tiger, Sivanesathurai Chandrakanthan, known as "Pillayan", was elected in May as chief minister of the eastern province, in a government down-payment on its promise of greater political power and economic prospects for eastern Tamils in exchange for support. On a recent afternoon in the port town of Trincomalee, the former child soldier presided over a meeting with four army generals. These men would once have killed each other.

But native villages are now off-limits and controlled by the army, and arrests and "disappearances" are common in urban areas. President Rajapaksa insists there will be "no peace and development" until the Tigers are defeated.

The Tigers' military setbacks are compounded by financial strains. According to *Jane's Intelligence Review*, they raised as much as $300m a year at their peak—mostly from abroad—giving them one of the highest budgets for a separatist group, second only to Colombia's Farc. But post-9/11, with the US and the European Union listing the Tigers as a terrorist group, dozens of financiers and arms smugglers have been arrested and millions in assets seized or frozen.

Observers note that the current offensive has yet to encounter the full weight of the Tigers forces. "The government has succeeded in significantly weakening the Tigers [but] they have a hardcore fighting unit that even by conservative estimates could run into several thousand," says Amantha Perera, a defence columnist for the *Sunday Leader* newspaper. In the past, the Tigers gave up territory to overextend army troops, he notes.

Karuna has said the Tigers may have chemical weapons they can deploy. Even if they are broken as a conventional fighting force, they could regroup in the dense northern jungles to wage a guerrilla war, Prabhakaran's speciality. And past experience dictates that when the Tigers are squeezed, terror becomes a useful tool. After a period of relative calm in the south, an explosion at a crowded Colombo market late last month wounded 45 people, a likely sign of more to come.

There is no doubt among watchers that a lasting peace will stay out of reach until the roots of Tamil nationalism are seriously examined. "Irrespective of what happens on the battlefield, what you will get is a military victor and not an end to the conflict," says Paikiasothy Saravanamuttu, director of the Centre for Policy Alternatives, a think tank in Colombo. "If not accompanied by a political strategy, we're not really out of the woods."

This story was reported with a grant from the Pulitzer Centre on Crisis Reporting

In Europe, Where's the Hate?

GARY YOUNGE

Over the past year or so the rural Italian idyll of Colle di Val d'Elsa has played host to a bitter battle for Enlightenment values. On one side, the hamlet's small Muslim community has raised a considerable amount of money to build a large mosque. Having gained the mayor's approval, the Muslims signed a declaration of cooperation with the town hall and even planted a Christmas tree at the site as a good-will gesture.

In response, other locals pelted them with sausages and dumped a severed pig's head at the site. On a wall near the site vandals daubed: "No Mosque," "Christian Hill" and "Thanks to the communists the Arabs are in our house!!!"

Such is the central dynamic in European race relations at present. It is probably not the dynamic you have heard most about. The most popular one making the rounds this side of the Atlantic involves hordes of Muslims, rabid with anti-Semitic and misogynistic views, running amok as they bomb, bully and out-breed their clueless liberal hosts in a bid to build a caliphate.

"Do you have a child back in England?" an elderly Los Angelena asked a British reporter on a recent *National Review* cruise.

"No," he said.

"You'd better start," she replied. "The Muslims are breeding. Soon, they'll have the whole of Europe."

Nor is it by any means the only dynamic. There *are* a handful of nihilistic young Muslims keen to bomb and destroy and a far larger number sufficiently disaffected that they are prepared to riot. There are also many Europeans keen to see equality and meaningful integration, defending civil liberties and opposing wars against predominantly Muslim lands.

But the primary threat to democracy in Europe is not "Islamofascism"—that clunking, thuggish phrase that keeps lashing out in the hope that it will one day strike a meaning—but plain old fascism. The kind whereby mostly white Europeans take to the streets to terrorize minorities in the name of racial, cultural or religious superiority.

For fascism—and the xenophobic, racist and nationalistic elements that are its most vile manifestations—has returned as a mainstream ideology in Europe. Its advocates not only run in elections but win them. They control local councils and sit in parliaments. In Austria, Belgium, Denmark, France and Italy, hard-right nationalist and anti-immigrant parties regularly receive more than 10 percent of the vote. In Norway it is

22 percent; in Switzerland, 29 percent. In Italy and Austria they have been in government; in Switzerland, where the anti-immigrant Swiss People's Party is the largest party, they still are.

This is not new. From Austria to Antwerp, Italy to France, fascists have been performing well at the polls for more than a decade. Nor are they shy about their bigotry. France's Jean-Marie Le Pen has described the Nazi gas chambers as a "detail of history"; Austria's Jörg Haider once thanked a group of Austrian World War II veterans, including former SS officers, for "stick[ing] to their convictions despite the greatest opposition." But the attacks of 9/11, the bombings in Spain and Britain and the riots in France gave the hard right new traction. The polarizing effects of terrorism facilitated the journey of hard-right agendas from the margins to the mainstream. Islamophobia became de rigueur. Recently German Chancellor Angela Merkel told a Christian Democrat party congress that "we must take care that mosque cupolas are not built demonstratively higher than church steeples."

In September 2006, British novelist Martin Amis told the *Times* of London: "There's a definite urge—don't you have it?—to say, 'the Muslim community will have to suffer until it gets its house in order.' What sort of suffering? Not letting them travel. Deportation—further down the road. Curtailing of freedoms. Strip-searching people who look like they're from the Middle East or from Pakistan. . . . Discriminatory stuff, until it hurts the whole community and they start getting tough with their children."

Far from being the principal purveyors of racial animus in Europe, Muslims are its principal targets. Between 2000 and 2005 officially reported racist violence rose 71 percent in Denmark, 34 percent in France and 21 percent in Ireland. With few governments collecting data on racial crime victims, it has been left to NGOs to record the sharp rise in attacks on Muslims, those believed to be Muslims and Muslim targets.

None of this means anti-Semitism and jihadism don't exist among Muslim communities in Europe. But it does provide a context for both. Muslims are a relatively tiny percentage of European citizens—there is a higher proportion of Asians in Utah than Muslims in Italy—and are overwhelmingly concentrated among the poor. More than 40 percent of Bangladeshi men in Britain under the age of 25 are unemployed. All of this excuses nothing but explains a great deal. According to a Pew Research

Center survey, the principal concerns of Muslims in France, Germany and Spain are unemployment and Islamic extremism. Integrating into a society that won't employ you, educate you or house you adequately is no easy feat. Participating in a political culture that scapegoats you is also tough. Attacked as Muslims at home and abroad, they defend themselves as Muslims. Every respected report in Britain has shown a direct link between the war in Iraq and recruitment to Islamist movements. And so the symbiosis of Islamophobes and Islamists is complete, with each thriving on polarization and prejudice: picking at scabs that might have healed, until the blood runs freely.

The most potent anti-Semites and bigots in Europe do not live in run-down housing projects but grace the corridors of power. They are not Muslim; they are Christian. The continent is not suffering from some new strain of bigotry imported from the Arab world or the Maghreb—it is simply suffering from one of its oldest viruses harbored among its most established ethnic populations.

UNIT 5

Terrorism in America

Unit Selections

Key Points to Consider

- Why does domestic terrorism receive less attention than international terrorism?

- What factors have contributed to the growth of hate groups in the United States?

- Should radical environmentalists and animal rights activists be treated as terrorists?

- Should the state have the right to take custody of children if the parents are members of a radical organization?

Student Website
www.mhcls.com

Internet References

America's War Against Terrorism
   http://www.lib.umich.edu/govdocs/usterror.html
Department of Homeland Security
   http://www.dhs.gov/dhspublic/index.jsp
FBI Home Page
   http://www.fbi.gov

Domestic terrorism remains a difficult topic for many in the United States. While Americans are willing to believe in "evil forces" with origins in other countries, many become uncomfortable at the thought of U.S. citizens as a source of political violence. Many refuse to believe that a system as free, open, and democratic as ours can spawn those who hate and wish to destroy the very system that has bestowed on them tremendous individual freedoms, including the right to political dissent.

American reactions to domestic terrorists vary. While many Americans are outraged by domestic terrorism, some terrorists, like Eric Rudolph, responsible for four bombings, including attacks on the Olympics in Atlanta, two women's clinics, and a bar, have achieved cult-hero status, with bumper stickers and T-shirts popularizing Rudolph's near-legendary flight from law enforcement officials. Groups like the Animal Liberation Front (ALF) and the Earth Liberation Front (ELF) continue to attract apologists searching for ways to justify or explain the violent behavior of otherwise 'good Americans.' Even the case of Timothy McVeigh, who was prosecuted and executed for the Oklahoma City bombing, has attracted some that continue to believe in an international conspiracy with origins in the Middle East, despite evidence to the contrary. This apparent schizophrenia is echoed in media reporting, public opinion, and public policy.

While the media demonizes the foreign terrorist, it tends to humanize native U.S. terrorists. Stories of American terrorists often emphasize a human-interest perspective. Stories about Minnesota's middle-class soccer mom, Jane Olson, or the young, idealistic, and obviously misguided "American Taliban," John Walker, or even the psychologically unbalanced log-cabin-recluse, Ted Kaczynski, make good copy and are designed to elicit sympathy or empathy in a larger audience. In its efforts to explain how or why 'good' Americans have gone 'bad,' the violence and victims are often ignored. A recent apology to veterans groups by the Secretary of Homeland Security for a DHS report that indicated that some veterans were attracted to or active in right-wing militia groups indicate that the topic of domestic terrorism is still a political minefield.

Public opinion and public policy are also subject to this apparent dissonance. While the American public and U.S. policymakers appear to care little about the legal rights or physical detention of foreigners suspected of association with terrorist organizations, the legal rights of domestic terrorists are often the subject of intense public scrutiny and debate.

The selections in this unit look at the problem of terrorism in the United States. The first article in this section provides a statistical overview of terrorism in the United States, 1997–2005. Next, David Holthouse from the Southern Poverty Law Center looks at the growth of hate group activity in the U.S. and provides

© The McGraw-Hill Companies, Inc./Jill Braaten, photographer

a brief overview of "the three most active and dangerous white supremacist hate group sectors in 2008." In the third article, Matt Rasmussen looks at the motives behind attacks carried out by radical environmentalists in the United States. He blames harsh sentencing on the efforts of an overzealous administration trying to distract from its failings " . . . to counter real terrorism." Next, Ashley Bohacik examines the violent tactics used by animal activists. Finally, Chris Selley examines the case of a Winnipeg mother whose three children were taken into custody by Child and Family Services because of her inflammatory rhetoric and involvement with white supremacy groups.

Incidents of Terrorism in the United States, 1997–2005

The geography of terrorism remains underexplored. By focusing on the spatial patterns of terrorist attacks, the settings and land uses in which attacks occur, and the methods used to perpetrate violence, this analysis helps build a theory of terrorism geography. Between 1 January 1997 and 11 September 2005, 178 terrorist incidents occurred in the United States. Analysis of these incidents suggests three insights. At the national scale, terrorism in the United States clustered in large urban areas, with regional differentiation of terrorist motives and targets. At the scale of individual attack sites, terrorist motivations pinpointed offices, clinics, and public spaces; right-wing violence, military, government, and infrastructural targets; and religious terrorism, commercial and special land uses. At the scale of individual interactions, terrorists crossed paths with victims in various ways. For example, the 2001 anthrax-attack letters and lone-wolf terrorism created alternative intersections of perpetrators with victims.

SAMUEL NUNN

Spaces can be at the heart of terrorist conflicts. Radical Islam's interest in Mecca and Medina is an example of a place-based spatial focus. In the 1960s Puerto Rican nationalist groups such as Los Macheteros executed attacks in the United States to promote independence of their homeland. In this sense, land control can be the strategic focus of terrorist campaigns. Past terrorist incidents in the United States targeted specific places—for instance, women's health clinics, ski resorts, or office buildings—in a strategic way in order to deliver messages to citizens and governments. Terrorists often perpetrate violence close to coveted real estate, and terrorist attacks reflect strategic spatial considerations embedded in targets and in methods used to commit crimes.

In any violent event, terrorist actors must either personally intersect the individuals, groups, or physical facilities targeted or have deposited timed explosives, firebombs, or other attack vectors designed to harm bystanders or property. Donald Black argues that the "geometry of terrorism" involves physical proximity combined with high social polarization, but his theory of collective terrorist violence says nothing about the spatial characteristics of terrorist targets or the functions performed at attack sites (2004). How and where do terrorist actors intersect victims in space? Criminology's routine activities theory predicts that criminal attacks occur where unguarded targets—that is, the victims of crime—go about their daily business of working, living, and playing (Felson 1998). A twist of terrorism

geography is that places are often the victims of terrorist attacks, as when places are targets because they host some activity—a government building, a health clinic, or a pristine natural environment, for example. The geography of terrorism requires a broader conception of victimization in which the places of terrorist incidents are an integral part of the messages such attacks deliver (Drake 1998). Understanding the geography of terrorism in the United States requires more attention to empirical questions about where attacks occur, such as:

- Terrorist incidents occur in different areas of a country. In the United States, have they occurred in clusters, or randomly across spaces of interest, people, or property? How are these locations linked to terrorist motivations? Which specific places are the most frequent settings for terrorist attacks?
- The functions performed at the spaces that constitute terrorist targets are indirect victims of the attack, and in this sense terrorist motivations are likely tied to certain types of settings for violence. To what extent can certain land uses be linked to higher risks of attack, different methods used, or terrorists' motivation or cause?
- How do terrorist actors intersect spatially with victims or property-based targets? Terrorists cross paths with victims, whether they be individuals or places, in a number of ways.

In the United States, terrorist actions frequently target places with facilities that perform specific functions. Attacks change the use of spaces, drive people from places, or create the threat of random violence in those places. From 1997 to 2005, close to zoo terrorist incidents have occurred in the United States. Even so, no one has systematically analyzed the spatial patterns of places where incidents occur, how place patterns connect to terrorist causes, the targets chosen for attack, the methods of attacks, the success or failure of attacks, or the types of land uses where terrorism occurs. Terrorist motivations influence the places and spaces that are targeted. If terrorism geography includes the interactions of place, motivation, and method in conducting terrorist attacks, then the theory and practice of terrorism geography need more attention.

In this article I identify the locations of religious, environmental, animal-rights, and other forms of terrorism. Certain types of facilities have borne the brunt of terrorist campaigns. Health facilities providing women's reproductive services have frequently been sites of anti-abortion violence. Environmental and animal rights terrorism have left footprints across amenity-rich regions. From a land-use perspective, certain kinds of terrorism have been more or less common. Specific land uses have links to distinct terrorist motives. Incidents can occur disproportionately among five kinds of land uses: commercial, infrastructure, private, public, or special. Special land uses include government facilities, laboratories, health clinics, and animal research sites. Commercial spaces include offices, stores, businesses, and media headquarters. Special land uses and commercial spaces hosted 70 percent of U.S. terrorist incidents during this period. For terrorist actors, using a specific target for violence is also an effort to spread fear among users of the targeted facility. Certain kinds of attacks—for example, anthrax letters and lone-wolf terrorists—create different spatial linkages among terrorist actors, victims, and their places of intersection.

The approach used here examines terrorist incidents at increasingly finer scales of spatial organization, from macrointeractions to microinteractions. It begins with the spatial distribution of terrorism across the continental United States. From there, the spatial scale reduces to regional differences in the incidence of terrorism. At the scale of individual incidents, certain land uses are the sites of terror attacks, which are identified, as are empirical linkages among land uses, methods, and motivations. At the largest scale, terrorist actors must cross paths with victims, and examples of terrorist incidents illustrate the different ways in which final closure occurs.

Defining and Measuring Terrorist Incidents, 1997–2005

The U.S. code of law defines domestic and international terrorism as "Activities that . . . involve acts dangerous to human life that are a violation of the criminal laws of the United States or of any State [and that] appear to be intended to intimidate or coerce a civilian population [,] to influence the policy of a government by intimidation or coercion[,] or to affect the conduct of a government by mass destruction, assassination, or kidnapping" (18 USC 113b). However, most offenders who are considered terrorists receive indictments and convictions as murderers, bombers, racketeers, arsonists, or other criminal violators. For instance, individuals arrested for arson may later become classified as terrorists if it is discovered that their motives were political. Law-enforcement officials, prosecutors, and the courts often define criminal acts as terrorism in an ex post act of judgment. How police authorities code crimes affects the count of terrorist incidents: Calling an attempted murder a hate crime may move it out of a terrorism classification. Some terrorist conspiracies involve the discovery or interdiction of what appear to be routine crime; for example, precursors of terrorist crime such as smuggling or identify theft. Charles Monroe noted that, during the 1970–1980 period, prosecutors charged domestic terrorists most frequently with racketeering violations, not violations of terrorism statutes (1982). Brent Smith and Kathryn Morgan showed that terrorism was the charge in 2 percent of 1,748 counts against domestic U.S. terrorists between 1980 and 1998 (1994). Racketeering, weapons, and explosives violations constituted more than half of all counts filed against domestic terrorists (Smith and others 2002). Obviously, different types of crimes qualify as terrorist incidents. Therefore, building a database for spatial analysis cannot fully identify the universe of terrorist incidents because determining that universe is impossible.

This analysis focuses on U.S. terrorist incidents that occurred in the lower forty-eight states from 1 January 1997 to 11 September 2005—four years before 9/11 to four years after that disaster. The sample of terrorist incidents analyzed conforms with the legal definition of terrorism used in the United States and comes from three compatible sources. The major source of data is the incident database built by the Memorial Institute for the Prevention of Terrorism (MIPT) Terrorism Knowledge Base (TKB), a comprehensive, broad-ranging, and systematic compilation of terrorist incidents in the world (MIPT 2005). The TKB includes incidents that are successful, incidents that fail, and intended attacks that were neither fully successful nor complete failures. The second source derives from U.S. Federal Bureau of Investigation (FBI) annual reports on domestic terrorism that classify terrorist-related activity into "terrorist incidents" (successful acts), "suspected terrorist incidents," and "preventions" (FBI 1997, 1998, 1999, 2000/2001). The third data source, published by the Anti-Abortion Violence Watch (AAVW), tracked the incidence of violence at clinics that delivered birth control and abortion services (Feminist Majority Foundation 2002).

The analysis defined terrorist incidents as: events included in the MIPT—TKB database, a total of 116 incidents; additional events in the FBI's annual reports through 2001, a total of 30 incidents; and anti-abortion violence documented by the AAVW as of May 2002, a total of 32 incidents. Altogether, 178 incidents occurred during the 1 January 1997–11 September 2005 period. The analysis used the following variables for each event:

- Cause (motive). This is the *mens rea* of terrorist crime: interests or motives linked to religion, the environment, animal rights, nationalism, right-wing politics, and race.
- How the attack was to occur (method). This is the *actus reus* of terrorist crime: arson or vandalism, armed attack or shooting, toxin attack, hijacking or robbery, bombing, or some other type of crime.
- Governmental jurisdiction of the targeted space (city, town, or village)
- Whether the attack was executed (success). The measurement of incidents includes planned but failed attempts: bombs that did not go off, letters unopened but dangerous because they were delivered, arson fires that did not start or spread, plans and plots discovered and foiled.
- Land-use classification of the space on which violence focuses (five land-use categories and several different settings—commerce, infrastructure, private use, public use, and special use. Land-use variables also help describe targets of the attack, including individuals, residential structures, health-care facilities, and government facilities.

Geographically and scientifically, we would like to see the spatial distribution of terrorist incidents in the United States in order to learn whether motives are linked to setting and jurisdiction and whether the success rates of terrorist incidents are uniform or vary across different jurisdictions, land uses, methods, or settings. The methods used to commit terrorist crimes may also be linked to motive, setting, land use, and place.

The Theoretical Context of Terrorism Geography

What is terrorism geography? Many terrorist campaigns have clear geographical motivations and spatial implications (Murphy 2003). The occupation of contested territory defines the Palestinian struggle against the Israelis (Noble and Efrat 1990). Controlling land was a primary motivation for the Shining Path's violence in Peru (Kent 1993), from the standpoint of Maoist guerilla strategy—for example, control first the countryside, then the cities—and as a more instrumental tactic to gain control over illicit drug production (Gorriti 1999, 111–113). Using a similar strategy, the Khmer Rouge captured and controlled Cambodian Land through systematic murders and disappearances of 1.4 million people. The Tamil Tigers are engaged in the capture and control of land as part of their insurgency in Sri Lanka (Laqueur 1999, 191–196;

Gourevitch 2005). Spanish terrorism linked to Basque Fatherland and Liberty (ETA) is aimed at establishing sovereign status for land in northern Spain and southern France (Whittaker 2005). However, with few exceptions, analyses of political violence in these locations say little about how space is related to the conduct, places, and tactics of these struggles. Space and place play remarkably low-key roles in most terrorism analyses (Flint 2003), and they deserve more attention.

A useful theoretical portal with geographical components is the work of the sociologist Donald Black. Expanding his earlier ideas about crime as a form of social control (1983), he conceives of terrorism as self-help among groups interested in addressing perceived problems, with one group waging collective violence on others to achieve something or to stop something (2004). Black invokes an arithmetic of intergroup relationships in which space is important to terrorist crimes. He focuses on the relationship between social geometry and physical proximity: His pure form of terrorism requires long social geometries (social distance in terms of ethnicity, religion, social class, corporate status, hierarchical authority, or some other form of extreme social polarization) and short physical proximity (people of different social geometries living in close proximity). Terrorism occurs where social distances are great and people are close. As Black notes, advanced technologies facilitate the spatial connection between victims and socially distant antagonists. Communications and transportation technologies shrink space, so persons once socially distant can now be close to their civilian enemies. Cellular technology and the Internet enable the coordination of attacks on civilians at long distances. Groups deliver attacks by using technologies such as letter bombs or toxins, shootings and assassinations, cyberattacks, airplanes, and improvised explosive devices. However, Black offers no further consideration of the spatial elements of terrorists and victims.

Early analyses of U.S. domestic terrorism glanced briefly at the role of places. An overview of U.S. terrorism by an FBI agent paid limited attention to geography, although the spatial implications of his analysis were evident (Monroe 1982). Monroe underscored the regularity of terrorist attacks in the United States (including Puerto Rico): 302 events across five years, an annual rate of sixty incidents. Geographical concerns elsewhere motivated much of the terrorist activity played out in the United States. These acts dealt not with control of U.S. land but with other nation's real estate: Puerto Rican nationalism, Croatian independence, or pro- and anti-Cuban violence. Monroe's summary of 1977–1981 terrorist events in the United States suggested both predictability and randomness. The usual spatial suspects—New York City and Los Angeles, for example—were places of planned political violence: 1981 bombings by Puerto Rican nationalists at New York's John F. Kennedy International Airport, New York stock exchanges, and nearby banks; targeted assassinations by an Armenian group in Los Angeles and a Croatian group's bomb attack on the New York State Supreme Court building. Less obvious locales such as Fort Collins, Colorado, and Evanston, Illinois, were places where terrorists planned violence.

Christopher Hewitt's data span 1955 to 1998 and came from a file of "over 2,700 terrorist incidents that have occurred in the United States and Puerto Rico since the early 1950s" (2000, 2). This reflects an annual rate of about sixty-three incidents. He showed the fatality rate from terrorism for the contiguous forty-eight states, reporting that eleven states had no terrorist fatalities during this period. States with the highest fatality rate per million population (three or more) were highlighted, suggesting four clusters: a western grouping (California, Nevada, and Idaho); a southeastern cluster (Louisiana, Alabama, Mississippi, and Florida); and two single states (South Dakota and New York). In a later analysis, covering U.S. terrorism to 2002, Hewitt did not mention terrorist incidents linked to the Earth Liberation Front (ELF) or the Animal Liberation Front (ALF), even though others had by then documented the spread of ecoterrorism (Hewitt 2003; Eagan 1996; Leader and Probst 2003).

Some methods of attack used in terrorism—bombing and lynching, for instance—have spatial roots. In his 1983 study of bomb-related crime in Dallas, Texas, Daniel Georges-Abeyie examined the 361 bomb threats involving racially stratified neighborhoods that had been reported during 1975 and found that the greater the racial diversity in a neighborhood the larger the number of bomb threats it reported. The sociodemographic structure of spatially bounded neighborhoods became linked to threats of violence. Georges-Abeyie found spatial differences in origin and receipt of bomb threats. He theorized that the racial composition of areas where crime occurs can be linked to a potential for terroristic violence—the use of bomb threats to intimidate or coerce—and suggested that areas with more racial diversity showed higher levels of potential violence. In this case, particular places, because of their sociogeographical characteristics, became targets of different kinds of terrorist threats.

Clusters of violent incidents are important to identify because terroristic violence in one area can affect surrounding areas. Stewart Tolnay, Glenn Deane, and E. M. Beck used county lynchings in ten southern states between 1895 and 1919—more than 2,200 lynchings during three five-year periods—to assess which of two models was more accurate: a contagion model, in which violence in one county is followed by violence in nearby counties, or a deterrence model, in which lynchings in one county lead to less violence in nearby counties. Their empirical analyses favored the deterrence model: "The intensity of mob violence in nearby areas was found to he negatively associated with the corresponding frequency in other areas" (1996, 811), Over time, this model would lead to uneven clusters of violence among counties. The question then becomes finding the place clusters.

These early analyses of terrorism geography fail to answer several questions. Terrorist violence focuses on specific, people or places, and, in order to, execute attacks, the agents of terrorism must cross paths with their victims at some point before or during an attack. The choice of targets is not unlimited but involves attack sites that satisfy the motivations and causes of terrorist groups, not to mention their need to execute successful attacks. Incident patterns result from the interaction of terrorist motivations, the places they attack, the target-site functions, and the methods they use. These interacting aspects of terrorism geography remain unexamined. From this, three questions deserve closer attention. First, based on terrorist causes, where do U.S. attacks occur? Second, what is the relationship between different land uses and the, risks, methods, and motivations of terrorist attacks? Third, how do terrorist actors intersect their victims in space?

Unpacking the Geography of Terrorism in the United States

Table 1 summarizes successful and unsuccessful terrorist incidents that took place in the United States between 1997 and 2005 by cause. The mens rea of these terrorist crimes—their political, social, or ideological motivation—consists of six motivational interests or causes: animal rights, the environment, nationalism, race, religion, and right-wing politics. Eighty percent of attacks stemmed from environmental, animal-rights, or religious causes. Agents of particular terrorist causes succeeded in their attacks at various rates. Pro-life incidents had an 84 percent success rate and Islamic causes, 64 percent. Environmental and animal-rights groups succeeded nine of every ten tries, but they primarily practiced vandalism and arson. Religiously motivated acts were the next most successful, and right-wing, antigovernment terrorist actors were the least successful. The relationship between the six general terrorist causes and success rates is weak but significant. The Pearson chi-square and contingency coefficient suggest that different terrorist motivations have different success ratios.[1]

As Table 2 shows, arson or vandalism, bombing, toxin attacks, and armed attacks or shootings are the most common criminal acts—the actus reus of terrorist crimes. The nominal statistical analysis indicates that the ways in which terrorists commit crimes are related to their motivations. Religious actors use bombs more frequently than do white supremacists, who use guns. Ecoterrorists tend to prefer arson or vandalism, as do religiously motivated agents and animal-rights terrorists.

The geographical distribution of incidents linked to terrorist causes or motivations is slightly clustered. Furthermore, terrorist causes focus on different types of targets. The approach used to see these differences compares regional clusters organized as all incidents, then compares the geographical distribution of religious and environmental causes. Mapping the U.S. places that were sites of 1997–2005 terrorist incidents revealed regional clusters. Figure 1 compares the volume of local place incidents and regional incident clusters. The clusters show regions composed of three cell-radius circular areas that distribute the sum of incidents

Table 1 Incidents of Terrorism in the United States, by Cause, 1 January 1997–11 September 2005[a]

General Causes Specific Causes	Number of Unsuccessful Incidents	Number of Successful Incidents	Total Number of Incidents	Percentage of Success by Each Cause	Percentage of Success by All Causes
Animal rights	1	18	19	94.7	10.7
Environment					
Antidevelopment causes	2	25	27	92.6	15.2
Antiglobalization causes	2	3	5	60.0	2.8
Antigovernment causes	0	1	1	100.0	0.6
Life sciences	1	9	10	90.0	5.6
Natural resources	1	19	20	95.0	11.2
All environmental causes				90.5	35.4
Nationalism				44.4	5.1
Anti-British causes	3	1	4	25.0	2.2
Cuban causes	0	2	2	100.0	1.1
Palestinian causes	2	1	3	33.3	1.7
All nationalist causes				44.4	5.1
Race (white supremacy)	8	7	15	46.7	8.4
Religion					
Islamic causes	8	14	22	63.6	12.4
Pro-life causes	6	31	37	83.8	20.8
Other religious causes	0	2	2	100.0	1.1
All religious causes				77.0	34.3
Right-wing politics	11	0	11	0.0	0.0
Total	45	133	178		100.0

[a]For the six general causes and success: Pearson chi-square = 55.5 (.001); nominal contingency coefficient = .49 (.001).
Sources: FBI 1997, 1998, 1999, 2000/2001; Feminist Majority Foundation 2002; MIPT 2005.

Table 2 Numbers of Terrorist Incidents in the United States, by Method and Cause, 1 January 1997–11 September 2005[a]

Method	Animal Rights	Environment	Nationalism	Race	Religion	Right- Wing Politics	All Causes
Arson or vandalism	15	61	2	0	20	0	98
Armed attack or shooting	0	1	1	7	2	3	14
Toxin attack	0	0	0	1	14	5	20
Hijacking or robbery	0	0	0	2	5	1	8
Bombing	1	4	3	3	20	2	33
Other	0	0	3	2	0	0	5
Total	16	66	9	15	61	11	178

[a]Pearson chi-square = 176.2 (.001); nominal contingency coefficient = .705 (.001).
Sources: FBI 1997, 1998, 1999, 2000/2001; Feminist Majority Foundation 2002; MIPT 2005.

Regional Clusters of Terrorism in the United States, 1977–2005, and Incident Rates per 100,000 Residents of Incident Sites, 2000

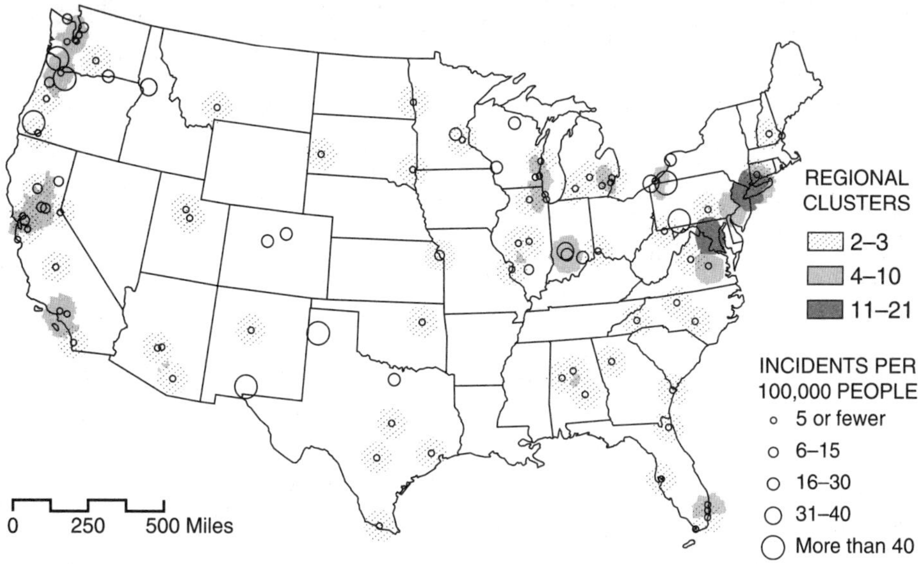

Figure 1 All incidents of terrorism in the United States: regional clusters, 1997–2005, and rates per 100,000 residents of incident sites, 2000.

Sources: FBI 1997, 1998, 1999, 2000/2001; MIPT 2005. (Cartography by the author)

per cell among a group of neighboring cells. Discrete clusters of incidents are visible along the Mid-Atlantic and West Coasts. The East Coast reflects the heaviest groupings of terrorist incidents in the New York City and Washington, D.C. metropolitan regions. U.S. terrorism also clusters disproportionately in the San Francisco and Southern California regions, as well as the entire Oregon-Washington coastal region. The most concentrated range of incidents occurred in the Boston-to-Washington urban corridor. The third pattern is centered around Chicago and the Great Lakes.

The population-weighted rate of incidence differs widely among the 113 places that witnessed terrorism—from less than 1 to 408 per 100,000 people. Normalizing rates into incidents per 100,000 people underscores how single incidents in small places inflate the rate of incidence. In larger population areas, this translates into low rates of incidence. Rural areas show higher rates. The 1997–2005 incident rate per 100,000 people was 0.2 in New York City (thirteen incidents among a population of 8 million in 2000) but 408 in Shanksville, Pennsylvania, site of a 9/11 airline crash (one incident among 245 people). Smaller areas show much larger normalized impacts. This is linked to the rural nature of many environmental attacks and the more general phenomenon of terrorist incidents in smaller jurisdictions. Nonetheless, the preponderance of events occurred in large metropolitan areas on both coasts.

This broad pattern masks a more meaningful relationship between terrorist causes and choice of attack sites. To illustrate how motivations influence cluster locations, Figures 2 and 3 compare regional clusters and incident rates of religious and environmental terrorism. These terrorist causes do not cluster in the same regions. Religious incidents arise in higher-density areas (lower rates per 100,000 people).

Ecoterrorism occurs in less dense areas (higher rates per 100,000 people). Ecoterrorism cluster on the Pacific Coast, with a few disconnected groups in the middle and upper Atlantic seaboard and another visible cluster of incidents around the Great Lakes. Religious clusters follow a southeastern arc, cutting through Washington D.C. and New York City. The arc moves as a function of pro-life violence, but it is anchored in the East by the concentration of religious incidents in Washington, D.C. and New York City, including the events of 9/11 and the October 2001 anthrax attacks.

Environmental groups use tactics that combine locational destruction and message delivery. Violence perpetrated against victims or their property commands them to honor the rights championed by terrorist agents. Areas with environmental amenities—national forests, scenic coastlines, and undeveloped or newly developing territories—often serve as targets. Sometimes the space itself is the object of violence; at other times the item destroyed is the primary message. A typical message advises people to stop developing certain kinds of resources. Animal-rights groups want organizations that affect nonhuman species to cease certain practices involving animals in processing or experimental facilities. To convince organizations not to use animals in laboratories, ALF activists burn or damage facilities that process animals and take actions against retail outlets that market mass consumerism and tourism. Environmental terrorism aims to stop activities or prevent events in certain spaces. Its primary focus is property; it seeks to protect life (Eagan 1996).[2] Environmental and animal-rights incidents pinpoint specific spaces and seek to stop certain activities from occurring there. They seek not to capture and control certain spaces but to alter the land uses or functions occurring there.

Incidents of Ecoterrorism in the United States, 1977–2005, and Incident Rates per 100,000 Residents of Incident Sites, 2000

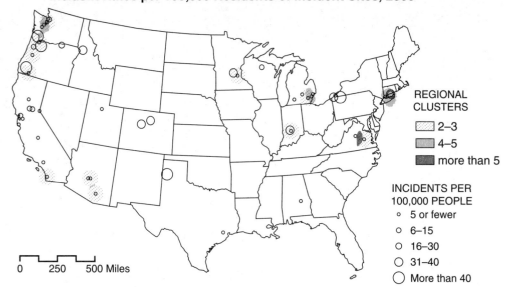

Figure 2 Incidents of ecoterrorism in the United States: regional clusters, 1997–2005, and rates per 100,000 residents of incident sites, 2000.

Sources: FBI 1997, 1998, 1999, 2000/2001; MIPT 2005. (Cartography by the author)

Incidents of Religious Terrorism in the United States, 1977–2005, and Incident Rates per 100,000 Residents of Incident Sites, 2000

Figure 3 Incidents of religious terrorism in the United States: regional clusters, 1997–2005, and rates per 100,000 residents of incident sites, 2000.

Sources: FBI 1997, 1998, 1999, 2000/2001; MIPT 2005. (Cartography by the author)

Religious motivations evidently generate different targets and have less uniform objectives. Religious terrorism creates more regional clusters than does ecoterrorism, but per-population incident rates are lower than are ecoterror rates. Religious causes are largely twofold: anti-abortion violence and violence on behalf of Islamic causes. In anti-abortion violence, terrorist agents try to convince citizens to stop using spaces as sites for abortions and birth-control services. They aim to shut down activity spaces. Conversely, Islamic causes seek not to stop activities performed at targeted sites

but to seriously disrupt routine activities and harm individual citizens and occupants of selected spaces. Major urban areas—Los Angeles, New York, and Washington, D.C.—were the sites of three-quarters of the incidents with apparent Islamic causes. Big cities—dens of iniquity, disorder, and chaos—were the preferred targets of Islamic attacks in sixteen of twenty-two incidents.

Turning now to spatial dynamics, terrorist incidents in the United States during the 1997–2005 period occurred in remarkably few locales (Table 3). Of the 25,000 or so

Table 3 Incidents of Terrorism in the United States, by Location, 1 January 1997–11 September 2005[a]

Location	Number of Incidents in Each Location	Cumulative Number of Incidents	Percentage of All Incidents	Cumulative Percentage of Incidents
New York, N.Y.	13	13	7.3	7.3
Washington, D.C.	10	23	5.6	12.9
Richmond, Va.	6	29	3.4	16.3
Bloomington, Ind.	4	33	2.2	18.5
Los Angeles, Calif.	4	37	2.2	20.8
Philadelphia, Pa.	4	41	2.2	23.0
Portland, Ore.	3	44	1.7	24.7
Albuquerque, N.Mex.	3	47	1.7	26.4
Miami, Fla.	3	50	1.7	28.1
Chico, Calif.	3	53	1.7	29.8
San Diego, Calif.	3	56	1.7	31.2
Twenty other locations	2	96	22.5	53.9
Eighty-two other locations	1	178	46.1	100.0

[a]The number of locations was reduced from 126 to 113 during geocoding, because suburban locations were combined with metropolitan areas when place-point data were missing (for example, West Hollywood became Los Angeles).
Sources: FBI 1997, 1998, 1999, 2000/2001; Feminist Majority Foundation 2002; MIPT 2005.

Table 4 Successful Terrorist Incidents in Selected U.S. Cities, 1 January 1997–11 September 2005

City	Percentage of Success in Each City	Number of Incidents in Each City	Number of Effective Incidents in Each City
New York, N.Y.	69	13	9
Washington, D.C.	30	10	3
Richmond, Va.	83	6	5
Bloomington, Ind.	100	4	4
Los Angeles, Calif.	50	4	2
Philadelphia, Pa.	80	4	3
Albuquerque, N.Mex.	100	3	3
Chico, Calif.	100	3	3
Miami, Fla.	66	3	2
Portland, Ore.	100	3	3
San Diego, Calif.	66	3	2

Sources: FBI 1997, 1998, 1999, 2000/2001; Feminist Majority Foundation 2002; MIPT 2005.

towns, townships, cities, and villages in the United States, only 113 (reduced from 126 because geocoding consolidated some suburbs into central cities) experienced the 178 terrorist incidents catalogued here. The usual spatial suspects reflected more incidents, but unexpected places had high counts as well. One-fourth of incidents occurred in only seven places. New York City, Washington, D.C., Los Angeles, Philadelphia, and Miami were among expected locales by virtue of their status as large cities with diverse targets and high population densities, but instances of terrorism also occurred in Richmond, Virginia, Bloomington, Indiana, Portland, Oregon, Albuquerque, New Mexico, Chico, California, and San Diego, California. A mix of motivations was evident in smaller venues.

Places have different levels of vulnerability to attack. The number of effective incidents—total incidents times success rate—shown in Table 4 allows a comparison of place riskiness. Bloomington, a college town in central Indiana, had as many incidents as did Philadelphia (four). But incidents in Bloomington had a 100 percent success rate, whereas Philadelphia's

Table 5 Terrorist Targets in the United States, by Land—Use Category and Success, 1 January 1997–11 September 2005[a]

General Land—Use Category Specific Land— Use Category	Number of Unsuccessful Incidents	Number of Successful Incidents	Percentage of Success for Each Category	Total Number of Incidents	Percentage of All Land-Use Categories
Commerce	11	41	79	52	29.2
Office	5	16	76	21	11.8
Retail facility	2	13	87	15	8.4
Business facility	1	7	88	8	4.5
Media office	3	5	63	8	4.5
Infrastructure	10	2	17	12	6.7
Transportation	7	2	22	9	5.1
Utility facility	3	0	0	3	1.7
Private uses	4	26	87	30	16.9
Residential structure	0	16	100	16	9.0
Construction site	1	10	91	11	6.2
Other sites	3	0	0	3	1.7
Public uses	0	11	100	11	6.2
Public space	0	8	100	8	4.5
Recreational space	0	3	100	3	1.7
Special uses	20	53	73	73	41.0
Health-care facility	6	30	83	36	20.2
Government facility	12	8	40	20	11.2
Animal facility	1	8	89	9	5.1
Laboratory	1	7	88	8	4.5
Total	45	133	75	178	100

[a]For the five general land-use categories and success: Pearson chi-square = 29.4 (.01); nominal contingency coefficient = .38 (.001).
Sources: FBI 1997, 1998, 1999, 2000/2001; Feminist Majority Foundation 2002; MIPT 2005.

rate was 75 percent. Bloomington had more effective incidents (and one fatality). Among the top eleven places of terrorist incidents, four small cities reflected 100 percent success rates. The larger cities stopped some attacks: Only 30 percent of the attacks in Washington, D.C. and 50 percent of those in Los Angeles attacks succeeded. The higher numbers of effective incidents in Richmond and Bloomington suggest a weaker preventive infrastructure against crimes of terrorism. The larger cities—Washington D.C., Los Angeles, Miami, San Diego, and New York City—show evidence of being best prepared to stave off attacks.

Targets of terrorist incidents vary (Table 5). More than half of all terrorist incidents were intended for five types of local settings, or targets: health-care facilities, offices, government facilities, residential structures, and retail facilities. From a land-use perspective, special uses, which typically have their own zoning categories, are the most vulnerable targets, followed by commercial areas.

An empirical relationship exists between land use and causes underlying terrorist incidents (Table 6). Pearson

chi-square tests and nominal contingency coefficient tests found a statistically significant linkage between land-use categories and terrorist causes. Viewed this way, special uses and commercial sites are the land-use categories at greatest risk of attack. Religious terrorists favor special land uses, then commercial spaces. Environmental actors prefer to attack commercial and private spaces. Terrorist motivations differ in their selection of attack methods (see Table 2) and targeted land uses (see Table 6). Specific methods of attack occur in particular land uses. Table 7 reports a significant relationship between terrorist methods and different types of land uses. Terrorist agents disproportionately attacked special land-use categories by using arson, vandalism, and bombings—all precursor crimes in which a terrorist perpetrator visits a targeted site, establishes an attack vector (deposits or hides an explosive device or firebomb, for example), and leaves.

Environmental terrorists target property, with more attacks outside in suburbs, outer growth zones, and exurban locales. The property is damaged by being bombed, burned, or

Table 6   Numbers of Terrorist Incidents in the United States, by Cause and Land—Use Category, 1 January 1997—11 September 2005[a]

Cause	Land—Use Category					
	Commerce	Infrastructure	Private Use	Public Use	Special Use	Total
Animal-rights	5	0	0	0	11	16
Environment	28	1	25	4	8	66
Nationalism	3	4	0	0	2	9
Race	4	2	2	7	0	15
Religion	12	2	2	0	45	61
Right-wing politics	0	3	0	0	8	11
Total	52	12	29	11	74	178

[a] Pearson chi-square = 159.2 (.001); nominal contingency coefficient = .687 (.001).
Sources: FBI 1997, 1998, 1999, 2000/2001; Feminist Majority Foundation 2002; MIPT 2005.

Table 7   Numbers of Terrorist Incidents in the United States, by Method and Land—Use Category, 1 January 1997–11 September 2005[a]

Method	Land—Use Category					
	Commerce	Infrastructure	Private Use	Public Use	Special Use	Total
Arson or vandalism	32	1	25	4	36	98
Armed attack or shooting	2	2	1	7	2	14
Toxin attack	5	1	1	0	13	20
Hijacking or robbery	4	2	0	0	2	8
Bombing	9	3	0	0	21	33
Other	0	3	2	0	0	5
Total	52	12	29	11	74	178

[a]Pearson chi-square = 111.82 (.001); nominal contingency coefficient = .621 (.001).
Sources: FBI 1997, 1998, 1999, 2000/2001; Feminist Majority Foundation 2002; MIPT 2005.

defaced. The property targeted must somehow be relevant to the terrorist, so that its choice delivers additional messages. When ecoterrorists firebomb a sport utility vehicle, the message may be a protest against gasoline-guzzling archconsumerism, an antiwar message, or a protest against globalization. A luxury house is fair game anywhere, and its destruction is a message that promotes more frugal living, less consumption, or less sprawl. Sometimes a particular space—timber mining in a specific forest, for example—from which ecoterrorists would like to banish development—is involved. This message goes beyond "no development" to include questions about natural resource use or who owns natural resource supplies. Ecoterrorism uses these messages to influence private and governmental decisions to develop natural resources.

The significant geographical relationships among terrorist motivation, targets, settings, and methods are more complex than they first appear. One way of probing this relationship more deeply is to ask how terrorist agents deliver and implement attacks. How do perpetrators traverse space to cross paths with victims (people or property)? Several alternative methods are available: bombing, shooting, and so forth (see Table 2). Even so, the extent to which terrorist actors must be close to the victim and the time of the attack vary. Usually, terrorist agents must visit the attack site at least once: They stash bombs, set fires, or shoot at a target situated in space. But perpetrators do not always have to visit the site of their planned attack.

Some long-distance terrorist attacks involve explosives, germs, bacteria, or viruses sent in letter or packages. Such attacks are unusual, with interesting twists to how spatial intersections between terrorists and victims occur. Here the attacker does not come into routine contact with the victim;

they are spatially separate, far apart. A technology designed to overcome spatial separation—the postal system—helps create the social proximity needed for terrorist violence.[3] Terrorist perpetrators and victims do not come face-to-face or physically intersect simultaneously in time and space. Instead, they are linked through physical items contained in envelopes or boxes. One spatial connection develops between the point of mailing and the point of receipt. The motivations behind letter terrorism are religion (sixteen incidents) or right-wing politics (three incidents).

Very few places served as sites for terrorist incidents using letters and mailed parcels. Among the 113 local sites, only six were linked to parcel-based attacks. New York City and Washington, D.C. were the top two. Philadelphia produced hoax anthrax letters to women's health clinics. In 1997, letter bombs from Cairo, Egypt arrived at a Leavenworth, Kansas prison, but they did not explode when opened. Boca Raton, Florida initiated the outbreak of mail-delivered anthrax spores on 2 October 2001. Government facilities, offices, and media offices were the only three targets of letter terror.

The largest event took place late in the fall of 2001. After 9/11, the Mid-Atlantic seaboard hosted a "Ping-Pong" game of anthrax and anthrax-threat letters. Table 8 depicts the sequence of anthrax letters and the states in which cases of anthrax were confirmed. The New York City and Washington, D.C. anthrax-attack letters were postmarked in Trenton, New Jersey during October. The anthrax attacks were nominally the product of Islamic perpetrators, but authorities never proved or disproved this.[4] They focused on media and government targets, linking a half-dozen cities and traveling in an intermittent wave up and down the Mid-Atlantic Coast. The anthrax attacks created a multiplace cluster comprising Boca Raton, Washington, Trenton, and New York City. One anthrax fatality in November, Ottilie Lundgren, lived in Oxford, Connecticut; the cause was suspected to be a cross-contaminated letter sent from Trenton to Wallingford, Connecticut. Her death evidently resulted from the 15 October anthrax letters, postmarked Trenton, sent to Sen. Thomas Daschle in Washington. Another cluster is a two-event set of reportedly noninfectious anthrax-threat letters sent on 15 October and 7 November to women's health clinics on the eastern seaboard. Authorities later prosecuted a pro-life bank robber, Clayton Waagner, for the distribution of these faux anthrax letters in the period between the real anthrax attacks.

The common way in which terrorists close the distance from their victim is through face-to-face violence. So-called lone wolves were responsible for five of the fourteen fatal incidents between 1997 and 2005 (see Table 8). These loners were not trying to capture or control specific spaces, but they did send clear messages that occupying public spaces can be dangerous. For terrorist loners, victimology is important. Their targets include nurses, doctors, racial or ethnic groups, or users of particular spaces and services.

People working in health clinics, people strolling down the street, or airline employees working at airport counters can be victims, and this randomness goes to the essence of terrorism. If lone-wolf terrorism sends a spatial message, it is that random violence can be applied directly to certain spaces.

The crimes of several lone wolves were classified as terrorism during the study period: Buford Furrow Jr., Benjamin Nathaniel Smith, Hesham Mohamed Hadayet, and James Charles Kopp. The terrorist physics of lone-wolf killers evokes the route they take through space on their way to executing terrorist crimes. At some point each of the four loners intersected his victim(s). Furrow shot dead a Filipino American postal carrier in Los Angeles. Smith took an automobile trip through Illinois and Indiana over the Fourth of July weekend in 1999. Figure 4 depicts his movement through public spaces, virtually all of it on Illinois and Indiana highways. Smith joined a drive-by shooting methodology with white supremacism, wounding and killing citizens who were moving through public spaces. In all, two people died from gunshot wounds and ten were wounded in six cities. Victims reflected nonwhite ethnicity and the misfortune of being present in public spaces along Smith's route. Smith ventured off the interstate highway network only to visit Bloomington, Indiana; then he headed to Salem, Illinois.

The travels of other lone-wolf terrorists would generate similar maps. On 4 July 2002 an Egyptian, Hesham Mohamed Hadayet, killed two people and wounded three at the EL AL Israel Airline ticket counter in the Los Angeles International Airport in the interest of ethnicity or radical Islam. In 1997 a Palestinian shot tourists atop the Empire State Building, striking a blow for Palestinian nationalism. In 1998 Kopp assassinated Barnett Slepian, a physician who performed legal abortions in Buffalo, New York. Slepian died in the private space of his personal residence; in his kitchen while preparing food.

Another loner, Clayton Waagner, robbed banks to pay for mailing the two waves of anthrax hoax letters to abortion clinics discussed above. By sending out more than 500 letters with fake anthrax powder, he instituted a web of spatial connections among family-planning clinics in the Midwest and on the East Coast. In October 2001 Waagner sent 250 hoax letters, postmarked Cleveland and Columbus, Ohio, Atlanta, Georgia, and Knoxville and Chattanooga, Tennessee, to clinics in seventeen states. The following month he mailed 270 letters to "clinics and pro-choice organizations in Eastern, Midwestern and Southern States" (National Abortion Federation 2004). Waagner, who claimed connections to the pro-life Army of God, was arrested in Cincinnati, then tried on federal terrorism charges in Philadelphia. To execute his campaign, Waagner traveled to eight cities: Philadelphia, Cleveland, Columbus, Cincinnati, Chattanooga, Knoxville, Atlanta, and Carrollton, Georgia.

Table 8 Sequence and Locations of Anthrax—Letter Attacks in the United States, 18 September—21 November, 2001

Date	Locations with Confirmed Anthrax Cases	Case Numbers[a]	Key Events
18 September			Five letters to the National Broadcasting Company, the *New York Post,* and the *National Enquirer* (Boca Raton, Florida) mailed in Trenton, New Jersey
22 September	New York	1	
25 September	New York	2	
26 September	New Jersey	3	
27 September	Florida,[b] New Jersey	4–5	
28 September	Florida, New York	6–7	
29 September	New York	8	
1 October	New York	9	
5 October			First fatality: case 5, Robert Stevens, *National Enquirer* photo editor, in Boca Raton, Florida
8 October			Letters to the District of Columbia (Senators Thomas Daschle and Patrick Leahy) mailed in Trenton, New Jersey
12 October			Senator Leahy's letter misrouted to Sterling, Virginia
13 October	New Jersey	10	Five *National Enquirer* employees test positive for anthrax in Boca Raton
14 October	New Jersey	11–12	Three investigators test positive in New York City
15 October	District of Columbia,[b] New Jersey	13–17	Clayton Waagner mails 250 fake anthrax letters to abortion and family-planning clinics in seventeen states and the District of Columbia
17 October			Twenty-eight House of Representatives staff members test positive for anthrax in the District of Columbia
18 October	New Jersey	18	U.S. Postal Service facility in Trenton, New Jersey closed
19 October	New Jersey	19	
23 October	New York	21	Second and third fatalities: cases 15 and 16, postal workers in Washington, DC
25 October	New York[b]	22	
26 October			U.S. Supreme Court building shut down
31 October			Fourth fatality: case 22, Kathy Nguyen, a hospital worker in New York City
7 November			Clayton Waagner posts 270 fake anthrax letters to locations in numerous states
14 November	Connecticut[b]	23	
21 November			Fifth fatality: case 23, Ottilie Lundgren of Oxford, Connecticut

[a] Cumulative number of cases identified by the Centers for Disease Control and Prevention.
[b] Anthrax cases that resulted in fatalities.
Source: Adapted from UCLA 2003.

Interpreting U.S. Terrorism Geography

Some of the findings of the preceding analyses are useful for building a stronger theoretical foundation for the geography of terrorism. Terrorist actions in the United States clustered in urban areas, and both their motives and their targets differed regionally. Religious, environmental, pro-life, and right-wing terrorism reflected different cluster patterns. When the patterns of terrorist incidents from 1997 to 2005 were reduced to the scale of individual attack sites, certain land uses exhibited higher risks of attack, as well as preferred methods of attack. Terrorists turned toward particular targets—offices, clinics, or public spaces—to send messages to a wider audience. Right-wing violence targeted military, government, and infrastructure targets. Religious terrorism

Benjamin Smith's Terrorist Spree in Illinois and Indiana, 1999

2 July
1. Chicago, Ill. Shoots at Jewish congregation; six wounded (Jews)
2. Skokie, Ill. Shoots pedestrian; one killed (African American)
3. Northbrook, Ill. Shoots into vehicle with two passengers (Asians)

3 July
4. Springfield, Ill. Shoots pedestrian; one wounded (African American)
5. Decatur, Ill. Shoots pedestrian; two wounded (African American)
6. Champaign-Urbana, Ill.: Shoots pedestrian; one wounded (Asian)

4 July
7. Bloomington, Ind. Shoots pedestrian; one killed (Asian)

5 July
8. Salem Ill. Kills himself after police chase

Figure 4   Benjamin Smith's terrorist spree in Illinois and Indiana, 1999.

Sources: AP 1999; CNN 1999; EmergencyNet News Service 1999. (Cartography by the author)

targeted commercial and special land uses. Commercial facilities and special land uses were the targets at greatest risk. When reduced to interactions across space, terrorist agents crossed paths with victims in different ways. Two cases showed how the 2001 anthrax letters and tone-wolf terrorism created different intersections of victim with perpetrator. The evolving lens of terrorism geography allows us to examine these findings.

Why do terrorist activities cluster in certain areas? Analysts believe that terrorist groups exhibit differences in operational networks and capacity to wage attacks over broader geographical areas (Drake 1998; van Meter 2002; Ettlinger and Bosco 2004). It may follow that the geographical clusters form where networks of potential perpetrators exist. Moreover, as seats of government, media, and business, metropolitan places abound with attractive targets for terrorist messages—transportation facilities, offices, clinics, houses, equipment, and dense concentrations of people. More targets mean greater vulnerability and higher risks of attack (Mitchell 2003). Alexander Murphy characterizes some areas as having "particularly high probabilities of conflict" (2003, 48).

Or the clustering of incidents in East and West Coast urban areas may be associated with a different set of dynamics. The 1997–2005 clusters fall in regions with sociodemographics that are more complex than simply high-density populations. The cluster sites also represent areas with greater social, religious, and ethnic diversity. Socially differentiated metropolitan regions establish a wide variety of social distances—differences in class, equality, ethnicity, cultural practices, political differences, and extreme social polarization

that result in large psychological and perceived sociological distances between those called "terrorists" and their victims—thus allowing terrorism to occur. Black argues that terror occurs in areas of great social distance and little physical distance (2004). Such combinations are most fruitful for terrorist violence. Another layer of social distancing to add to this is that, "between 1983 and 2004, refugees [were] resettled across many metropolitan areas in the United States, with 30 areas receiving 72 percent of the total. The largest resettlement areas [were] in established immigrant gateways in California (Los Angeles, Orange County, San lose, Sacramento), the Mid-Atlantic region (New York) and the Midwest (Chicago, Minneapolis-Saint Paul), as well as newer gateways including Washington, DC; Seattle, WA; and Atlanta, GA" (Singer and Wilson 2006, 1), Filtered through Black's ideas about social distance, it is possible that refugees from political conflict add to the social distances inherent in urban density; increasing, the potential for terrorism. Clearly, U.S. border-control policies since 9/11, built on the fear that foreign conflicts can be imported from volatile world regions, have made the nation's borders less porous to foreign immigrants and refugees. Among the refugees whom Audrey Singer and Jill Wilson documented between 1983 and 2004, period. large numbers came from Russia, Yugoslavia, Iran, Somalia, Iraq, and Ethiopia, all nations experiencing significant levels of political, nationalist, and ethnic terrorism (2006, 7).

However, the social-distance hypothesis does not explain other sets of U.S. terrorism. In pro-life and environmental violence, terrorist agents are not necessarily operating from spaces of extreme social polarization. The physical locations of targets hit by environmental terrorism are far from dense, socially differentiated metropolitan areas, situated instead in less heterogeneous rural and exurban settings. The selection of targets is driven by the nature of a setting like undeveloped land or by the nature of activities at an attack site. Perpetrators of anti-abortion violence are not necessarily socially distant from their targets either; instead, they are interested largely in stopping the functions performed by their targets or at the physical site of the attack (at a clinic, for example). In both of these instances the characteristics of the setting, not simply social distance, determine the targets. Black does not recognize this fact in his speculations about terrorist motivations, so his theory of terrorism geometry is not an effective predictor of where the next attack may occur. The analysis presented here, which identifies regions and locales where terrorist incidents occurred in the past, offers at least some probabilistic predictive value.

Another aspect of U.S. terrorism geography is that jurisdictions exhibit different levels of vulnerability to crimes of terror. Some cities are at greater risk than are others. Metropolitan regions offer the wide choice of targets and the potential social distances that can fuel terrorism, but jurisdictions do not possess the same capacities to forestall attacks. Washington, D.C. must be the most well-defended jurisdiction despite the 9/11 attack and notwithstanding the 2002 sniper shootings. As one indirect benefit of defense against terrorism, previous research suggested a connection between antiterrorist measures in the nation's capital and a downward trend in crime. The number of daily police reports of crimes dropped while higher homeland-security alerts were in place (Klick and Tabarrok 2005). Terrorism-prevention programs may increase police presence in the community and, in doing so, lower rates of other local crimes and improve local capacity to stop planned incidents. New York City's success rate during the 1997–2005 period was 69 percent. By 2005 the city's antiterrorism initiatives were thought to be strong and innovative (Finnegan zoos). One example of that strength occurred in 2003, when New York City authorities uncovered a plot to bomb subway stations (Horowitz 2005).

The identification of certain land uses as frequent and dangerous targets for various terrorist incidents and motivations or causes is another ingredient of terrorism geography. Different parts of the United States have different levels of risk. The absence of people does not mean the absence of attack risks. Ecoterrorism focuses on environmentally attractive natural areas or exurban fringes of metropolitan regions. Open public and private spaces under development pressures are likely targets, and they are difficult to defend. However, specialized land uses—government facilities, health clinics, or laboratories—appear to have been at greatest risk between 1997 and 2005. Many critical infrastructure facilities locate in specially zoned land-use categories: utilities, transportation, or health care, for example). Islamic terrorism in the United States focused on offices and commercial spaces, areas where citizens conduct the daily commerce of Western capitalism.

Terrorism geography reduces ultimately to the intersection of terrorist agents and their victims. In the United States, lethal terrorist violence frequently occurs in public spaces. Lone-wolf terrorists take advantage of travel in such spaces to execute crimes that target victims who are in the same public spaces. Consider how the terrorism landscape of Washington would look if authorities had labeled John Allen Muhammad and Lee Boyd Malvo's October 2002 killings "terrorism." The two so-called Beltway Snipers successfully used a terroristic method—targeted assassination via shootings—thirteen times in the public spaces of Northern Virginia, killing ten people, wounding three, and generating raw terror throughout the Washington metropolitan area. Their success intimidated and coerced citizens or government officials—by, for example, demanding money from the latter—into different patterns of behavior. Muhammad and Malvo called themselves "God" and left a tarot card at a killing site, suggesting some religious motivation. But, by classifying the crimes as "routine homicides," officials largely ignored potential terroristic motivations. Like Benjamin Smith, Muhammad and Malvo utilized public spaces as the settings within which they selected targets and launched their attacks. They were distant from their victims, for they used a scoped rifle to close the final space between killer and victim. The anthrax attacks were a more distant method, using postal attack vectors to close the physical distance between terrorist agents and their victims and to push terrorist incidents across the threshold into private space. In these instances, terrorists have no face-to-face intersection with their victims.

The Future of Terrorism Geography

The nuances of terrorism geography run a gamut, from macroclusters of incidents across the continental United States, to preferred targets of terrorist causes, to ultimate intersections of terrorist actors and their victims. Researchers have examined terrorism in ways that marginalize the characteristics of place—they have not clearly recognized the importance of the setting in which violence occurs. Nor have they acknowledged that the functions of places play a part in the delivery of terrorist messages. By focusing on differences in the patterns of attacks across space, the settings and land uses in which attacks Occur, and the methods by which terrorist violence is perpetrated, geographers can strengthen the geography of terrorism and, possibly, build better public-safety policies designed to prevent incidents. More research is also needed to examine the spatial patterns of terrorist crimes in countries other than the United States. Can the empirical pictures developed from U.S. examples be applied elsewhere and used to better understand terrorism geography?

Notes

1. The Pearson chi-square tests a null hypothesis that the relative frequencies of occurrence of observed events follow a specified frequency distribution. The nominal contingency coefficient tests the strength of association of the cross-tabulated frequencies. Values range from 0 (no association) to 1 (the theoretical maximum possible association). Statistically significant relationships suggest an empirical relationship between nominal variables such as terrorist motivations, methods, and land uses.

2. How should arson and bombings be classified? The perpetrator can never be completely sure a human will not be harmed if the tactic is successful—people can burn up inside offices or be injured or killed in various ways by remote explosions. Some incidents have involved individuals targeted for violence by ecoterrorists (Leader and Probst 2003). One subgroup of ecoterrorism—animal-rights extremists—has moved from property damage to personal mayhem. In a 1999 British case, an animal extremist group tortured and maimed a British filmmaker (Molland 2004).

3. It could be argued that the system of mail delivery by the U.S. Postal Service is a form of routine activity that occurs six days a week, follows well-known temporal patterns, and takes place in predictable, specific places. Furthermore, mail is typically "unguarded," in the sense that people rarely take special precautions when they open parcels.

4. So far, a massive investigation by the FBI has not succeeded in building a case for indicting anyone responsible for the fall 2001 incidents. Thus, only the letters were available to suggest the cause. Although the perpetrator(s) appear to have been Muslims, some believe that the cause was not Islamic in origin. Scientists evidently believed that the sophistication of the anthrax virus could only have originated in U.S. laboratories, so the focus shifted from Islamic extremists to scientists capable of synthesizing the anthrax bacteria. By the fall of 2006, further assessments had suggested that the anthrax bacteria were not as technically sophisticated as originally reported. For this analysis, therefore, I classified the attacks as having an Islamic cause.

References

AP [Associated Press]. 1999. Suspect in Racial Shooting Spree was Well Known in College Town. AP release, 5 July, posted on the Link-ups Web page "July 4th, 1999 Midwest Shooting Spree." [www.saxakali.com/communityLinkups/july_4th.htm].

Black, D. 1983. Crime as Social Control. *American Sociological Review* 48 (1): 34–45.

———. 2004. The Geometry of Terrorism. *Sociological Theory* 22 (1): 14–25.

CNN [Cable News Network]. 1999. Untitled CNN release, 5 July, posted on the Link-ups Web page "July 4th, 1999 Midwest Shooting Spree." [www.saxakali.com/communityLinkups/july_4th.htm].

Drake, C.J.M. 1998. *Terrorists' Target Selection.* New York: St. Martin's Press.

Eagan, S. P. 1996. From Spikes to Bombs: The Rise of Eco-Terrorism. *Studies in Conflict & Terrorism* 19 (1): 1–18.

Emergency Net News Service. 1999. Shooting Spree Suspect Kills Himself during Chase. EmergencyNet News Service report, 5 July. [www.emergency.com/1999/smithpg.htm].

Ettlinger, N., and F. Bosco. 2004. Thinking through Networks and Their Spatiality: A Critique of the US (Public) War on Terrorism and Its Geographic Discourse. *Antipode* 36 (2): 249–271.

FBI [Federal Bureau of Investigation]. 1997. *Terrorism in the United States.* Washington, D.C.: Federal Bureau of Investigation.

———. 1998. *Terrorism in the United States.* Washington, D.C.: Federal Bureau of Investigation.

———. 1999. *Terrorism in the United States.* Washington, D.C.: Federal Bureau of Investigation.

———. 2000/2001. *Terrorism in the United States, 2000/2001.* Washington, D.C.: Federal Bureau of Investigation.

Felson, M. 1998. *Crime and Everyday Life.* 2nd ed. Thousand Oaks, Calif.: Pine Forge Press.

Feminist Majority Foundation. 2002. Clinics Arsoned/Bombed 97–02. *Anti-Abortion Violence Watch,* 16 May, 1. Map. [www.feminist.org/rrights/aavw35.pdf].

Finnegan, W. 2005. The Terrorism Beat: How Is the N.Y.P.D. Defending the City? *New Yorker,* 25 July, 58–71.

Flint, C. 2003. Terrorism and Counterterrorism: Geographic Research Questions and Agendas. *Professional Geographer* 55 (2): 161–169.

Georges-Abeyie, D.E. 1983. The Social Ecology of Bomb Threats: Dallas, Texas. *Journal of Black Studies* 13 (3): 305–320.

Gorriti, G. 1999. *The Shining Path: A History of the Millenarian War in Peru.* Translated by R. Kirk. Chapel Hill: University of North Carolina Press.

Gourevitch, P. 2005. Tides of War: After the Tsunami, the Fighting Continues. *New Yorker,* 1 August, 54–63.

Hewitt, C. 2000. Patterns of American Terrorism, 1955–1998: An Historical Perspective on Terrorism-Related Fatalities. *Terrorism and Political Violence* 12 (1):1–14.

———. 2003. *Understanding Terrorism in America: From the Klan to Al Qaeda.* London: Routledge.

Horowitz, C. 2005. Anatomy of a Foiled Plot. In *The Best American Crime Writing* 2005, edited by O. Penzler and T. H. Cook, 177–190. New York: Harper Perennial.

Kent, R. B. 1993. Geographical Dimensions of the Shining Path Insurgency in Peru. *Geographical Review* 83 (4): 441–454.

Klick, J., and A. Tabarrok. 2005. Using Terror Alert Levels to Estimate the Effect of Police on Crime. *Journal of Law and Economics* 48 (1): 267–279.

Laqueur, W. 1999. *The New Terrorism: Fanaticism and the Arms of Mass Destruction.* Oxford: Oxford University Press.

Leader, S. H., and P. Probst. 2003. The Earth Liberation Front and Environmental Terrorism. *Terrorism and Political Violence* 15 (4): 37–58.

MIPT [Memorial Institute for the Prevention of Terrorism]. 2005. Terrorism Knowledge Base. Data Screens Set for U.S. Incidents Only, 1 January 1997 through 11 September 2005. [www.tkb.org/IncidentRegionModule.jsp].

Mitchell, J. K. 2003. Urban Vulnerability to Terrorism as Hazard. In *The Geographical Dimensions of Terrorism,* edited by S. L. Cutter, D. B. Richardson, and T. J. Wilbanks, 17–25. New York: Routledge.

Molland, N. 2004. Chronicle of direct actions, 1999–2004. Formerly at [www.animalliberationfront.com/ALFront/alf_summary.htm].

Monroe, C. P. 1982. Addressing Terrorism in the United States. *Annals of the American Academy of Political and Social Science* 463 (1): 141–148.

Murphy, A. B. 2003. The Space of Terror. In *The Geographical Dimensions of Terrorism,* edited by S. L. Cutter, D. B. Richardson, and T. J. Wilbanks, 47–52. New York: Routledge.

National Abortion Federation. 2004. Anti-Abortion Extremists /Clayton Waagner. *Clinic Violence.* [www.prochoice.org/ about_abortion/violence/clayton_waagner.html].

Noble, A. G., and E. Efrat. 1990. Geography of the Intifada. *Geographical Review* 80 (3): 288–307.

Singer, A., and J. H. Wilson. 2006. *From "There" to "Here": Refugee Resettlement in Metropolitan America.* Living Cities Census Series. Washington, D.C.: Brookings Institution.

Smith, B. L., and K. D. Morgan. 1994. Terrorists Right and Left: Empirical Issues in Profiling American Terrorists. *Studies in Conflict and Terrorism* 17 (1): 39–57.

Smith, B. L., K. R. Damphousse, F. Jackson, and A. Sellers. 2002. The Prosecution and Punishment of International Terrorists in Federal Courts: 1980–1998. *Criminology & Public Policy* 1 (3): 311–337.

Tolnay, S. E., G. Deane, and E. M. Beck. 1996. Vicarious Violence: Spatial Effects on Southern Lynchings, 1890–1919. *American Journal of Sociology* 102 (3): 788–815.

UCLA [University of California-Los Angeles]. 2003. American Anthrax Outbreak of 2001. University of California—Los Angeles, School of Public Health, Department of Epidemiology. [www.ph.ucla.edu/epi/bioter/detect/antdetect_intro.html].

Van Meter, K. M. 2002. Terrorists/Liberators: Researching and Dealing with Adversary Social Networks. *Connections* 24 (3): 66–78.

Whittaker, D. J., ed. 2005. Spain. In *The Terrorism Reader,* 125–138. New York: Routledge.

DR. SAMUEL NUNN is a professor of criminal justice at Indiana University—Purdue University, Indianapolis, Indiana 46204.

The Year in Hate

Number of Hate Groups Tops 900

DAVID HOLTHOUSE

From white power skinheads decrying "President Obongo" at a racist gathering in rural Missouri, to neo-Nazis and Ku Klux Klansmen hurling epithets at Latino immigrants from courthouse steps in Oklahoma, to anti-Semitic black separatists calling for death to Jews on bustling street corners in several East Coast cities, hate group activity in the U.S. was disturbing and widespread throughout 2008, as the number of hate groups operating in America continued to rise. Last year, 926 hate groups were active in the U.S., up more than 4% from 888 in 2007. That's more than a 50% increase since 2000, when there were 602 groups.

As in recent years, hate groups were animated by the national immigration debate. But two new forces also drove them in 2008: the worsening recession, and Barack Obama's successful campaign to become the nation's first black president. Officials reported that Obama had received more threats than any other presidential candidate in memory, and several white supremacists were arrested for saying they would assassinate him or allegedly plotting to do so.

At the same time, law enforcement officials reported a marked swelling of the extreme-right "sovereign citizens" movement that wreaked havoc in the 1990s with its "paper terrorism" tactics. Adherents are infamous for filing bogus property liens and orchestrating elaborate financial ripoffs.

Somewhat surprisingly, it wasn't just the usual suspects from the white supremacist underworld who sought to exploit the country's economic turmoil and political strife. A key 2008 hate group trend was the increasing militancy of the extremist fringe of the Hebrew Israelite movement, whose adherents believe that Jews are creatures of the devil and that whites deserve death or slavery.

These radical black supremacists have no love for Barack Obama, calling him a "house nigger" and a puppet of Israel. They preach to inner-city blacks that evil Jews are solely responsible for the recession. The rhetoric of white-skinned hate group leaders in 2008 was equally alarming. Last September, for example the cover of *National Socialist* magazine depicted then-presidential nominee Barack Obama in the crosshairs of a scope, with the headline "Kill This Nigger?"

What follows is a detailed look at the three most active and dangerous white supremacist hate group sectors in 2008: Ku Klux Klan groups, neo-Nazis, and racist skinheads.

Ku Klux Klan

Reversing a generally declining trend since 2000, Klan groups in the United States increased significantly in 2008, from 155 chapters to 186. Seventeen new chapters belong to the Brotherhood of Klans Knights of the Ku Klux Klan (BOK), which during the past five years has grown into the largest Klan organization in the country. In 2008, the Marion, Ohio-headquartered BOK launched a handful of chapters in Canada, linking up with the Aryan Guard, a fast-growing white nationalist group based in Alberta.

A smaller but likewise rapidly expanding Klan group, the United Northern and Southern Knights of the Ku Klux Klan, which in 2007 absorbed the National Aryan Knights, more than doubled its number of chapters and tripled its geographic reach last year, going from 11 chapters in eight states to 24 chapters in 24 states.

The continued rise of the United Northern and Southern Knights and the BOK paralleled the decline of the Imperial Klans of America (IKA). Since 2005, the IKA has shriveled from 39 chapters in 26 states to just six chapters in five states. Last year, it suffered a crippling blow when a Meade County, Ky., jury delivered a $2.5 million judgment against members of the IKA, including $1 million against IKA leader Ron Edwards, in a lawsuit brought by the Southern Poverty Law Center on behalf of a mixed-race teenager who was assaulted by IKA thugs in Kentucky.

Beyond the IKA trial, the biggest Klan story for the mainstream media in 2008 was the murder of a 43-year-old Tulsa, Okla., woman during a backwoods Klan initiation ritual near Bogalusa, La. According to law enforcement investigators, the victim was recruited over the Internet to join the Sons of Dixie, a tiny KKK faction led by Raymond "Chuck" Foster. Foster allegedly shot the woman in the head after she changed her mind about joining the Klan.

Blipping on the media's radar last December was the National Knights of the Ku Klux Klan, whose imperial wizard,

Ray Larsen, called for all Klansmen "worldwide" to wear black armbands and fly the American flag upside down on Jan. 20, the day of Barack Obama's inauguration.

Neo-Nazis

A slight drop in the number of neo-Nazi chapters last year from 207 to 194 was attributable largely to the dissolution of National Vanguard after its leader, Kevin Alfred Strom, was convicted in January 2008 on child pornography charges. (Strom was released last fall after serving prison time.)

Another major neo-Nazi leader, American National Socialist Workers Party "Commander" Bill White, also suffered legal troubles in 2008, culminating in his December indictment on several federal felony counts for posting death threats on his website or by making them by phone. Along with the threats, White often posted the home addresses of perceived enemies, ranging from Canadian human rights attorney Richard Warman (in an item subtly titled "Kill Richard Warman") to *Miami Herald* columnist Leonard Pitts to officials of the Southern Poverty Law Center.

When the seven-count federal indictment came down, White was already jailed in Chicago on separate charges. He was arrested last October and extradited from Roanoke, Va., where he owns apartments in black neighborhoods, to face a federal obstruction of justice charge for allegedly threatening the foreman of a Chicago jury that convicted neo-Nazi leader Matt Hale in 2004 of soliciting the murder of a federal judge. Still, despite White's legal and personal financial turmoil (he declared bankruptcy last June), the ANSWP grew last year from 30 chapters in 26 states to 35 chapters in 28 states, making it the second-largest neo-Nazi organization in the country, after the National Socialist Movement (NSM).

Apart from its usual literature dispersals, book burnings, swastika lightings, and its annual "Hated and Proud" hate rock festival, the NSM in 2008 targeted Latino immigrants with sizable "illegal invasion" protests in Washington, D.C., and Omaha, Neb. Subjected for years to movement ridicule for their brown-shirt uniforms, NSM national and state chapter leaders also voted at the group's National Congress last April to switch to "more militant looking" black BDUs (Battle Dress Uniforms). Even with the makeover, the NSM lost 30 chapters last year (it later added 26, for a net loss of six chapters) after leader Jeff Schoep abandoned his family and relocated NSM headquarters from Minneapolis to Detroit in January 2008, reportedly to move in with a new girlfriend of dubious Aryan purity.

Nevertheless, the NSM benefited from diminished competition as the formerly dominant National Alliance continued its long decline, shrinking to 11 chapters in nine states. Similarly, Aryan Nations, another one-time powerhouse, withered to 11 chapters in 10 states. White Revolution gained no ground, ending the year as it began with a dozen chapters.

Two upstart neo-Nazi groups emerged in 2008. The League of American Patriots, which held its inaugural meeting last March 29, appears to be comprised of former National Vanguard members. The second newcomer, Knights of the Nordic Order, was founded by "two former captains of the Aryan Brotherhood," a notorious white supremacist prison gang, according to its website.

Racist Skinheads

The total number of racist skinhead crews, driven by the addition of a couple of new organizations, rose from 90 in 2007 to 98 last year.

Relatively inactive in 2007, Hammerskin Nation, long a force to be reckoned with in the racist skinhead subculture, came back in a big way in 2008. The diminished tally of Hammerskins chapters (which dropped from 15 to 12) is misleading, as it represents the merging of smaller chapters and Hammerskin leaders weeding out weaker outfits, rather than a real drop in the organization's strength and membership. On the contrary, the Hammerskins last year stepped up recruiting while forging new bonds with other skinhead groups and hosting dozens of hate rock concerts, white power cookouts, Mixed Martial Arts prizefight viewing parties and other widely promoted events.

The Confederate Hammerskins (CHS), the organization's southeastern regional division, kept particularly busy, beginning last March with a St. Patty's Day concert in Central Florida that was heavily attended by skins from across the country. Represented crews included Volksfront, Blood & Honour American Division, Atlantic City Skins, Troops of Tomorrow, and The Hated. Members of the Outlaws Motorcycle Club, a notorious biker gang, also attended.

A close Hammerskins ally, the Portland, Ore.-based Volksfront, held its first annual "Althing" gathering last Aug. 29-Sept. 1 on private land purchased by Volksfront in rural Missouri, about an hour's drive north of St. Louis. Part three-day hate rock blowout, part skinhead summit, the Althing was held in the "Samuel Weaver Memorial Hall," named after white supremacist Randy Weaver's son, who was killed by federal agents during the infamous Ruby Ridge standoff in 1992 (Weaver's wife and a U.S. marshal were also killed). Among the white supremacist leaders who attended was veteran skinhead organizer David Lynch, leader of the resurgent Sacramento, Calif.-based crew American Front.

Last December, more than 100 skinheads from at least five states gathered in Florida for a "Martyr's Day" party, co-sponsored by CHS, Volksfront and American Front, that featured a keynote address phoned in from prison by Richard Kemp, a member of the white supremacist terrorist group The Order. Martyr's Day commemorates the 1984 death of Order founder Bob Mathews, who died in a shootout with the FBI.

Another noteworthy development in the skinhead sector was the severe weakening of the Vinlanders Social Club (VSC), a skinhead coalition that began in 2003 and grew to become Hammerskin Nation's primary rival. Plagued by infighting, criminal prosecutions and desertions, the Vinlanders made no public appearances in 2008, limiting their activities to private beer bashes. Three inner-circle Vinlanders, including co-founder Eric "The Butcher" Fairburn, were convicted last year of a March 2007 racially motivated attack on a homeless black man in downtown Indianapolis. At his sentencing hearing last August, Fairburn publicly renounced the skinhead movement.

Formerly aligned with the VSC, the Keystone State Skinheads (KSS) distanced their group from the Vinlanders, changed their name to Keystone United and recast themselves as media-friendly "pro-white" activists. Keystone mouthpiece Keith Carney denounced hooliganism in several newspaper and television interviews. Last October, the group held a "Leif Ericson Day Celebration," honoring the Viking explorer, in a Philadelphia public park on the banks of the Schuylkill River. In contrast to the screaming hate rock performed by Absolute Terror and Total War at the annual Keystone-sponsored "Uprise" concert in January 2008, which was held in a secret location, Celtic folk musicians provided entertainment at the two-faced crew's "family-friendly" event.

In contrast to KSS, the United Society of Aryan Skinheads (USAS) made no effort to revamp its image in 2008. Formed in recent years inside California's state prison system, the USAS continues to espouse white-power skinhead ideology and grow into a strong presence throughout Southern California as members are paroled. The USAS went from a single chapter in 2007 to nine chapters in 2008, including three separate crews in San Diego, the group's base of operations in the outside world. Though populated almost entirely by ex-cons, the USAS, unlike most prison-based white supremacists, actually maintains a powerful racist identity and rarely compromises principles in favor of criminal profits.

One major new racist skinhead group surfaced in 2008: the Supreme White Alliance, or SWA. Co-founded by Kentucky skinhead Steven Edwards, son of Imperial Klans of America leader Ron Edwards, the SWA by year's end boasted eight chapters in as many states, an active website and a substantial online presence on MySpace as well as on the white nationalist social networking site New Saxon. The group's vice president is former IKA member Jarred Hensley, who served more than a year for his role in the hate crime assault that led to the SPLC lawsuit. "Out of prison and back on the streets," Hensley posted on MySpace last July upon his release. "It's gr88 to be a Skinhead!" Last October, former SWA probate Daniel Cowart was arrested in Tennesee with another skinhead he met online for allegedly plotting to assassinate Barack Obama after killing 88 black students (88 is neo-Nazi code for the phrase "Heil Hitler"). The SWA claimed that Cowart had been kicked out prior to hatching the plan.

Green Rage

Radical environmentalists are caught between their love of the Earth, trespass of the law, and the U.S. government's war on terror.

MATT RASMUSSEN

People like to think of the courtroom as a crucible of justice, but to me it's always seemed a diluter of passions. The atmosphere is restrained, so respectful and genteel it's easy to forget that people's lives hang in the balance. The system has a way of straining out emotion. It is designed to objectify, to control the soaring passions that created the need for the courtroom in the first place. The perpetrators and the victims pour their passions into the settling ponds of the attorneys, and the attorneys, in turn, pour the diluted stuff into the deep vessel of the judge, and, by extension, into the even deeper water of The System.

If you sat in the gallery of a federal courtroom in my hometown of Eugene, Oregon, last summer and watched as six young men and women entered guilty pleas in a string of environmentally motivated arsons—crimes that the federal government describes as the most egregious environmental terrorism in the nation's history—you might have wondered where the passion had gone. One by one, in a windowless chamber, the defendants answered perfunctory questions posed by Judge Ann Aiken, who sat Oz-like in the highest chair. One by one, they listened to descriptions of the crimes they were accused of committing. One by one, they accepted the government's offer of plea bargains, and one by one, they said the word.

"Guilty."

Kevin Tubbs, thirty-seven, an animal rights activist who migrated to Eugene from Nebraska, mumbled the word and shook his head. Kendall Tankersley, twenty-nine, who holds a degree in molecular biology, choked it out through a gathering sob. Stanislas Meyerhoff, twenty-nine, who wants to study auto mechanics, said it with an odd sort of let's-get-this-over-with politeness. They addressed Judge Aiken as "your honor" and "ma'am."

In the gallery, reporters scribbled. Federal prosecutors with American flag pins affixed to somber blue suits looked on dispassionately. Sentencing dates were set, and the prosecutors, seeking lengthy terms, asked the judge to employ guidelines issued under counter-terrorism laws when considering how much time each should serve.

The crimes to which the six confessed included seventeen attacks, all but one of them arson or attempted arson. The actions took place in five western states between 1996 and 2001. No one was injured. Sport utility vehicles were burned at a Eugene car dealership. So was a meat-packing plant in Redmond, Oregon. Other targets included federal facilities in Wyoming and California and Oregon, where wild horses and burros were let loose and buildings burned down. And in the most notorious action, a spectacular nighttime blaze high in the Rockies destroyed several structures at the Vail ski area. Many of the attacks were followed by communiqués issued under the banner of the Earth Liberation Front, a shadowy, leaderless offshoot of the group Earth First!, and by its sister group, the Animal Liberation Front.

Prosecutors say those who did the crimes took extraordinary means to conceal their involvement. They met in secret gatherings they called "book club" meetings, discussing details such as computer security, target surveillance, and lock-picking. They required that each attendee describe actions they took to avoid detection while traveling to the meeting sites. They used nicknames and code words. They called their criminal actions "camping trips," and dubbed the timing devices they attached to incendiary bombs "hamburgers."

"Terrorism is terrorism—no matter the motive," FBI director Robert Mueller said in January 2006, after the Bush administration announced indictments in an investigation it calls Operation Backfire. "The FBI is committed to protecting Americans from all crime and all terrorism, including acts of domestic terrorism on behalf of animal rights or the environment."

Many were appalled. How could anyone possibly use that singularly loaded word to describe these acts? Where is the moral equivalence between burning an SUV in the dead of night (and doing as much as you can, given the nature of the business at hand, to see that no one gets hurt) and ramming a 767 into a skyscraper? When Eugene's daily newspaper, the *Register-Guard*, used the word *eco-terrorism* to describe the investigation, at least one reader took its editors to task, writing that the paper "appears to confuse arson occurring within the context of a nonviolent campaign with terrorism." The paper opted for the softer-sounding *eco-sabotage* thereafter.

Chelsea Dawn Gerlach is twenty-nine now. Under the terms of her plea bargain, she'll likely spend ten years in prison—assuming she cooperates with government prosecutors as they continue their investigation. If she had been found guilty at trial of all the government had accused her of, she could have been given a life sentence. (Federal prosecutors are seeking life sentences for the majority of those indicted in the Operation Backfire investigation, yet, according to the U.S. Sentencing Commission, the average sentence for arsonists in 2003 was just around seven years.) Along with Meyerhoff, Gerlach is an alum of South Eugene High, a school with a sterling reputation in the heart of Eugene's liberal, affluent south side. In fact, all six of those who entered guilty pleas had close ties to Eugene, as did four others who awaited trial at the time of this writing and three more who had fled the country.

By the time she was in her early twenties, Gerlach had come to believe that Western culture was having a ruinous effect on the global environment, that the Earth faced environmental catastrophe. She felt compelled to do something about it. At some point, passion and frustration drove her over the boundary of her country's laws. Playing by the rules, it seemed, was doing no damn good. At some point, according to the details of her plea bargain, she found herself at the base of Vail Mountain, watching flames light the night sky, awaiting the return of another ELF operative, Bill Rodgers, who had set the fires. Two days later, she found herself at the Denver Public Library, composing a claim of responsibility on a computer that couldn't be traced to her. The message said ELF took the action "on behalf of the lynx," whose habitat would be harmed by an expansion at Vail. "For your safety and convenience, we strongly advise skiers to choose other destinations until Vail cancels its inexcusable plans for expansion," Gerlach wrote.

Skiers did not stop coming to Vail. The arson attack sparked a wildfire of popular condemnation that was directed toward those responsible and, by unfair association, toward more mainstream environmentalists who had also been fighting the expansion. Ultimately, Vail's owners got $12 million from their insurers and the expansion whistled through.

Last summer, in that Eugene courtroom, Gerlach reached her day of reckoning with the system. She, too, said the word. "Guilty." Then she asked the judge if she could read a statement. Gerlach, who has straight black hair and a round, welcoming face, gathered herself and took a deep breath. The words tumbled out in a rush:

"These acts were motivated by a deep sense of despair and anger at the deteriorating state of the global environment and the escalating inequities within society. But I realized years ago this was not an effective or appropriate way to effect positive change. I now know that it is better to act from love than from anger, better to create than destroy, and better to plant gardens than to burn down buildings."

Gerlach admitted to participating in nine of the seventeen attacks described in the government's indictment. In addition to the Vail arson, she served as a lookout as other operatives put

incendiary devices next to a meat-packing plant in Eugene; she tried to burn down a Eugene Police Department substation; she participated in an ELF arson that did more than $1 million in damage at an Oregon tree farm that grew genetically modified poplar trees; she helped topple an electrical transmission tower in the sagebrush-and-juniper country east of Bend. And on Christmas night in 1999, she sat in a van that she and her friends had named "Betty" and served as lookout as others placed buckets of diesel fuel next to a Boise Cascade office in Monmouth, Oregon. The buckets ignited and destroyed an eight-thousand-square-foot building, doing $1 million in damage. Then Gerlach sent out an ELF communiqué: "Let this be a lesson to all greedy multinational corporations who don't respect ecosystems. The elves are watching."

The first time I came to Eugene I wondered what all the fuss was about. I knew its reputation well—a university town, a hotbed of liberal activism, home to Ken Kesey and other '60s holdouts. But when I drove through the arterials and back streets on the north side of the city I realized that much of Eugene is just plain old suburbia—ranch homes, tidy lawns, and conservative values.

After a decade of living and working in Eugene, I know this about the place: It's a slice of America, profoundly divided along fault lines of politics, values, and culture. On the south side of the Willamette River, which bisects the city, you'll find the liberal Eugene of renown, full of University of Oregon faculty and tie-dyed hippies who attend the freewheeling Oregon Country Fair each July. Conservative Eugene is on the north side of the river, full of satellite dishes and American flags and folks who favor the traditional charms of the Lane County Fair in August.

There are divisions within the divisions, just as there are in America at large. There are monied fiscal conservatives and working-class Bush supporters. There are affluent liberals who vote Democrat and there are the more disheveled activists who have no patience for the compromises made by mainstream liberals. Those who committed the ELF arsons, and their supporters, come from this latter milieu.

If there is a physical heart of the radical environmental movement in Eugene, it is a leafy precinct of old wooden houses just west of downtown, known as the Whiteaker neighborhood. An outsider—someone from, say, Cedar Rapids, Iowa, or St. Petersburg, Florida, or Provo, Utah, or from any of a thousand bastions of conventional American culture, including many corners of Eugene—might fixate on a curbside cardboard box offering "free stuff," or a do-your-own-thing piece of art in a front yard, a dreadlocked couple strolling hand in hand, a FUCK BUSH sign, a flash of tattooed flesh, a braless woman, a pair of ratty Carhartt cutoffs, a pierced tongue, eyebrow, nose, belly button, or neck, and feel a skosh uncomfortable.

Whiteaker rose to national prominence in 1999, after perhaps a couple dozen of its residents—young adults who described themselves as anarchists—helped foment the lawlessness at the World Trade Organization conference in Seattle. Suddenly "the Eugene anarchists" were a cause célèbre.

Reporters from the BBC, the *Los Angeles Times,* CNN, the *Wall Street Journal,* and other major outlets descended on Eugene, their editors demanding analysis pieces explaining what the hell had happened in Seattle. In Eugene, there was a good deal of uneasy eye-rolling. Local civic leaders reacted with a mix of revulsion and denial to the notion that their city was Anarchy Central. The consensus was that the whole thing had been blown out of proportion.

No one knows how many anarchists there really are in White-aker; they don't keep membership rolls. At least some of those who donned black garb in Seattle were kids doing what kids the world over often do: immerse themselves in an adrenaline-charged cause that's greater than oneself. Not all of Eugene's anarchists are callow youths, though. Some are genuine, stead-fastly committed, and deep-thinking.

Eugene's brand of anarchy is "green anarchy." Unlike old-style industrialist anarchists, green anarchists are primarily concerned with the effects of civilization on the global environment. They are more radical in their thought than, say, Marx-ists are. They would certainly agree that capital accumulates in a fashion that creates a wealthy elite at the expense of the exploited masses, but their critique goes far beyond that. Their central precept is not that civilization needs to be reconstructed, but rather that it needs to be overthrown in its entirety and never replaced. Things started to go wrong, they contend, when humans first domesticated plants and animals.

The nexus between the green anarchists, the Earth Libera-tion Front, and those ensnared in the government's investiga-tion is not perfect. Several of the defendants don't claim to be advocates of the green anarchy movement now, if they ever were. And some of them, it seems, had not thought through the intellectual justifications of their actions in a formal sense—perhaps they just felt in their gut that things like SUVs and animal slaughterhouses and plantations that grow genetically modified trees were wrong. Whatever their motivations, their actions and rhetoric match up quite well with the principles of the green anarchist philosophy.

If they are in need of intellectual mentorship, Eugene's green anarchists have a resource close at hand. John Zerzan is in his sixties, a graduate of Stanford and San Francisco State University and one of the foremost anticivilization thinkers in the world. In the '60s he was a Marxist and a Maoist and a Vietnam protester and a devotee of the Haight-Ashbury psy-chedelic scene. He now believes that Paleolithic humans and the few remaining primitive cultures provide the best models for how humans should subsist. His books include *Elements of Refusal, Future Primitive,* and *Against Civilization: Readings and Reflections.* He is an editor of *Green Anarchy,* which calls itself "an anticivilization journal of theory and action." He was a confidant of Theodore Kaczynski during the Unabomber trial.

On a sunny afternoon last summer, I sat down with Zerzan on his shady back deck. His house is small and tidy, a wooden bungalow that sits near a busy one-way just south of the White-aker neighborhood. I asked him if he thought too much had been made of the Eugene anarchists after the WTO riots.

"60 Minutes was here. You can't say that would have hap-pened just because we have a good idea," he said. Then he

switched to the recent indictments. "All of the people who have been arrested in this thing used to live here in Eugene. There was a lot happening here, and that whole neighborhood [White-aker] was the key part. Now it's quieter."

I had never before spoken with Zerzan, although I knew that he lived in Eugene; around town, he's taken for granted in the way that minor celebrities who live in small cities often are. He has a salt-and-pepper beard, straight bangs, and a quiet, almost patrician demeanor that I found disarming. He seems younger than his age.

I asked him if he thought the arsons outlined in the gov-ernment's indictment had done any good. He pointed out that most of the actions were followed by anonymous communiqués explaining precisely why the actions were taken. The combina-tion of action and explanation can be quite powerful, he said.

Zerzan clearly struggles with the question of violence. Of Kaczynski, he said he found him "lacking in the basic kind of human connection that most people have." He hopes that the anticivilization movement will prevail without great bloodshed, although he quickly adds "my anarchist friends mainly laugh at me for being too hopeful." Humans, he believes, may very well forge a new way of living on Earth, or, rather, return to old ways of living on Earth, before utter environmental collapse imposes a Malthusian end.

"You can't make the revolution happen by promising people less," he said. Then he swept his hand out in front of him, tak-ing in his house, the sound of cars and trucks hurtling past, the hum of the city, of human civilization. "You can't say all of this is more. This is becoming more sterile and cold and fucked up by the minute."

Down at Sam Bond's Garage, in the heart of Whiteaker, organic beer is served up in old jam jars. Tots in hemp smocks frolic on the wooden floor. A black t-shirt hangs on a wall sporting a skull and crossbones on the front and "Whiteaker" in pirate scrawl beneath.

It's a Sunday night in June, and the place is filling up fast. There's a disco ball hanging from old wooden rafters in the eatery's barnlike interior space. Two large ceiling fans beat the air, but a thermometer on the wall reports eighty-three degrees nonetheless. The usual customers, the ones who just came by for beers or a bite to eat or to chat with friends, seem a bit bewil-dered by the gathering crowd. A middle-aged man shoulders up to the bar to settle his tab and a young woman inquires if he's here for the rally. When the man asks what rally, she says, "It's for Free Luers. He got twenty-three years for burning up three SUVs." Soon the hall is full, a standing-room-only crowd of perhaps two hundred.

Jeffrey "Free" Luers is a skinny kid from suburban Los Angeles who is serving his fifth year in prison. In 2000, when he was twenty-one, Luers and an accomplice were arrested for setting fire to three SUVs in the middle of the night at a car lot near the University of Oregon (a separate action from those included in the Operation Backfire indictment). A Eugene judge sentenced Luers, who refused all of the government's plea bargain offers, to nearly twenty-three years in prison. The authorities say they made an example of Luers to forestall further crimes; activists say they made a martyr of him. Luers remains unrepentant. In a recent message to his supporters, he said, "I got careless, I got sloppy. I slipped up. I got caught."

I find a seat at the bar and order an ale. An acquaintance recognizes me and squeezes over to say hello. He points to a man sitting at a table in the center of the hall. Amid the young tattooed-and-pierced set and the older pony-tailed-and-sandaled set, this man is conspicuous. He looks as if he just walked in from an engineering convention. He has a conservative haircut, wears chino slacks, and keeps his reading glasses tucked in his left shirt-pocket. He's perhaps in his late sixties, and sits next to his tastefully dressed, bespectacled wife.

"That's Luers's dad," my friend says, and then pauses. "Just think—he'll probably never see his son out of prison again."

The elder Luers, whose name is John, shuffles up to a small stage at one end of the room. He leans on a cane as he walks. Rallies for his son have been held annually for the past few years, and Luers notes that this is one of forty-three around the world on this day. "The crowds just keep getting bigger," John Liters says. "We are so grateful for the support you have shown our son."

I introduce myself later and ask if he speaks with writers and he says politely but firmly, "No we don't."

There are other speakers. Jeffrey Luers may be the poster child of the government's crackdown on so-called environmental terrorists, but this night most are preoccupied with the recent arrests. This crowd refers to the government's Operation Backfire investigation as The Green Scare, seeing it as an all-out effort to discourage environmental activism and dissent. Many have been interrogated by FBI agents, and many believe their phones are tapped.

One of the organizers of the rally speaks up and says "we know what real terrorism is" to loud applause. Misha Dunlap of the Civil Liberties Defense Center, a Eugene nonprofit that has lent assistance to Luers and to the more recent defendants, gives an update. Then anticivilization author and thinker Derrick Jensen takes the stage. He asks any FBI agents in the audience to please raise their hands. When no one does, he shrugs and says, "Worth a try." Then he says, "What you're doing is wrong and I plan on seeing you brought to justice." More applause and a few boisterous hoots. Jensen speaks for more than an hour about environmental holocaust and resistance, and the audience is rapt.

When someone mentions the name Jake Ferguson, the room erupts in a chorus of hisses. Ferguson, a former Whiteaker insider, is the government's primary informant in the Operation Backfire case. He has not been charged in any of the crimes, but has admitted to being a key operative in many of them. He agreed to wear hidden recording devices when speaking with fellow activists, and now his name is anathema in Whiteaker—a stop sign just a few blocks from Sam Bond's has been defaced to read STOP JAKE.

Ferguson may bear the epithet "snitch," but many radical activists consider the six who have accepted plea bargains to be snitches too. Still, there is an unmistakable aroma of violence in the green anarchists' attitude toward Ferguson. A typical posting on the Portland Independent Media Center website, which has served as a clearinghouse among activists for information and

commentary on the Operation Backfire case, described Ferguson as "the worst type of scum on earth." Another writer added, "jake admitted being a snitch to people in the community after the story broke. why he can still talk is a good question." (It's worth noting, though, that Ferguson had suffered no physical harm at the time of this writing, at least not to my knowledge. The talk may be streetwise and tough, but the vast majority of Eugene's radical activists would never intentionally harm another person or animal.)

I leave Sam Bond's before the music starts—a hip-hop duo is on the bill. Outside, the night air is cool. It feels good to be out of that space, not just because of the stifling heat, but because of the intensity in the room.

I find my car and drive through the quiet streets of Whiteaker. Downtown is empty except for a trio of homeless youths hanging out on a corner by the city library. The curtains are drawn in most of the homes in my own south side neighborhood. The crowd at Sam Bond's may be ready for the revolution, but the rest of the world just seems to want a good night's sleep.

T he operation backfire indictment is sixty-five pages long and identifies the first building the Eugene arsonists burned down as the Oakridge Ranger Station, just up the road from Eugene. On the night of October 30, 1996, a motorist saw the flames and called 911. When firefighters drove into the parking lot, nails stuck in the tires of their trucks. The building was too far gone to save. By morning, it was a pile of cinders.

The Oakridge arson was one of the first subjects I wrote about after returning to my native Northwest. I had just left a job as a newspaper reporter on the East Coast, and had taken another job, editing a small magazine that covers National Forest issues. Nothing like this had ever happened in Oregon. People were shocked.

Within the region and throughout the federal government the presumption was immediate. This was the work of environmental extremists. Two nights earlier, someone had torched a Forest Service pickup truck at a ranger station seventy miles to the north, and had left graffiti including "Forest Rapers" and "Earth Liberation Front." They had also scrawled the letter A with an extended crossbar—the symbol of the anarchist movement. No one claimed responsibility for the Oakridge fire, but many people assumed both acts were done by the same people.

Dan Glickman, President Clinton's Secretary of Agriculture, who oversaw the Forest Service, told reporters then that he had "absolutely no tolerance for individuals or groups that engage in terrorism." Jack Ward Thomas, who was chief of the Forest Service, said, "This is what people do who do not understand how to operate in a democracy."

But to me, and to many in the mainstream environmental community, these assumptions made no sense. At the time of the arson, environmentalists had just scored a major victory in the steep forestlands just a few miles away from Oakridge.

In the early 1990s, the Forest Service had proposed a salvage-logging project on the slopes bordering nearby Warner Creek. The area had burned in 1991, leaving behind a patch-work of both blackened wood and healthy trees. When a Eugene judge ruled the Forest Service's plan legal under the notorious Salvage Logging Rider in 1995, protesters sprang into action. They built barricades, dug trenches, and fashioned makeshift structures to keep logging equipment out. Then, in the summer of 1996, after activists had maintained the blockade for nearly a year, the Clinton administration ordered the Forest Service to shelve its plans to log Warner Creek (and more than 150 other controversial sales around the West).

So why would an environmentalist of any stripe decide, just months later, to burn down the Oakridge Ranger Station?

Aboveground activists did all they could to distance themselves from the act. The Oregon Natural Resources Council, fearing a public relations disaster, offered a $1,000 reward to anyone who provided information leading to the conviction of those responsible.

Years passed with no arrests. There were rumors that the fire had been an inside job, the work of a disgruntled employee. The Forest Service built another ranger station, a fetching structure with two stories and broad eaves, in exactly the same spot where the other had stood. Then, last summer, Kevin Tubbs, one of the six who accepted the government's plea bargain offer, owned up to the deed.

At the Warner Creek blockade, Tubbs, curly-haired and deeply committed to the cause, had kept vigil atop a structure built from logs; if anyone tried to move the thing, he said, it would collapse and send him falling down the steep mountain-side to his death. In Eugene's federal courtroom, wearing standard-issue Lane County Jail garb, with close-cropped hair, and looking a little middle-aged, he admitted to this:

> On the night of the arson, he drove two fellow activists, Ferguson and Josephine Sunshine Overaker, east from Eugene to the vicinity of the Oakridge Ranger Station and dropped his passengers off. According to the account read in court by U.S. assistant attorney Stephen Peifer, Ferguson and Overaker placed incendiary devices around the ranger station. They threw nails onto the parking lot to slow down emergency responders and then the three drove back toward Eugene. They took back roads to avoid detection. They paused at a covered bridge near the town of Lowell and tossed the gloves they had used while committing the crime into the dark waters of a reservoir. The incendiary devices worked as intended and the ranger station was destroyed.

Despite Tubbs's confession, Timothy Ingalsbee, one of the leaders of the Warner Creek effort, still has trouble accepting the notion that environmentalists burned down the ranger station. Tall and lanky and gentle of manner, Ingalsbee holds a doctorate in environmental sociology from the University of Oregon. After the Warner Creek battle, he had wanted to work with the Forest Service to establish the site as a permanent wildfire research station within the National Forest system. "What the fire did was to destroy that opportunity," he said. "I had excellent professional relationships with the Oakridge Forest Service staff, and after the fire that ended."

Mainstream environmentalists reacted with the same sense of puzzlement and disgust to the majority of the attacks described in the Operation Backfire investigation. And while many on the left are critical of the aggressiveness with which the federal government has pursued the case—viewing the millions spent as evidence of the Bush administration's overzealousness in its war on terror and a convenient distraction from the failings of the administration to counter real terrorists—virtually no one in the environmental community believes the attacks have done anything but harm.

"It's bad for our cause all around. It stinks," Rocky Smith told *High Country News* in the days after the Vail attack. Smith, a Colorado environmentalist, had worked tirelessly to fight the Vail expansion through legal means. "There are lots of reasons to hate Vail," he said, "but not enough to justify arson."

S o, why? Those who are directly involved in the cases—those who are under indictment or who have accepted plea bargains—won't talk about motives. Most of those who are closest to them won't say anything either. Government prosecutors have indicated that there may be more indictments, and many activists are afraid to talk openly about the actions and those who allegedly committed them.

It's hard, though, to escape the conclusion that the main motivation of the Eugene arsonists was sincere, passionate conviction.

"I believe these arsons were a result of total frustration," one Whiteaker activist who knows several of the defendants told me over coffee. "It's just very painful to witness, so clearly, the rape of the planet."

Consider the story of Bill Rodgers. He was forty at the time of his arrest, making him the oldest of those indicted in the Operation Backfire investigation. Authorities describe him as a ringleader in the group of arsonists—they say he served as a sort of mentor to Gerlach, for one. Police arrested him last December at the modest bookstore and community center he ran in Prescott, Arizona. Two weeks after his arrest, he put a plastic bag over his head and suffocated himself.

In a farewell letter, he wrote, "Certain human cultures have been waging war against the Earth for millennia. I chose to fight on the side of bears, mountain lions, skunks, bats, saguaros, cliff rose and all things wild. I am just the most recent casualty in that war. But tonight I have made a jail break—I am returning home, to the Earth, to the place of my origins."

Here's what activists like Rodgers believe: They believe we face a crisis of mass extinction, caused by civilization. They believe the atmosphere is being spoiled, the climate pitching on the verge of ruinous change, because of civilization. They believe our bodies are being poisoned and so are our spirits, by civilization.

They've considered the state of the planet and they've decided against some hopeful half critique. They've looked all the way down into the pit and, rightly or wrongly, come to the conclusion that the whole damn thing is undeniably, irretrievably messed up. The government is wrong, mainstream culture is wrong, the tokenist sellout environmental community is wrong, civilization itself is wrong.

The green anarchists are historical determinists, as are Marxists and Christian fundamentalists. Their worldview is based on more, though, than extrapolations of weighty political treatises or divinations of holy texts. It is based on the work of scientists such as E. O. Wilson and Jared Diamond and respected, peer-reviewed biologists and climatologists and ecologists the world over whose work suggests that human activity is having a calamitous effect on the Earth's natural systems.

Globalization. Capitalism. Greed. Civilization. Call it what you will. It will end, the green anarchists insist, whether by means of environmental collapse, violent revolution, or the collective enlightening of human consciousness.

"We are now witnessing the final days of Western Civilization," declared a recent posting on the Portland Independent Media Center website. "As this civilization decays around us—as the wars spread and the natural disasters increase in frequency—and as those trapped by western culture slowly break from their cognitive dissonance and open their hearts and minds, a new reality will begin to reveal itself. Our task is to let this transformation take its course, and to speed it along where we can."

History is littered with historical determinists who were convinced the revolution was just around the corner. A few were right, most were wrong. And history is full of social upheavals in which true believers decided the cause was so great that they would step beyond the boundaries of law. Some have been vindicated by history, some scorned.

When I consider the ELF arsonists, I find myself thinking of the militant nineteenth-century abolitionist John Brown. So appalled was Brown by the institution of slavery that he tried to spark a revolution. He thought all that was needed was a firm nudge and the whole South would erupt in a slave rebellion. He was wrong, and was caught. His actions enraged the southern populace, and the system against which he struggled prosecuted him, convicted him, and hanged him.

At the time he was viewed as a crazed visionary whose quixotic strivings had changed nothing. But as the forces of abolition gained strength—as the real revolution unfolded—he became something much more potent. He became a symbol. Over the course of decades, what was first considered lunacy and extremism came to be regarded as courage and righteousness.

Years from now, when we have a clearer understanding of the full damage we have done to the Earth, is it possible the ELF arsonists will be remembered in similar fashion?

When Activists Attack
Companies Square Off against Animal Rights Groups

In December 2006, the New York Stock Exchange announced that it would begin listing medical research company Life Sciences Research on its electronic trading platform, Arca. This was great news for the New Jersey research facility, as investors and traders would now be able buy and sell shares more easily. The bad news, however, came in the following day's headlines.

ASHLEY BOHACIK

L ife Sciences Research, Inc., is the parent of Huntingdon Life Sciences (HLS), a scientific research company that periodically uses animal testing to develop cures for diseases such as cancer and AIDS. Animal rights activists have long protested HLS' operations—while also targeting connected individuals and associated companies—with some even invoking illegal methods including intimidation, physical violence, vandalism and identity theft. In response to the NYSE listing, however, two activist groups, Stop Huntingdon Animal Cruelty (SHAC) and Win Animal Rights (WAR) shifted the brunt of their protest activities to the stock exchange itself and vowed to continue campaigning until the listing was reconsidered.

This was not the first time the NYSE had come under fire on this matter. When it had considered listing Life Sciences Research in 2005, animal rights activists launched numerous protests and harassed NYSE employees, trading groups and other financial services providers. Under such activist pressure, the stock exchange removed the listing minutes before the opening bell on September 7, 2005.

Observers criticized the decision, and in April 2006 a full-page ad was published in the *New York Times* declaring that the NYSE was yielding to what were essentially terrorist threats.

Since then, SHAC has launched "Operation Fight Back," a renewed campaign against the NYSE. Since January 2007, activists have begun organizing protest activities against the NYSE and its European counterpart Euronext, as well as the exchange's shareholders, specialists and members. WAR, a radical animal rights group based in New York, also launched its own "Operation Helter Skelter" campaign against the NYSE in January 2007. The current campaigns have led to organized protests against the financial industry in both the United States and in various countries in Europe, primarily the United Kingdom. Activists have also carried out demonstrations against companies in other industries, specifically those that hold shares of Life Sciences Research.

Violent Tactics

While the current campaigns by SHAC and WAR against the NYSE have consisted primarily of protests (both at offices and the homes of company executives), in the past some animal rights protesters have conducted illegal and harassment-type activities. And in limited instances, such methods have already been used in the campaign against HLS.

In May 2007, for example, members of the Animal Liberation Front (ALF) allegedly vandalized the property of a financial advisor of a targeted company by spray-painting messages on his home and vehicle. And as part of the 2005 campaign against the NYSE, SHAC members posted the contact information of hundreds of NYSE employees on its website, and ALF claimed responsibility for acts of vandalism at two New York yacht clubs used by employees of a firm that intended to trade shares of Life Sciences Research. SHAC activists have also posted personal information of employees (including social security numbers and bank information) as well as instructions for bypassing security at targeted firms' offices on SHAC's website. Additionally, activists have used smoke and pipe bombs to further harass and intimidate companies connected to HLS.

> **The activists smashed a window at the house and then inserted a garden hose. The decision to use water to flood the house was a second choice—after the activists ruled out arson.**

In October 2007, activists from ALF claimed responsibility for vandalism and other property damage at the house of a UCLA scientist who conducts nicotine research on animals. Specifically, the activists smashed a window at the house and then inserted a garden hose in an effort to flood the premises. Importantly, the letter claiming responsibility also indicated that the decision to use water to flood the house was a second choice—after the activists ruled out arson in that particular instance. A statement later released by the UCLA scientist confirmed the attack and indicated that the activists caused between $20,000 and $30,000 worth of damage to the home.

The use of water to flood a target's house is a new tactic for some members of the animal rights movement, and there is the potential for the method to now spread among other militant activists, due to the success of the attack and the interconnectivity of animal rights groups. While this particular incident involved a UCLA scientist, there is a possibility that activists could use this tactic as part of other campaigns, including those against the NYSE, in which activists have specifically targeted individual employees. That said, the activists claiming responsibility for the flood incident indicated that arson remains a preferred method for direct actions by some of the most extreme members, specifically when activists are looking to cause significant property damage.

While it is unlikely that a majority of activists in the animal rights movement will resort to illegal or harassment activity that poses a danger to humans or results in significant property damage, lone individuals or small activist cells undertaking such action remains a cause for concern. Lone actors, who carry out direct actions in support of the cause, either with or without the tacit approval of recognized animal rights organizations, remain a real and lasting threat.

Combating Activist Operations

In November 2006, Washington enacted the Animal Enterprise Terrorism Act (AETA), further strengthening protection for animal researchers and associated companies against extremist tactics, many of which had not been envisioned in the Animal Enterprise Protection Act of 1992. The AETA expanded offenses covered under federal law to include threats, harassment and other intimidation methods that do not "physically disrupt" animal enterprises, but instead elicit fear among employees. This can include anything from making false bomb threats to posting home telephone numbers of company workers. The legislation covers persons or companies affiliated with animal enterprises in addition to individual employees, and includes graded penalties—up to life imprisonment—that are based on the level of financial damage or bodily injury sustained from an extremist act.

While AETA addresses many important issues not included in earlier legislation, some are concerned that the act will not eliminate illegal or harassing activities. In fact, previous attempts to curtail such activities have actually provoked activists in some cases.

Following the sentencing of two members of SHAC for their efforts to shut down Huntingdon Life Sciences, an anonymous group of animal rights extremists carried out a retaliatory attack for the "unfair conviction" of the activists in September 2006.

A spokeswoman for ALF later stated that the incident served as an indication that the underground animal rights movement intended to increase its efforts. Despite the attempt by the government to "send a message" to activists by prosecuting several

extremists, animal activists would use the case as motivation to carry out additional undercover attacks in order to further their agenda, according to ALF.

Following the passage of the AETA, other extremist animal rights protest groups indicated that the new act would only provoke further underground activity. Activists who previously only employed legal tactics were concerned that they would face prosecution by the government due to the new measures regardless, and therefore were considering more militant actions as little incentive remained to stay "above ground" and face detection by officials.

In a press release from the North American Animal Liberation following the attack at the UCLA scientist's home, representative Jerry Vlasak stated that due to harassment of activists by campus police at the school during regular protests, underground—and more militant—members of the movement had come forward to escalate operations.

As direct actions carried out by some animal rights extremists have continued in recent years, it is unlikely that militant members of the movement will be deterred by the measures included in the AETA. Animal rights extremists will continue their efforts targeting various animal enterprises and affiliated companies, as there are a large number of activists who are willing to risk potential repercussions in the name of the larger animal rights movement.

> **There are a large number of activists who are willing to risk potential repercussions in the name of the larger animal rights movement.**

Corporations Fight Back

In many instances, companies are unable to take action against activists. Despite the militant actions of the few, the protests carried out by most groups, while disruptive, are perfectly legal, which prevents police or security officials from intervening. Even in home protests, police are limited based on the activists' constitutional right to demonstrate, and other prevailing laws and guidelines. In fact, during one home protest in New York, a neighbor of the targeted individual who threw objects at the activists became the subject of a police report filed by the protesters.

While some companies have increased security measures at their offices and conducted new security assessments of their physical sites, others have taken different measures to increase protection. In the United Kingdom, a rapidly growing number of corporate directors have applied for governmental permission to withhold personal information, such as home addresses, from the country's register of directors, maintained by Companies House. In general, the register allows subscribers on the Companies House website to access information on company directors, but a rising number of executives have attempted to keep certain details private by instead using the address of their accountant or solicitor.

Companies have also used the judicial system to protect their employees and customers. In 2006, animal rights activists sent anonymous letters to shareholders of a targeted company, threatening that if they did not sell their shares, their personal details would be published on an activist website. The company was able to obtain a court injunction banning any unnamed party from contacting shareholders. As the letters were anonymous, however, officials indicated that it would be difficult to ensure that they did not follow through on the threat.

In many of the instances involving animal rights groups obtaining personal information about shareholders or employees of various companies, it remains unclear what methods they used to obtain such data. There is the possibility that some of the information was collected using animal rights sympathizers—or even members—within the affected company or organization, leading some to fear an insider threat.

Countermeasures should safeguard employees who remain vulnerable due to the relative ease of obtaining private information.

Additionally, open source data centers present another relatively easy method for activists to obtain personal data. Countermeasures by affected corporations should also safeguard employees who remain vulnerable due to the relative ease of obtaining this private information.

Continued Activities

Protests and other actions by members of SHAC and WAR have continued since the launch of their campaigns against the NYSE and affiliated companies. Despite efforts to curtail their activities, it is unlikely that the most extreme members of these groups will be deterred by the AETA or otherwise. Furthermore, some animal activists will only be further emboldened by their previous success against the NYSE in 2005, prompting a prolonged campaign to once again force the exchange to remove the Life Sciences Research listing. But for other companies facing similar pressure from activist groups, additional security measures and renewed legal action may prove to be an effective option to mitigate the risk to their employees and facilities.

ASHLEY BOHACIK is an intelligence analyst for Total Intelligence Solutions' Global Fusion Center in Arlington, Virginia.

White-Pride Mom

Her kids remain in custody, but she's not giving up: 'this is war'.

CHRIS SELLEY

One of the most contentious child-custody cases in recent memory began on a Tuesday morning in March, when a seven-year-old arrived at a suburban Winnipeg school with a swastika drawn on her arm—just as she had on Monday, when her teacher had scrubbed it off. Monday's swastika was the girl's handiwork, but her mother had redrawn it, in keeping, she says, with her distraught daughter's wishes. She now describes it as "the stupidest thing I've ever done in my life."

The school famously notified Winnipeg Child and Family Services, which took the girl and her two-year-old brother into custody. Four months later, on CFS orders, they remain with their maternal grandmother; they see their mother just two hours a week, she claims. Since March, she has dumped her husband, branding him a "flamboyant bigot." She says she's retained the services of family lawyer Regan Thatcher, and she's been presenting her beliefs as a kinder, gentler version of white nationalism, swapping the Nazi flag in her home for a banner reading "White pride world-wide," according to a news report. Though she remains in regular contact with Canadian white-supremacist icon Paul Fromm and has received support from August Kreis, leader of the Aryan Nations, she insists white pride is "not about hating. It's about having love for yourself, love for your race, pride within."

Maclean's discovered less guarded comments on race relations under the online handle "aryanprincess1488," which the woman admits is hers (though she claims her ex-husband and another friend occasionally used it too). ("14/88" is shorthand for the "14 words" and "88 precepts" of the late David Lane, a member of a neo-Nazi terrorist group. 88 can also stand for HH—the eighth letter of the alphabet, repeated—or "heil Hitler.") "If it were up to you," aryanprincess1488 asked last August, "would you sacrifice yourself and your children to save our entire race? There would be a 100 percent guarantee that all Jews would be destroyed." A week later, returning to the discussion, the poster conceded, "I hate Jews, really I do, a lot." Aryanprincess1488's other

contributions include musings on travelling back in time to "warn Hitler about the consequences of being allies with the Japs," and, in May 2005, complaining that Winnipeg is "infested with Indians and other such inferiors." But she insists the comments don't reflect reality. "In a discussion forum, it's a little different," she says. "You're online, you're discussing a topic and you want the topic to go further." Even off the web, however, she's not shy about her opinions. She doesn't deny the Holocaust, for example, but she suggests only 271,368 Jews died in Hitler's "so-called death camps," and thinks "the real Holocaust happened in Dresden under Churchill's thumb."

But despite her odious beliefs, the case has exposed a remarkably broad consensus that child services authorities should not seize children solely because of their parents' political extremism. There is a "fundamental value, recognized in the Charter of Rights," says Nick Bala, an expert on family law at Queen's University, "that parents have a presumptive right to raise their children—and that children have a presumptive right to live with their parents." Political beliefs alone should never infringe upon that right, he argues. Neither the "glorification" nor the "preaching" of hatred on their own are legitimate grounds for intervention, argues Noa Mendelson Aviv, director of the Canadian Civil Liberties Association's Freedom of Expression Project. She says such a policy would be an "inappropriate, offensive and dangerous" expansion of "state surveillance." And while David Matas, senior legal counsel for B'nai Brith, has argued that indoctrination to racial hatred is a form of child abuse, it seems even Winnipeg CFS disagrees. The agency won't discuss the case, but a spokesperson insists "a parent or guardian's religious, political or other views do not determine if a child is in need of care."

In fact, most family lawyers, law professors and child services professionals contacted by *Maclean's* say while agencies sometimes overreach, they don't intervene solely on political grounds. Thatcher could not be reached for comment, but a case file obtained by the *Winnipeg Free Press* mentions concerns about drug and alcohol use, "the parents' behaviour and associates," and allegations the girl had missed dozens of days of school—all disputed by her mother.

On Sept. 24, CFS will have to satisfy a judge at the family division of the Manitoba Court of Queen's Bench that the kids remain in need of protection, and that it has a reasonable plan to eventually get them back with their mother. Child custody orders frequently demand that parents address issues such as those CFS claimed to find in the home, and if parents refuse to comply, cases can drag on for years. But the mother denies any such problems existed. She wants the custody order tossed out and her kids returned, and while the judge could do that, Winnipeg lawyer Len Fishman says it's rare to win a case simply on the grounds that child services didn't meet the standard for intervention. She can appeal the decision, but she says she's unsure how she'll pay even her current legal bills. In any event, she seems to be in no mood for conciliation. "The government of my country has told me I am a bad mother for holding these beliefs," she insists. "I will not deny them, I will not stand down. This is war."

UNIT 6

Terrorism and the Media

Unit Selections

Key Points to Consider

- How do terrorist organizations use the Internet?

- Can regulation of the Internet help in the war on terror?

- What impact has hip-hop music had on terrorist recruitment?

Student Website
www.mhcls.com

Internet References

Institute for Media, Peace and Security
http://www.mediapeace.org
Terrorism Files
http://www.terrorismfiles.org
The Middle East Media Research Institute
http://www.memri.org

The media plays an important role in contemporary international terrorism. Terrorists use the media to transmit their message and to intimidate larger populations. Since the hijackings at Dawson's field in Jordan in 1970 and the massacre at the Munich Olympics in 1972, international terrorists have managed to exploit the media and have gained access to a global audience. The media provides terrorists with an inexpensive means of publicizing their cause and a forum to attract potential supporters. In the age of independent fund raising, terrorists have become increasingly dependent on accessible media coverage.

As media coverage has become more sophisticated, terrorist organizations have become increasingly conscious of their interactions with the press. Managing public relations, drafting press releases, and arranging interviews have become important functions, often delegated to individuals or groups in the semi-legal periphery of the organization.

The impact of the increasingly symbiotic relationship between terrorists and media has been two-fold. On the one hand, the media has provided terrorists with real-time coverage and immediate 24-hour access to a global public. As long as the explosion is big enough and the devastation horrific enough and there are cameras close by, media coverage of the incident is guaranteed. Holding true to the old axiom "if it bleeds, it leads," the media seems only too willing to provide terrorists with free, unlimited, and at times indiscriminate coverage of their actions.

On the other hand, the media also provides terrorists with a means of ventilation, potentially reducing the number of violent incidents. This outlet subtly influences terrorists to function within certain, albeit extended, boundaries of social norms, as grave violations of these norms may elicit unintended or unwanted public backlash and a loss of support. In light of these contradictory tendencies, the debate about media censorship or self-censorship continues.

The Internet and new media have provided terrorists with instant, unfiltered access to a new audience. Terrorists are becoming increasingly less dependent on traditional or "big" media. As the "YouTube" generation engages in political discourse, the terrorists' use of this medium will continue to grow.

The articles in this unit explore the relationship between terrorism and the media. Philip Seib discusses the use of the media by Al-Qaeda and argues that, in addition to Bin Laden's video performances, "there are hundreds of online videos that proselytize, recruit, and train the Al-Qaeda." Next, Paul Piper, a reference librarian, discusses how terrorists use the Internet. He identifies some of the most popular and noteworthy terrorist and anti-terrorist websites.

Andrew Potter examines attempts by Islamic extremists to recruit members among urban youths. As they attempt to capitalize on cultural alienation among young American blacks, terrorist organizations are using hip-hop music to recruit a new generation of "gangsta jihadis." Next, Feisal Mohamed discusses the role of the Internet in disseminating radical Islamic ideas. He argues that the medium of dissemination is as important as the content of the messages. Finally, Cohen and Küpçü argue that the rise of stateless enemies and Internet organization heralds a new type of war. They propose that the U.S. Congress needs to implement legislation to address this change in warfare.

The Al-Qaeda Media Machine

PHILIP SEIB, JD

Like an aging rock star who has dropped out of the public eye, Osama bin-Laden occasionally decides to remind people that he's still around. He makes video appearances that first appear on Arabic television channels but which the world quickly sees on television or on multiple websites. Bin-Laden's message is "Hey, they haven't caught me yet," which cheers up his fans, but his threats and pronouncements are mostly terrorist boilerplate. For all the parsing of his sentences and scrutinizing of the color of his beard, hardly anything in his videos helps us better understand and combat terrorism.

Meanwhile, significant Al-Qaeda media efforts go largely unnoticed by news organizations and the public. This myopia is characteristic of an approach to antiterrorism that focuses on Bin-Laden as terror-celebrity while ignoring the deep-rooted dynamism of a global enemy. Most jihadist media products make no mention of Bin-Laden, but they deserve attention because they are vital to Al-Qaeda's mission and to its efforts to extend its influence. Al-Qaeda has become a significant player in global politics largely because it has developed a sophisticated media strategy.

> . . . Al-Qaeda . . . cultivates an even larger audience through masterful use of the media . . .

Lacking a tangible homeland—other than, perhaps, scattered outposts in the wilds of Waziristan—Al-Qaeda has established itself as a virtual state that communicates with its "citizens" and cultivates an even larger audience through masterful use of the media, with heavy reliance on the Internet. For every conventional video performance by Bin-Laden that appears on Al-Jazeera and other major television outlets, there are hundreds of online videos that proselytize, recruit, and train the Al-Qaeda constituency.

Growth of the Media Machine

The Al-Qaeda media machine has grown steadily. Al-Qaeda and its jihadist brethren use more than 4,000 websites to encourage the faithful and threaten their enemies. The Al-Qaeda production company, As-Sahab, released 16 videos during 2005, 58 in 2006, and produced more than 90 in 2007. Like a Hollywood studio, As-Sahab has a carefully honed understanding of what will attract an audience and how to shape the Al-Qaeda message.

You won't get As-Sahab's videos from Netflix, but any web user can easily find them, and the selection is wide. In 2006, the Global Islamic Media Front, an Al-Qaeda distribution arm, offered "Jihad Academy," which includes footage of attacks on U.S. troops, insurgents assembling improvised explosive devices (IEDs), prospective suicide bombers reading their last testaments, and general exhortations to join the war against the United States, Israel, and other foes.

Another distributor with ties to Al-Qaeda, Ansar al-Sunnah's Media Podium, produced "Top 20," a selection of filmed IED attacks on U.S. forces in Iraq "in order to encourage the jihad and the competition between the mujahideen to battle and defeat their enemy." For this greatest hits video, criteria for selection included "the degree of security conditions while filming the operation's site" and "precision in hitting the target."[1]

With the stirring music and graphic images of an action movie, the videos fortify the resolve of the Al-Qaeda faithful and, even more important, capture the attention of 15-year-olds in cyber cafes—the next generation of Al-Qaeda warriors. Al-Qaeda takes recruitment seriously, recognizing that potential martyrs require convincing that their sacrifice will be noble and worthwhile. Once inspired by the videos, the prospective jihadist might move on to a web posting such as "How To Join Al-Qaeda," which tells him: "You feel that you want to carry a weapon, fight, and kill the occupiers. . . . Set a goal; for example, assassinating the American ambassador—is it so difficult?"[2]

Spreading the Message

As-Sahab is part of the media department Bin-Laden established when Al-Qaeda formed in 1988. The first message to emerge was that Al-Qaeda was a brave underdog facing the monstrous Soviet Union. Soon thereafter, Al-Qaeda announced its resolve to take on other purported enemies of Islam. In 1996, Bin-Laden issued his "Declaration of War on the United States" and used the Al-Qaeda media machinery to spread the call for jihad.

Before a U.S. air strike killed him in June 2006, Abu Musab al-Zarqawi, the self-proclaimed head of Al-Qaeda in Iraq, took this kind of media work to a new level. He first displayed his grisly flair for using media when terrorists abducted American businessman Nicholas Berg and beheaded him in Iraq in 2004, with Zarqawi apparently the executioner. The terrorists video-taped the beheading and presented it on a website, from which it was copied to other sites and downloaded 500,000 times within 24 hours.[3]

The following year, Zarqawi began an online magazine, *Zurwat al-Sanam* (The Tip of the Camel's Hump, meaning ideal Islamic practice), which featured 43 pages of text, including stories about fallen jihadists, and photographs of Osama bin-Laden and George W. Bush.[4] Later, Zarqawi's "information wing"—which included his own online press secretary—released "All Religion Will Be for Allah," a 46-minute video with scenes including a brigade of suicide bombers in training. As *The Washington Post* reported, the video was offered on a specially designed web page with many options for downloading, including Windows Media and RealPlayer versions for those with high-speed Internet connections, another version for those with dial-up, and one for downloading it to play on a cell phone.[5] Production quality has become more sophisticated, with many videos now including subtitles in several languages and some featuring 3-D animation.[6]

Al-Qaeda-related operations outside the center of the Middle East have also copied the As-Sahab look, as we can see in the Al-Qaeda organization's video productions in the Islamic Maghreb. Videos of the December 2006 attack in Algeria on a convoy of employees of Halliburton subsidiary Brown & Root-Condor and the April 2007 attacks in Algiers featured the professional technical quality of As-Sahab productions. Terrorism experts speculated that an Al-Qaeda condition for its affiliating with the North African Salafist Group for Call and Combat was an upgrade of the local group's media competency.[7]

Even cartoons depicting children as suicide bombers are easily available on the web, and Hamas's Al-Aqsa Television has featured children's programming that extols martyrdom. On one popular program on this channel, *Pioneers of Tomorrow*, a Mickey Mouse-like character became a martyr when he refused to turn over his family's land to Israelis. In another episode, the child host of the show sang, "We can defeat the colonialist army. We have regained our freedom through bloodshed and the wrath of fire. If we receive good tidings, we will meet our death with no hesitation."[8] It is hard to calculate the damage that the poisonous residue of such fare may cause over time.

Through news reports, satellite television provides Al-Qaeda and the public with graphic representations of Al-Qaeda's work and occasional glimpses of Bin-Laden himself. More significantly, the Internet supplies more detailed versions of what the news media have covered, all the while furthering operational connectivity and a sense of cohesion. Michael Scheuer observed that "the Internet today allows militant Muslims from every country to meet, talk, and get to know each other electronically, a familiarization and bonding process that in the 1980s and early 1990s required a trip to Sudan, Yemen, Afghanistan, or Pakistan."[9] As author Gabriel Weimann noted, *Sawt al-Jihad* (*Voice of Jihad*), an Al-Qaeda online magazine, reflects the multiple purposes of such ventures: "Orchestrating attacks against Western targets is important, but the main objective remains that of mobilizing public support and gaining grassroots legitimacy among Muslims."[10]

Training Opportunities

A further aspect of this effort to build a web-based constituency is an online library of training materials explaining how to mix ricin poison, how to build a bomb using commercial chemicals, how to sneak through Syria and into Iraq, and other such advice. Experts who answer questions on message boards and chat rooms support some of these items.

Another Al-Qaeda online magazine, *Muaskar al-Battar* (Camp of the Sword), underscored the value of online instruction: "Oh Mujahid brother, in order to join the great training camps you don't have to travel to other lands. Alone in your home or with a group of your brothers, you too can begin to execute the training program."[11] To enhance cyber security for such connections, the online *Technical Mujahid Magazine* was begun in late 2006 to instruct its readers about electronic data security and other high-tech matters.

During the past few years, the online training curriculum has expanded to include small-unit infantry tactics and intelligence operations such as collecting data, recruiting members of state security services, and setting up phone taps. Readers have downloaded this material in places such as Australia, Canada, Germany, Great Britain, and Morocco, and it has turned up when law enforcement raided cells in those countries. Some intelligence experts argue that online training has its limits—that technical skills and tradecraft require more than web-based instruction. But although Al-Qaeda's students might be able to glean only rudimentary knowledge from Internet sources, it is enough to make them dangerous.[12]

> **. . . the online training curriculum has expanded to include small-unit infantry tactics and intelligence operations . . .**

Information Operations

The Al-Qaeda leadership has stressed Internet use in directives to its citizens/followers, as was illustrated in this message carried on one of its websites:

> Due to the advances of modern technology, it is easy to spread news, information, articles, and other information over the Internet. We strongly urge Muslim Internet professionals to spread and disseminate news and information about the Jihad through e-mail lists, discussion groups, and their own websites. If you fail to do this, and our site closes down before you have done this, we may hold you to account before Allah on the Day of Judgment. . . . We expect our website to be opened and closed continuously. Therefore, we urgently recommend to any Muslims that are interested in our material

to copy all the articles from our site and disseminate them through their own websites, discussion boards, and e-mail lists. This is something that any Muslim can participate in easily, including sisters. This way, even if our sites are closed down, the material will live on with the Grace of Allah.[13]

This appreciation of the value of the Internet is nothing new for Al-Qaeda. Even when under attack by U.S. forces in late 2001, Al-Qaeda fighters in Afghanistan clung to their high-tech tools. A Pakistani journalist who was on the scene wrote that while retreating, "every second Al-Qaeda member was carrying a laptop computer along with his Kalashnikov."[14]

The Internet allows access to an almost infinite array of information providers and is attractive for other reasons, as well. For terrorist organizations, the Internet is preferable to satellite television because it provides unmatched opportunities to reach a global audience with video productions without having to rely on any particular television channels. In addition, using the Internet avoids problems associated with distribution of a physical product. Instead of establishing clearing houses to mail videos—a process that law enforcement agencies were able to disrupt—these groups now rely on pirated video-editing software and websites onto which material may be uploaded for their followers to access. These sites feature items such as the 118-page "Comprehensive Security Encyclopedia," which was posted in 2007 with detailed instructions about improving Internet and telephone security, purchasing weapons, handling explosives, transferring funds to jihadist groups, and other useful hints.[15]

One of the masters of this craft was Younis Tsouli, a young Moroccan whose *nom de cyber-guerre* was "Irhabi007." Based in England, Tsouli provided technical skills needed by Al-Qaeda after it left Afghanistan and established an online headquarters. He assisted Zarqawi when he used the Internet as part of his war plan in Iraq. Tsouli was adroit at hacking into servers that he then used to distribute large video files. (One of his hacking victims was the computer system of the Arkansas Highway and Transportation Department.)

Arrested in London in 2005 and sent to prison by a British court in 2007, Tsouli understood the effectiveness of the Internet in reaching potential recruits for Al-Qaeda's cause. The 2006 U.S. *National Intelligence Estimate* acknowledged the importance of this: "The radicalization process is occurring more quickly, more widely, and more anonymously in the Internet age, raising the likelihood of surprise attacks by unknown groups whose members and supporters may be difficult to pinpoint."[16]

By mid-2007, some Al-Qaeda-related websites were broadening their agendas. "Media jihad" included entering online forums with large American audiences in order to influence "the views of the weak-minded American" who "is an idiot and does not know where Iraq is." The "weak-minded" were to be targeted with videos showing U.S. troops under fire and with false messages purportedly from American soldiers and their families lamenting their involvement in the Iraq war. At the same time, web forums for Islamist audiences featured information gleaned from Western news reports, such as poll results showing lack of public support for the war and, occasionally, information about weapons systems that news stories published.

Worldwide Recruiting

Beyond the material directly addressing warfare, such websites devote some of their content to ideological and cultural issues that are at the heart of efforts to win the support of young Muslims. Because Al-Qaeda's leaders believe this will be a long war, they see appealing to prospective jihadists and enlarging their ranks as crucial to their eventual success. The number of English-language jihadist sites has been growing, with approximately 100 available as vehicles for militant Islamic views. Some of these operate overtly. In October 2007, the *New York Times* profiled a 21-year-old Saudi-born American living in North Carolina whose blog extols Bin-Laden's view of the world. He includes videos designed to appeal to North American and European Muslims who are angry about the Iraq war and are responsive to claims that Islam is under siege.

The number of English-language jihadist sites has been growing, with approximately 100 available as vehicles for militant Islamic views. Some of these operate overtly.

This blogger had apparently not violated any U.S. laws, so he continued his online efforts, reaching—he claimed—500 regular readers. Although some law enforcement officials want to shut down such sites and prosecute their proprietors, some terrorism experts propose that such sites be allowed to operate in public view because they may provide insights into terrorist thinking and operations.[17]

Al-Qaeda's recruiting efforts have targeted British and American Muslims, such as a 2006 video that described rapes and murders allegedly committed by U.S. soldiers in Iraq. Released to mark the first anniversary of the 7/7 bombings in London, the video featured Bin-Laden's deputy, Ayman al-Zawahiri; Shehzad Tanweer, one of the London bombers, who died during the attack; and Adam Gadahn, also known as "Azzam the American," who grew up in California.

Tanweer, delivering his final testament in English with a Yorkshire accent, said: "We are 100 percent committed to the cause of Islam. We love death the way you love life. . . . Oh, Muslims of Britain, you, day in and day out on your TV sets, watch and hear about the oppression of the Muslims, from the east to the west. But yet you turn a blind eye, and carry on with your lives as if you never heard anything, or as if it does not concern you. . . . Oh, Muslims of Britain, stand up and be counted. . . . Fight against the disbelievers, for it is an obligation made on you by Allah." To this, Gadahn added, "It's crucial for Muslims to keep in mind that the American, the British, and the other members of the coalition of terror have intentionally targeted Muslim civilians."[18]

Among more recent videos aimed at a U.S. audience is "To Black Americans," which features Zawahiri criticizing Colin Powell and Condoleezza Rice and introducing video clips of Malcolm X talking about the unfair treatment of African-Americans. (These video clips date back to the Vietnam War years.) This video resembles Cold War-era communist propaganda, and it does not appear to have caused much of a stir, but it gives some indication of where Al-Qaeda's propaganda efforts are heading.

Terrorist organizations see young Muslims in non-Islamic countries as likely prospects for recruitment, and so they use media tools to stoke anger about purported economic and political discrimination. Al-Qaeda is apparently trying to create an online community where members of the Muslim diaspora will feel at home. Once they are part of this "community," they can view a steady stream of jihadist messages of varying degrees of subtlety.

Al-Qaeda recognizes the value of developing online networks. Chris Zambelis wrote, "The Internet enables like-minded militants to associate and communicate anonymously in cyber social networks. This process reinforces their sense of purpose and duty and encourages solidarity with the greater cause."[19] Extending such efforts beyond an Arabic-speaking core of support is a crucial part of Al-Qaeda's expansion.

Terrorist organizations . . . use media tools to stoke anger about purported economic and political discrimination.

YouTube and other such sites make videos like "To Black Americans" easily available, which differentiates today's propaganda from its antecedents during the Cold War and earlier. It can reach a global audience instantly. Just how big that audience really is remains open to question, but as Al-Qaeda increases its video production output, it seems to be operating on the theory that at least some of its messages will reach their desired viewers.

During the second half of 2007, U.S. forces in Iraq shut down at least a half-dozen Al-Qaeda media outposts in that country. One house the U.S. raided in Samarra contained 12 computers, 65 hard drives, and a film studio. The American military effort to halt such media operations relied in part on the belief of General David Petraeus that "the war is not only being fought on the ground in Iraq but also in cyberspace."[20] Petraeus's concern relates to an issue raised in the U.S. Army and Marine Corps Field Manual, *Counterinsurgency*—insurgents attempt to shape the information environment to their advantage by using suicide attacks and other such tactics to "inflate perceptions of insurgent capabilities."[21]

Cyberspace Warfare

Information dominance is a modern warfare tenet that is increasingly important, particularly if conventional military strength accompanies the effective exercise of soft power. Al-Qaeda understands the limitations of its own use of "hard power"—the coercive force of terrorist attacks—and continues to expand its conceptual approach to information warfare. Recognizing the pervasiveness of the information delivered by satellite television and the Internet and the influence of news organizations ranging from the BBC to Al-Jazeera, Al-Qaeda is now offering, in the words of Michael Scheuer, "a reliable source of near real-time news coverage from the jihad fronts for Muslims." From Iraq and Afghanistan, wrote Scheuer, Iraqi insurgents and Taliban forces produce, on an almost daily basis, combat videos, interviews with their commanders, and graphic footage of retaliatory measures against locals who cooperate with American or U.S.-backed forces.[22]

This effort reflects Al-Qaeda's dissatisfaction with Arab news organizations as vehicles for its media products. Zawahiri has criticized Al-Jazeera, in particular, because it refused to be a mere conveyor belt for Al-Qaeda videos, dared to edit Bin-Laden's pronouncements rather than show them in their entirety, and gave airtime to Al-Qaeda's critics. Because of As-Sahab's video producers' technical expertise, Al-Qaeda can now set itself up as a third force that provides a message different from Western media and the new generation of Arab news providers.

Zawahiri has said that what he calls "jihadi information media" have been "waging an extremely critical battle against the Crusader-Zionist enemy" and have "demolished this monopoly" by confronting conventional media organizations. Taking things a step further, in late 2007, Zawahiri offered to participate in an online interview in which he would take questions from individuals and news organizations.[23]

To some extent, this might be mere gamesmanship on the part of Al-Qaeda. By making himself available for a cyberspace chat, Zawahiri taunts those who have been hunting him for years. By holding a "news conference," the Al-Qaeda leadership positions itself on a plane comparable to that where "real" governments operate. By using new media to communicate with the rest of the world, Al-Qaeda stakes a claim to being an exponent of modernity.

By holding a "news conference," the Al-Qaeda leadership positions itself on a plane comparable to that where "real" governments operate.

One is tempted to dismiss these maneuvers as just another distracting ploy by murderous thugs, but for those who see Al-Qaeda's cadres as heroic defenders of Islam—and their numbers are substantial—this exercise is evidence of legitimacy, despite Al-Qaeda's vilification by much of the world.

The inadequate responses to Al-Qaeda's media messages heighten the danger. Even a flawed argument has appeal when we allow it to stand in an intellectual vacuum. Moderate Muslims and non-Muslims who do not accept the idea that prolonged conflict is inevitable must recognize this reality and act on it in a sophisticated, comprehensive way.

This means providing a steady stream of videos and other materials through the new media that many members of the Al-Qaeda audience use. This counter-programming should not feature defensive, pro-American content, but rather should concentrate on undermining Al-Qaeda's purported nobility, such as by reminding the audience how many Muslims have died in the terrorist attacks and insurgent warfare Al-Qaeda instigated.

Osama bin-Laden will undoubtedly pop up in another video before long. Note what he says, but then look to the always expanding reservoir of jihadist media to see what Al-Qaeda is really up to.

Notes

1. www.archive.org/details/jihad-academy; www.archive.org/details/top_20.

2. "On Islamist Websites," MEMRI (Middle East Media Research Institute), Special Dispatch Series no. 1702, 31 August 2007.

3. Naya Labi, "Jihad 2.0," *The Atlantic Monthly* (July/August 2006): 102.

4. Robert F. Worth, "Jihadists Take Stand on Web, and Some Say It's Defensive," *New York Times,* 13 March 2005.

5. Susan B. Glasser and Steve Coll, "The Web as Weapon," *Washington Post, 9* August 2005.

6. Craig Whitlock, "The New Al-Qaeda Central," *Washington Post,* 9 September 2007.

7. Andrew Black, "Al-Qaeda in the Islamic Mahgreb's Burgeoning Media Apparatus, *Jamestown Foundation Terrorism Focus,* vol. IV, issue 14, 15 May 2007.

8. "On Hamas TV Children's Program," Middle East Media Research Institute, Special Dispatch Series no. 1793, 27 December 2007.

9. Michael Scheuer, *Imperial Hubris* (Washington, DC: Brassey's, 2004), 81.

10. Gabriel Weimann, *Terror on the Internet* (Washington, DC: United States Institute of Peace, 2006), 44.

11. Steve Coll and Susan B. Glasser, "Terrorists Move Operations to Cyberspace," *Washington Post,* 7 August 2005, A 1.

12. Michael Scheuer, "Al-Qaeda's Media Doctrine," *Jamestown Foundation Terrorism Focus,* vol. IV, issue 15, 22 May 2007;

"The Role and Limitations of the 'Dark Web' in Jihadist Training," Stratfor Terrorism Brief, 11 December 2007.

13. Weimann, *Terror on the Internet,* 66.

14. Abdel Bari Atwan, *The Secret History of Al-Qaeda* (Berkeley, CA: University of California Press, 2006), 122.

15. Even F. Kohlmann, "The Real Online Terrorist Threat," *Foreign Affairs* 85, no. 5 (September-October 2006): 117; Middle East Media Research Institute, "Islamist Websites Monitor 82, 84," Special Dispatch Series no. 1543, 13 April 2007.

16. National Intelligence Council, *National Intelligence Estimate,* "Trends in Global Terrorism: Implications for the United States," April 2006, Key Judgments (Unclassified).

17. Michael Moss and Souad Mekhennet, "An Internet Jihad Aims at U.S. Viewers," *New York Times,* 15 October 2007; Michael Moss, "What To Do About Pixels of Hate," *New York Times,* 21 October 2007.

18. "American Al-Qaeda Operative Adam Gadahn, Al-Qaeda Deputy al-Zawahiri, and London Bomber Shehzad Tanweer in New al Sahab/Al-Qaeda Film Marking the First Anniversary of the 7/7 London Bombings," Middle East Media Research Institute (MEMRI), Special Dispatch Series no. 1201, 11 July 2006; Jessica Stern, "Al-Qaeda, American Style," *New York Times,* 15 July 2006.

19. Chris Zambelis, "Iraqi Insurgent Media Campaign Targets American Audiences," *Jamestown Foundation Terrorism Focus,* vol. IV, issue 33, 16 October 2007.

20. Jim Michaels, "U.S. Pulls Plug on Six Al-Qaeda Media Outlets," *USA Today,* 4 October 2007.

21. *The U.S. Army-Marine Corps Counterinsurgency Field Manual* (Chicago, IL: University of Chicago Press, 2007), 5.

22. Scheuer, "Al-Qaeda's Media Doctrine."

23. Shaun Waterman, "Zawahiri Pledges Online Chat," *United Press International,* 17 December 2007.

PHILIP SEIB is Professor of Journalism and Public Diplomacy at the University of Southern California. He holds an AB from Princeton University and a JD from Southern Methodist University. Professor Seib has authored and edited numerous books, including *Beyond the Front Lines: How the News Media Cover a World Shaped by War,* and the recently published *New Media and the New Middle East.* His next book, *The Al-Jazeera Effect: How the New Global Media Are Reshaping World Politics,* will be published in the summer of 2008.

From *Military Review,* by Philip Seib, May/June 2008, pp. 74–80. Published by U.S. Army Command, Combined Arms Center.

Nets of Terror

Terrorist Activity on the Internet

I approached this article with both fascination and some trepidation.

My original interest was piqued by a Knight Ridder news article written in late September of 2007[1] claiming that the Internet was the new terrorist frontier. I have to admit the concept of terrorists openly advertising on the web seemed astounding. Though we all know anything is possible on the Internet, it also seemed like a media ploy to drum up more fear. Two websites referred to in the articles, Jihad University and Terrorist 007, proved to be something other than specific websites. However, this opened the door to thinking about how terrorists were using the Internet, if at all. On one hand, what better way to spread propaganda, recruit volunteers, and raise funds than via the web? On the other hand, didn't this open one's group to infiltration and subsequent destruction?

PAUL PIPER

Just what is a terrorist anyway? The word has become ubiquitous and been used to describe individuals, nations, policies, religions, and on the other end of the spectrum, abusive spouses, angry drivers, and even "tough love" parenting.

The decision to write the article raised other more personal concerns. Would these sites be in English? I can't read Arabic and online translation services are faulty. Would the sites be password guarded? And, if so, how would potential recruits get the passwords? Would I be monitored for visiting them (either by our government, the terrorist group, or both)? What might the consequences of such monitoring be? The last thing I wanted was to end up taped to a chair under mercury vapor lights and have sand drizzled into my eyes—particularly after an all-expenses-paid government flight to Gitmo.

Terrorism: Defining the Concept

Terrorism is an emotionally charged word. It is also overused and misused, referring to anything from a suicide bomber to an abusive husband to a politician of different stripes. Section 2331 of Chapter 113b of the Federal Criminal Code defines terrorism as "[A]ctivities that involve violent or life-threatening acts; that are a violation of the criminal laws of the United States or of any State; and appear to be intended (i) to intimidate or coerce a civilian population; (ii) to influence the policy of a government by intimidation or coercion; or (iii) to affect the conduct of a government by mass destruction, assassination, or kidnapping; and . . . (C) occur primarily within the territorial jurisdiction of the United States . . . [or] . . . (D) occur primarily outside the territorial jurisdiction of the United States . . ."[2] However, even this language can seem vague and even contradictory, particularly when examining rules of armed conflict. Some of the numerous other definitions are also contradictory.

Several overarching concepts apply when discussing terrorism. The first is the concept of warfare. Terrorist states and organizations often claim that they are at war and that this status justifies so-called terrorist acts. While according to the Geneva Convention, this is debatable, it does bring to light another concept, the concept of rules of engagement, torture, and so forth. If the rules of warfare or engagement are created by the "opposition," then the terrorists often refuse to follow them, claiming a disenfranchised or marginalized contribution in creating the rules. The concept of Jihad, or Holy War, is an example of warfare that operates under very different rules of engagement than many countries, including those who signed the Geneva Convention, would recognize.

Another concept is innocent civilians. Civilians, innocent or not, are often killed in warfare. The distancing and deceptive military term is "collateral damage." However, the term terrorism implies the actual targeting of civilians, such as the 9/11 attack. Many terrorist groups would argue there are no such things as civilians. From this standpoint, one could ask if the nuclear bombings of Hiroshima and Nagasaki, which targeted primarily civilians, would today be considered terrorism or warfare.

The third concept is "illicit activity," meaning "crimes" outside actual killing and torture. Many terrorist groups are impoverished and resort to drug trade, smuggling, theft, kidnapping for ransom, and other illicit activities to fund their cause. These crimes are of course justified by the "higher cause" of their battles.

A fourth concept, related to the first, is perspective. The Israelis and Palestinians offer a prime example. Depending which side one is on, it's easy to overlook or amplify the atrocities done by both entities.

With all these concepts plus other factors, one can see that the term itself is extremely messy. Groups identified by one government, or consortium of governments, as terroristic may consider the other side the true terrorists. Given the confusion and complexity, this article will feature groups considered terrorist by our own and other Western governments in hope of demonstrating how such groups use the web to function.

Terrorist Use of the Internet

Terrorists use the Internet in a variety of ways. While this article will concentrate on websites, and, to a minor degree, chat rooms, bulletin boards, blogs, forums, and discussion groups, other significant Internet uses also benefit terrorists. Terrorists use the Internet quite simply because it is easy and inexpensive to disseminate information instantaneously worldwide and relatively uncensored.

Information and Data Mining

The Internet is rife with information of potential use to terrorist groups. For example, these groups could find maps, satellite photos (Google Earth), blueprints, and information on transportation routes, power and communication grids and infrastructures, pipeline systems, dams and water supplies, explosive-device instructions, biological and nuclear weapons, and much, much more. It was no accident that the U.S. and many other governments scrambled after 9/11 to reclassify and remove information from the web. According to a *USA Today* article[3] quoting an AP release, the U.S. government alone pulled over 1 million documents from public view, many from the web. In some ways, much of this was futile, since a large proportion of this material was archived in various ways, but it still represented a wake-up call to the availability and accessibility of information that could prove harmful in the wrong hands.

Once documents and information, such as those listed above, are obtained, the Internet provides an excellent communication medium for sharing such information among sympathetic groups.

Recruitment

This is a loaded category. Obviously, certain groups attempt, via traditional advertising and propaganda techniques (rhetoric and images playing on fears and desires) to attract volunteers to their cause. In the case of terrorism, the recruitment is often based on political and/or religious rhetoric. But a basic fact is often overlooked—much marketing is oriented toward young adults, the most prolific Internet users, who, by their younger age, are consequently among the most susceptible to propaganda.

The Site Institute [http://www.siteinstitute.org], although no longer extant (morphing into the Site Intelligence Group [http://www.siteintelgroup.org], extensively monitored Al-Qaeda's Internet communications in the early 2000s. It documented an extensive effort to recruit fighters to travel to Iraq and fight. Potential recruits, typically identified through secret chat rooms and bulletin boards, were fed a diet of religious fundamentalism and anti-American rhetoric, as well as training manuals. Most of those targeted were young men—angry, bored, and easily manipulated.

Fundraising

While similar to all-out recruitment in techniques, fundraising is often more open and blatant. Websites for "popular" terrorist organizations often have links such as "What You Can Do" or "How Can I Help." Visitors to such websites are often monitored and researched; likely candidates (repeat visitors and those who stay for long periods of time) are contacted and offered additional information or asked for assistance.

Networking and Information Sharing

They say that information, like love, is only useful if it's shared. Terrorist groups by necessity share information, whether how to manufacture explosives, obtain fraudulent passports, perform identity theft or by holding news events, publishing manifestoes, or supplying logistical and tactical information. While typically relying on password-guarded forums, chat rooms and bulletin boards (using products such as Pal Talk), a number of large-scale terrorist groups, such as Hamas, have become less centralized and more extensively networked. Information is often mirrored at many sites with sites functioning in a parallel fashion, although with local emphasis. This way wholesale disruption of information flow can be circumvented if one site crashes.

Information sharing also includes sharing information mined from other legitimate sites, as well as the online distribution of newsletters, magazines, reports, and analyses. Publications such as *The Terrorist's Handbook* [http://www.capricorn.org/akira/home/terror.html], *The Anarchist Cookbook* [http://www.anarchistcookbookz.com/download.html], *The Mujahadeen Poisons Handbook* (available from a charming site called TheDisease.net— http://thedisease.net/functions.php?PHPSESSID=35ecd4 2d8c5c82507b03643c3e05485d&arcanum=nbc/chemical/ Mujahideen_Poisons.pdf], *The Encyclopedia of Jihad* (in Arabic), and the *Sabotage Handbook* are all available with a bit of digging.

Logistics and Tactical/Strategic Planning

The Internet cannot be separated, qualitatively, from any other means of communication, in that terrorists are just as likely to use cell phones, radios, and face-to-face communication to communicate tactical and strategic planning. We know now that Al-Qaeda operatives used email extensively to plan the 9/11 attacks. According to Gabriel Weinmann,[4] Hamas largely uses chat rooms to coordinate attacks and plan operations across Gaza, the West Bank, Lebanon, and Israel. Information, such as maps, photographs, directions, and technical details of explosives, is often encoded or encrypted.

Cyberterrorism

There is no standardized definition of cyberterrorism. The concept previously focused on hacking or cracking into computers for the purpose of disruption. Potential targets are numerous, e.g., telecommunication systems, defense systems, medical facilities, power grids, transportation, and so forth. The FBI's definition[5]—"the use of cyber tools to shut down critical national infrastructures (such as energy, transportation, or government operations) for the purpose of coercing or intimidating a government or civilian population"—fit this criteria. Lately however, the scope has expanded. The National Conference of State Legislatures [http://www.ncsl.org/programs/lis/CIP/cyberterrorism.htm] defines cyberterrorism this way:

> The use of information technology by terrorist groups and individuals to further their agenda. This can include use of information technology to organize and execute attacks against networks, computer systems and telecommunications infrastructures, or for exchanging information or making threats electronically. Examples are hacking into computer systems, introducing viruses to vulnerable networks, website defacing, denial-of-service attacks, or terrorist threats made via electronic communication.

Under this definition, particularly the last clause, many terrorist groups are culpable, but so are anti-terrorist groups trying to take down terrorist websites.

While cyberterrorism remains an area of great concern, since the majority of all operations of any significance worldwide are computerized and use networks, there have been no major significant attacks on any national infrastructures involving terrorist groups. However, this remains an area of grave concern for most international defense and security organizations.

Terrorist and Anti-Terrorist Websites

Most terrorist groups either do not have websites; have sporadic websites or sites that continually change URLs; appear in languages—or alphabets—foreign to most of us; or are very difficult to locate. As always, one starts with Google searches. Limiting to country and using blog searches also yields results. I had some limited success using Wikipedia (the links at the bottom of the article) as well as lists compiled by some of the sites below. You can also monitor Who is [http://www.whois.com] the official domain registry for particular words or phrases (such as Al-Shaheed) and examine the results. Clicking on the resulting links can be quite fruitful. If you have access to various mail groups, searching these and other discussion groups can help, as well as examining the little literature in the field. Once found, links on existing terrorist websites often link to other organizations. The World of Islam Portal [http://www.worldofislam.info] is an exceptional portal into Islamic culture, but, some of its numerous links to sites, forums, and organizations may reach questionable sites.

Terrorist groups use websites for a number of reasons and feature particular categories of information: organization history, biographies, writings, speeches, ideological and political aims, field reports, maps, and news. Some even provide gift shops. Information on sites is typically biased. Some sites, particularly some of the Iraqi sites, glorify all kinds of violence, while others feature only violence by their enemies, downplaying their own.

Information about Terrorist Groups

A number of sites, e.g., the Middle East Media Research Institute (MEMRI) [http://www.memri.org], track the web presence of terrorist organizations. In its words, MEMRI "explores the Middle East through the region's media. MEMRI bridges the language gap which exists between the West and the Middle East, providing timely translations of Arabic, Persian, Turkish, Urdu-Pashtu media, as well as original analysis of political, ideological, intellectual, social, cultural, and religious trends in the Middle East." This organization provides continuous updates of sites it considers Jihadist, particularly those hosted by U.S. servers [http://www.memri.org/iwmp.html]. Many of these reports contain URLs to websites. MEMRI also publishes lists of sites with a brief description, a photo of the homepage, and the URL. MEMRI's information is considered authoritative and high quality and is often used for translation services.

The best source for URLs of terrorist websites is the Internet Anthropologist [http://warintel.blogspot.com]. The Internet Anthropologist exemplifies citizen involvement in monitoring terrorist activity on the Internet. Written by a man who calls himself Gerald, the blog has many offerings, including a list of websites hosted by reputed terrorist groups, primarily Islamic; a database of 24,000 names and bios of known terrorists; a specialized terror search engine, and even an anti-terrorist toolbar. This site is a bit confusing to use, so try going directly to its site map.

The Southern Poverty Law Center [http://www.splcenter.org] tracks sites with possible connections to domestic national terrorist activity, such as known hate groups. Many of these groups, such as white separatist skinheads, advocate violence and are linked to domestic terrorism. This site provides a map [http://www.splcenter.org/intel/map/hate.jsp] of acknowledged hate groups in the U.S. Groups are divided into Black Separatist, Christian Identity, General Hate, Ku Klux Klan, Neo-Nazi, Neo-Confederate, Racist Skinhead, and White Nationalist. This site does not give URLs; however, you can search Google to find sites for the groups listed.

Founded in 1913, the Anti-Defamation League (ADL) documents violent and prejudicial activities targeted primarily against Jewish people. In addition to international activities, it has posted archives [http://www.adl.org/learn/Events_2001/events_archive_2004_print.asp] of extremist events. Perhaps more importantly, its online newsletter, *Terrorism Update* [http://www.adl.org/main_Terrorism/default.htm], is quite adept at ferreting out recent developments in national and global terror. A recent issue reveals the name of a North Carolina Jihadist blogger; the fact that Al-Qaeda has released videos formatted for cell phones; and the identification of a new English website for the Popular Front for the Liberation of Palestine (PFLP). While perhaps a bit peripheral to the scope of this article, the ADL is also in the forefront of attempting to combat hate speech on the Internet [http://www.adl.org/main_internet].

The Memorial Institute for the Prevention of Terrorism [http://www.mipt.org] is a nonprofit, nationally recognized think tank responsible for creating databases and sharing information on terrorism. This organization was established in 2000 primarily as a response to the 1995 bombing of the Alfred P. Murrah Federal Building in Oklahoma City. It has been active in a number of areas including bioterrorism, research exercises and simulations, public safety, technical research, legal projects, and case studies and reports. Its board of directors includes leaders from academia, business, and government. This group offers web users several databases, referred to on the site as "knowledge bases." One of these, the Terrorism Knowledge Base [http://www.mipt.org/TKB.asp] is a sophisticated tool that allows a user to search for groups, incidents, leaders and members, and cases by geographic region. Various tools offer an array of capabilities, such as incident statistics by several variables, group reports and information, and graphing tools. Among other capabilities, these tools allow one to explore the relationships between different groups. While the Institute currently documents and abstracts 43 terrorist groups, it does not provide website or Internet activity on them.

Terrorism Central [www.terrorismcentral.com], sponsored by the Potomac Institute for Policy Studies, is dedicated, in its words, to "building a central information repository [on terrorism] comprising original and secondary sources spanning over four decades of research." While the site doesn't have extensive information on terrorists and the Internet, it does have an extensive list of terrorist organizations and a section of documents (full-text) relating to cyberterrorism and information warfare.

The Federation of American Scientists offers—in a rather bland web presence—what it terms the Intelligence Resource Program [http://www.fas.org/irp]. This program is primarily dedicated to intelligence work and, though unadorned, provides copious online reports, hearings, and the like dedicated to this topic. In addition, they provide an extensive list of worldwide intelligence agencies. Specific to terrorism, this site provides a number of online reports [http://www.fas.org/irp/threat/terror.htm], including the State Department's Pattern's of Global Terrorism Reports dating back to 1989. One of the more useful features of this site for identifying terrorist organizations is a list of groups that may fall into the category of terrorist; note that liberation movements, substance cartels, and other para-state entities are also included here There are currently descriptions of 385 groups but no URLs.

GlobalSecurity.org [http://www.globalsecurity.org] claims to be "the leading source of background information and developing news stories in the fields of defense, space, intelligence, WMD, and homeland security." The organization, which began in 2000, caters primarily to journalists and the media. It hosts an extensive list of global military organizations divided by country [http://www.globalsecurity.org/military/world]. These military organizations, agencies, and groups all have highly detailed write-ups. There is some very useful information in here about para-military groups, many of which have terrorist intentions.

While it may seem a major oversight to not include an in-depth analysis of the Department of Homeland Security (DHS) [http://www.dhs.gov] here, there isn't enough relevant information to justify it. In the past several years, the DHS has morphed into a gigantic and often labyrinthine bureaucracy. Its website reflects this and makes it difficult to ferret out information on terrorist organizations and their web/Internet activities. To give credit, the organization seems very focused on internal, national coordination.

> **While it may seem a major oversight to not include an in-depth analysis of the Department of Homeland Security (DHS) here, there isn't enough relevant information to justify it.**

More useful for this article is the list hosted by the U.S. Department of State of foreign terrorist organizations (FTOs) [http://www.state.gov/s/ct/rls/fs/37191.htm], even though it only amounts to a rather basic list of 42 organizations with no annotations or website links. The State Department also publishes an annual review of global terrorism, along with other relevant related documents [http://www.state.gov/s/ct/rls].

The U.S. Institute of Peace [http://www.usip.org] is "an independent, nonpartisan, national institution established and funded by Congress." The organization is dedicated to the art of peacemaking and peacekeeping. It has a considerable collection of online publications, among them a collection of terrorism and counterterrorism documents. Of these, take particular note of www.terror.net by Gabriel Weinmann [http://www.usip.org/pubs/specialreports/sr116.html] available in PDF. This pivotal work details the variety of methods that terrorists use to manipulate the Internet for their purposes. Weinmann has expanded greatly on this paper in his recent book *Terror on the Internet: The New Arena, the New Challenges,* published by the U.S. Institute of Peace in 2006. I recommend this book highly to anyone interested in pursuing this topic.

Examples of Terrorist Websites

As previously mentioned, terrorist websites are notoriously unstable. Groups often play cat-and mouse with their enemy, which leads to transitive URLs. Websites are often crashed by well-meaning citizen geek-groups. For example followers of the Jawa Report [http://mypetjawa.mu.nu] were credited with taking down the original Taliban site. Attackers often hack sites or use denial of service (DoS) attacks. The U.S. government, to my knowledge, does not have a policy of crippling or eliminating these websites, although it does monitor them.

Terrorist organizations also suffer from the labile nature of revolutionary struggle, fracture internally, have problems with critical mass and funding, and suffer severe casualties. None of these leads to a robust Internet life.

Islamic Terrorism

These sites can disappear or change URLs as quick as the wind, so the URLs below may no longer be current. Accessing cached copies in Google or other search engines, as well as archived copies on the WayBack Machine [http://www.archive.org/index.php], typically yields good results.

No terrorist group of the time has the cachet and household recognition as Al-Qaeda, which in Arabic means "the base." Currently led by the nefarious and elusive Osama Bin Laden, Al-Qaeda is an international Sunni Islamic organization founded in 1988. It has bases and training centers in many countries, primarily in the Middle East, Africa, and Asia, and has many sympathetic groups and apostles. Al-Qaeda does not have a central website; rather, it uses a network of sites that disseminates news, speeches, mandates, polemics, etc. These sites mirror many of Al-Qaeda's cells. Gabriel Weinmann[6] estimates there are as many as 50 such sites. Examples of these cells are groups such as al Muhajiroun and the Supporters of Shareeah [http://www.geocities.com/suporters_of_sharia].

For scholars interested in examining the early central Al-Qaeda sites, the original URL was http://www.alneda.com; another early URL is http://www.news4arab.org. As-Sahab, Al-Qaeda's media and production arm, uses the al-Ekhlaas forum [http://www.ek-ls.org/forum] to distribute information and videos.[7] This forum is however, password-protected and in Arabic.

Iraq

Iraq has become a central battlefield for many different factions of violent Islamic fundamentalists and terrorists. As the smattering of examples that follow demonstrate, there are many terrorist websites with strict Iraq ties that are often sympathetic to Islamic resistance as a whole.

The Al-Zarqawi [http://www.alamer.biz/ameer/home.html] (Arabic-only) website is dedicated to the followers of Abu Musab al-Zarqawi. Zarqawi was a Jordanian-born terrorist who formed the group Al-Qaeda in Iraq sometime in the 1990s. He was killed in 2006. He was known primarily for focusing anger and military rage on U.S. troops in Iraq, whom he considered invaders. A Sunni, he also severely criticized Shiite Muslims in Iraq.

The Ansar website [http://www.al-ansar.biz] represents Ansar al Sunna, a conglomerate of terrorist factions formed in 2003. The website first aired the video of the beheading of American citizen Nicholas Berg. This airing unwittingly led to its web demise by crashing the Malaysian-hosted server with excessive traffic and drew enormous attention to their site. While many terrorist sites downplay their own actions and amplify the atrocities of their enemies, this site, and many of the younger, angrier cooperatives, take the opposite approach, tapping into sentiments of violent anger.

The Islamic Army in Iraq (IAI) [http://www.iaisite-eng.org] is a Baathist mujahideen organization dedicated to getting foreign troops out of Iraq. Its website has an English option. Choices include Military Operations and Filmed Operations, which feature footage of "our brothers" blowing up an American Humvee and other acts of violence against American troops. The site also includes Media Statements, Political Statements, Jihad information, and a forum [http://alboraq.info/forumdisplay.php?f=72].

Juba, a self-proclaimed soldier of the IAI, has created a site called Baghdad Sniper [http://www.baghdadsniper.com] (English available). "I am not a criminal. . . . I am not bloodthirsty . . . I just defend our land you invaded . . . defend our children [from] whom you stole their happiness and their right to live in peace."

Subhanaka Forum [http://sobhank.com/vb] posts communiqués by jihad groups in Iraq, while http://www.iraqipa.net posts videos and messages. Both of these sites are in Arabic. The blog MNHATT [http://kjgafd.blogspot.com], also in Arabic, is sympathetic to Jihad in Iraq.

Saraya Sa'd Ibn Abi Waqas [http://www.sarayasaad.com] has posted videos of attacks on American convoys; the group Shabkat Qawafil Al-Islam [http://kwaflislam.com/vb/index.php] hosts a forum for Islamic State of Iraq communiqués. Both sites are in Arabic.

While the media and politicians often attempt to paint a cohesive and evolutionary picture of the current war in Iraq, serious scholars realize the complexities of populations, issues, politics, and economies. Although offensive, websites such as these offer alternative interpretations to a complex reality.

Palestine

The Palestinian militant group Hamas uses numerous sites to target and address many populations. Its primary site, the Palestine Information Center [http://www.palestine-info.info], is available in eight languages and incredibly elaborate. The site welcomes you with music and features news, graphics, comments, reports, analysis, and much more. It is obviously a site that stretches out a friendly, virtual arm and hand to the Western visitor.

Hamas, a Palestinian Sunni Islamic group founded in 1987 during the first Intifada, or uprising against Israeli rule, currently hold a majority of elected seats in the Palestinian Legislature. Its military wing is considered terroristic by many countries worldwide.

Other Hamas sites include the Palestine Gallery [http://www.palestinegallery.com], which is in Arabic only, and the Izz ad-Din al-Qassam Brigades [http://www.alqassam.ps/english], a site for the military wing of Hamas, which is in English. Numerous other websites, such as the Hamas-run Al-Fateh.net, which, according to Israeli news, recruits children for martyrdom, exist as well.

Hamas was among the first terrorist groups to use the Internet,[8] publishing the U.K.-based *Filastin al-Muslimah* online in the late 1980s.

Lebanon

The Hezbollah (aka Hizbollah, Hizbu'llah—Party of God) site is in Arabic but has an English-language version, Islamic Resistance in Lebanon [http://english.hizbollah.tv/index.php]. The Hezbollah is a group of Lebanese Shiite militants, formed in 1982, as a reaction to the Israeli invasion of Lebanon. It had numerous early ties to Iran and was particularly influenced by the beliefs of the Ayatollah Khomeini.

Extremely media-savvy, the Hezbollah operates al-Manar [http://www.almanar.com.lb/NewsSite/HomePage.aspx], a radio and television station. Al-Manar TV is a high-production site that broadcasts in English and offers text, audio, and video streams of national, regional, and world news that is slanted toward Islamic resistance and unity.

Iran

Iran is currently recognized as a terrorist state by a number of Western countries. The President's homepage [http://www.president.ir/eng/government] links to an extensive list of government websites, including the Ministry of Defense [http://www.mod.ir]. The Revolutionary Guards Corps of Iran (Army of the Guardians of the Islamic Revolution) [http://www.shahid.ir], a radical branch of the Islamic Republic of Iran's military, is accused of executing numerous terrorist acts and sponsoring terrorist training camps within the borders of Iran. An Islamic news site with ties to this group is Tabnak [http://tabnak.ir].

Afghanistan

The Taliban, who also use the moniker "Islamic emirate of Afghanistan," are a group of extreme Sunni Islamic fundamentalists who seized control of Afghanistan using weapons the U.S. had given them to fight Russian invaders. Their previous website, viewable on the WayBack Machine at http://www.alemarah.org, was taken down by a group of self-described terrorist fighters. Its new site, in Arabic, is http://www.alemarah.110mb.com.

After 9/11, the Taliban were accused of harboring Bin Laden and driven from power in Afghanistan by U.S. and allied forces. They have continued to have a presence, however, and, according to some military strategists, are rebuilding forces.

Examples of Non-Islamic Terrorist Sites

Spain

Basque separatists and the movement for Basque independence dates back to early 19th-century battles with the Crown of Spain. Currently, the movement is thriving, and Basque people reflect every aspect of tolerance and intolerance, from live-and-let-live to violent terrorists. The Euskadi Ta Askatasuna (ETA) movement of Basque separatists, a terrorist group, originally used a website called Euskal Herria Journal [http://www.igc.apc.org/ehj] to espouse their beliefs. Though the site has been repeatedly hacked and is no longer active, you can view it on the WayBack Machine.

Basque News [http://www.eitb24.com] is in English and, while embracing the Basque culture, may provide links to more violent organizations. It is primarily a centrist publication with an excellent overview of the breadth and diversity of this group.

Japan

The group Aleph [http://english.aleph.to], formerly known as Aum Shinrikyo, is a religious organization/cult that relies on a pastiche of beliefs from Buddhism, Hinduism, Christianity, and other spiritual practices. Aum Shinrikyo was never a stranger to controversy, criticized early on for its recruiting methods and treatment of disciples. Its cult took a demonic turn in 1993, however, when it began manufacturing sarin and stockpiling weapons. Several assassination attempts were also blamed on the group. It was the orchestrated sarin gas attack on the Tokyo subway system on March 20, 1995, that catapulted this group to international notoriety. While the current group, re-named Aleph in 2000, claims to have severed any ties with terrorism, it is still considered a terrorist organization and is highly monitored. Its website contains a seemingly innocuous selection of dogma and readings.

Sri Lanka

Tamil Eelam [http://www.eelam.com], or Tamil Nation, is a perfect example of how the definition of terrorism often lies in the eyes of the beholder. This ethnic minority considers itself to be waging a legitimate war for recognition against the Sinhala government. The site endorses the Tamil Tigers as freedom fighters; however, many nations, including the U.S., consider them to be terrorists. The group, unlike FARC (see below) and Hamas, but similar to the Basque Separatists, is attempting to gain its own country status. The site is in English and offers insight into the group's history, politics, and news.

Colombia

The Revolutionary Armed Forces of Colombia (FARC) [http://www.farcep.org] is a Marxist-Leninist organization founded in 1964 within Colombia that fights the Colombian government for a political voice. FARC has been involved in killings and kidnappings, as well as the cocaine trade. Its website was hosted by a Swiss IP (the site is currently down) in Spanish with an English option. Previous examples of this site can be examined on the Internet Archive.

Philippines

The Communist Party of the Philippines/New People's Army (CPP/NPA) [http://www.philippinerevolution.net] has a very advanced website in English and Tagalog that details the history of the CPP and the NPA, as well as featuring press releases, documents, publications, photographs, videos and songs, among other information. This site has been hacked several times but is currently up and running.

Miscellaneous Sites

Certain websites are no longer active but played a formative role in web presence for the pursuit of terrorist activities. Examples include Assam [http://www.assam.com], a propaganda site for jihad in Afghanistan, Chechnya, and Palestine; 7hj7hj [7hj.7hj.com], which taught visitors how to hack into government networks and contaminate websites with worms and viruses; and the Islamic Studies and Research Center [http://www.drasat.com], a news site for Islamic fundamentalists and terrorists.

Jihadunspun [http://www.jihadunspun.net] is an interesting and controversial site. Considered by some parties to be sponsored by terrorists and by others to be a CIA front, Jihadunspun is a large Canadian website (currently attempting to move to Malaysia) that claims to offer an uncensored version of the U.S. war on terror. The site appears Islamic in origin and contains articles, news feeds, both mainstream and what they call "uncensored" regional reports and information, and a members-only area and forum.

The mail group alt.security.terrorism [http://groups.google.com/group/alt.security.terrorism/topics], a member of the Google Groups fiefdom, is comprised of people dedicated to tracking and discussing terrorist activities. This site is quite active and represents a wide variety of opinions. There are many references to news items, actions, political issues, etc.

Language Issues

There is no way to underestimate the power of language. Many sites by organizations large and small that are labeled as terrorist, or engage in activities that are by definition terroristic, do not publish in English. Scholars and interested parties who wish to harvest information from these sites and don't read the language are at the mercy of translators, who are often expensive, or, worse yet, must rely on horrible web-based translation devices. Only use these devices, which are often language-selective and only translate short sections of text, as a last resort. If used sparingly and with caution, these devices can, however, give one an idea of what a site is about.

Several of the more "legitimate" terrorist groups, for example, the Hezbollah, offer sites in English as well as their native language. Groups such as the Hezbollah obviously realize that in today's world, offering an alternative to the mainstream English-speaking media's perception of their organizations is a necessary spin. These sites are rich in propaganda, alternative scenarios, arguments, philosophies, and often feature donation and/or recruitment options. Anyone truly interested in researching an organization such as Hezbollah should consider the information on these sites critical.

Conclusion

If we consider the Internet analogous to geography, virtual space as it were, we begin to witness a mirror or map of the world and its inhabitants. Terrorist groups, in all their variety and complexity, feel compelled to stake a claim to this virtual territory. Their methods vary from those of extremely nationalistic groups, such as the Tamil Tigers or the Basque Separatists, for whom a single website is their resident home, to Al-Qaeda, a group less concerned with national boundaries and more with the boundaries of hearts and minds. Al-Qaeda, just as a multinational corporation, is a product of the 21st century and operates with a fluidity that largely ignores national boundaries.

The Internet presence of terrorists and terrorist organizations is in a rudimentary phase. It is still aimed at staking out and defining territory; at information sharing, recruitment, fund raising; etc. Elements of these missions will probably always remain. However, terrorist actions in the real world will eventually be mirrored in virtual space. Cyberterrorism will mirror the suicide bombings and roadside attacks and 9/11s of our physical geography and its scale and human sacrifice will likely increase.

I am tempted to end this article on a positive note, but an ongoing examination of these cultures of violence has not increased my hope for peaceful resolution or co-existence. Some situations may be more easily healed. Groups such as FARC who are fighting for a voice in government may be appeased by obtaining that voice and cease their violent ways. But other groups, such as Al-Qaeda, will continue to fight their perceived enemies, roughly defined as the Western world, indefinitely. One can only hope for brilliant politicians and world leaders, a more tightly defined global community, as well as adequate defenses, to shepherd us safely through the 21st century and beyond.

References

1. Blumenthal, Les, "Cyberspace: The Final Frontier in the War on Terror," *Knight Ridder Tribune,* Sept. 21, 2007.

2. The Office of the Law Revision Counsel, U.S. House of Representatives, Jan. 2, 2006, June 26, 2008 [http://uscode .house.gov/download/pls/18C113B.txt].

3. Bass, Frank and Herschaft, Randy, "1M archived pages removed post-9/11" Associated Press, *USA Today,* March 13, 2007, June 20, 2008 [http://www.usatoday.com/news/ washington/2007-03-13-archives_N.htm].

4. Weinmann, Gabriel, "Terror on the Internet: The New Arena, the New Challenges," U.S. Institute of Peace Press, Washington, D.C. 2006.

5. FBI Testimony of Dale L. Watson, executive assistant director, Counterterrorism/Counterintelligence Division, FBI, before the Senate Select Committee on Intelligence, Feb. 6, 2002. "The Terrorist Threat Confronting the United States" [http://www.fbi .gov/congress/congress02/watson020602.htm 6/23/2008].

6. *Ibid.* Weinmann, Gabriel.

7. Private email communication with Dr. Rusty Shackleford, 6/18/2008.

8. *Ibid.* Weinmann, Gabriel.

Jihad with a Hip-Hop Pose Is an Easier Sell with Youth

ANDREW POTTER

International terrorism came to Ottawa a few weeks ago in the form of Mohammed "Big Dawg" Babar, the al-Qaeda supergrass and star prosecution witness in the trial of Momin Khawaja, an Ottawa man accused of plotting with a group to blow up a London nightclub in 2004. In the opening moves of a trial that featured rooftop snipers across from the courthouse and airport-level security inside, Babar testified to Khawaja's involvement in what he called "the J"—for jihad.

While the most newsworthy aspect of this is that Khawaja, the first Canadian charged under our post-9/11 Anti-terrorism Act, is finally being tried after four years of legal wrangling, what is fascinating is the combination of gangsta slang and jihadist pieties—a sort of hip-hop jihad—that emerges in the email and surveillance-tape evidence. In one typical email exchange, a London contact named Omar Kyam wrote to Khawaja, "How's it's goin' niggas, everything OK?" Khawaja replied, "Yeah, bro, got home safe. How bout you niggas? Everything cool?"

'Yeah, bro, got home safe. How bout you niggas?' Momin Khawaja writes in one email.

At one point, the cultural dissonance generated by one too many "inshallah, niggas" got to be a bit much for Ontario Superior Court Justice Douglas Rutherford, who noted that the term niggas appeared "to cover a broad ambit." By way of explanation, Babar told Rutherford, "In one sense, niggas means everyone involved. But to understand which niggas are niggas, you have to know the people and understand from the email who he was referring to." To which Rutherford dryly replied, "That clears up how unclear it is."

It is widely thought that the post-9/11 "clash of civilizations," to the extent to which it exists at all, is between Islam and Christianity, which is why George W. Bush took so much heat for his early, clumsy attempts at framing the fight against terrorism as a crusade. The real opponent to Islamic fundamentalism, though, is not Christianity. What Islamic fundamentalists find far more objectionable than the West's religion is our worship of things like Wal-Mart, Britney Spears, and credit cards.

What is striking then is the form that resistance to the West among urbanized Islamic youth, or at least these ones, is taking. It consists of what the social critic Mark Lilla has called "a universal culture of the wretched of the earth"—a set of symbols and attitudes stolen wholesale from the streets of New York, Chicago and Los Angeles by way of hip-hop music videos. From the native reserves of northern Ontario to the *banlieues* of Paris, the gangsta pose of American black males has become the archetypical way of responding to cultural alienation, and young jihadis are just the latest to fall for its charms.

But who can blame them? As it is described in books like Lawrence Wright's *The Looming Tower,* the traditional training for al-Qaeda sounds extremely unpleasant: move to the mountains of Pakistan where there are hardly any girls around, live in the dust, pray a lot, and eat bad food. It's the sort of ascetic existence that isn't going to attract a lot of recruits from urban centres. For disaffected Muslim youth in London or Paris or Ottawa on the other hand, a combination of devout Islamic principle and hip-hop street cred would be pretty hard to resist.

But here's the thing. In North America, the gangsta pose isn't a threat to the system—it is the system. Gangsta culture is nothing more than streetwise capitalism, an idea nicely explored in the 2007 film *American Gangster.* It is not despite, but because of, his numerous gun and drug charges that Snoop Dogg now has a hit reality show, while 50 Cent has parlayed his nine bullet wounds into a fortune based largely on an investment in vitamin water. But, for jihadis, the gangsta pose is part of a deadly campaign to throw some serious terror into the system's workings, if not to bring it down entirely.

Khawaja's trial is deadly serious business. Five of his alleged co-conspirators were convicted of numerous terrorism charges in 2007, and will spend most of what remains of their wasted lives in a British prison. For all of Babar's wit and gangster charm, he was at one point a very scary dude. He was an associate of Mohamed Sidique Khan, the 7/7 bomber who killed six people and injured dozens when he blew himself up at the

Edgeware Road train station. Babar has pleaded guilty in U.S. District Court to five terrorism charges related to the organization of a jihad training camp and the purchase of bomb-making equipment, and agreed to testify in foreign terrorism trials in exchange for a reduction in his otherwise guaranteed 70-year sentence.

Our romantic familiarity with the pose helps make hip-hop jihad the threat it is. Partly it is that many of us share with jihadis an underlying unease with the homogeneity and decadence of global pop culture, but more worrisome still is that it makes the jihadist message that much more palatable to youth.

It is natural to be wary of turbaned men training and praying in the mountainous wilds of Pakistan—it is so culturally alien that we can't help but see it as a threat. But gangsta jihadis? They're kinda cool, a bit sexy even, and that's where the danger lies: that otherwise decent kids, wallowing in the usual confusions of adolescent rage and anxiety, will find meaning and purpose in the embrace of what Mohammed Babar so disarmingly calls "the J."

The Globe of Villages: Digital Media and the Rise of Homegrown Terrorism

Feisal G. Mohamed

We have been told that the August 2006 plot to attack several U.S.-bound flights departing from London's Heathrow Airport was hatched largely by Muslim Britons. This is becoming a familiar story. Earlier this summer, the Royal Canadian Mounted Police foiled a homegrown Toronto cell in its attempt to blow up Parliament with a fertilizer bomb similar to that used by Timothy McVeigh in the Oklahoma City bombing. The July 7, 2005, attacks on London buses and subways were carried out largely by British citizens, and this was not the first such occurrence: two Britons traveled to Tel Aviv in 2003 to conduct a suicide bombing of a nightclub that killed three and wounded sixty.

This country too has produced its share of accused or convicted jihadists. The "Lackawanna Six," all American citizens of Yemeni heritage, were arrested in 2002 for attending an al-Qaeda camp in Afghanistan—much like Hamid Hayat, a second-generation Pakistani-American, who was convicted last year, albeit on dubious evidence, for receiving jihadist training in Pakistan. Iyman Faris, an American citizen born in Kashmir, was sentenced to twenty years in prison in 2005 for participating in a plan to attack the Brooklyn Bridge. These men are joined by several other Americans who have been found guilty of providing material or logistic support to Islamist terrorists: Marwan Othman el-Hindi, Uzair Paracha, Junaid Babar, and Ali al-Timimi and his "Virginia jihadists." I say nothing of the Miami "cell" arrested in June 2006 for conspiring with al-Qaeda, whose members seemed more interested in using terrorist funds to buy a new wardrobe than in waging holy war; or of Naveed Haq, whose attack on a Jewish community center in Seattle this August killed one and injured five (it has been suggested that he acted entirely on his own and has a history of mental illness); nor am I concerned with such converts as José Padilla, Richard Reid, and the three recently arrested in connection with the attempt to explode passenger jets over the Atlantic: Don Stewart-Whyte, Brian Young, and Oliver Savant. (One wonders if these men turned to violence after converting to Islam or if they converted to Islam so that they might engage in spectacular anti-Western violence.)

As yet we have not been offered a satisfactory explanation of this political or religious zealotry. The terms by which foreign terrorism is made scrutable are quite familiar by now: faced with a lack of opportunity in the Arab world and the humiliations—real and imagined—dealt to one's coreligionists, desperate youth come to see themselves as engaged in cosmic warfare against iniquity and turn to violence. In this vein, Mohammed Atta, the ringleader of the September 11 attacks, is held up as the paradigmatic modern terrorist. Despite his education and residence in Germany, he became hostile toward the West upon return to his native Egypt, where his world-class training as an engineer fitted him only for unemployment, and where he saw the birthplace of one of the world's great civilizations reduced to a satrapy prostrating itself before the Western tourist dollar. Such a narrative of the development of a terrorist has provided comfort in the West across the political spectrum. The conservative finds in it an irreconcilable clash of civilizations: no matter how much we give to these people they still hate us; best to have a firm hand. The liberal finds in it evidence of universal outrage over the evils of global capitalism and American foreign policy: if Western industry, and particularly big oil, had a shred of regard for the prosperity of the Arab majority, if the United States did not prop up Arab tyrants and simultaneously inflict suffering on the Palestinians and Iraqis, there would be no terrorists.

But the phenomenon of Western jihadists is harder to explain than this suggests. If religion is the explanation for terrorism—if we argue that Iran and Saudi Arabia have used their oil wealth to assure the global spread of retrograde ideas in both of Islam's major sects, so that each one now strives to outdo the other in paranoia—we still cannot entirely explain why lunatic Muslim clerics have found an audience among young men born into liberal societies. And if politics and economics are the explanation for terrorism, why is it that those who are stakeholders in affluent Western democracies feel directly involved in political struggles taking place on the other side of the planet?

The real question is, what makes the religion and politics of radical Islam seem to apply to the situation of a Muslim in London, Toronto, or Brooklyn? This is not the same as the question that is often identified as pressing: whether Muslim immigrants in the West are assimilating into the host culture.

Many immigrant communities show little regard for assimilation. Any walk through a self-respecting Chinatown, for example, will reveal a significant number of individuals making a life in the West that is culturally closer to the motherland than to their adopted home. Those who clamor for fuller assimilation of Muslims reveal their discomfort with the increasingly multicultural complexion of the West in a way only tangentially related to this particular minority group; they use terrorism as a cover for their dislike of foreign dress, beliefs, and manners. Nor can the isolation of the Muslim community—imposed from within and without—be regarded as the key motivation for violence. Isolation has always been, and ever will be, a condition of immigrant life, and there are many fewer obstacles faced by Muslims today than have been peacefully overcome by the Asian, Jewish, Irish, Italian, Mexican, Native, and African Americans who have suffered most in the long and continuing struggle to broaden this country's promise of dignity and prosperity.

Present-day conditions of immigration do seem, however, to foster an especially keen sense of unity between diaspora and kin country. The first such condition is the mobility of the modern world, which produces a constant state of traffic between East and West. Rather than arrival en masse and slow adaptation, the modern immigrant community is in a state of constant exchange with the mother country. Those who immigrate will travel home regularly; many who reside in the West will do so temporarily; this allows cultural and emotional bonds with non-Western society to remain firmly intact.

The exchange of people across East and West, however, may not be as important as it seems at first glance. Even the influence of itinerant Muslim preachers may not be as decisive as it looks. A good deal has been done, in England especially, to crack down on radical clerics; perhaps that country has learned the lesson of its seventeenth-century civil wars, fired as they were from the Puritan pulpit. But a recent survey by the Federation of Student Islamic Societies suggests that the vast majority of young British Muslims get their ideas outside of the mosque. The underground meeting and the website are the crucial milieus of the radical subculture.

It is the means by which ideas, rather than people, are exchanged that is the real issue, and especially the way in which modern communications make it possible to identify exclusively with one's kin country while living elsewhere.

One of the consequences of the Internet is its generation of communities of readers without geographical association. As a technology bound to the distribution of physical objects, the printed page necessarily reflects the values of a given locale. If we were still shackled to print—and I mean the cast-metal-striking-paper kind, not the ink or laser jet variety—the cost of delivering al-Qaeda propaganda to East London would be prohibitive; the lack of broad demand would make it a hopeless venture. The dissemination of ideas on the web is not married to the local market; once one has a functioning computer and an active Internet connection, it is just as easy to access al-Jazeera as it is FoxNews. The market forces governing such access have shifted profoundly, so that where one lives is no longer an index of what one reads or thinks. This may be why a recent Pew study found that many of the most obnoxious ideas of the Arab world are alive and well in Europe: for example, 56 percent of the British Muslims surveyed claimed that Arabs did not carry out the September 11 attacks, as compared to 53 percent in Jordan, 41 percent in Pakistan, and 47 percent in Nigeria. This may also be why many young Muslims born and raised in the West are more radical in their religious views than their parents are. Greater technological savvy seems to foster, rather than to diminish, the influence of Eastern delusion.

What I am suggesting here goes beyond the now-redundant claim that the Internet has been an important means by which Islamism organizes itself. As the *Washington Post* observed in August 2005, attacks on al-Qaeda camps in Afghanistan have led to the creation of virtual training facilities. "To join the great training camps you don't have to travel to other lands," one Saudi magazine claims, "alone, in your home or with a group of your brothers, you too can begin to execute the training program." Michael Dartnell's recent book *Insurgency Online* shows how the Internet has allowed non-state actors to achieve new levels of organization and thus to exert previously unimaginable political influence. Even Michael Chertoff has emerged from the Department of Homeland Security's thick cloud of bureaucracy to shed some light on this front, claiming in a recent issue of the *Atlantic Monthly,* that "we have to look at the onset of virtual terrorism—virtual jihad—where groups radicalize themselves over the Internet."

The shortcoming of such commentary is that it commits what Marshall McLuhan described as the cardinal sin of media studies: it focuses on content rather than on the medium itself. We miss the point in claiming that the jihadists are visiting the wrong websites. What is really significant is that the Internet has made it possible for new human relationships to emerge. "The medium is the message," in McLuhan's famous phrase, "because it is the medium that shapes and controls the scale and form of human association and action."

It is a commonplace of cultural history to say that vernacular print and its reading public helped to create the idea of the modern nation-state. Electronic communications are causing this idea to dissolve. Individuals are led into a mystique of participation in affairs across the globe, from one laptop in East London to another in the mountains outside of Jalalabad. And in electronic media this mystique of participation is the end itself, rather than argument and explanation. No longer is society bound by the rational interpretation of the physical and social world that print generates—the anvil on which the liberal tradition was forged. Instead it is being rent asunder as various groups are drawn to the visceral totems of image-based media. Though McLuhan thought that the sense of universal participation generated by electronic media would put an end to parochialism, quite the opposite has occurred. Rather than his global village, we have become a globe of villages; we live in a cacophony of hidebound parochialisms where individuals seek association only with those to whom they relate by way of primordial intuition.

Mcluhan may have been correct to say that the most "backward," the least literate parts of the world would take up the new media most eagerly, but he did not foresee the conflicts that the new media might create within a multicultural West. The liberal state, with its dependence on rational association, is dissolving into a collection of masses united by the parochialisms of "religion" and "culture," a phenomenon to be observed among Muslims and non-Muslims alike.

Can a little Internet surfing really do all that? Yes, and to illustrate why it is so, allow me a moment of autobiography. I was once reading a Philip Roth novel and came across the phrase, "Newark was all of Jewry to me"—I can't remember which one it was; it could have been any of Roth's works. This single statement made me realize more about my own ethnicity than any other I have encountered before or since. As with Roth, everything I had grown up recognizing as a part of my ethnic heritage—Egyptians don't play sports, drink, or curse; they wear their religion lightly, laugh from the soul, and are moved to outrage only when their children underachieve at school—had been learned from the hundred or so households of Egyptian emigrés in my hometown of Edmonton, Canada, nearly all of whom, men and women, I proudly stress, were university-educated professionals. Only after reading Roth's statement did it occur to me that though I had always identified myself as Egyptian-Canadian, my sense of what was Egyptian had little connection to the seventy-two million individuals living a world away in Egypt, most of whom eke out a subsistence living using agricultural techniques that have not changed in the past millennium.

At the same moment, I saw that my sense of identity was very much like that of an author with whom it should be doubly antithetical: he being a Jewish American and I a Muslim Canadian. And recognizing this unexpected proximity made me realize that a minority experience much like my own had found its way into the mainstream of North American life. This led me along a chain of ideas to the point with which I began this essay: that isolation has always been, and always will be, a condition of immigrant life.

But had I grown up in the age of the blogosphere, I might have found a radically different narrative by which to explain my minority experience. If I had spent my time surfing the Net rather than reading novels, I might have been more prone to isolate myself with my coreligionists rather than to see myself as having a specifically Western experience of the world. This is also the great irony that homegrown jihadists fail to see: though they may feel a mystique of participation with the plight of Muslims on the other side of the planet, it is only a mystique. Looking at their blogs shows just how thoroughly their lives and hopes partake in the Western version of self-indulgent, egocentric adolescence. Toronto's *Globe and Mail* has provided a look at the blog of Zakaria Amara, leader of that city's homegrown jihadists, which reveals this sensibility: underneath the Islamist rhetoric one finds a teenager confused by his raging hormones, convinced that the older generation has accepted a corrupt world and fallen into lethargic inaction—and anxious over college applications. Had he been reading Roth rather than the ravings of zealots to which the Internet provides too-ready access, he might have found quite a different sympathetic voice to help him make sense of himself and the world around him.

This is not to say that current efforts to crack down on radical Islam are entirely misguided. No civil society should tolerate a cleric who advocates its destruction and incites his listeners to do the necessary work. The move in Britain to observe mosques and to expel radical imams is entirely appropriate. But if Western Muslims are to carve out their own identity as other minorities have done—neither "assimilated" nor clinging to the bigotries of the motherland—the brand of identity to which electronic media contribute must also be addressed. A robust censorship of radical websites would only address content; we also need to promote real literacy and the concomitant primacy of reason. If the new vogue for religion-based schooling is allowed to flourish, it must force students to become "people of the book," to use the Prophet Muhammad's phrase. Emphasizing only science and religion, with little regard for a humanities curriculum of literature and history, creates an intellectual environment where parochialism flourishes.

It is through literacy that we become rational observers of both West and East, and it is through literacy that Muslims can reclaim the long intellectual and artistic traditions that have been occluded by the rise in the twentieth century of Saudi Wahhabism, Iranian radical Shiism, and the Arab world's histrionic opposition to the state of Israel. Only then will Muslims themselves tear the veil of false holiness off a radical Islam that is itself a cover for the political tyrannies of today's Middle East.

Feisal G. Mohamed is assistant professor of English at Texas Tech University and a Milton scholar.

Congress and the "YouTube War"

Michael A. Cohen and Maria Figueroa Küpçü

The United States is "fighting a different kind of enemy" in its War on Terror, or so says President Bush. He's right. For the first time since the days of the Barbary pirates, America is doing active battle not with a rival nation, but with a non-state actor (al Qaeda) that lacks a geographical home, is motivated by ideology more than territorial ambition, and whose victories are defined in non-military terms. It is an enemy that uses communication technology, public opinion, and the global 24-hour news cycle to wage its battles. It is, in a very real sense, the first "YouTube War" of the twenty-first century.

The rise of al Qaeda is a sign of the era in which we live. With the spread of economic and political liberalization, with the advent of new communication technology, and with the gradual erosion of state power and influence, individuals, organizations, and institutions are enjoying an unprecedented opportunity to affect international events. The rise of the non-state actor stands to become the most resonant characteristic of global affairs at the dawn of the twenty-first century.

Yet the stateless nature of this different kind of enemy is not being reflected in America's current anti-terrorism strategy. In fact, the United States is wielding a military approach against its jihadist foes that is straight out of a twentieth-century playbook. President Bush has chosen to wage this "different kind of war" in Iraq, in a manner reminiscent of the Balkan wars, the conflict in Rwanda, and even the Vietnam War—a territorial, resource-based conflict between rival ethnic and religious groups competing for the spoils of political power.

The New Global Environment

Five years after the attacks of September 11, it is long over-due for the United States to factor this new global environment into its approach for fighting the War on Terror. For five years, Congress has followed the White House's lead in fighting terrorism, with rather uncertain results. In recent congressional elections, the manner in which America is fighting the War on Terror was rarely debated. But, as the 110th Congress implements a legislative agenda for the next two years, it is of critical importance that it do more than simply articulate the fact that America is fighting a "different kind of war"—and instead ensure that the United States fight that war differently.

To be sure, broader American success in the War on Terror can only come when the albatross of U.S. involvement in Iraq comes to an end. It has been, and will continue to be, near impossible to wage an effective war against a non-state actor so long as America is mired in a state-based civil war that is weakening its global credibility and diverting its attention and resources. The drawdown of American troops in Iraq would help to refocus America's antiterrorism agenda on al Qaeda and remove from its jihadist enemies the rallying cry of opposition to the continued occupation. The president's recent protestations notwithstanding, Iraq is not where the War on Terror will be won or lost. What happens in Iraq will not stop the jihadists from waging their civilizational struggle against the United States.

America is mired in a generation-long battle and what is needed today is a comprehensive antiterror strategy that takes into full account the attributes and characteristics of the enemy that America is facing. In the immediate term, that means re-calibrating the efficacy of military power in a war against non-state actors, focusing on the tools of public perception to win the war of ideas, and above all, utilizing the capabilities, knowl-edge, and resources of constructive non-state actors on behalf of U.S. foreign policy goals.

The Trap Called Iraq

There is probably no more venerated—and well-funded—public institution in American society than the U.S. military. Few in Congress have openly questioned the effectiveness of the military as a tool for fighting terrorism. But America's mil-itary has significant limitations when it comes to defeating a non-state actor enemy such as al Qaeda. In the wake of Septem-ber 11, the Bush administration (understandably) made military power the tip of the sword in America's response and the U.S. military effort in Afghanistan remains the most effective tactic that has been employed against al Qaeda: removing the terror-ists' home base, dispersing their leaders, and severely degrading the group's ability to wage attacks against America.

The war in Iraq, on the other hand, has tragically laid bare the limitations of using military force when fighting a non-state actor. Prior to September 11, Osama bin Laden and his top cohorts expressed a willingness, even desire, for the United States to invade and occupy a Muslim country. They saw the benefits of a long, protracted struggle between the United States and an Islamic enemy—and they have reaped great rewards from the U.S. war in Iraq. Instead of focusing U.S. political, military, and economic power on fighting terrorism, preventing Afghanistan from again becoming a base of operations for al Qaeda, and organizing an antiterror coalition of like-minded nations, Washington has mired the nation in an internecine, sectarian conflict. Above all, the war in Iraq has shown the limitations of U.S. political will and military might. No longer is America perceived as the invincible, benevolent power that it was before it invaded Iraq. As a result, America's deterrent power has been significantly and fundamentally eroded.

It may be the ultimate irony of America's post-9/11 warrior ethic that the law enforcement officials who prevented the bombing of trans-Atlantic flights to the United States last summer have done as much or more to directly protect the American people than the troops who have rotated through Iraq. This, of course, is not to impugn the soldiers who are fighting and dying in Iraq, but instead the leaders who sent them there. During the 2004 presidential campaign, Senator John Kerry was excoriated by the Bush camp for intimating that the War on Terror could be treated as a law enforcement matter. When one considers how easily the 9/11 attacks could have been prevented by effective coordination among America's law enforcement agencies, one can't help but wonder whether the senator was on to something. The reality is that, in an era of asymmetric threats and non-state actors, the sledgehammer of American military force is not necessarily the best means of protecting America's interests—sometimes, it's just old-fashioned police work.

Winning the War of Ideas

In April 2003, it seemed for a moment that the dominant image of the Iraq war would be the toppling of the Saddam Hussein statue in Baghdad's Republic Square. Instead, it is likely to be the pathetic, hooded, and tortured Iraqis at Abu Ghraib prison, the Internet videos of Iraqi insurgents attacking American troops, or a defiant Saddam at the gallows.

In the era of the non-state actor, public perception is crucial, but soldiers don't do public relations. They fight wars and they kill their enemies—and few have been more effective at this essential skill than the U.S. military. But few armies have been more unprepared for the public relations element of twenty-first century conflict. As Thomas Ricks' recent book, *Fiasco*, makes clear, the U.S. military is unsuited for fighting counterinsurgencies. The rampant disclosures of abuse, which culminated in the Abu Ghraib scandal, were largely the result of sending well-trained military units into a guerrilla conflict in a strange land, where years of military training provided little preparation for the daily challenge of armed occupation. The result was a precipitous decline in America's standing around the world, even among its allies. Recent polling data shows that strong majorities in Germany (78 percent) and Great Britain (56 percent) agreed that the United States was doing a "bad job" of promoting human rights. In a similar poll taken in 1998, fewer than one in four Germans (24 percent) and Britons (22 percent) held that view.[1]

The importance of public perceptions was not lost on America's enemy. As former Central Intelligence Agency (CIA) deputy director John E. McLaughlin has noted, al Qaeda today is driven primarily by "ideology and the Internet." Right now, the morbidly curious can log onto YouTube.com and other viral video sites that popularize free content through the Internet or any number of jihadist websites to see videos of the killing of American soldiers and Improvised Explosive Device (IED) attacks against coalition troops. As disturbing as these images are, they provide graphic evidence of al Qaeda's success in using Iraq to create a prime recruiting tool for the terrorists of tomorrow. As a recent memo by the director of strategic communications at the U.S. embassy in Baghdad points out, "Insurgents, sectarian elements, and others are taking control of the message at the public level." The level of sophistication from insurgent forces is extraordinary, attacks on U.S. forces are filmed from multiple angles with high-resolution optics. Footage is actually edited and soundtracks feature religious statements. According to a recent *Newsweek* article, "U.S. officials believe insurgents attack American forces primarily to generate fresh footage." This contrasts greatly with the normal U.S. response to military actions taken in Iraq—a press release.[2]

However, the White House continues to blame public relations failures for undermining U.S. effectiveness in the War on Terror. In a *Los Angeles Times* op-ed in early 2006, former secretary of defense Donald Rumsfeld bragged about the new "strategic communications framework" put forward by the Pentagon to get out America's story. This past October, word leaked that the Pentagon plans to ramp up its communications effort by creating a rapid response media unit. But even the best communications plan is mere window dressing if you don't have a good story to tell. A November 2006 *Atlantic Monthly* profile of Karen Hughes was illuminating in this regard. The top U.S. public diplomat noted how hard it was for her to "sell" America in the Arab world because of the conflict in Iraq.

Iraq notwithstanding, recalibrating the public perception of U.S. foreign policy must be front and center in the minds of the new Congress. It is a great irony of the War on Terror that, while sizable percentages of Muslims are rejecting violence and, in particular, suicide bombings, this has not translated into a more positive view of the United States and its foreign policy objectives. In the five most predominately Muslim countries, sizable majorities continue to express markedly negative views of America and, in particular, the War on Terror.

Yet Washington's public diplomacy efforts have sputtered. Since 2003, the State Department has been justly faulted for its lack of an overall strategy, qualified staff, and culturally sophisticated approach to public diplomacy—and for not utilizing the lessons of private-sector campaigns more effectively.[3] Reinvigorating the effort will require not only presidential involvement, but also genuine public measures to improve America's image overseas.

These can run the gamut from small but meaningful initiatives such as the opening (rather than the closing) of American libraries in foreign locales, increased student exchange programs, foreign scholarships, and wide-ranging public health initiatives to the more vigorous engagement of American business, nonprofits, and even public relations firms in changing perceptions of the United States around the world. When fighting an enemy as media savvy as al Qaeda, Washington needs to take far more seriously the crucial importance of public perception in the YouTube era.

Utilizing Non-State Actors

The universal recognition of organizations like al Qaeda is a clear example of the success of non-state actors in placing themselves on the world's radar screens. But just as terrorist groups have been able to project themselves, so too have individuals, organizations, and corporations shown the ways in which altruistically minded non-state actors can change the world for the better. In an era of growing privatization in foreign affairs, the United States needs to do more to use these influential non-state actors to further foreign policy objectives.

Take the example of Rita Katz, a freelance intelligence gatherer, whose company, the Search for International Terrorist Entities Institute (SITE), provides some of the most up-to-date intelligence about terrorist organizations. Katz and others in the freelance intelligence field have been extraordinarily effective at ferreting out time-sensitive and actionable intelligence resources. At a time when only several dozen people in the FBI have proficiency in Arabic, policymakers should look more closely at individuals like Katz for clues that will uncover a terrorist attack before it occurs. Moreover, groups like SITE or the Investigative Project, headed by Steve Emerson, have shown an ability to harvest public sources of information in areas that traditional intelligence-gatherers eschew.

As Emerson notes, America's intelligence agencies are hindered by a bureaucratic culture that is overly compartmentalized, resists information-sharing, and has an innate distrust of open source information, which is why outside groups "can do a lot more."[4] But private intelligence is but one piece of the puzzle. There are numerous other examples of non-state actors furthering national security by drawing on the work of political consultants who advise opposition movements in former Yugoslavia, Georgia, and Ukraine; of trial lawyers who seek to hold state sponsors of terrorists legally responsible; and military contractors who train modern armed forces.

The Bush administration has used some of these groups in isolated circumstances, but the practice of actively drawing on the know-how of non-state actors should become a fundamental element of foreign policy. With Congress' urging, government agencies should be creating departmental liaisons specifically geared toward reaching non-state actors and utilizing their discrete expertise.

Regulating Military Contractors

Above all, Congress must draft commonsense guidelines for non-state actors to develop relationships that are based on transparency, accountability, and oversight. Consider the case of military contractors. In Bosnia, these groups provided essential security support for U.S. peacekeeping troops. In Afghanistan, private military contractors (PMCs) helped U.S. forces attack al Qaeda leaders and recruit proxy Afghan armies. In Iraq, PMCs are the backbone of the U.S. occupation, providing essential administrative and security services. According to recent Pentagon estimates, there are currently 25,000 private security contractors (PSCs) engaged in Iraq. This private army of contractors represents the second-largest contingent of armed personnel serving in Iraq who provide essential support to America's overburdened military. Since April 2003, the Labor Department estimates that more than 670 contractors have been killed—a total greater than all non-U.S. coalition fatalities combined.[5]

Yet few are asking the difficult questions about their responsibilities. Many firms operate in a gray zone beyond congressional oversight, military codes of conduct, and even international law. For example, in the United States, only recently have legislative changes made it possible for PSCs to be held accountable under the Uniform Code of Military Justice, the legal code that applies to U.S. military personnel. This attempt at enhancing accountability on the battlefield is a step in the right direction, though it remains to be seen if it is actually implementable. While certain international conventions apply to armed civilians, enforcement of these rules is discretionary and has been generally nonexistent. In Iraq, if a contractor kills an Iraqi civilian, there is virtually no legal recourse for the victim's family. The involvement of civilian contractors in military roles also creates operational challenges. Private security contractors are outside the official chain of command and control. But, to the average Iraqi citizen, the actions of contractors are indistinguishable from those of soldiers. They are just more Americans carrying guns—uniform or no uniform. As a result, illegal actions by PSCs reflect directly—often negatively—on their home country.

Clearly, America's reliance on PSCs is growing faster than Washington's ability or inclination to regulate them. Congressional action is long overdue.

Supporting Those "Supporting Democracy"

In addition, Congress and the Bush administration need to do a better job of standing up for individuals and organizations that work to promote democracy overseas. For more than a decade, foreign funds, not only from sympathetic foreign governments, but from a number of non-state actors, nongovernmental organizations (NGOs), and wealthy individuals, have flowed freely into nascent democracies. This seed capital has paid for political expertise, civic organizing, and public relations programs that have helped propel democratic movements.

But in January 2006, Russian president Vladimir Putin signed legislation oppressively regulating non-governmental organizations in Russia. The bill created a government agency with a mandate to monitor more than 400,000 civil society groups now in existence and shut down those whose activities "contradict the constitution or the laws of the Russian Federation." This effort was widely perceived as a direct attack on a fledgling Russian democracy.

Yet while the Bush administration protested, the complaints were half-hearted and lacking true diplomatic muscle. Restricting the work of NGOs is a shot across the bow to the administration's stated policy of encouraging the spread of democracy. Moreover, when U.S. international credibility is in decline, NGOs and advocacy groups can play a unique role in circumventing diplomatic channels and promoting objectives fundamental to national interests. But they need diplomatic support. The success of President Vladimir Putin's efforts at stifling democracy advocates may encourage emulation otherwise. Congress should take up the issue of NGOs operating freely in Russia today as it did the issue of Jewish *refuseniks* in the past.

Engaging the Business Community

Last November, a G-8 sponsored conference of global business leaders debated how they might help in the fight against terrorism.[6] The results were achievable ideas for cross-border collaboration: improved monitoring of terrorist activity in the financial, telecommunications, and Internet sectors, and agreement to prioritize sectors that were potential targets of a terrorist attack, such as infrastructure, international trade supply chains, and centers of tourism. Heads of international transport unions, banks, agricultural and industry conglomerates, and even the World Diamond Council offered models of how new standards and information-sharing could help to expose havens of criminal activity. Above all, business leaders acknowledged that thus far their efforts have been reactive—protecting employees and assets—but precious little effort has been put toward proactively countering terrorist operations.

Initiatives to harness the resources and innovation of the private sector are encouraging. Collaboration between business and government to fight terrorism can be especially effective when implemented at the local and regional level. But this is no easy task. Government officials are often unable to speak the language of non-state actors and the communication gap has frustrated a number of well-intentioned proposals. Congress must ultimately ensure that the engagement of the private sector is abetted with incentives and leadership, so that segmented actions become a sum greater than their parts.

Congress, in short, has an opportunity to change the course of the War on Terror and ensure that America is fighting this "different kind of enemy" in a different and effective manner. To do so, Washington must recognize the changing nature of global relations, which offers greater opportunities for non-state actors, but also demands of them greater responsibilities. Doing so is a complicated endeavor, but it must become a defining feature of U.S. foreign policy. To successfully wage the War on Terror requires more than tough talk and the sword of military tactics—it requires a fundamental rethinking of the forces driving global affairs in the twenty-first century.

References

1. "American and International Opinion on the Rights of Terrorism Suspects," Program on International Policy Attitudes, University of Maryland, July 17, 2006, at http://www.worldpublicopinion.org.
2. Scott Johnson, "We're Losing the Info War," *Newsweek,* January 15, 2007.
3. "U.S. Public Diplomacy: State Department Efforts Lack Certain Communication Elements and Face Persistent Elements," Government Accountability Office report, May 2006.
4. Michael Isikoff and Mark Hosenball, "How Clarke Outsourced Terror Intel," *Newsweek,* March 31, 2004.
5. See www.globalsecurity.org, updated August 2006.
6. Global Forum for Partnerships between States and Businesses to Counter Terrorism, Moscow, November 30, 2006.

MICHAEL A. COHEN and **MARIA FIGUEROA KÜPÇÜ** are co-directors of the Privatization of Foreign Policy Initiative at the New America Foundation.

From *World Policy Journal,* by Michael A. Cohen and Maria Figueroa Kupcu, 23:4 (Winter 2007), pp. 49–54. Copyright © 2007 by The World Policy Institute. Reprinted by permission of MIT Press Journals.

UNIT 7

Terrorism and Religion

Unit Selections

Key Points to Consider

- Why is it important to understand terrorist ideologies?

- Why is the identification of moderate Muslims important?

- Do Islamic schools contribute to the problem of terrorism?

Student Website
www.mhcls.com

Internet References

Free Muslims Against Terrorism Jihad
http://www.freemuslims.org/news/articles.php?article=140
Islam Denounces Terrorism
http://www.islamdenouncesterrorism.com
Religious Tolerance Organization
http://www.religioustolerance.org/curr_war.htm

Over the past decade, the topic of religion has played an increasingly prominent role in discussions of international terrorism. Fears of a resurgence of fundamentalist Islam have spawned visions of inevitable clashes of civilizations. Even before the events of September 11th, the term religious terrorism had become a staple in the vocabulary of many U.S. policymakers.

While there is currently no commonly accepted definition of religious terrorism, one should note that in the popular press the term religious terrorism is often used as a euphemism for political violence committed by Muslims. It is naïve to presume that all political violence committed by members of a particular religious group is necessarily religious violence. The relationship between religion and political violence is much more complex.

Experts have noted that many of today's religious terrorists were nationalists yesterday and Marxists the day before. Unlike their historical predecessors like the *Thugs* in India who killed to sacrifice the blood of their victims to the Goddess *Kali,* today's religious terrorists see violence as a means of achieving political, economic, and social objectives. Religion is often seen as a means, rather than an end in itself. In many cases religious ideologies have taken over where other ideologies have failed.

Ideologies are systems of belief that justify behavior. They serve three primary functions: (1) They polarize and mobilize populations toward common objectives; (2) They create a sense of security by providing a system of norms and values; and (3) They provide the basis for the justification and rationalization of human behavior. Ideologies do not necessarily cause violence. They do, however, provide an effective means of polarizing populations and organizing political dissent.

While the emergence of religious ideologies signals an important shift in international terrorism, the role of religion in international terrorism is often exaggerated or misunderstood. Religion is not the cause of contemporary political violence. It does, however, provide an effective means for organizing political dissent. In some parts of the world political extremists have infiltrated the mosques, temples, and churches and have managed to hijack and pervert religious doctrine, superimposing their own views of the world and encouraging the use of violence.

The three articles in this unit provide an overview of the relationship between religion and terrorism. In the first selection, Dale Eikmeier highlights the basic tenets of Qutbism. He argues that an understanding of the enemy's ideology is crucial to long-term success against terrorism. The second article argues that distinguishing between moderate and extremist Muslim groups

© D. Falconer/PhotoLink/Getty Images RF

is essential. It focuses on the difficulty and importance of identifying moderate Muslim groups which may serve as an antidote to radical Islam and offers a six question litmus test to identify groups that "merit support and consideration." The last selection in this unit examines the role of Islamic schools in terrorist training. It argues that highly educated individuals are more likely to be involved in major attacks than those who attended religious schools.

Qutbism: An Ideology of Islamic-Fascism

Dale C. Eikmeier

The recently published *National Military Strategic Plan for the War on Terrorism* (NMSP-WOT) is to be commended for identifying "ideology" as al Qaeda's center of gravity.[1] The identification of an ideology as the center of gravity rather than an individual or group is a significant shift from a "capture and kill" philosophy to a strategy focused on defeating the root cause of Islamic terrorism. Accordingly, the plan's principal focus is on attacking and countering an ideology that fuels Islamic terrorism. Unfortunately, the NMSP-WOT fails to identify the ideology or suggest ways to counter it. The plan merely describes the ideology as "extremist." This description contributes little to the public's understanding of the threat or to the capabilities of the strategist who ultimately must attack and defeat it. The intent of this article is to identify the ideology of the Islamic terrorists and recommend how to successfully counter it.

Sun Tzu wisely said, "Know the enemy and know yourself; in a hundred battles you will never be in peril."[2] Our success in the War on Terrorism depends on knowing who the enemy is and understanding his ideology. While characterizing and labeling an enemy may serve such a purpose, it is only useful if the labels are clearly defined and understood. Otherwise, overly broad characterizations obscure our ability to truly "know the enemy," they diffuse efforts, and place potential allies and neutrals in the enemy's camp. Unfortunately, the War on Terrorism's use of labels contributes a great deal to the misunderstandings associated with the latter. The fact is, five years after 9/11 the NMSP-WOT provides little specific guidance, other than labeling the enemy as extremist.[3] This inability to focus on the specific threat and its supporting philosophy reflects our own rigid adherence to political correctness and is being exploited by militant Islamists portraying these overly broad descriptions as a war against Islam. As David F. Forte states "We must not fail . . . to distinguish between the homicidal revolutionaries like bin Laden and mainstream Muslim believers."[4]

Knowing the enemy requires an understanding of militant Islam's ideology and recognizing that it is the militants' "center of gravity."[5] Their extremist ideology has been called many things, "Militant Islam," "Salafism," "Islamism," "Wahhabism," "Qutbism," "Jihadism," and even "Islam."[6] Since most ideologies reflect the integration of various related concepts, theories, and aims that have evolved over time into a broader body of thought, no label is entirely perfect and all are subject to critique. However, it appears that President Bush has ended the debate and accepted "Islamic-Fascism" as the ideological label.[7] While Islamic-Fascism immediately conjures up images of an evil to be resisted and is therefore useful as a public relations term, intellectually it does little for the serious students of Islam or the strategic planners charged with its defeat.

So what is this ideology we label Islamic-Fascism? What are its sources, theories, aims, and who are its proponents? The answers to many of these questions can be found in a collection of violent Islamic thought called Qutbism.[8] Qutbism refers to the writings of Sayyid Qutb and other Islamic theoreticians, e.g., Abul Ala Maududi and Hassan al Banna, that provide the intellectual rationale underpinning Islamic-Fascism. Qutbism is not a structured body of thought from any single person (despite its name), source, time, or sect; rather it is a fusion of puritanical and intolerant Islamic orientations that include elements from both the Sunni and Shia sects of Islam that have been combined with broader Islamist goals and methodologies. Qutbism integrates the Islamist teachings of Maududi and al Banna with the arguments of Sayyid Qutb to justify armed jihad in the advance of Islam, and other violent methods utilized by twentieth century militants. Qutbism advocates violence and justifies terrorism against non-Muslims and apostates in an effort to bring about the reign of God. Others, i.e., Ayman Al-Zawahiri, Abdullah Azzam, and Osama bin Laden built terrorist organizations based on the principles of Qutbism and turned the ideology of Islamic-Fascism into a global action plan.

The Foundation: Puritan Islam

Qutbism is structured on a common foundation of puritan Islamist orientations such as Wahabbi, Salafi, and Deobandi.[9] These orientations share several traits and beliefs:

- A belief that Muslims have deviated from true Islam and must return to "pure Islam" as originally practiced during the time of the Prophet.[10]
- The path to "pure Islam" is only through a literal and strict interpretation of the Quran and Hadith, along with implementation of the Prophet's commands.[11]
- Muslims should individually interpret the original sources without being slavishly bound to the interpretations of Islamic scholars.[12]
- That any interpretation of the Quran from a historical, contextual perspective is a corruption, and that the majority of Islamic history and the classical jurisprudential tradition is mere sophistry.[13]

The Architects: Islamist Theoreticians

While puritan Islamic orientations set the foundation, it was Islamist theoreticians who built Qutbism's intellectual framework. One of the founding fathers of modern Islamist thought is Abul Ala Maududi

(1903–1979), a Deobandi alumni.[14] Maududi believed the Muslim community's decline resulted from practicing a corrupted form of Islam contaminated by non-Islamic ideas and culture. Maududi reminded Muslims that Islam is more than a religion; it is a complete social system that guides and controls every aspect of life including government.[15] He believed tolerance of non-Muslim rule and non-Islamic concepts and systems was an insult to God. Therefore, the only way Muslims might practice pure Islam and assume their rightful place in the world is through the establishment of Islamic states, where Islam rules independent of non-Islamic influences. These Islamic states would eventually spread Islam across the globe and establish God's reign. Maududi argued the only practical way to accomplish Islamic rule is through jihad.

Maududi explained his concepts in *Jihad in Islam.*

In reality Islam is a militant ideology and programme which seeks to alter the social order of the whole world and rebuild it in conformity with its own tenets and ideals. "Muslim" is the title of that International Militant Party organized by Islam to carry into effect its militant programme. And "Jihad" refers to that militant struggle and utmost exertion which the Islamic Party brings into play to achieve this objective.

Islam wishes to destroy all States and Governments anywhere on the face of the earth which are opposed to the ideology and programme of Islam regardless of the country or the Nation which rules it.

It must be evident to you from this discussion that the objective of Islamic "Jihad" is to eliminate the rule of an un-Islamic system and establish in its stead an Islamic system of State rule. Islam does not intend to confine this revolution to a single State or a few countries; the aim of Islam is to bring about a universal revolution.[16]

Maududi's *Jihad in Islam* articulated the goals of an evolving Islamist ideology by reiterating the strategic objective of global Islamic rule and designating jihad as the way to achieve it. Thinkers like Hassan al Banna, in *Jihad,* Muhammad Adb al Salam Faraj, *The Neglected Duty,* and Sayyid Qutb, *In the Shade of the Quran* and *Milestones* espoused similar ideas and attempted to put them into practice.[17]

Hassan al Banna (1905–1949), founder of the al-Ikhwan al-Muslimun (Muslim Brotherhood), believed, like Maududi, that a revival of "pure Islam" was the antidote to Western domination and a cure for the malady infecting the Muslim world.[18] A charismatic leader and organizer, al Banna implemented the Islamist vision by organizing the Muslim Brotherhood in 1928 with the objective of establishing government rule on the basis of Islamic values.[19] His approach was gradualist rather than revolutionary. By providing basic services to the community including schools, mosques, and factories he sought popular support for Islamist goals through persuasion.[20] However, despite this, al Banna never articulated a practical method for taking power.[21] Additionally, al Banna's domineering personality and micro-managerial leadership style created a fragile organization that fragmented following his death in 1949.

Hassan al Banna's lasting legacy was reminding Muslims that the Quran says jihad against un-believers is an obligation of all Muslims. He also argued that jihad was not just the defense of Muslim lands but a means "to safeguard the mission of spreading Islam."[22] The idea of jihad to spread Islam and to establish the Islamic state was then expanded by his contemporary Sayyid Qutb.

Sayyid Qutb (1906–1966) is regarded by some as the founding father and leading theoretician of the contemporary extremist movement.[23] According to William McCants of the US Military Academy's Combating Terrorism Center, our jihadi enemies "cite Sayyid Qutb repeatedly and consider themselves his intellectual descendants."[24] Qutb became one of the leading spokesmen and thinkers of the Muslim Brotherhood, persuasively advocating the use of violence to establish Islamic rule and like Maududi inspired thousands to take up the cause of "establishing God's rule on earth."[25] Unlike al Banna who tried to build an Islamic society from the bottom up, Qutb changed the strategy by developing a top-down approach that focused on removing non-Islamic rulers and governments.

Qutb argued that the entire world, including the Muslim, was in a state of *jahiliyah,* or ignorance where man's way had replaced God's way.[26] According to Qutb, since jahiliyah and Islam cannot co-exist, offensive jihad was necessary to destroy jahiliyah society and bring the entire world to Islam.[27] Until jahiliyah is defeated, all true Muslims have a personal obligation to wage offensive jihad. When Qutb added offensive jihad to the widely accepted concept of defensive jihad, Qutb broke with mainstream Islam and ridiculed Muslim scholars:

Those who say that Islamic Jihad was merely for the defense of the "home land of Islam" diminish the greatness of the Islamic way of life and consider it less important [than] their "homeland." . . . However, [Islamic community] defense is not the ultimate objective of the Islamic movement of jihad but it is a mean of establishing the Divine authority within it so that it becomes the headquarters for the movement of Islam, which is then to be carried throughout the earth to the whole of mankind. . . .[28]

Thus offensive jihad against non-Muslims in the cause of spreading Islam and the rule of God was not only justified, it was glorious.

In addition to offensive jihad Sayyid Qutb used the Islamic concept of "takfir" or excommunication of apostates.[29] Declaring someone takfir provided a legal loophole around the prohibition of killing another Muslim and in fact made it a religious obligation to execute the apostate. The obvious use of this concept was to declare secular rulers, officials or organizations, or any Muslims that opposed the Islamist agenda a takfir thereby justifying assassinations and attacks against them. Sheikh Omar Abdel Rahman, who was later convicted in the 1993 World Trade Center attack, invoked Qutb's takfirist writings during his trial for the assassination of President Anwar Sadat.[30] The takfir concept along with "offensive jihad" became a blank check for any Islamic extremist to justify attacks against anyone.

Fawaz A. Gerges, who claims to have interviewed Islamic terrorists in several countries, states "Qutb showed them the way forward and . . . they referred to [him] as a *shadhid,* or martyr." He describes how "jihadis look up to Qutb as a founding spiritual father, if not the mufti, or theoretician of their contemporary movement."[31] Ayman al-Zawahiri credits Qutb's execution in 1966 for lighting the jihadist fire. Al-Zawahiri claims Qutb dramatically altered the direction of the Islamist movement by forcefully driving the idea of "the urgent need to attack the near enemy" (rulers and secular governments in Muslim countries).[32]

Qutb's theory of unrestricted jihad ". . . against every obstacle that comes into the way of worshiping God and the implementation of the divine authority on earth . . ." is the intellectual basis behind the exhortations of Abdullah Azzam and Ayman al-Zawahiri and ultimately the establishment of Osama bin Laden's al Qaeda.[33]

The Contractors

Qutb's disciples, Abdullah Azzam and Ayman al-Zawahiri, introduced Osama bin Laden to Qutb's ideology. Azzam first met bin Laden when he lectured at King Adbul Aziz University in Jeddah, Saudi Arabia, where bin Laden was studying under Mohammad Qutb, Sayyid's brother.[34] In response to the Soviet invasion of Afghanistan, Azzam left Saudi Arabia and established the *Maktab al-Khadamat* or "Services Offices" in Pakistan to organize, train, and support international mujahideen fighting in Afghanistan. Bin Laden joined Azzam in 1984 and supported the mujahideen effort through his *Bait ul-Ansar* or "House of Helpers." Azzam's mentorship provided the young bin Laden the practical experience to develop the logistical and organizational skills necessary for recruiting, training, and funding a jihadi network with global reach. After the Soviet withdrawal from Afghanistan, Azzam attempted to shift the jihadi effort to Palestine. This shift created a rift with bin Laden—who was under the ideological mentorship of Ayman al-Zawahiri—over the direction of the organization. Conveniently for bin Laden, Azzam was killed in Peshawar by assassins in November 1989 and bin Laden assumed full control of the Maktab.[35]

Ayman al-Zawahiri, a prolific writer on Qutb's ideas, met Osama bin Laden during the Afghan war. Their close relationship resulted in the 1989 merger of the Maktab and Egyptian Jihad that formed al Qaeda. Al-Zawahiri served as the organization's ideologist while bin Laden was the organizer and leader.[36] Al-Zawahiri authored al Qaeda's manifesto *Knights Under the Prophet's Banner* which clearly links the Islamist's goal with Qutb's strategy of unrestricted jihad.[37] Significantly, it explains al Qaeda's rational for attacking the "far enemy" (the US, Israel, and other non-Muslim powers) first.[38]

The "far enemy first" strategy was revolutionary as it overthrew the accepted "near enemy strategy" of al Banna, Qutb, Azzam, and Faraj.[39] This shift was the result of careful strategic decisionmaking by al-Zawahiri and bin Laden. It is only natural to assume that the two compared the failures of the Muslim Brotherhood, al-Jamaa al-Islamiya, Egyptian Jihad, and other organizations to prevail over the "near enemy," to the successes of the Afghan mujahideen in their victory over the Soviets. They reasonably concluded that the "far enemy" strategy was the wiser course of action.[40]

- Advantages of Jihad against the infidel "far enemy."
  - Unifies and rallies international Muslim support.
  - Allows greater sanctuary in supportive states.
  - Is easier to portray as the defense of Islam and a religious obligation.
  - Attacks the source of power behind "apostate regimes."
  - Is easier because infidel countermeasures are limited and less effective.
- Disadvantages of Jihad against the "near enemy."
  - Splits Muslims and localizes support.
  - Subjects the organization to more effective state security organs.
  - Geography and political factors limit internal sanctuary.
  - Local politics versus religious issues confuse the members and the people, weakening their resolve.
  - Western support to apostate regimes not affected.

For these reasons al Qaeda in the 1990s focused its efforts on the "far enemy" and the United States in particular. Zawahiri and bin Laden pushed a shift from small isolated extremists attacking local apostate regimes to clear-cut and unified jihad against infidels. The intent was not so much as to destroy the West, but rather to unify Muslim masses behind al Qaeda's goals.[41] The intent of progressively spectacular attacks against US and Western interests was to drive the United States from the Middle East, thus weakening apostate Muslim regimes and increasing al Qaeda's prestige. They intended the attacks of 9/11 to provoke an inevitable infidel retaliation that would rally ordinary Muslims to global jihad in defense of Islam. Al-Zawahiri and bin Laden thought that by changing the target of the Qutbist strategy, they could turn the struggle into a war between Islam and the West. Naturally, pro-western secular regimes in Muslim lands would be the first casualties of this war. As these regimes fell they would be replaced by Islamic rule; thus setting the initial stage for further Islamic conquests.

Osama bin Laden's chief contribution to Qutbism may be his management and organizational skills. The Muslim Brotherhood's collapse after al Banna's death demonstrated the fragility of hierarchical organizations dependent on a single leader. It can be assumed that bin Laden as a business management student and protégé of Azzam learned from al Banna's mistakes and designed al Qaeda as a networked organization of franchises rather than a conventional hierarchical organization. His organizational design facilitated the rapid globalization of Qutbism and distribution of resources, while building durability and protective firewalls between cells.

Whether al Qaeda's leadership is the central planning and controlling hub or only the ideological center of loosely affiliated groups is debatable.[42] What is clear is that al Qaeda cells share Qutbist ideology and goals. This is why it is essential that the *National Military Strategic Plan for the War on Terrorism* correctly identifies ideology, not the leadership or organization of a particular group, as the center of gravity. The question then becomes how best to attack it.

Attacking the Center of Gravity

There are five "lines of operations" to be utilized in the attack on Qutbism, the ideological center of gravity for the Islamic-Fascist movement. Four of these lines are entirely the responsibility of the Muslim world: The message, the messenger(s), the ideology's supporting institutions, and the institutions of the counter-ideology. A fifth line lies in both the Muslim and non-Muslim worlds and is the defense of the universally accepted values, norms, and principles of modern civilization. Any successful strategy for the War on Terrorism requires synchronized efforts along all five lines to pressure and eventually collapse the ideological center of gravity. In theory this would strip al Qaeda and its affiliates of their source of power and bring victory in the war against the jihadi.

First Line of Operation: Attack the Message

The first and most important line of operation is attacking the Qutbist message. While the West has a supporting role, it is ultimately the responsibility of the Islamic world to lead this effort.[43] Obviously, only moderate Islam can undermine Qutbism's theological foundations. The most credible weapons in this attack are the voices of mainstream Muslims and scholars. Abdal-Hakim Murad, a British Muslim, explains:

Certainly, neither bin-Laden nor his principal associate, Ayman al-Zawahiri, are graduates of Islamic universities. And so their proclamations ignore 14 centuries of Muslim scholarship, and instead take the form of lists of anti-American grievances and of Koranic quotations referring to early Muslim wars against Arab idolaters. These are followed by the conclusion that all Americans, civilian and military, are to be wiped off the face of the Earth. All this amounts to an odd and extreme violation of the normal methods of Islamic scholarship. Had the authors of such fatwas followed the norms of their religion, they would have had to acknowledge that no school of mainstream Islam allows the targeting of civilians. An insurrectionist who kills non-combatants is guilty of *baghy,* "armed aggression," a capital offense in Islamic law.[44]

Moderate Islam's faithful should be given the encouragement and tools required to make their voices heard, so they might direct fellow Muslims who have let anger mislead them to a more radical ideology.

Creditability of a message relies not only on logic and reasoning but also on the credentials of the messenger.

One method of rescuing the jihadi from Qutbism is "hujjat" or proof. Yemeni Judge Hamoud Al-Hitar believes that terrorism has an intellectual base and it can be defeated intellectually.[45] He uses hujjat in theological dialogues that challenge and then correct the wayward beliefs of the jihadi. Hitar believes that moderate Islam can rescue the jihadi whom he believes are ordinary people that have been led astray by al Qaeda propaganda. His successful record of rehabilitation has piqued the interest of several countries that see his methodology as a powerful anti-terrorism technique.[46]

Mohammed VI, the King of Morocco, in response to the 2003 Casablanca bombings, took a number of steps to attack the extremist's message and recapture a large segment of Moroccan society (disillusioned youth) that had fallen under the influence of radical imams. He established special training programs for imams and a unique program to train female religious guides. The King's establishment of the Council of Religious Scholars, a group responsible for issuing religious edicts, was well received by Muslims.[47]

Respected Islamic leaders increasingly are speaking out against Islamic-Fascism. Sheikh-ul-Islam, Talghat Tajuddin, the Supreme Mufti of the Commonwealth of Independent States, recently challenged all Muslims to resist extremism and defend Islam:

Violent, extremist Islamists invoke on their own head the true jihad. Challenging all the peoples of the Earth, and first of all mainstream Islam, professed by the overwhelming majority of the Islamic world, these forces put themselves in opposition to Islam. And reacting against them is a religious, moral, social, and political duty of each Muslim.[48]

Attacking the message also requires a paradigm shift for moderate Muslim spokesmen. Defending Islam as a religion of peace and tolerance with the subliminal objective of blunting Western criticism of Islamic extremism does little to help in defeating the terrorist or saving Islam. These spokesmen need to shift to the offensive, targeting their rhetoric and philosophy against their own disillusioned people in an effort to expose Islamic-Fascism for the evil it is. This is probably the only way they will extract themselves and their followers from the catastrophic plague infecting Muslim culture and threatening world peace. Failure to actively pursue such a strategy might suggest that the problem is not with extremism but with the basic tenets of Islam.

Second Line of Operation: Attack the Messenger

Creditability of a message relies not only on logic and reasoning but also on the credentials of the messenger. Many of Qutbism's proponents are individuals with questionable religious credentials, yet they claim religious authority. These misrepresentations can be their achilles heel and the means to discredit them and their message. With the exception of Abul Ala Maududi and Abdullah Azzam, none of Qutbism's main theoreticians trained at Islam's recognized centers of learning. Although a devout Muslim, Hassan al Banna was a teacher and community activist. Sayyid Qutb was a literary critic. Muhammad Abd al-Salam Faraj was an electrician. Ayman al-Zawahiri is a physician. Osama bin Laden trained to be a businessman. As Muslims, al Banna, Qutb, Faraj, al-Zawahiri, and bin Laden may have the right to claim a singular understanding of God's will, the intent of the Prophet, and how Muslims should live. However, the more formally and rigorously trained, moderate Islamic scholars exercising the collective wisdom of 14 centuries of Islamic theology should be able to challenge and refute their extreme Qutbism positions.

Third and Fourth Lines of Operation: Attack Islamic-Fascism's Supporting Institutions and Support Mainstream Islamic Institutions

The third and fourth lines of operation are mirror images, one being the negative image of a positive. Moderate Islam and Islamic-Fascism essentially have the same institutional support structures which fall into three categories; educational, financial, and informational. Educational institutions include schools, universities, mosques, and centers. Funding for these institutions include private donations, charities, endowments, and state sponsorship. Informational institutions include centers, dedicated media, independent media, state controlled media, and organizational outreach. The tactic that moderate Muslims and those fighting against extremism should use is to restrict and close those institutions advocating Qutbism while promoting others that offer positive alternatives. Actions along these two lines complement one another and should be synchronized to obtain the most effective synergistic results.

Societies not only have the right to self-defense, but an obligation to protect themselves against Islamic-Fascism's use of unrestricted jihad. Aclaim of religious obligation or freedom does not supplant the right to self-defense. Simply put, the murder of non-Muslims cannot be protected under the guise of Islamic religious or cultural freedom. Therefore, any religious or secular institution supporting Qutbism should be restricted or closed. There are recognized governmental and religious authorities with the ability to enact the appropriate legislation that would facilitate restrictions on or the closing of Qutbist institutions. Conversely, institutions that provide alternatives to Qutbism or support moderate Islam need to be recognized and supported. The measures taken by the King of Morocco and others are clear examples of what can be done. Only by enabling advocates and disciples of moderate Islam can we expect to counter the siren-call of Qutbism and its associated terrorism.

Fifth Line of Operation: Inoculation

While the Muslim world wrestles with the future of Islam the rest of the world must inoculate itself against the ideology of Islamic-Fascism. Inoculation not only enables continued resistance to the spread of Islamic-Fascism but sets the stage for its eventual elimination. Inoculation comes in two ways. The first is the answer to the wartime question, what are we fighting against. The second form of inoculation answers the question, what are we fighting for. The answer to these two questions serves to immunize the societal body against the corrupting message of Islamic-Fascism. It has the associated benefit of strengthening society to fight for the elimination of such a message or philosophy.

Inoculation requires information campaigns and the education of individuals regarding the anti-human rights and religiously intolerant agenda of the Qutbists. The most effective weapon we might utilize in this campaign is the Qutbists' own words and writings. Exposing the greater society to writings promoting world conquest, the murder of non-Muslims, and total submission to a particular view of what the world should be would go a long way in alerting nations to the threat they need to be prepared to resist.

The second half of the inoculation explains to the various societies what they must protect and promote. Towards this end an information campaign is required in an effort to promote a vigorous defense of what many nations term "universally accepted values." These universal values are perhaps best summarized in the United Nations' Universal Declaration of Human Rights and the United States Bill of Rights. Treaties, conventions, constitutions, courts, and tradition have further defined these values, the result being an established and widely accepted body of norms and goals for civilized behavior. The objective in this part of the inoculation is to promote the superiority of values and principles so that societies worldwide might enthusiastically defend them against the threat posed by the Islamic-Fascists.

Conclusion

The 9/11 hijackers and London's 7/7 bombers were not poor, uneducated, and hopeless men without futures. They had futures, but were seduced by an extremist ideology disguised as an obligation to God. The *National Military Strategic Plan for the War on Terrorism* correctly identifies ideology as the center of gravity. It recognizes that this is a war of ideas between competing social and religious systems, one offering the promise of individual liberty and the other, Islamic-Fascism. To successfully defend freedom against the threat poised by Islamic-Fascism, global leaders and individuals must understand the foundation of Qutbism as primarily derived from Sayyid Qutb. Understanding Qutbism, exposing and discrediting it as an extremist theology and strategy is the most direct course to the defeat of the Islamic-Fascist movement's center of gravity and victory in the War on Terrorism.

Notes

1. *Center of Gravity,* Primary Sources of Moral or Physical Strength, Power, and Resistance; Joe Strange, *Centers of Gravity & Critical Vulnerabilities* (Quantico, Va.: Marine Corps Univ. Foundation, 1996), p. ix.

2. Sun Tzu, *The Art of War* (London, Eng.: Oxford Univ. Press, 1963), p. 84.

3. Chairman of the Joint Chiefs of Staff, *National Military Strategic Plan for the War on Terrorism* (Washington, 1 February 2006), http://www.defenselink.mil/qdr/docs/2005-01-25-Strategic-Plan.pdf, p. 3.

4. David F. Forte, *Religion is Not the Enemy,* http://www.nationalreview.com/comment/comment-forte101901.shtml.

5. *Center of Gravity,* Strange, p. ix.

6. Personal interview with Dr. Sherifa Zuhur, 31 July 2006; Email exchange with William McCants, 6 August 2006; Email exchanges with Dr. Andrew Bostom, July-August 2006.

7. "Bush: U.S. at War with 'Islamic Fascists," *CNN.com,* 10 August 2006, http://www.cnn.com/2006/POLITICS/08/10/washington.terror.plot/index.html.

8. William McCants, *Problems with the Arabic Name Game,* http://www.ctc.usma.edu/research/Problems%20with%20the%20Arabic%20Name%20Game.pdf, see also, Thomas O'Connor, *Islamist Extremism: Jihadism, Qutbism, and Wahhabism,* http://faculty.ncwc.edu/toconnor/429/429lect14.htm.

9. Islamism and Islamist are terms describing the worldwide puritanical Islamic revival movement that seeks to replace secular governments with Shari'a law and establish theocracies throughout the world. See O'Connor.

10. Khaled Abou El Fadl, *Islam and the Theology of Power,* http://www.islamfortoday.com/elfadl01.htm.

11. Ibid.

12. Ibid.

13. Ibid.

14. Abdul-Majid Jaffry, *Maulana Maududi's Two-Nation Theory,* http://www.witness-pioneer.org/vil/Articles/politics/mawdudi2.html. *Who was Abu Alaa Maududi?* http://www.thewahhabimyth.com/mawdudi.htm.

15. Abu al-Ala Mawdudi, *Human Rights, the West and Islam,* http://www.jamaat.org/islam/Human-RightsPolitical.html#Human; Abdul-Majid Jaffry; G. F. Haddad, *A Word About Mawdudi's Ideas,* http:// www.sunnah.org/history/Innovators/mawdudi2.htm; Abdul-Majid Jaffry.

16. Sayyeed Abdul-Ala Maududi, *Jihad in Islam* (Lahore, Pakistan: Islamic Publications), pp. 8, 9, and 24, http://www.islamistwatch.org/texts/maududi/maududi.html.

17. Online library, preface by Dr. A. M. A. Fahmy of the International Islamic forum, http://www. youngmuslims.ca/online_library/books/jihad/. Muhammad Adb al Salam Faraj, *The Neglected Duty,* trans., Johannes Jansen (New York: MacMillian Publishing, November 1986). Syed Qutb, *In the Shade of the Quran,* trans. by A. A. Shamis (Riyadh, Saudi Arabia: WAMY International, June 1995), [World Assembly of Muslim Youth is a Saudi nongovernmental organization that promotes Wahhabism.], http://www.youngmuslims.ca/online_library/tafsir/syed_qutb/; Syed Qutb, *Milestones* (American Trust Publications, December 1991), http://www.youngmuslims.ca/online_library/books/milestones/hold/index_2.asp.

18. Trevor Stanley, "Hassan al-Banna: Founder of the Muslim Brotherhood, Ikhwan al-Muslimum," *Perspectives on World History and Current Events,* 2005, http://www.pwhce.org/banna.html.

19. Yasser Khalil, *Hassan al-Banna–A Great Muslim and Teacher of Da'wa,* http://www.jannah.org/articles/hassan.html.

20. Ibid.

21. Stanley.

22. Hassan al-Banna, "Why Do the Muslims Fight," contained in *Jihad in Modern Islamic Thought A Collection,* ed., Sheikh Abdullah Bin Muhammad Bin Humaid, http://www.majalla.org/.

23. Fawaz A. Gerges, *The Far Enemy: Why Jihad Went Global* (Bronxville, N.Y.: Sarah Lawrence College) prologue, http://www.cambridge.org/us/catalogue/catalogue.asp?isbn=9780521791403.

24. McCants.

25. Sayyid Qutb, "The Right to Judge," contained in *Jihad in Modern Islamic Thought A Collection; Who was Sayyid Qutb,* http://www.thewahhabimyth.com/qutb.htm.

26. Jahiliyah, literally "ignorance," is a concise expression for the pagan practice of the days before the advent of the Prophet Muhammad (S. A. W.). Jahiliyah denotes all those world-views and ways of life which are based on rejection or disregard of heavenly guidance communicated to mankind through the Prophets and Messengers of God; the attitude of treating human life—either wholly or partly—as independent of the directives of God. http://www.islam101.com/selections/glossaryJ.html. See also, Sayyid Qutb, "The Right to Judge."

27. Qutb, "The Right to Judge."

28. Sayyid Qutb, "On Jihad," in *Jihad in Modern Islamic Thought A Collection.*

29. Takfir or takfeer. The term refers to the practice of excommunication or declaring that a Muslim individual or a Muslim group is apostate or non-believers. Some consider the punishment for being a Takfir death, http://atheism.about.com/library/glossary/islam/bldef_takfir.htm, http://www.pwhce.org/takfiri.html.

30. Gerges.

31. Ibid.

32. Ibid.

33. Ibid.

34. Kenneth Katzman, *Al Qaeda: Profile and Threat Assessment,* Congressional Research Service Report for Congress, the Library of Congress, 17 August 2005, http://www.fas.org/sgp/crs/terror/RL33038.pdf.

35. Ibid.

36. Christopher Henzel, "The Origins of al Qaeda's Ideology: Implications for US Strategy," *Parameters,* 35 (Spring 2005), http://www.carlisle.army.mil/usawc/Parameters/05spring/henzel.htm.

37. Youssef H. Aboul-Enein, "Ayman Al-Zawahiri's Knights under the Prophet's Banner: The al-Qaeda Manifesto," *Military Review* 85 (January–February 2005), http://usacac.army.mil/CAC/milreview/English/JanFeb05/JanFeb05/Bbobjan.pdf; Michael G. Knapp, "Distortion of Islam by Muslim Extremists," *Military Intelligence Professional Bulletin* (July–September 2002), 37–42; Nimrod Raphaeli, *Ayman Muhammad Rabi' Al-Zawahiri: The Making of an Arch Terrorist,* http://www.jewishvirtuallibrary.org/jsource/biography/Zawahiri.html; Henzel.

38. Henzel.

39. Abd al-Salam Faraj, author of *The Neglected Duty,* was a Qutbist who lead the assassination conspiracy against Anwar Sadat. He was a forceful voice that advocated attacks against the "near enemy," apostate Muslim regimes.

40. For a similar conclusion, see Giles Kepel, *The War for Muslim Minds: Islam and the West,* trans., Pascale Ghazaleh (Cambridge, Mass.: Belknap Press, 2004), pp. 1–2.

41. Henzel.

42. Katzman.

43. See Sami G. Hajjar, "Avoiding Holy War: Ensuring That the War on Terrorism is Not Perceived as a War on Islam," in *Defeating Terrorism: Strategic Issues Analysis,* ed., John Martin (Carlisle, Pa.: US Army War College, Strategic Studies Institute, January 2002), p. 17, http://www.strategicstudiesinstitute.army.mil/pubs/display.cfm?PubID=273.

44. Abdal-Hakim Murad, *Bin Laden's Violence is a Heresy Against Islam,* http://www.islamfortoday.com/murad04.htm.

45. James Brandon, "Koranic Duels Ease Terror," *The Christian Science Monitor,* 4 February 2005, p. 1, http://www.csmonitor.com/2005/0204/p01s04-wome.html.

46. Peter Willems, "The Dialogue Committee is Known Internationally," *Yemen Times,* http://www.yementimes.com/article.shtml?i=799&p=community&a=2.

47. Scheherezade Faramarzi, "Female Preachers Graduate," *Associated Press,* 4 May 2006.

48. Sheikh-ul-Islam, Talghat Tajuddin in a speech "The Threat of Islam or the Threat to Islam," Moscow, 28 June 2001, trans., M. Conserva, http://www.islamfortoday.com/tajuddin01.htm.

COLONEL DALE C. EIKMEIER is a strategic planner at the US Army War College's Center for Strategic Leadership. He has held a variety of command and staff assignments in CONUS, Europe, the Middle East, and Asia. He recently served as a strategist with the Multinational Forces-Iraq where he worked with the Iraqi National Security Advisor's staff. He also served as a staff augmentee planner with the J3, US Central Command, Forward, in support of Operation Enduring Freedom.

From *Parameters,* by Dale Eikmeier, Spring 2007 pp. 85–97. Published in 2007 by U.S. Army War College. Reprinted by permission.

In Search of Moderate Muslims

JOSHUA MURAVCHIK AND CHARLES SZROM

Ever since his first post-9/11 speech summoning the nation to a war against terrorism, President Bush has stressed that "our war is against evil, not against Islam." Indeed, his administration has branded the terrorists as "traitors to their own faith"—outlaws who are "trying, in effect, to hijack Islam itself."

There is no reason to doubt the sincerity of such pronouncements. But they also reflect a strategic imperative—namely, to prevent the jihadists from attracting wide support in the Muslim world. The goal of Bush's policy is, rather, to call forth the Muslim majority *against* the acts and ideology of the terrorists. As the Middle East scholar Daniel Pipes has put it: "radical Islam is the problem and moderate Islam the solution."

This is one facet of U.S. policy on which there has been virtually no dissent. But it begs the question: what exactly is moderate Islam, and where can we find it?

The term itself is perhaps unfortunate. "Moderate" implies a lesser quantity or degree of something. A moderate leftist, for example, is not too far left. Is a "moderate Muslim" not too Islamic? To put it this way is to concede that Islam is, properly understood, antithetical to the West, and that at issue is only the intensity of the antipathy. By implication, this is to accept that terrorism is a natural corollary of an exacting fidelity to Islamic tenets—the very premise we presumably deny.

It is true that Islam's fierce dogma of monotheism insists that the world in its entirety must come to acknowledge Allah and the teachings of his unique messenger. Passages of Islamic Scripture imply a relentless war until this goal is achieved. But, as always with Scripture, contrary inferences may be drawn from other passages. In any case, non-Muslims clearly cannot accept a Muslim doctrine of war against them and, if need be, will surely meet war with war. At the same time, it is scarcely the place of non-Muslims to tell Muslims how pious their practice ought to be or how intense their devotion to their faith. If the premise of our fight against terrorism is that Muslims must become less devout, then the prospects for success will be both poor and beyond our control.

When we speak of moderate Muslims as a counterweight to extremists, then, what we seek has nothing to do with the ardor of their religious convictions. Rather, it centers on the acceptance or rejection of pluralism. In this view, Muslims may still hope and pray for the eventual recognition by all mankind of the truth of Muhammad's message. (Christians and Jews do something similar.) But they may not take up the sword to hasten the advent of that goal or pursue disputes among or within countries by violent means. That implies democratic methods and a spirit of tolerance.

But if this explains what we mean—or ought to mean—by moderate Muslims, where can we find them, and how can we tell the real thing?

Kamran Bokhari is a one-time adherent of Islamism who broke with its ideology and is now a student of radical Islam and the director of Middle East analysis for the private intelligence firm StratFor. Bokhari has developed a useful taxonomy to distinguish among four different groups who are often all identified as moderate Muslims.

The first are ordinary citizens of Muslim countries for whom faith but not politics is central to their lives. They pray daily, fast during Ramadan, make the Haj if they can afford to, but evince little interest in public affairs. Constituting a kind of silent majority, they do not participate in violent actions, and mostly do not support them.

The second group of moderates is made up of regimes, like those in Egypt or Jordan, whose "moderation" consists in alignment with the West. A third group comprises secular liberals who are largely in sympathy with the political and cultural values of the West; well-known examples include the late Egyptian novelist Naguib Mahfouz and the Iraqi writer Kanan Makiya.

Finally, there are various self-described Islamists who dissent from the violent ways or extreme doctrines of other Islamists. These "moderate Islamists," so it is claimed, are searching for an analog to European Christian Democracy: to wit, a political stance that is in some sense inspired or informed by religious ideals but is neither dogmatic nor exclusionary.

Bokhari's first two categories—the apolitical silent majority and the Western-allied regimes-are what they are. The former, precisely on account of their quiescence, are not likely to carry much political weight, and the latter, while valuable, not only are incapable of delivering victory in the war against terror but, through their denial of political freedoms, probably also feed terrorism. It is rather among the third and fourth groups—secular liberals and moderate Islamists—where new leverage or assets in the war against terror may perhaps be found.[1] And it is these two groups and, sometimes, the relationship between them that have been the focus of the greatest amount of conjecture and debate.

Secular liberals are of course the group with the greatest affinity for democracy and other Western values.[2] Unfortunately, the results of recent elections in Egypt, Iraq, and the Palestinian Authority seem to have proved that their views command little allegiance in the Muslim Middle East, especially when stacked up against the apparently irresistible force of Islamism. Nonetheless, in Egypt, despite pervasive vote rigging, the secularist Ayman Nour won 8 percent of the vote for the presidency against Hosni Mubarak in 2005. The same year, in Iraq, Iyad Allawi's Iraqi List won a similar percentage, and other secular parties also won some seats in parliament. These groups represent minorities, but not negligible ones.

In the Palestinian Authority, the secular Fatah lost narrowly in 2006 to Hamas and, according to polls, would almost surely win a rematch today. While secular, Fatah is historically anything but liberal; in fact, it was a pioneer of terrorism. Yet today, while hardly purged of terrorists, it counts some important liberals in its camp, notably Prime Minister Salam Fayad and Foreign Minister Riad Malki.

The example of Fatah is a reminder that, for decades, the region's dominant ideologies—Baathism, pan-Arab Nasserism, Arab socialism, Communism—were strongly secular and often anti-religious in character. In the 20th century, the Muslim Middle East embraced a variety of authoritarian secular ideologies; is it not conceivable that it might some day embrace democratic secularism as well? Although secular liberals are very much in the minority, and we cannot invest our regional interests in them alone, they are the embodiment of the values that we wish to nurture. Even as we seek other allies, it would be moral and political folly to abandon them.

This brings us to the Islamist movement, or to certain elements of it. Originating in 1928 in Egypt's Muslim Brotherhood, Islamism took wing following the triumph of the 1979 Iranian revolution, which gave birth to the first "Islamic Republic." As it has spread, so has it become increasingly variegated. Some factions, starting with al Qaeda, are violent in the extreme. Others eschew violence or, after having once embraced it, have now come to renounce it.

It is among these non-violent Islamists that moderates—genuine or illusory—have been sighted. Virtually everywhere in the Middle East, Islamist groups are in opposition, and often they are the most powerful opposition force on the scene. As victims themselves of human-rights abuses like arbitrary arrest and torture, they often espouse democracy and human rights, and at least in the near term they may be the ones with the most to gain from free elections. That is why, in the context of America's turn to democracy promotion, they have appeared to be theoretically plausible allies.

Early advocates of such an alliance have included some (but hardly all) indigenous liberals. Anguished by their own weakness in the face of oppressive regimes, they have looked to the Islamists, with their larger and more devoted followings, as a counterweight. The thought is nothing new. In *Sugar Street* (1957), the third volume of his magnificent "Cairo Trilogy," the novelist Naguib Mahfouz portrays two activist brothers, a Communist and an Islamist, in pre-Nasser times. To the dismay of the Communist, meetings hosted by his Islamist brother draw much larger crowds; but an elder comrade in whom he confides reassures him that, ultimately, the Islamists will serve the Communists' objectives:

Don't you see that they use our language when appealing to the mind and speaking of socialism in Islam? Even reactionaries feel obliged to borrow our vocabulary. If they pull off a revolution before we do, they will realize at least some of our objectives. They will not be able to stop time's progressive motion.

The current iteration of this tale began with the 2000 imprisonment of Saad Edin Ibrahim, the dean of Egyptian dissidents. Conducting a jail-house dialogue with Islamist prisoners, Ibrahim came away convinced that they could be valuable allies. He wrote:

Based on my 30 years of empirical investigation into these parties—including my observations of fellow inmates during the fourteen months I spent in an Egyptian prison—I can testify to a significant evolution on the part of political Islam. In fact, I believe we may be witnessing the emergence of Muslim parties that are truly democratic, akin to the Christian Democrats in Western Europe after World War II.

By the time of the 2006 war in Lebanon, spurred perhaps by anger over Israel's military actions, Ibrahim went further, depicting Islamists in general-not only peaceful ones—as the region's true democrats:

The Arab people do not respect the ruling regimes, perceiving them to be autocratic, corrupt, and inept.... [M]ainstream Islamists with broad support, with developed civic dispositions, and with services to provide are the most likely actors in building a new Middle East. In fact, they are already doing so through the Justice and Development party (AKP) in Turkey, the similarly named PJD in Morocco, the Muslim Brotherhood in Egypt, Hamas in Palestine, and, yes, Hizballah in Lebanon.

Ibrahim's openness to Islamists was echoed somewhat more continuously by the respected Egyptian scholar Amr Hamzawy of the Carnegie Endowment for International Peace:

In today's Arab world, Islamists have assumed the role once played by national liberation movements and leftist parties. They are the mass movements of the 21st century.... Like all successful movements, Islamists have been able to distill a long, complex philosophical tradition into simple slogans that have quickly supplanted the pan-Arabism and socialism that dominated the region until the 1970s. As a result, in most countries Islamists represent the only viable opposition forces to existing undemocratic regimes.

Hamzawy, like others, has in mind especially the Muslim Brotherhood, the granddaddy of all Islamist groups and the one that in Egypt's 2005 parliamentary elections bested the ruling National Democratic party in most of the (carefully chosen) districts in which it entered candidates. The Brotherhood thereby demonstrated its potential to challenge the power of the incumbents. This result may have had something to do with the fact that, a year earlier, it had issued a "reform initiative" stressing "respect for partisan plurality, free elections, and the rotation of power" as well as (in the words of its spokesman) "complete equality in rights and duties" for Egypt's Christian Copts and women. To underscore its new stance, in 2004 the Brotherhood even began to replace its traditional slogan, "Islam is the answer," with a new one: "Freedom is the answer." (The change attracted more notice than the Brotherhood's subsequent reversion to the original in time for the 2005 election.)

At first, the American government was unmoved by the arguments of Ibrahim and Hamzawy. Secretary of State Rice reaffirmed U.S. policy: "we're going to respect Egyptian laws.... We have not engaged the Muslim Brotherhood and . . . we won't." But others began to voice an interest in dialogue and even cooperation. According to Joshua Stacher, an Egypt specialist at Syracuse University,

> Empirical evidence demonstrates that the Brotherhood is just as committed—if not more committed—to civil nonviolence than other democracy movements that the United States has belatedly supported in places such as the Philippines, South Africa, and Indonesia. Yes, the Brotherhood is socially conservative. But the group is also politically pragmatic, believes in institutional development, and responsibly opposes authoritarian government.

A less bold but more influential statement of the same perspective appeared in *Foreign Affairs* under the title, "The Moderate Muslim Brotherhood." According to its authors, Robert S. Leiken and Steven Brooke, both of the Nixon Center, Egypt's Islamists would not only speed democratization by counterbalancing authoritarian regimes but serve other U.S. policy goals as well. While, they wrote, "critics speculate that the Brotherhood helps radicalize Muslims, in fact it appears that the Brotherhood works to dissuade Muslims from violence, instead channeling them into politics and charitable activities." Indeed, in Egypt, rather than "pursuing a divisive religious or cultural agenda," the Brotherhood "followed the path of toleration."

The *Foreign Affairs* essay grew out of a report commissioned by an arm of the American government and presented at a State Department seminar. This in itself signaled a new official interest in an opening to the Brotherhood—a group that, after all, held 88 seats in the Egyptian parliament. Last April, some Brotherhood legislators, including Mohammed Saad al-Katatni, the leader of the group's parliamentary bloc, attended a reception for a visiting U.S. congressional delegation hosted by the American ambassador, Francis J. Ricciardone. When Ricciardone came under criticism for this supposed faux pas, a "senior U.S. official" reassured *Newsweek* that "the invite to el-Katatni was 'cleared' by the State Department."

And indeed the interest of the U.S. government in talking to representatives of the Brotherhood is easy to understand. Had not Washington hobbled itself in the Iranian crisis of 1979 by having previously acquiesced in the shah's demand that we have no contact with his opposition? Nevertheless, to talk with the Brotherhood was one thing, to look to it as a force for democracy or moderation quite another.

In their essay, Leiken and Brooke make much of the Brotherhood's participation in Egyptian elections, contrasting this to the stance taken by the likes of Abu Musab al-Zarkawi, head of al Qaeda in Iraq, who threatened to treat all voters as "infidels." Jihadists, they write, "loathe the Muslim Brotherhood . . . for rejecting global jihad and embracing democracy." But how much is proved when a group that is excluded from power espouses democracy? As Abdul Rahman al-Rashed, the Saudi journalist who now heads the al-Arabiya television network, has put it, "The problem is not in giving power to Islamists—the problem is that [afterward] it will be impossible to take it out of their hands by democratic means."

In the case of the Brotherhood, one powerful reason to heed al-Rashed's warning is the fact that the organization is not itself democratic. Instead, it is headed by a "General Guide" who is elected for life by the fifteen-member General Guidance Council. Nor is the council itself elected by the rank-and-file; rather, it

perpetuates itself by selecting new members to fill vacancies as they occur. The entire structure of the organization is top-down, resembling the so-called "democratic centralism" of Western Communist parties. And the membership is secret.

It may be objected that the group is officially outlawed in Egypt and therefore forced into clandestine practices. But it enjoys enough breathing room to have run an open and highly successful national-election campaign, so surely it could democratize itself if this were among its priorities. A better glimpse into the group's ethos was offered in 2005 when, splitting away from the movement, some members complained in a public statement that the Brotherhood's internal dictum was: "I listen and I obey."

As for the Brotherhood's endorsement of women's rights, the only female among the hundred-plus candidates fielded in the 2005 election signified her own views in an article she wrote for the Brotherhood website entitled, "Men are Superior to Women." And as for minorities, when an Alexandria court ruled in April 2006 that the interior ministry should allow citizens of the Baha'i faith to list their religion on identity cards, Brotherhood members of parliament responded with outrage, arguing in debate a month later that adherents of Baha'i were apostates who deserved death. Finally, contrary to the Brotherhood's protestations of democratic conviction, statements in its literature and by some leaders confirm that it aims to create a new caliphate over the Islamic world.

If the Brotherhood is lacking in democratic credentials, what of its claim to moderation? True, the group does not engage in violence and has strongly condemned terror bombings in Egypt and some other Arab countries. On the other hand, it applauds the killing of Israelis in general and of Americans in Iraq. In an interview with an Egyptian weekly, General Guide Muhammad Mahdi Akef formulated the position as follows:

> The Muslim Brotherhood movement condemns all bombings in the independent Arab and Muslim countries. But the bombings in Palestine and Iraq are a [religious] obligation. This is because these two countries are occupied countries, and the occupier must be expelled in every way possible. Thus, the movement supports martyrdom operations in Palestine and Iraq in order to expel the Zionists and the Americans (translation by MEMRI).

This statement consciously makes no mention of a country called Israel. As Akef explained on another occasion, "There is nothing in our dictionary called 'Israel,'" only "Zionist gangs that occupied an Arab land after kicking out its residents." In a similar vein, Akef has called the Holocaust a "myth." The symbol of the Muslim Brotherhood is a Qur'an bracketed by crossed swords, and its pronouncements—like the chants of its demonstrators—continue to affirm the importance of jihad. Its website, moreover, features an article explicitly rejecting any attempt to define jihad "in an apologetic way that stresses only the dimension of individual self-discipline." Rather, jihad can, "of course, entail the use of force when peaceful means are not successful."

Leiken and Brooke, among others, argue that some younger Brotherhood members hold more liberal views. No doubt; but as the Brotherhood worked on a new party platform late last year, the elders seemed firmly in control. The draft program, leaked to the press, contained a number of relatively liberal formulations, but it also explicitly advocated the exclusion of women and non-Muslims from the nation's highest offices. More startling, it sought the creation of a Supreme Ulama Council as a supervisory body above Egypt's civilian government—a Sunni version of the Iranian system of theocracy.

The Egyptian Brotherhood is the original Islamist group, but today there are scores, perhaps hundreds, of others. To start with, national branches of the Brotherhood exist all over the Arab world. The exact relationship among them is murky, both because of the group's secrecy and because, although organized by country, the Brotherhood does not believe in countries but in a transnational caliphate. (When challenged on his statement that he would prefer to be ruled by a Muslim foreigner than an Egyptian Christian, the General Guide reportedly responded *"toz fi Masr,"* a colloquialism that translates roughly as "screw Egypt.") Nonetheless, the national branches do appear to vary considerably in the degree of their militancy.

The Syrian version, for example, is probably the most moderate, and has allied itself strongly with secular forces—liberal and otherwise—against the long-incumbent Baathist regime. Its head, Ali Sadreddin Bayanouni, has publicly criticized the Egyptian Brotherhood's draft platform, arguing that "adopting the democratic system means accepting its results. . . . We don't need, in Egypt or Syria, an article stating that the president or prime minister should not be a woman."

By contrast, the Brotherhood's Palestinian version is the Islamic Resistance Movement, or Hamas. Although some detect moderation even here (see, for example, "Hamas: The Perils of Power" by Hussein Agha and Robert Malley in the *New York Review of Books*, March 9, 2006), Hamas revealed its true attitude toward democracy in its armed putsch in Gaza and its openly expressed ambition to repeat the act in the West Bank. As for "peace," the group backs its implacable demand for the destruction of Israel with a war of terror against Israeli civilians checked only by Israel's retaliatory assassination of its leaders. Hamas's resistance to territorial compromise is embedded in its charter, which declares that

> the land of Palestine is an Islamic Waqf consecrated for future Muslim generations until Judgment Day. It, or any part of it, should not be squandered: it, or any part of it, should not be given up.

Nor is Hamas willing to stop once it has thrown the Jews into the sea. Its charter adds: "the same goes for any land the Muslims have conquered by force." In other words, after Tel Aviv come Andalusia, Tours, and the suburbs of Vienna.

Still more diverse than the Brotherhood's various branches is the array of splinter groups that have broken away from it. In Egypt, for example, the Brotherhood's renunciation of violence in the 1970s—a step taken under duress—led to the formation of Islamic Jihad and Jamaat al-Islamiya. The former, which spawned Osama bin Laden's lieutenant Ayman al-Zawahiri, carried out the 1981 assassination of President Anwar Sadat. The latter staged the 1997 massacre of 58 foreign tourists at Luxor.

On the other hand, there have also been splitoffs in a moderate direction. Most notable is the Hizb al Wasat (Party of the Center), which broke away in the 1990s and applied for legal recognition. When the government refused to license it, a portion of al Wasat's members returned to the Brotherhood, giving rise to suspicions that it had all along been a ploy to create a front (the Brotherhood itself not being allowed to act as a party). But for a decade since then,

al Wasat's top leader, Abu Elela Madi, and those of his followers who did not return to the Brotherhood, have tried repeatedly to become licensed and in the process have forged a profile at variance with the Brotherhood's.

In the group's latest application for official recognition, women make up a quarter of the "founders," a list that also included a handful of Copts (although they later withdrew). Elela Madi himself insists that "we are against religious parties that are based on a religious basis and adopt the theocratic thinking of clergymen." He has also denounced the "idea of a caliphate" as "not supported with a single decisively clear [Islamic] text." In 2005, when one of us asked Elela Madi whether his party favored continued recognition of Israel, he replied that it had taken no position on the matter but that he himself did.

Aside from the various sections and offshoots of the Brotherhood, other Islamist groups have emerged out of the fanatical Wahhabi sect of Saudi Arabia, and from the various non-Arab reaches of the Muslim world, notably Iran, Southeast Asia, and Turkey.

Turkey's Justice and Development party (AKP) is especially noteworthy because of the strategic importance of that country and its historic role, forged by Ataturk, as a model of secularization. In addition, this party provides the rare example of an Islamist group that has held power won democratically, having polled pluralities of 34 percent in 2002 and 46 percent in 2007.

In office, it is true, the AKP has peeled back some elements of Kemalist secularism. Thus, AKP mayors have imposed restrictions on the sale of alcohol, while Prime Minister Tayyip Erdogan has proposed amending the constitution to repeal its ban on the wearing of headscarves in universities. Some observers have warned of more subtle and potentially far-reaching measures of Islamization, such as seeding the judiciary with Islamist magistrates.

On the other side of the ledger, however, the AKP has improved the treatment of Kurds, enacted certain legal rights for women, and maintained Turkey's alliance with the U.S. as well as friendly ties to Israel and the pursuit of union with Europe. On balance, then, the AKP's performance to date arguably strengthens the thesis that there is little to fear from Islamists who are voted into office. Yet some caveats must be added. For one thing, the AKP had shed much of its Islamist skin *before* being elected. For another, it has governed under two powerful constraints. Externally, the EU's criteria for membership leave little room for Islamization, at least as long as Turkey continues to pursue admission. Internally, the army continues to act as guarantor of the Kemalist tradition, having previously suspended democracy four times. Although the AKP's strong electoral base may inhibit such military intervention today, the party is not free to disregard the sensitivities of the generals. Would it show a different face if free of these constraints? Who is to say?

As this incomplete survey suggests, the sheer number and variety of Islamist groups make it difficult to sort and assess them. So does the absence of any Rome or Moscow to unite them or set down a central line. Another problem is uncertainty as to whether their behavior in power would match their pronouncements in pursuit of power, or, in the case of Turkey, whether they would continue to rule as they do if the pressure on them relaxed. Still another complicating factor is that the groups have often evolved in their thinking.

One recent example: Abdel-Aziz el-Sherif, predecessor of Ayman Zawahiri as the chief of Egyptian Islamic Jihad, and the author of *Basic Principles in Making Preparations for Jihad,* a canonical text for al Qaeda and other violent jihadists, has just issued a new work from his Cairo prison cell that recants his earlier opinions and proscribes violence against civilians. Although this is literally a jail-house conversion, it bespeaks an ideology lacking heavy theoretical anchors.

On top of this, Islamist groups have a certain history of dissimulation. Bin Laden, Zawahiri, and their ilk are quite frank in their mania, but others are cagier. The Muslim Brotherhood's website sometimes says one thing in Arabic and something quite different in English. And, in common with much of the rest of the Muslim world, these groups play monotonous semantic games with the word "terrorism," claiming to reject it but applauding the murder of Israeli infants as "resistance."

Such habits of dissimulation extend even to the U.S. In this country there are few avowedly Islamist organizations, but several groups have abetted or fronted for the radicals The American Muslim Council (AMC), for example, defines itself as "a political movement for the civil rights and justice for all Americans," and its representatives have been feted at the White House and delivered benedictions for the House of Representatives. But the AMC evidently prefers Islamic theocracy to the American system of government. Using what is almost certainly an apocryphal quotation, one of its publications explains:

> As America today touts democracy as though it is morally engraved, it might do well to remember the astute observation of the esteemed British scholar and philosopher, George Bernard Shaw, who said about Muhammad: "I believe that if a man like him were to assume the dictatorship of the modern world he would succeed in solving the problems in a way that would bring much-needed peace and happiness."

The AMC has gone so far as to include a paean to the mastermind of 9/11 on its website: "Osama bin Laden has said he seeks the liberation of the Muslim world from American dominance. He is one man, sitting silently in a cave, praying five times a day to a force unseen, believing in the power that delivered to the others the freedom of their nations."

All of the difficulties of assessment would disappear if, at bottom, all Islamists were alike. Daniel Pipes has suggested that "mak[ing] a distinction between the mainstream Islamists and the fringe ones [is] like making a distinction between mainstream Nazis and fringe Nazis. They're all Nazis, they're all the enemy."

Is this the case? Suppose that, to continue Pipes's analogy, there had been Nazis who clearly rejected violence, as some who call themselves Islamists have done. Would they not have been meaningfully distinguishable from Hitler's crew? An anathema so sweeping as Pipes's can lead to classifying individuals or groups wrongly, or overlooking important transformations in attitude.

In this connection, a dispute over an American-based group between Pipes and one of us (Muravchik) may hold implications for the broader question of how we should treat the various currents of Islamism. The dispute concerns the U.S. based Center for the Study of Islam and Democracy (CSID), which espouses democracy and includes in its ranks both secularists and Islamists. In 2004, Carl Gershman, the president of the National Endowment for Democracy (NED), spoke at a CSID conference, drawing an attack from Pipes at the time and another one last year. Defending Gershman on COMMENTARY's blog *contentions,* Muravchik pointed out that he, too, had addressed a CSID conference, thus eliciting another broadside in which Pipes accused both Gershman and Muravchik of being "amateurs" on the subject of Islam (true, but hardly dispositive).

In his response to Muravchik, Pipes quoted a statement issued by "the truly moderate Muslim intellectual leaders associated with the Center for Islamic Pluralism." Naming a few CSID figures, the statement labeled the group "a front for some of the most obnoxious members of the 'Wahhabi Lobby' in America."

Among those CSID figures named was Abdulwahab Alkebsi. An American who emigrated from Yemen over 27 years ago, Alkebsi is a practicing Muslim who calls himself a secularist and among other posts has served as the director of Middle East programs at the NED. A vocal supporter of the U.S. war in Afghanistan, he has denounced bin Laden and al Qaeda in the strongest terms and has unequivocally condemned suicide bombings in Israel. Critics in the Egyptian press recently attacked Alkebsi as an "American traitor" and one of the "American [Trojan] horses" in the Arab world.

But the centerpiece of Pipes's 2004 critique of Gershman, from which the whole dispute flowed, had been another figure in CSID. This was Kamran Bokhari, nailed by Pipes as a former spokesman for al Muhajiroun, a group so fanatic that it praised the 9/11 attacks on America. Bokhari is the same scholar whose taxonomy of Islamism we have drawn on for this article. He had indeed been an Islamist and had joined al Muhajiroun in the mid-1990s while a student at Southwest Missouri State University; but he left the group when he recognized its radicalism, years before 9/11. No longer considering himself an Islamist, but remaining a devout Muslim, Bokhari has written one of the boldest essays about Muslims and terrorism that we have seen. He did it, moreover, not for outside consumption but in the *Muslim Public Affairs Journal,* whose readers are mainly fellow Muslims. This is his message:

> The threat to Islam and Muslims does not come from the United States or the West; rather, it comes from the extremists who operate freely within our midst. It is high time that Muslims end their silence about terrorism under the guise of supporting "legitimate armed freedom struggles." The attacks of September 11, 2001, should have been a wake-up call for Muslims everywhere that there is something wrong with their communities, that they have neglected to take stock of a cancer of extremism that has now grown into a beast of global proportions. . . . While the vast majority of Muslims do not support terrorism, the fact is that they also do not do anything against it. Poisoned by conspiracy theories on how the American and Israeli intelligence agencies were behind 9/11, a large number of Muslims are focusing on the "war against Islam and Muslims" and hence fail to see that radical and militant Islamists are waging a far more lethal war against Islam and Muslims.

This is exactly the message Americans have been hoping that Muslim opinion leaders would address to their religious brethren. It is also presumably what Daniel Pipes meant when he said that "moderate Islam is the solution." Yes, it comes from a former Islamist. But is that a bad thing or a good thing? Such cold-war heroes as Whittaker Chambers, Sidney Hook, Arthur Koestler, Milovan Djilas, and many others were former Communists. Few can understand the malign logic of a totalitarian ideology as well as those who have been inside it themselves—or inside cognate ideologies like the socialism of Britain's Labor Foreign Minister Ernest Bevin, who invented NATO, or of the Portuguese leader Mario Soares, who led the pivotal fight to snatch his country from the grasp of the Communists in 1974.

Is it possible that former Islamists could play a role akin to that of former Communists, or that moderate Islamists could approximately resemble anti-Communist socialists? To close our eyes to this possibility is to handicap ourselves—a handicap illustrated, as it happens, by Pipes's reliance on the Center for Islamic Pluralism as an exemplar of the "moderate Islam" he himself seeks. For this center is largely a one-man operation run by Stephen Schwartz, a former Trotskyist who converted to Islam in 1997. In speaking to Muslim audiences he adopts the middle name of Suleiman, but how many Muslims does Pipes believe are ready to look to Schwartz for leadership? If he is the answer to our search for "moderate Islam," then our prospects are dim indeed.

To be open to Islamist moderates or to Islamists-in-transition does not mean to hold back from critical scrutiny. In most Islamist groups, as our discussion of the Muslim Brotherhood makes clear, there is little moderation to be found. Nevertheless, one reason to favor talking even to some who are not moderates is that we should not miss the opportunity to probe weaknesses in their ideology. As compared with Communism, Islamism has the advantage of being genuinely rooted among Muslims in a way that Communism was never rooted among the "proletarians" for whom it claimed to speak. Communism, on the other hand, enjoyed the advantage of looking hopefully to an imaginary future, whereas Islamism, problematically, looks to an imaginary past; its ideal is to live like the Prophet and his companions. But this is a hopeless model. Not even the most extreme jihadist is prepared to trade his house for a tent, his car for a camel, his Kalashnikov and explosives for a sword and spear? Perhaps that dreary vision is why so many prefer to focus on the enticements that await them in the beyond.

In addition, there are others worthy of more sympathetic consideration. Besides the Turkish AKP and the Egyptian al Wasat, there is the new Wasatia party in the Palestinian territories. A particularly intriguing case, this last group was founded in March 2007 by Muhammad Dajani, director of the American Studies Institute at al-Quds University in Ramallah and a former Fatah member. Wasatia represents an attempt to create an alternative to both Fatah and Hamas. It calls for a two-state solution and recognizes Israel's right to exist. As for the "right of return" for Palestinian refugees, Dajani says: "Why create such a big obstacle to the peace process when it is just not practical?" Wasatia argues strongly against the violence practiced by Hamas and many of Fatah's proxies. Dajani puts it this way: "Our goal is to teach youth that suicide bombing is not Islam."

In considering these and other groups, it is even possible to set out some basic criteria by which to judge whether they are indeed parties with whom America might pursue a constructive relationship. That their politics are informed by religious values is not in itself a disqualification; nor need they be explicitly pro-American, although it would be hard to cooperate with any who are consistently anti-American. As we see it, there are six questions to be asked of any such group.

- Does it both espouse democracy and practice democracy within its own structures?
- Does it eschew violence in pursuit of its goals?
- Does it condemn terrorism?
- Does it advocate equal rights for minorities?
- Does it advocate equal rights for women?
- Does it accept a pluralism of interpretations within Islam?

Any group that meets these six criteria seems to us to merit support and cooperation, and groups that go a long way toward meeting them deserve at least a second look. To be sure, it would be a grievous error to chase after Islamists at the expense of the secular liberals who are our most natural allies. Even if the numbers of such liberals are small, they are our natural soul mates, and we should embrace them as warmly as they wish to be embraced by us. But just as we once found friends and allies among those who had come through the Communist mill, so we may also find friends and allies, or at least people with whom we can cooperate, among moderate Islamists or those who have come through the Islamist mill. In this connection, too, we would do well to recall that some renegades from Communism (the name of Jay Lovestone comes to mind) evolved into full-fledged anti-Communists only by stages.

Communism, for a time, seemed as if it might triumph. When he defected from Moscow's service, Whittaker Chambers wrote famously that he had joined history's losing side. By contrast, radical Islamism is a fragile and perishable ideology, and, unless we surrender, there is little possibility that it will triumph. The only question is how much damage it will do before it implodes, and the answer may be a very great deal. So long as we do not fall for the first Muslim Brother who gives us a wink and a smile, anyone who can help us to forestall the worst is worth our trouble to cultivate.

Notes

1. There is yet another formation not included in Bokhari's typology. This comprises a variety of Islamic theologians working to construct interpretations of Muslim scripture that sustain moderation, modernity, and tolerance. In the long run, this could prove to be the most important group of all, but for the time being it has little political weight.

2. "Secular" in this context is not tantamount to atheist or agnostic. Rather it signifies belief in a separation of mosque and state analogous to the practice in most of the West.

JOSHUA MURAVCHIK, a resident scholar at the American Enterprise Institute (AEI), is working on a book about Arab and Muslim democrats. **CHARLES SZROM** is a research assistant at AEI.

The Madrassa Scapegoat

PETER BERGEN AND SWATI PANDEY

M adrassas have become a potent symbol as terrorist factories since the September 11 attacks, evoking condemnation and fear among Western countries. The word first entered the political lexicon when the largely madrassa-educated Taliban in Afghanistan became the target of a U.S.-led strike in late 2001. Although none of the September 11 terrorists were members of the Taliban, madrassas became linked with terrorism in the months that followed, and the association stuck. For Western politicians, a certain type of education, such as the exclusive and rote learning of the Qur'an that some madrassas offer, seemed to be the only explanation for the inculcation of hate and irrationality in Islamist terrorists.

In October 2003, for example, Secretary of Defense Donald H. Rumsfeld wondered, "Are we capturing, killing or deterring and dissuading more terrorists every day than the madrassas and the radical clerics are recruiting, training and deploying against us?"[1] In the July 2004 report of the National Commission on Terrorist Attacks Upon the United States, commonly known as the 9-11 Commission, madrassas were described as "incubators of violent extremism," despite the fact that the report did not mention whether any of the 19 hijackers had attended a madrassa.[2] In the summer of 2005, Rumsfeld still worried about madrassas that "train people to be suicide killers and extremists, violent extremists."[3] As the United States marked the fourth anniversary of the September 11 attacks in the autumn of 2005, several U.S. publications continued to claim that madrassas produce terrorists, describing them as "hate factories."[4]

Yet, careful examination of the 79 terrorists responsible for five of the worst anti-Western terrorist attacks in recent memory—the World Trade Center bombing in 1993, the Africa embassy bombings in 1998, the September 11 attacks, the Bali nightclub bombings in 2002, and the London bombings on July 7, 2005—reveals that only in rare cases were madrassa graduates involved. All of those credited with masterminding the five terrorist attacks had university degrees, and none of them had attended a madrassa. Within our entire sample, only 11 percent of the terrorists had attended madrassas. (For about one-fifth of the terrorists, educational background could not be determined by examining the public record.) Yet, more than half of the group we assessed attended a university, making them as well educated as the average American: whereas 54 percent of the terrorists were found to have had some college education or to have graduated from university, only 52 percent of Americans

can claim similar academic credentials. Two of our sample had doctoral degrees, and two others had begun working toward their doctorates. Significantly, we found that, of those who did attend college and/or graduate school, 48 percent attended schools in the West, and 58 percent attained scientific or technical degrees. Engineering was the most popular subject studied by the terrorists in our sample, followed by medicine.

None of the apparent masterminds of the five terrorist attacks had attended a madrassa.

The data raise questions about what type of education, if any, is actually more likely to contribute to the motivation or skills required to execute a terrorist attack. Researchers such as Dr. Marc Sageman have argued that madrassas are less closely correlated with producing terrorists than are Western colleges, where students from abroad may feel alienated or oppressed and may turn toward militant Islam.[5] Given that 27 percent of the group attended Western schools, nearly three times as many as attended madrassas, our sample seems to confirm this trend. The data also show a strong correlation between technical education and terrorism, suggesting that perpetrating large-scale attacks requires not only a college education but also a facility with technology. This type of education is simply not available at the vast majority of madrassas.

These findings suggest that madrassas should not be a national security concern for Western countries because they do not provide potential terrorists with the language and technical skills necessary to attack Western targets. This is not to say that madrassas do not still pose problems. To the extent that they hinder development by failing properly to educate students in Asian, Arab, and African countries and that they create sectarian violence, particularly in Pakistan, madrassas should remain on policymakers' minds as a regional concern.[6] A national security policy focused on madrassas as a principal source of terrorism, however, is misguided.

The Truth about Terrorist Education

"Madrassa" is a widely used and misused term. In Arabic, the word means simply "school."[7] Madrassas vary from country to country or even from town to town. They can be a day or boarding school, a school with a general curriculum, or a purely religious school attached to a mosque.[8] For the purposes of our study, "madrassa" refers to a school providing a secondary-level education in Islamic religious subjects.[9] We examined information available in U.S., European, Asian, and Middle Eastern newspapers; U.S. government reports; and books about terrorism to determine which of the 79 terrorists responsible for the five major attacks attended such madrassas. In the one instance when a terrorist was found to have attended a madrassa and later a university, we classified him as a graduate of both types of schools. Attacks in which information about the terrorists' education was scant, such as the 2000 attack on the USS *Cole* and the 2004 Madrid train bombings, were excluded from the study.

The 1993 World Trade Center Bombing

On February 26, 1993, a truck bomb exploded in the parking garage beneath the twin towers of the World Trade Center, killing six people and injuring more than 1,000. Ringleader Ramzi Yousef had hoped the bomb would kill tens of thousands by making one tower collapse onto the other. The 12 men, including Yousef, responsible for this first World Trade Center bombing were the best educated of any group we studied. All of them had some college education, with most having studied in universities in the Middle East and North Africa, and two having graduated from Western colleges. The spiritual guide of this terrorist cell, the Egyptian cleric Sheik Omar Abdel Rahman, had a master's degree and had started on his doctoral dissertation at Al Azhar University in Cairo—the Oxford of the Islamic world. Yousef, the mastermind of the plot and the nephew of the operational commander of the September 11 attacks, obtained a degree in engineering from a college in Wales. None of the attackers appeared to have attended a madrassa.

The 1998 Africa Embassy Bombings

On August 7, 1998, nearly simultaneous bombings at the U.S. embassies in Tanzania and Kenya killed 224 people. The attacks were the largest perpetrated by Al Qaeda at the time and catapulted the group and its leader, Osama bin Laden, into the public eye. The 16 attackers who orchestrated the bombings were found largely to be part of a local Al Qaeda cell. This group of men had one Western-born member, Rashed Daoud al-Owhali, who hailed from Liverpool and claimed to have been indoctrinated not at a madrassa but by audio tapes about the Afghan jihad. Recent attacks in Madrid and London have shown that immigrants and the children of immigrants living in Europe may be more dangerous than far-flung madrassa graduates. Sageman, along with scholars such as Olivier Roy and Robert S. Leiken, have noted that living in the West alienates many immigrants and has a strong correlation to Western-based terrorist activity.[10] The Africa group demonstrates another trend that later reappeared in the 2004 Madrid bombings: the formation of ties between the undereducated (and easily influenced or even criminal) and the well educated. Seven of the 16 plotters in the Africa group attended college, with two, Wadih El-Hage and Ali Mohamed, attending Western schools.

The September 11 Attacks

In the most devastating terrorist attack to date, 19 hijackers crashed three planes into the World Trade Center and the Pentagon, with a fourth plane crashing in rural Pennsylvania; nearly 3,000 people were killed. The four pilots who led the September 11 attacks all spent time at universities outside of their home countries, three of them in Germany. As the 9-11 Commission detailed, the plot took shape in Germany as they were completing their degrees.[11] The lead hijacker, Muhammad Atta, had a doctorate in urban preservation and planning from the University of Hamburg-Harburg in Germany. The 15 "muscle hijackers" vary in educational background. Little is known about some of them, including Khalid al-Mihdhar, who met the pilot, Nawaf al Hazmi, while fighting in Bosnia. Indeed, several of the terrorists we studied, if they were not well educated, were so-called career jihadists with experience fighting in regions such as Bosnia and Afghanistan. Still, even of the muscle group, six of the 15 had completed some university studies. Finally, we also examined the so-called secondary planners, who had overall control of the operation, many of whom were longtime Al Qaeda operatives, and found that all of them had attended college in Europe or the United States. Khalid Sheikh Muhammad, the operational commander of the September 11 attacks, had obtained a degree in engineering from a college in North Carolina.

Despite the fact that much of the information about the educational backgrounds of the September 11 planners and pilots has been widely reported, otherwise sophisticated analysts persist in believing that they were the products of madrassas. In his 2005 book *Future Jihad*, Walid Phares, a professor of Middle Eastern studies at Florida Atlantic University and a frequent commentator on U.S. television, explained that Wahhabism "produced the religious schools; the religious schools produced the jihadists. Among them [were] Osama bin Laden and the nineteen perpetrators of September 11."[12] In fact, bin Laden did not attend a religious school when he was growing up in Jeddah, Saudi Arabia, studying instead at the relatively progressive, European-influenced Al Thagr High School and later at King Abdul Aziz University, where he focused on economics.[13] From what is available on the public record, it seems that none of the 19 hijackers attended madrassas.

Madrassas should not be a national security concern for Western countries.

The 2002 Bali Nightclubs Bombing

Islamist terrorists attacked two tourist hotspots in Bali in October 2002, killing more than 200. As was the case with the Africa embassy bombings, the Bali attack was aimed at Western targets, in this case tourists, in a non-Western country. Yet, unlike the previous examples, Bali is the only terrorist attack to have been perpetrated in part by terrorists who attended madrassas. Nine of the 22 perpetrators attended the Al Mukmin, Al Tarbiyah Luqmanul Hakiern, and SMP Pemalang pesantran—Islamic schools of a kind particular to Indonesia.

Most Indonesian madrassas are part of the state school system and teach a broad range of subjects. Pesantren, however, such as Al Mukmin, operate outside of this system and are generally boarding schools. The curriculum at pesantren usually focuses on religion and often offers practical courses in farming or small industry.[14] This constellation of schools, particularly Al Mukmin, provided many recruits to Jemaah Islamiyah, the militant Islamist group that seeks to create fundamentalist theocracies in countries across Southeast Asia.

Even in the Bali attacks, however, five of the 22 members of the group had college degrees, particularly the key planners. The mastermind of the Bali plot, Dr. Azahari Husin, who was killed in a shootout with Indonesian police in November 2005, obtained his doctorate from the University of Reading in the United Kingdom prior to becoming a lecturer at a Malaysian university.[15] Noordin Muhammad Top attended the same Malaysian school. The third mastermind, Zulkarnaen, also known as Daud, studied biology at an Indonesian college. Azahari and Top are also suspected of involvement in the 2005 Bali bombings that killed 22 people.

The July 7, 2005, London Bombings

The July 7, 2005, bombings of three subway stations and a bus in London killed 56 people, including the suicide bombers, and were the work of homegrown British terrorists with suspected Al Qaeda ties.[16] The initial news coverage of the attack featured hyperventilating reports that the four men responsible had attended madrassas. One such piece in the *Evening Standard* stated that three of the bombers attended madrassas, which it termed "haven[s] for so-called Islamic warriors."[17] In fact, three of the four suicide attackers had some college education, and none attended a madrassa until adulthood, when their attendance consisted of brief visits lasting for periods from a few weeks to a few months. The suicide bombers made a conscious decision to travel halfway around the globe to attend radical Pakistani madrassas after they had already been radicalized in their hometown of Leeds in the United Kingdom.

Of the four suicide attackers, Hasib Hussain, a man of Pakistani descent, attended Ingram Road Primary School in Holbeck and began his secondary education at South Leeds High School. Although he did not take his postsecondary school subject exams, he held a GNVQ, or vocational degree, in business studies. He visited Pakistan in 2003, when he was likely 16 or 17, after making a pilgrimage to Mecca. It was around this time that, back in England, he began socializing with two of the other bombers, Shehzad Tanweer and Muhammad Sidique Khan, with whom he frequented the Stratford Street mosque and the Hamara Youth Access Point, a teenage center in Leeds. Khan and Tanweer have similar backgrounds of elementary and secondary education in the United Kingdom. Khan later studied child care at Dewsbury College, and Tanweer studied sports science at Leeds Metropolitan University. Similar to Hussain, Tanweer traveled to Pakistan to study briefly at a madrassa in 2004, at the age of 21. The fourth bomber, Jamaican-born Germaine Lindsay, attended Rawthorpe High School in

Huddersfield in the United Kingdom and converted to Islam at the age of 15.[18] Local influences appeared to play a far greater role in the radicalization of these young men than did their brief trips to Pakistani madrassas.

Where Are Terrorists Really Educated?

History has taught that terrorism has been a largely bourgeois endeavor, from the Russian anarchists of the late nineteenth century to the German Marxists of the Bader-Meinhof gang of the 1970s to the apocalyptic Japanese terror cult Aum Shinrikyo of the 1990s. Islamist terrorists turn out to be no different. It thus comes as no surprise that missions undertaken by Al Qaeda and its affiliated groups are not the work of impoverished, undereducated madrassa graduates, but rather of relatively prosperous university graduates with technical degrees that were often attained in the West.

Bin Laden, Al Qaeda's leader, is the college-educated son of a billionaire; his deputy, Dr. Ayman al-Zawahiri, is a surgeon from a distinguished Egyptian family. Ali Mohamed, Al Qaeda's longtime military trainer, is a former Egyptian army major with a degree in psychology who started work on a doctorate in Islamic history when he moved to the United States in the mid-1980s. Other Al Qaeda leaders worked in white collar professions such as accounting, the vocation of Rifa'i Taha, a leader of the Egyptian terrorist organization known as the Islamic Group, who signed on to Al Qaeda's declaration of war against the United States in 1998.

Immigrants and their children in Europe may be more dangerous than madrassa grads.

Our findings suggest that policymakers' concerns regarding madrassas are overwrought. More than half of the terrorists that we studied took university-level courses, and nearly half of this group attended Western schools. The majority of the college-educated group had technical degrees, which sometimes provided skills for their later careers as terrorists. Yousef's degree in electrical engineering, for example, served him well when he built the bomb that was detonated underneath the World Trade Center in 1993. It was the rare terrorist who studied exclusively at a madrassa, and only one terrorist managed to transition from madrassa to university, suggesting that madrassas simply should not be part of the profile of a terrorist capable of launching a significant anti-Western attack. Only in Southeast Asia, as seen in the Bali attack in 2002, did madrassas play a role in the terrorists' education. Yet, even in this example, the madrassa graduates paired up with better-educated counterparts to execute the attacks. Masterminding a large-scale attack thus requires technical skills beyond those provided by a madrassa education.

Because madrassas generally cannot produce the skilled terrorists capable of committing or organizing attacks in Western countries, they should not be a national security concern. Conceiving of them as such will lead to ineffective policies, and cracking down on madrassas may even harm the allies that Washington attempts to help. In countries such as Pakistan, where madrassas play a significant role in education, particularly in rural areas, the wholesale closure of madrassas may only damage the educational system and further increase regional tensions. One of Gen. President Pervez Musharraf's plans to reduce extremism, expelling foreign students and dual citizens, may be effective in reducing the number of militant Arabs studying in Pakistan but may also harm neighboring countries such as Afghanistan, which rely on Pakistani madrassas, by leaving thousands of poor Afghans without any education.[19]

Cracking down on madrassas may even harm the allies that Washington attempts to help.

This is not to suggest that Western countries should ignore madrassas entirely. To the extent that they remain a domestic problem because they undermine educational development and spawn sectarian violence, particularly in Pakistan, Western policymakers should remain vigilant about working with local governments to improve madrassas, as well as state schools. Efforts at observation and regulation might be more usefully directed toward European Islamic centers such as the Hamara Youth Access Point, where the London bombers gathered. Armed with a more realistic understanding of religious schools, particularly the differences in the curricula they provide across countries and regions, policymakers can hone their strategy with respect to madrassas. Only by eliminating the assumption that madrassas produce terrorists capable of carrying out major attacks can Western countries shape more effective policies to ensure national security.

Notes

1. "Rumsfeld's War-on-Terror Memo," May 20, 2005, http://www.usatoday.com/news/washington/executive/rumsfeld-memo.htm (reproducing memo titled "Global War on Terrorism" to Gen. Dick Myers, Paul Wolfowitz, Gen. Pete Pace, and Doug Feith, dated October 26, 2003).

2. *The 9/11 Commission Report: The Final Report of the National Commission on Terrorist Attacks Upon the United States* (New York: W.W. Norton, 2004), p. 367.

3. Donald Rumsfeld, interview by Charlie Rose, *Charlie Rose Show,* PBS, August 20, 2005.

4. Alex Alexiev, "If We Are to Win the War on Terror, We Must Do Far More," *National Review,* November 7, 2005; Nicholas D. Kristof, "Schoolyard Bully Diplomacy," *New York Times,* October 16, 2005, sec. 4, p. 13.

5. See Marc Sageman, *Understanding Terrorist Networks* (Philadelphia: University of Pennsylvania Press, 2004).

6. For a detailed study of the relationship between madrassas and violence in Pakistan, see Saleem H. Ali, "Islamic Education and Conflict: Understanding the Madrassahs of Pakistan" (draft report, United States Institute of Peace, July 1, 2005).

7. Febe Armanios, "Islamic Religious Schools, *Madrasas:* Background," *CRS Report for Congress,* RS21654 (October 29, 2003), p. 1, http://fpc.state.gov/documents/organization/26014.pdf.

8. Ibid., pp. 1–2.

9. Ibid., p. 2.

10. See generally Olivier Roy, *Globalized Islam: The Search for a New Umma* (New York: Columbia University Press, 2004); Robert S. Leiken, "Europe's Angry Muslims," *Foreign Affairs* 84, no. 4 (July/August 2005): 120–135.

11. *9/11 Commission Report,* pp. 160–169.

12. Walid Phares, *Future Jihad: Terrorist Strategies Against America* (New York: Palgrave Macmillan, 2005), p. 63.

13. Peter Bergen, *The Osama bin Laden I Know: An Oral History of Al Qaeda's Leader* (New York: Free Press, 2006), chap. 1.

14. Uzma Anzar, "Islamic Education: A Brief History of Madrassas With Comments on Curricula and Current Pedagogical Practices" (draft report, March 2003).

15. Richard C. Paddok, "Terrorism Suspect Dies in Standoff," *Los Angeles Times,* November 10, 2005, p. A4.

16. See Peter Bergen and Paul Cruickshank, "Clerical Error: The Dangers of Tolerance," *New Republic,* August 8, 2005, pp. 10–12.

17. Richard Edwards, "On Their Way to Terror School," *Evening Standard,* July 18, 2005, p. C1.

18. Ian Herbert, "Portrait of Bomber as a Dupe Fails to Convince Bereaved," *Independent,* September 24, 2005, p. 16.

19. Naveed Ahmad, "Pakistani Madrassas Under Attack," *Security Watch,* October 8, 2005, http://www.isn.ethz.ch/news/sw/details.cfm?ID=12418.

PETER BERGEN is a Schwartz fellow at the New America Foundation and an adjunct professor at the School of Advanced International Studies at Johns Hopkins University. **SWATI PANDEY** is a researcher and writer at the Los Angeles Times.

From *The Washington Quarterly,* by Peter Bergen and Swati Pandey, 29:2 (Spring 2006), pp. 117–125. Copyright © 2006 by the Center for Strategic and International Studies (CSIS). Reprinted by permission of MIT Press Journals.

UNIT 8

Women and Terrorism

Unit Selections

Key Points to Consider

- Why are the experiences of women often misunderstood?

- Why do terrorist organizations recruit women?

- Should female terrorists be viewed as "portents of gender equality"?

- How should governments respond to the threat of female terrorists?

Student Website
www.mhcls.com

Internet Reference

Foreign Policy Association—Terrorism
   http://www.fpa.org/newsletter_info2478/newsletter_info.htm

Women are often portrayed as victims of political violence. The fact that women have played a critical role in the evolution of contemporary international terrorism is too frequently ignored. In the 1970s women like Ulrike Meinhof and Gudrun Ensslin of the German Baader-Meinhof Gang, Mara Cagol of the Red Brigades in Italy, Fusako Shigenobu of the Japanese Red Army, and Leila Khaled of the Palestine Liberation Organization held key roles in their organizations and significantly influenced the development of modern terrorism.

Today, while often less visible than their male counterparts, women are once again actively involved in international terrorism. Women like American Lori Berenson, a former anthropology student at MIT, who became involved with the Tupac Amaru Revolutionary Movement (MRTA) and Shinaz Amuri (AKA Wafa Idris), a 28-year-old volunteer medic who became a young Palestinian heroine after she killed herself in a suicide bombing, are the role models for a new generation of women bent on creating terror.

In the first article, Mia Bloom examines the motives of women who choose to become suicide bombers and discusses potential reasons for recruitment of women by terrorist organizations. She concludes that despite their increased involvement these women are not likely to become "portents of gender equality." In the second article, Judith Miller interviews two would-be women suicide bombers in Israel's Hasharon prison. Based on her interviews and a review of the expert literature on the subject, she explores how governments can best respond to this threat. Finally, Alisa Stack-O'Connor examines how and why terrorist organizations use women in their attacks. Focusing on their propaganda value, the obstacles they face, and the tactical advantage they provide, she emphasizes the importance of women's role in terrorist organizations.

Female Suicide Bombers

A Global Trend

MIA BLOOM

Ever since Muriel Degauque, a Belgian convert to radical Islam, blew herself up in Iraq last November, questions have surfaced about the growing role of women in terrorism. Degauque's attack occurred on the same day that Sajida Atrous al-Rishawi's improvised explosive device (IED) failed to detonate at a wedding in Amman. This apparent growing trend of women bombers has the general public and counterterrorism specialists concerned because of its implication that women will be key players in future terrorist attacks.

Yet the recent focus on female suicide bombers neglects the long history of female involvement in political violence. In reality women have participated in insurgency, revolution, and war for a long time. Women have played prominent roles in the Russian Narodnaya Volya in the nineteenth century, the Irish Republican Army, the Baader-Meinhof organization in Germany, the Italian Red Brigades, and the Popular Front for the Liberation of Palestine. Historically, however, women have mostly played supporting roles. "Society, through its body of rules and its numerous institutions, has conventionally dictated [women's] roles within the boundaries of militancy. Assisting in subordinate roles is welcomed and encouraged. Actually fighting in the war is not." [1] Most often, the primary contribution expected of women has been to sustain an insurgency by giving birth to many fighters and raising them in a revolutionary environment.

Women are now taking a leading role in conflicts by becoming suicide bombers—using their bodies as human detonators for the explosive material strapped around their waists. The first female suicide bomber, a seventeen-year-old Lebanese girl named Sana'a Mehaydali, was sent by the Syrian Socialist National Party (SSNP/PPS), a secular, pro-Syrian Lebanese organization, to blow herself up near an Israeli convoy in Lebanon in 1985, killing five Israeli soldiers. Of the twelve suicide attacks conducted by the SSNP, women took part in six of them. From Lebanon, the incidence of female bombers spread to other countries—Sri Lanka, Turkey, Chechnya, Israel, and now Iraq. Out of the approximately seventeen groups that have started using the tactical innovation of suicide bombing, women have been operatives in more than half of them. [2] Between 1985 and 2006, there have been in excess of 220 women suicide bombers, representing about 15 percent of the total. [3] Moreover, the

upsurge in the number of female bombers has come from both secular and religious organizations, even though religious groups initially resisted using women.

Their participation in suicide bombings starkly contradicts the theory that women are more likely to choose peaceful mechanisms for conflict resolution than men are—that women are inherently more disposed toward moderation, compromise, and tolerance in their attitudes toward international conflict. [4] (In fact, most existing notions of women in the midst of conflict portray them as *victims* of war rather than as perpetrators.) Complicating these notions of femininity further is the fact that the IED is often disguised under a woman's clothing to make her appear pregnant, and so beyond suspicion or reproach. On April 25, 2006, Kanapathipillai Manjula Devi, used such a tactic to penetrate a military hospital in Colombo, Sri Lanka. Posing as the wife of a soldier on her way to the maternity clinic, she gained access to the high-security facility. [5] She had even visited the maternity clinic for several weeks prior to her attack to maintain her cover. [6] The advent of women suicide bombers has thus transformed the revolutionary womb into an exploding one.

Why do women become suicide bombers? Motives vary: to avenge a personal loss, to redeem the family name, to escape a life of sheltered monotony and achieve fame, or to equalize the patriarchal societies in which they live.

In many instances, the women are seeking revenge. Consider, for example, the women who join the Liberation Tigers of Tamil Eelam (LTTE), which is based in the Tamil areas, in the northern and eastern provinces, of Sri Lanka. [7] According to anthropologist Darini Rajasingham-Senanayake, the government has committed organized violence against the Tamils through a systematic campaign of disappearances, rape, checkpoint searches, and torture—as well as the elimination of whole villages in remote areas. [8] Moreover, in the midst of conflict, the government forces have not been mindful to differentiate civilians from combatants and militants.

These oppressive tactics, along with civilian deaths, have soured the Tamil population on the government's assurances of devolution and equal rights, which in turn has emboldened the LTTE and solidified their control of Jaffna.[9] Rajasingham-Senanayake explains, "In this context militant groups who infiltrate camps have little difficulty in recruiting new cadres from deeply frustrated and resentful youth, men and women, girls and boys."[10] In fact, the atrocities need not even hurt a Tamil woman directly for her to join the LTTE, as long as they affect the Tamil community as a whole:

> Witnessing rape . . . hearing about rape from other villagers and the Army's killing of Tamil youth (girls and boys arrested by the Sri Lankan Army) . . . and the feeling of helplessness in not being able to defend against the Sri Lankan Army are the main reasons for the girls joining the LTTE.[11]

As the example of the Tamil women demonstrates, women generally become involved, at least initially, for personal, rather than ideological, reasons. In Chechnya, to give another example, the female operatives are called 'Black Widows,' because many were the sisters, mothers, or wives of Chechen men killed in battles with federal troops.[12]

Zarema Muzhikhoyeva was one such widow. On July 10, 2003, she was arrested carrying a homemade bomb on Tverskaya-Yamskaya Ulitsa.

> Muzhikhoyeva [admitted to having been] recruited by Chechen rebels as a suicide bomber, in exchange for $1,000 in compensation to her relatives to repay for jewelry she had stolen from them. . . . When the rebels sent her to Moscow to carry out her mission, she changed her mind and got herself arrested by police.[13]

Muzhikhoyeva was the first bomber to be captured alive. When the court sentenced her to the maximum of twenty years despite the fact that she had opted not to explode her cargo, Muzhikhoyeva shouted, "Now I know why everyone hates the Russians!"—adding that she would return and "blow you all up."[14] This powerful image resonated throughout the Chechen community. Even though Muzhikhoyeva had done the right thing, the Russian court had not granted her any leniency, radicalizing her even more in the process.

However, while women usually become suicide bombers in response to a personal tragedy, some may also believe they can change their society's gender norms through militant involvement. According to Clara Beyler, a counterterrorism analyst in Washington, D.C., and formerly a researcher for the International Policy Institute for Counterterrorism in Herzliya, Israel,

> There is a difference between men and women suicide attackers: women consider combat as a way to escape the predestined life that is expected of them. When women become human bombs, their intent is to make a statement not only in the name of a country, a religion, a leader, but also in the name of their gender.[15]

Again, the Chechen Black Widows provide strong support for this idea. Historically, a woman's most relevant role in Chechen society was to raise children, form their characters, and make them strong so that they became warriors for the Islamic faith (*mujahideen*) when they grew up. Even after they were allowed to be a part of battles, female insurgents were initially used merely to supply medical aid, food, and water to the men; they also carried weapons and ammunition across enemy territory and maintained the guerrillas' morale. At the Dubrovka theater siege, for example, the men took care of the explosives and intimidation, while the women distributed medical supplies, blankets, water, chewing gum, and chocolate. Though the women allegedly toyed threateningly with their two-kilo bomb belts, they did not control the detonators—the men retained control of the remotes.[16]

The Black Widows, on the other hand,

> choose to die as a bomber in order to show the strength of the resistance. They can wear kamikaze bomb-belts, or drive a truck that is full of explosives. Chechen guerrillas are inspired with the image of Khava Barayeva—the first to walk the way of martyrdom. Chechen rebels . . . write poems and songs about her.[17]

The use of female operatives, especially by a religious militant organization like the Chechen Al Ansar al-Mujahideen, is significant. Until recently, a female bomber was almost certainly sent by a secular organization. In effect,

> [t]he growth in the number of Chechen female suicide bombers signaled the beginning of a change in the position of fundamentalist Islamic organizations regarding the involvement of women in suicide attacks—a change that [has since] become devastatingly apparent.[18]

The idea of violence empowering women had already spread through the West Bank and the Gaza Strip. On January 27, 2002, Wafa Idris became the first Palestinian woman to perpetrate an act of suicide terror. A twenty-seven-year-old aid worker for the Palestinian Red Crescent Society from the Al-Am'ari refugee camp near Ramallah, she was carrying a backpack with explosives:

> The bomb in her rucksack was made with TNT packed into pipes. Triacetone triperoxide, made by mixing acetone with phosphate, is ground to a powder. In a grotesque parody of the domestic female stereotype, it is usually ground in a food mixer, before being fed into metal tubes.[19]

On the way to delivering it to someone else, she got stuck in a revolving door, detonating the explosives.[20] She killed one Israeli civilian and wounded 140 others.

Though her death was allegedly accidental, it instantly transformed her into a cult heroine throughout the Arab world. The military wing of Fatah, the Al-Aqsa Martyrs Brigades, took responsibility for the attack three days later. Birzeit students appealed for more women to emulate Idris. Commenting on Idris's death, female students stated, "The struggle is not limited strictly to men. . . . It's unusual [for a Palestinian woman to martyr herself], but I support it. . . . Society does not accept this idea because it is relatively new, but after it happens again, it will become routine."[21] And in an editorial entitled, "It's a Woman!" *Al-Sha'ab* proclaimed:

It is a woman who teaches you today a lesson in heroism, who teaches you the meaning of Jihad, and the way to die a martyr's death. It is a woman who has shocked the enemy, with her thin, meager, and weak body. . . . It is a woman who blew herself up, and with her exploded all the myths about women's weakness, submissiveness, and enslavement. . . . It is a woman who has now proven that the meaning of [women's] liberation is the liberation of the body from the trials and tribulations of this world . . . and the acceptance of death with a powerful, courageous embrace.[22]

The Al-Aqsa Martyrs Brigade even set up a special unit to train female suicide bombers and named it after Wafa Idris.[23] "We have 200 young women from the Bethlehem area alone ready to sacrifice themselves for the homeland," bragged one Al-Aqsa leader.[24] Matti Steinberg, a former special advisor on Arab affairs to the Israeli government, described how a Hamas bimonthly publication—dedicated to women—was replete with letters to the editor from Palestinian women asking for permission to participate directly in the conflict and asserting their right to be martyrs.[25]

Palestinian women have torn the gender classification out of their birth certificates, declaring that sacrifice for the Palestinian homeland would not be for men alone; on the contrary, all Palestinian women will write the history of the liberation with their blood, and will become time bombs in the face of the Israeli enemy. They will not settle for being mothers of martyrs.[26]

This participation of Palestinian women in violence had global reverberations. In 2002, Indian security forces twice went on high alert, in January and again in August, to guard against possible attacks by female suicide bombers. The suspects sprang from two Pakistan-based Islamic organizations, Jaish-e-Mohammed and Lashkar-e-Taiba, both associated with Al Qaeda. In March 2003, *Asharq Al-Awsat* published an interview with a woman calling herself 'Um Osama,' the alleged leader of the women *mujahideen* of Al Qaeda. The Al Qaeda network claimed to have set up squads of female suicide bombers—purportedly including Afghans, Arabs, Chechens, and other nationalities—under orders from bin Laden to attack the United States:

We are preparing for the new strike announced by our leaders, and I declare that it will make America forget . . . the September 11 attacks. The idea came from the success of martyr operations carried out by young Palestinian women in the occupied territories. Our organization is open to all Muslim women wanting to serve the (Islamic) nation. . . .[27]

The involvement of Palestinian women in suicide bombings has also had an extreme impact on the cultural norms of Palestinian society. Palestinians have long had a set of rules that describe and limit gender roles (although Palestinian women have been mobilized politically since the 1960s). These rules have dictated the separation of the sexes and restricted women to the private sphere—particularly in rural areas. Through violence, women

have placed themselves on the frontlines, in public, alongside men to whom they are not related. This has resulted in a double trajectory for militant Palestinian women—convincing society of their valid contributions while at the same time reconstructing the normative ideals of the society.[28]

At the same time, it is difficult to ascertain whether terrorist organizations are actually employing women out of a heightened sense of gender equality. According to Farhana Ali, an international policy analyst at the RAND Corporation:

The liberal door that now permits women to participate in operations will likely close once male jihadists gain new recruits and score a few successes in the war on terrorism. At the same time that a Muslim woman is indispensable to male-dominated terrorist groups and the war effort, she also is expendable. The sudden increase in female bombers over the past year may represent nothing more than a riding wave of al-Qaeda's success rather than a lasting effort in the global jihad. . . . [T]here is no indication that these men would allow the mujahidaat to prevail authority and replace images of the male folk-hero.[29]

Indeed, the drive to recruit women as suicide bombers may actually be little more than a tactical response to the need for more manpower. Besides adding women to their numbers, insurgent organizations can shame the men into participating, in the style of right-wing Hindu women who goad men into action by saying, "Don't be a bunch of eunuchs."[30] This point is underscored by the bombers themselves. A propaganda slogan in Chechnya reads: "Women's courage is a disgrace to that of modern men."[31] And in the martyrdom video Ayat Akras—an eighteen-year-old Palestinian woman who set off a bomb in the Supersol supermarket in Jerusalem—taped before she blew herself up, she stated, "*I am going to fight* [emphasis added] instead of the sleeping Arab armies who are watching Palestinian girls fighting alone"—an apparent jab at Arab leaders for not being sufficiently proactive or manly.[32]

It appears that insurgent organizations in Iraq are similarly inspired. Although women form a very small number of the bombers in Iraq, the message is that men should not let women do their fighting for them. On March 29, 2003, within weeks of the U.S. invasion of Iraq, two women (one of whom was pregnant) perpetrated suicide attacks against the Coalition forces. Then, on April 4, 2003, Al-Jazeera television played a video of two Iraqi women vowing to commit suicide attacks: "We say to our leader and holy war comrade, the hero commander Saddam Hussein, that you have sisters that you and history will boast about." In a separate video, another woman, identified as Wadad Jamil Jassem, assumed a similar position: "I have devoted myself [to] Jihad for the sake of God and against the American, British, and Israeli infidels and to defend the soil of our precious and dear country."[33]

Terrorist groups may also find women useful as suicide bombers because of the widespread assumption that women are inherently nonviolent. Women can bypass, for example, Israel's restrictive checkpoints and border policy, which has proven fairly effective against Palestinian insurgent organizations inside the occupied territories. Since the mid-1990s, it has been almost impossible for unmarried men under the age of forty to get permits to cross the border into Israel. Women don't arouse suspicion like men and blend in more effectively with Israeli civilians: "Attacks perpetrated by women have tended to be those where the terrorist planners needed the perpetrator to blend in on the Israeli 'street.' These female terrorists . . . westernize their appearance, adopting modern hairstyles and short skirts."[34] This is reminiscent of the ways in which women in Algeria transformed their appearance to participate in the FLN revolution against the French occupation during the Battle of Algiers in the early 1960s. The use of the least likely suspect is the most likely tactical adaptation for a terrorist group under scrutiny. Terrorist groups have therefore looked further afield for volunteers, to women and children.

A growing number of insurgent organizations are also taking advantage of the fact that suicide bombing, especially when perpetrated by women and young girls, garners a lot of media attention, both in the West and in the Middle East. Attacks by women receive eight times the media coverage as attacks by men, again largely because of the expectation that women are not violent. Realizing this, the Al-Aqsa Martyrs Brigades have drawn propaganda mileage from their female bombers.[35] The image of women defying tradition to sacrifice their lives for the Palestinian cause has drawn more attention to the despair of the Palestinian people. "Suicide attacks are done for effect, and the more dramatic the effect, the stronger the message; thus a potential interest on the part of some groups in recruiting women." [36]

This tactic also makes the terrorists appear more threatening by erasing the imagined barriers between combatants and noncombatants, terrorists and innocent civilians. This is the underlying message conveyed by female bombers: terrorism has moved beyond a fringe phenomenon; insurgents are all around you. For secular militant Palestinian groups at least, Akras's death demonstrated that they are not all religious fanatics who believe that God will grant them entrance to Paradise or reward them with seventy-two virgins (*houris*). Nor are the leaders all gripped by a burning desire to see all females locked behind black veils. For them, the involvement of women is meant to signal that they are waging a political war, not a religious one—and the suicide bombings are a carefully planned and executed part of a precise political strategy.[37]

Degauque's attack raises an added element of female converts, of which there are thousands in Europe, married to Muslim men and willing to make the sacrifice. Increasingly, bombers in Iraq have been female converts to Islam and not Arab women. On June 2, 2006, a woman known only as Sonja B, a German convert to Islam, was seized in Germany, foiling her planned attack in Iraq. After his arrest last November in Morocco with sixteen other militants suspected of terrorist activities, Mohamed Reha, a Moroccan Belgian affiliated with the Moroccan Islamic Combat Group (GICM), claimed, "The partners of several suspected terrorists being detained in Belgium are ready to carry out suicide attacks in Morocco."[38] He continued: "Many Muslim women whose husbands were arrested in Belgium would like to become involved in Jihad, the holy war. [I was asked] to help them by finding someone to train them and supply them with explosives." According to Belgian

sources, an Algerian named Khalid Abou Bassir, who claims to be the coordinator for Al Qaeda in Europe, was designated to lead a team of female suicide bombers.[39]

Converts are a particularly dangerous group, not only because they can evade most profiles, but also because they carry European passports. Also, like in most faiths, converts may feel the need to prove themselves and can be more radical in their views than are people born into the faith—thus making them more susceptible to extremist interpretations of Islam. Converts, male as well as female, may very well be a key resource in the future for terrorist organizations. Pascal Cruypennick was arrested in Belgium for sending suicide bombers to Iraq; other converts, like Richard Reid and Jose Padilla, are also in custody. In Belgium, as in many other countries in Europe, it appears converts are leading the charge to jihad in Iraq.

Are women suicide bombers portents of gender equality in their societies?

Unlikely. Fanaticism and death cults generally do not lead to liberation politics for women. Women may exhibit courage and steely resolve as terrorists, but if they are part of a system that affords them unequal status, then feminism doesn't apply. [40] It is telling that the women who participate in suicide bombings are usually among the most socially vulnerable: widows and rape victims. In fact, in several instances, the women were raped or sexually abused not by representatives of the state but by the insurgents themselves. As such they are stigmatized, and thus easily recruited and exploited.

> Those who send these women do not really care for women's rights; they are exploiting the personal frustrations . . . of these women for their own political goals, while they continue to limit the role of women in other aspects of life.[41]

The evidence that males in terrorist organizations exercise control over the women is also strong. Palestinian female cadres are not welcomed into the paramilitary terrorist factions, which remain dominated by men. Even in the Al-Aqsa Martyrs Brigades, women are not welcomed by the ranks of the male fighters. And in Sri Lanka, where women constitute 30 percent of the suicide attackers and form crucial conventional fighting units, few women are among the top leadership. Beyler remarks:

> It is mostly men who govern this infrastructure. . . . Women are rarely involved in the higher echelons of the decision-making process of these groups. Women may volunteer, or . . . be coerced to conduct a murderous strike, but the woman's role is ultimately dictated by the patriarchal hierarchy that rules Palestinian society and its terrorist groups.[42]

In fact, the LTTE has attempted to compel married Tamil women, including retired female cadres, to adopt more traditional and conservative forms of dress (the sari and head coverings) and not wear trousers in LTTE-controlled areas.

However, some may argue that there is a difference between the lower-ranking female operatives in terrorist groups and the women who are planners and leaders, such as Ulrike Meinhof, who provided the intellectual backbone of the Baader-Meinhof organization. The assassination of Czar Alexander II in 1881 was also organized by a woman, and many other nineteenth-century revolutionaries were female. Nevertheless, in many cases, women's participation in violence did not lead to their equal status in the societies that formed subsequent to the revolutions. It is interesting to note that the women who played violent roles in revolutionary movements in Iran, Palestine, and Algeria were not included in the leadership of the successor regimes.

The problem lies in the fact that these women, rather than confronting archaic patriarchal notions of women and exploding these myths from within, are actually operating under them. These include a well-scripted set of rules in which women sacrifice themselves; the patriarchal conception of motherhood, for example, is one of self-denial and self-effacement. In a sense, martyrdom is the ultimate and twisted fulfillment of these ideals. So, the spectacle of female suicide bombers doesn't challenge the patriarchy as much as provide evidence of its power. The message female suicide bombers send is that they are more valuable to their societies dead than they ever could have been alive.

Notes

1. Lucy Frazier, "Abandon Weeping for Weapons: Palestinian Women Suicide Bombers," http://www.nyu.edu/classes/keefer/joe/frazier.html (accessed November 21, 2003).

2. "From Jerusalem to Jakarta and from Bali to Baghdad, the suicide bomber is clearly the weapon of choice for international terrorists." Quoting Don Van Natta, Jr., "Big Bang Theory: The Terror Industry Fields its Ultimate Weapon," New York Times, August 24, 2003, sec. 4, 1.

3. Yoram Schweitzer, ed., Female Suicide Bombers: Dying for Equality? Jaffee Center for Strategic Studies, Memorandum 84, August 2006, 8.

4. Emile Sahliyeh and Zixian Deng, "The Determinants of Palestinians' Attitude Toward Peace with Israel," International Studies Quarterly 47 (4) (December 2003): 701.

5. Arjuna Guwardena, "Female Black Tigers: A Different Breed of Cat," in Schweitzer, ed., Female Suicide Bombers, 87.

6. Tamil sources, interview by Mia Bloom, July 2006.

7. In July 1997 three national human rights commissions established in 1994 found that there had been 16,742 disappearances since July 1988.

8. Darini Rajasingham-Senanayake, interview by Mia Bloom, Colombo, Sri Lanka, October 25, 2002.

9. Robert I. Rotberg, ed., Creating Peace in Sri Lanka: Civil War and Reconciliation (Cambridge, Mass.: World Peace Foundation and the Belfer Center for Science and International Affairs, 1999), 9.

10. Rajasingham-Senanayake in ibid., 62.

11. Tamil sources, personal correspondence with the author, November 26, 2003.

12. There is some dispute about whether the Black Widows are in fact widows. Irina Bazarya argues that many are not widows but have been a product of societal forces predisposing

and molding them to become militants as an expression of Ayat, traditional Chechen mores (Ph.D. thesis, University of Cincinnati, forthcoming).

13. Anatoly Medetsky, "Court Tries Alleged Tverskaya Bomber," St. Petersburg Times, March 30, 2004.

14. Steven Lee Meyers, "From Dismal Chechnya, Women Turn to Bombs," New York Times, September 10, 2004.

15. Clara Beyler, "Messengers of Death: Female Suicide Bombers," http://www.ict.org.il/articles/articledet.cfm?articleid=470.

16. Anne Speckhard and Khapta Akhmedova, "Black Widows: The Chechen Female Suicide Terrorists," in Schweitzer, Female Suicide Bombers, 63–90.

17. Ibid.

18. Yoram Schweitzer, "A Fundamental Change in Tactics," Washington Post, October 19, 2003, B03.

19. Giles Foden, "Death and the Maidens," The Guardian, July 18, 2003.

20. Agence France Presse, April 12, 2002.

21. Kul al-Arab (Israel), February 1, 2002.

22. Al-Sha'ab (Egypt), February 1, 2002.

23. Sophie Claudet, "More Palestinian Women Suicide Bombers Could Be On The Way: Analysts," Middle East Times, March 1, 2002.

24. Graham Usher, "At 18, Bomber Became Martyr and Murderer," The Guardian, March 30, 2002.

25. Matti Steinberg, interview by Mia Bloom, September 2002.

26. According to Dr. Samiya Sa'ad Al-Din, Al-Akhbar (Egypt), February 1, 2002.

27. "Bin Laden Has Set Up Female Suicide Squads: Report," Arab News, Dubai, March 13, 2003.

28. Frazier, "Abandon Weeping for Weapons."

29. Farhana Ali, "Muslim Female Fighters: An Emerging Trend," Terrorism Monitor 3 (21) (November 3, 2005).

30. Amrita Basu, "Hindu Women's Activism and the Questions it Raises," in Patricia Jeffrey and Amrita Basu, eds., Appropriating Gender: Women's Activism and Politicized Religion in South Asia (London: Routledge, 1998).

31. Dimitri Sudakov, "Shamil Besaev Trains Female Suicide Bombers," Pravda, May 15, 2003.

32. Libby Copeland, "Female Suicide Bombers: The New Factor in Mideast's Deadly Equation," Washington Post, April 27, 2002, C1.

33. Cited by Roman Kupchinsky in "'Smart Bombs' with Souls," Organized Crime and Terrorism Watch 3 (13) (April 17, 2003).

34. Yoni Fighel, "Palestinian Islamic Jihad and Female Suicide Bombers," October 6, 2003, www.ict.org.

35. Scott Atran argues that as a result of Akras's martyrdom, Saudi Arabia sent 100 million dollars to fund the Al-Aqsa Intifada.

36. Claudet, "More Palestinian Women Suicide Bombers Could Be On The Way."

37. Usher, "At 18, Bomber Became Martyr and Murderer."

38. AFP report, cited by De Standaard.

39. The use of women remains a point of contestation among different streams of Salafism in Al Qaeda Central. The

recently killed Abu Musab al-Zarqawi certainly had no qualms about using women in Iraq or Jordan, but other militants, like Samir Azzouz, have thus far refused. As long as the majority of suicide bombers in Iraq come from the Gulf, the numbers of women will remain low since neither the Saudis nor other more conservative Wahhabis will permit women to go on jihad.

40. Foden, "Death and the Maidens."

41. Ibid.

42. Clara Beyler, "Using Palestinian Women as Bombs," *New York Sun,* November 15, 2006.

MIA BLOOM is assistant professor of international affairs at the University of Georgia. She is the author of *"Dying to Kill: The Allure of Suicide Terror"* (2005).

The Bomb under the Abaya

JUDITH MILLER

The suicide vest, stuffed with explosives, nails, ball bearings and various metal fragments, weighed close to 40 pounds. But it felt "like roses on my shoulders," Shefa'a al-Qudsi told me when I interviewed her this spring in an Israeli security prison near Tel Aviv. "I was even more eager to do it after I put the vest on," said the now 31-year-old Palestinian from Tulkarem. "Many would have died. No fence in the world would have stopped me."

Wafa al-Biss, who is now 23, had the opposite reaction when she tried on the explosive pants she had been given for her mission. "I told them the pants were too tight and too heavy," she said, tugging at her headscarf with her scarred fingertips as she recounted her conversation with the men who were sending her to kill and die. "They said: 'Don't worry. We have a bigger size for you!' I looked in the mirror and didn't recognize myself," al-Biss told me, her eyes welling with tears. "And I thought: What am I doing here?"

The two women with their opposite reactions to the prospect of becoming human bombs had been brought together by Israeli counterterrorism officials in Ward 12 of Hasharon Security Prison, an austere facility a half-hour drive north of Tel Aviv. The sprawling, multi-story concrete structure, surrounded by concertina wire and florescent-lit guard towers, is located in the Plain of Sharon where lush citrus groves embrace the prison in a sea of green. Clearly visible from a major highway, tens of thousands of Israeli commuters pass the unmarked facility each day en route to Tel Aviv.

Wafa al-Biss and Shefa'a al-Qudsi live among more than 60 other Palestinian women involved in terrorism—would-be bombers, spotters, supporters of and counselors to future *shaheeds* and *shaheedas,* male and female martyrs, as Palestinians call them. Twelve of some 22 women who have participated since 2002 in such suicide missions survived and are now confined here and in similar prisons, where Israeli intelligence officials have been studying them intensively. Cynics may say that these women prisoners were the beneficiaries of second thoughts, but Israeli officials assert that most of them, including Shefa'a al-Qudsi, were either apprehended before they could reach their targets, or, as in the case of Wafa al-Biss, discovered too late that the devices they were wearing were faulty.

What Israeli officials have more difficulty explaining is why they chose to sacrifice themselves to kill Israelis. Why are so many so eager to do something so profoundly contrary to the human instinct for survival?

Because I found conflicting and only partial answers in the many books that have already been written on suicide attacks, I went to the gates of Hasharon prison to talk to the women themselves. Since Israel has in detention among the largest number of people who have tried and failed to carry out *istishhad,* or religiously blessed self-sacrifice—nearly half of the 380 aspiring suicide bombers since 2002 have failed or were stopped before carrying out their missions—it seemed a natural place to start.

What led Palestinians to this deadly choice? Were the motives similar to those of the seemingly endless reservoir of suicide bombers who have killed so many Iraqis and Americans in Iraq? Are the motives similar to those of suicide bombers in Afghanistan, where U.S. soldiers and Afghan civilians alike now face growing peril? Are New Yorkers and other Americans likely to confront suicide attacks like those that Israelis, Sri Lankans, Turks and others have endured?

The prison holding more than 60 Palestinian women was clean but icy cold on the spring morning that my translator and I arrived. Escorted by male and female prison guards armed with mace and revolvers, we were guided through a labyrinth of wire and steel, along long, narrow corridors separated by several thick steel doors and gates to Wards 11 and 12, where veterans of failed suicide missions and other serious security crimes are held.

Each ward has two tiers of cells, which vary in size, holding one to 10 prisoners. They surround a small open-air courtyard where the women eat in good weather, talk, read, play cards, and exercise. On the day of my visit, several were walking there, arm-in-arm. Others were sweeping the courtyard or wiping the narrow windows of the thick doors of the cells that confine them at night and during the day unless they are eating, praying, exercising, or studying Hebrew or other courses the prison offers. Shefa'a al-Qudsi, unusual among Palestinian women suicide bombers, who tend to be better educated than their male counterparts, earned her high school diploma here.

Most of the women in Ward 12 are members of Hamas, the militant Islamic group that wants to create an Islamic Palestinian state in all of Israel and refuses to recognize the existence of the Jewish state. Almost all wore headscarves.

Why are so many so eager to do something so profoundly contrary to the human instinct for survival?

Soon after we entered the ward, a tall, stern-looking young prisoner—the unit's designated political leader in *hijab* and *jilbab,* a full-length traditional dress—approached my male translator and me. She was all business: Who were we? she asked, her eyes narrowing. What did we want?

We were journalists, I replied—from America, in my case.

"We don't like America because of the war in Iraq and your support for the Zionists and Jews," she declared abruptly and turned away.

The other women watched her carefully. As the ward's spokesperson, she defined what the women could say. This was the party line, and I sensed I would soon hear it again from the women who had agreed to meet me separately.

Ward 11 had four such "leaders"—one from each of the factions represented here, the Palestine Liberation Organization's Fatah, the two leading militant Islamic groups—Hamas and Islamic Jihad—and the leftist, secular Popular Front for the Liberation of Palestine. The women, permitted to wear their own clothes, buy and cook their own food if they can afford it, are also allowed to celebrate holidays and visit with their families—if only through glass partitions and monitored telephones. Also in contrast to American jails where personal items are severely restricted, several of the women had numerous photographs and personal memorabilia in their cells, along with television sets. They watch what they want, the women told me, which in these wards were mostly soap operas and Al Jazeera, the Qatari-owned satellite news station that champions Arab causes and praises suicide bombers in Palestine and Iraq as "martyrs."

I was unprepared for the children. When I entered Ward 12, one of the ward's two infants was being fed by her mother and fussed over by other inmates. Israel, I was told, lets babies remain with their mothers until they are two years old. Some of these women decided to become suicide bombers or support terrorism when, or perhaps because they were pregnant, or like Shefa'a, had an infant at home.

"We try to live our lives," Shefa'a al-Qudsi told me. "But prison is a graveyard for the living."

Shefa'a al-Qudsi had been in prison for five years, since she was 26. Her daughter, Diana, was a year old when the police arrested her at her parents' house hours before she was supposed to carry out her suicide attack at a hotel disco in Netanya, a beach town north of Tel Aviv. Now her daughter, whom she has rarely seen in prison, is six. Eager to be reunited with her, she is scheduled to be released in October.

"Although I've spent the best years of my life in here," she said. "I regret nothing. What I did was not wrong."

Shefa'a al-Qudsi is one of 10 children. She says she had a "good and comfortable life, everything I needed" before deciding to sacrifice herself for Palestine. A younger brother was also arrested en route to his own suicide attack in February 2002, two months before she was picked up. Shefa'a is also rare in having actively sought recruitment and planning her own attack.

"The guys wanted me to do the operation in Hadera," she said, referring to another neighboring seaside Israeli town. "But I had worked for eight years as a hair dresser, often in Israel. I had some Israeli clients and knew Netanya like the back of my hand. There was a hotel there with a dancing hall, a beautiful place by the sea. A lot of Orthodox Jews live nearby; it was usually crowded. Because the Israelis demolished everything beautiful in our lives, I wanted to do the same to them.

"I chose Netanya," she said proudly. "I told the guys: bring me the explosives; I'll do the rest." She also decided to disguise herself as a pregnant woman to avoid suspicion.

Several things led her to act, she told me. First was Israel's occupation. Life had become intolerable since the onset of the second Intifada in September 2000, the Palestinian uprising that followed the collapse of peace talks between Palestinians and Israelis which had limped along since the 1993 Oslo peace accords, a period of great hope turned sour. While young Palestinians threw stones during the first Intifada, between 1987 and 1993, they discovered a more devastating weapon in round two. Suicide bombings soared after September 2000, with the visit of Israeli Prime Minister Ariel Sharon to Jerusalem's Temple Mount, sacred to Jews, and also the site of the Al Aqsa mosque, which Muslims revere. His visit was the flashpoint for the second, so-called "Al Aqsa" intifada. In January, 2002, a young Palestinian woman named Wafa Idris was catapulted into Palestinian celebrity by becoming the forty-seventh Palestinian suicide bomber—but the first woman to kill herself while murdering Israelis. Her picture was everywhere in the West Bank and Gaza—on Palestinian TV, on posters. Poets wrote songs in her honor. Women named daughters after her.

Shefa'a told me that Idris's example had inspired her. "She opened the door for women to do something important in our struggle," she said. "Til Wafa, women had just helped jihad by making food. I thought: We can do more."

Living conditions on the occupied West Bank and Gaza deteriorated as the second Intifada dragged on. "Two of my cousins were killed, my brother was jailed. The army invaded our city and demolished houses. A war raged inside me: Should I, or should I not do something? The Israelis were killing us like rats and nobody was doing anything, not the Arabs, nobody. And I thought: No one will help us. I must make these dogs know how we feel. Even bullets that miss make noise."

Then her youngest brother was arrested. "Mahmoud was only 15 but prepared to be a martyr" she said. He is now serving an 18-year sentence in another security prison. "My family and I were shocked. But I was ashamed to be doing nothing."

Though not politically active, she persuaded them at a local mosque to help her become a suicide bomber.

Through a cousin, she contacted the *shabbab*—"the guys" from the Al Aqsa Martyrs Brigade, sponsored by the late Yasir Arafat's secular Al-Fatah. Though she had not been politically active, she persuaded them at a local mosque to help her become a suicide bomber. They initially hesitated, she recalled, asking about her daughter.

"I told them that my body would be a bridge to a better future that my daughter would walk over," she said. "Yes, I would die, but I would help give her a better life, a future without occupation. I was placing her fate in Allah's hands."

In the days before her attack, she kept her daughter close by as she read the Koran and prayed. While her family suspected something was wrong, since she was not normally religious, they said nothing. The plot was foiled only after an informant disclosed her plans to the Israelis, she complained bitterly. She was arrested the night before she was to receive a coded cell-phone message signaling the start of the operation: "The wedding has begun."

I sensed that al-Qudsi's motives *were* more complex, and as we talked, this seemingly determined young woman's confidence flagged as she recounted her failed marriage and the other disappointments that made martyrdom so attractive. While all of her siblings had finished college, she had dropped out of high school at 16 "to marry the man I loved," her first cousin. But Essam had humiliated her by marrying a Romanian while working in Europe and asking her for a divorce. At 19, she returned to her parents' home, rejected, a single mother with dubious remarriage prospects. Essam eventually asked her to remarry him after his second wife left him and their two children to return to Romania, she said. But she refused, "as a matter of dignity."

Al-Qudsi now claims to be optimistic about the future. Given her sacrifice, she says, "many jobs will be waiting for me." She may work in the part of the Palestinian Authority still run by Yasir Arafat's Fatah, or at the "prisoners club," which has paid her family 1000 shekels a month since her incarceration—about $350 a month, not an insignificant sum in economically hard-pressed Palestine whose average per capita annual income is under $1,000. Her father has opened a new cafe in Tulkarem. With her enhanced social status as a would-be *shaheeda,* she looks forward to working with men now, she said. "I've had more than enough of women in jail," she laughed. But she does not want to remarry, to go "from one prison to another."

She has become "more political" and "closer to God" in prison, she says. She has also perfected her Hebrew. "We need to know the language of our enemy to better confront him, she said, a giggle softening the threat she is still determined to convey.

Would she discourage her daughter Diana from emulating her path towards martyrdom? I asked her. "I will teach her that education is the most important thing in life," she replied. "But our children can be shot coming home from school. The best of our children become martyrs, whether or not they want to be. So if she wanted to do this, I wouldn't try to stop her."

I f Shefa'a al-Qudsi was a willing human weapon in her people's asymmetric war against an overwhelmingly powerful enemy, Wafa al-Biss, 23, is her opposite—the quintessential victim.

Now in the second year of a 12-year sentence, she was deeply distraught on the day she agreed to speak to me. She had never really wanted to become a suicide bomber, she told me tearfully. Life and bad luck had given her no choice. Born into wretched poverty in Jabalya refugee camp in Gaza, one of 12 children, she said that much of her body and fingertips had been burned in a freak cooking accident at home the year before her failed mission. She had been coaxed, no, coerced into becoming a martyr by "Abul Khair," an older man from the Al-Aqsa Martyr's Brigade. "I wish I had never met him," she said bitterly.

With her lovely face and soft voice, Wafa al-Biss was not at all what I expected from what I had read about her and seen on videotape. Hours after her arrest on June 6, 2005 at the Erez crossing, the main transit point between Israel and Gaza, Israeli intelligence had hauled her before reporters to discuss her failed mission. Her neck and hands were still covered with scars and bandages from the kitchen gas explosion in her home months earlier.

At the press conference, according to several articles, Wafa al-Biss was a study in defiance—the model would-be martyr. Her greatest wish, her "dream" since childhood, she declared, was martyrdom. "I believe in death," she told reporters. Her target was an Israeli hospital, perhaps even Soroka Hospital in Beersheba, where she had been treated for her burns, which had probably saved her life. "I wanted to kill 20, 50 Jews. Yes!" she exclaimed, "even babies. You kill our babies!"

She might have succeeded had the Shin Bet, Israel's domestic security service, not warned checkpoints to be on the lookout for a female suicide bomber from Gaza. When a soldier noticed something odd in the young woman's gait as she entered the transit hall, she was ordered to stop and remove her long, dark cloak. Stranded between a metal turnstile behind her and an iron gate in front of her, Wafa al-Biss found herself alone in the evacuated hall. As military surveillance cameras recorded her every move, a solider ordered her again to disrobe and drop her bomb.

She had never really wanted to become a suicide bomber. She had been coerced by an older man.

Panicked and frustrated, Wafa al-Biss decided to kill herself anyway. Security camera video shows her reaching into her right pocket to pull the detonator string. But instead of exploding in a lethal mass of fire, smoke, and metal shards, the string came out in her hand. Again and again she thrust her hand into her pocket, pushing the detonator. The cameras dispassionately record her failed mission's final moments—Wafa al-Biss, alone in the hall, screaming and crying, clawing at her face—condemned to live.

"I don't care about Jews and Arabs," she told me in the prison; she had never been political. Israelis at Soroka, where she had spent three months with her burns, treated her with "respect and dignity," she said. "They had been very kind," she said. "But I still wanted to kill myself."

She had tried to do so even before the gas accident, on her birthday in November 2004, that had scarred her body, deformed the fifth digits of both hands, and left her fingertips and chin discolored. Long before that, she told me, she had been in despair. She had grown up desperately poor. Her father was "primitive." He rarely let her go out except to school or the mosque. He and her brothers beat her. She tried to throw herself out a window at age 18, but courage failed her. "Islam says you can't kill yourself. I was afraid of the shame for my family," she said.

"If my family had been normal, if I could have afforded to have been treated in America, if I could wear my hair and live my life like yours," she said, "I would never have thought about killing myself."

Instead, she said, she approached a group known to be associated with the "Resistance." Would they accept her as a martyr?

At first, the man she came to know only as Abul Khair, whom she met secretly at Al Shifa Hospital in Gaza, urged her to think it over. Despite the reverence that fellow Gazans showed martyrs and their families, she hesitated. She called him a week later to say she had changed her mind.

"But they hunted me like prey," she recalled. "Abul Khair kept calling," she said. "He told me a guy they were counting on had backed out of an operation; they needed me. 'Look at your future,' they told me. 'No one will ever marry you.' I knew it was true. I was not good at school. I had no future."

She agreed to meet him again, this time at the Haifa mosque. Would God grant her anything she wanted in paradise? she asked him. "Would he give me new skin?"

Yes, he told her.

"What did death feel like?" she pressed him.

She wouldn't feel anything, she quoted him as saying. "It's like a pin prick."

"I wanted to believe him," she told me. "He looked religious, like someone you could trust. He told me I was very brave. He made me feel important." She agreed to become a shaheeda.

'Look at your future,' they told me. 'No one will ever marry you.' I knew it was true. I had no future.

When she returned home, upset and crying, her mother sensed something was wrong. "I lied and told her that my finger hurt. Her mother made her some food and told her it would be better soon, "*inshallah,*" Wafa said. If her mother sensed what Wafa was about to do, she didn't let on, she insisted.

As the day of her operation approached, Wafa grew despondent. She had gone to a safe house in Gaza twice with young men who picked her up in a car on a corner near her home. Being in the company of men who were not family members was religiously and culturally forbidden in conservative Palestine. She initially feaired they would "harm my dignity as a woman," she told me. Instead, they escorted her to a nondescript house on

the edge of her city where she was asked to try on the explosive pants, test the detonator—a gift to the Al-Aqsa group from its ostensible rival, Hamas—and videotape a political statement about the need to kill Jews. "I didn't feel that way; I told them I wanted to say something else," she said.

Ultimately, however, she complied. She was taped reading the statement and holding a Kalashnikov—for the first time ever, she says. "It was heavy."

The day before her operation, she kept to herself, cried, prayed, and tried cheering herself up by serenading her two pet canaries with a song she sang for me that morning in prison—a popular prisoner anthem in many Arab countries. "I am running away from my cage, said the bird," as Wafa began humming.

"And the bird said: Hide me with you . . . as a tear came out to his eye.

And he said his wings are broken,

And he can no longer fly."

The morning before her attack, she woke up in terror. She called Abul Khair to tell him she had changed her mind. "But they threatened me," she said. "They said they would bring the belt to my house and explode it on me." She relented and accompanied them to the safe house, she said, where she spent the night before the attack.

The day of her attack, June 21 , 2005, "was the hardest day of my life." She had failed at this as she had "so many other opportunities in my life."

She expected little now, she told me. No one was helping her; no group was paying or supporting her parents, she said. One day, she hoped to marry, but her pained expression suggested she knew this was unlikely. Perhaps she would be able to have her burns treated, she said. She would replace the birds, which had died since she went to jail.

While Shefa'a al-Qudsi's story of her failed suicide bombing was consistent over time with what she had told her Israeli interrogators soon after her arrest, Wafa's account was not. Who was the real Wafa al-Biss: the proud patriotic bomber who boasted of her desire to slaughter Jews, even babies, at the hospital that had saved her life? Or the tearful victim of a sophisticated martyrdom recruiting organization who had failed to kill herself, if not others, only because of a defective detonator? Which al-Biss was I to believe?

Smadar Perry, a journalist for the Israeli newspaper Yediot Ahranot who has interviewed over a dozen would-be male and female martyrs in her many trips to Israeli prisons and detention centers, told me that what these prisoners say soon after their arrest is usually more reliable than what they are encouraged to say later on by fellow inmates and political mentors in jail.

What Wafa al-Biss omitted from her saga, however, shows how hard it is to understand the motives of suicide bombers and how complex those motives can be. She still had enough pride or shame to conceal from me facts that would have highlighted her despair. For unlike al-Qudsi, she was not motivated by the nationalist and religious reasons she claimed soon after her arrest. And it was not her long-standing "dream" to become a martyr. Nor did she act primarily because of Israel's occupation, though the Al-Aqsa Martyr's Brigades, which had given her the bomb, driven her to the crossing, and shown her how to blow herself up, would have us beUeve that. Rather, she acted in large part because those she had loved and trusted the most had abandoned her.

She did not tell me, for instance, as NBC News reported a few days after her arrest and press conference, that she had been engaged to be married, or that her fiance had broken off their engagement after her disfiguring accident. Nor did she say that, according to a Palestinian friend whose son Wafa had befriended at Soroka Hospital, she had resisted leaving after her three-month stay. Wafa's friend recalled how she had to be removed on a stretcher, crying and pleading not to be returned home.

In Gaza, she grew ever more despondent. While Israeli doctors at Soroka had strongly recommended counseling, her brothers had objected: neighbors might think she was crazy, bringing further shame upon the family.

Finally, although Wafa had told me her parents knew nothing of her plans, this, too, conflicted with what she told Israeli interrogators. Security sources told me that soon after her arrest she told them that although her parents had initially disapproved of her mission, they ultimately encouraged her. The video she told me had been made in the Al-Aqsa safe house, for instance, was actually taped on the second floor of her own home, with her parents' approval. Her own mother had helped her dress the morning of her attack. When the zipper of the explosive-laden pants tore as she was putting them on, her mother sewed it back up.

Wafa Al-Biss, the ultimate victim, is the exception among suicide terrorists, says Yoram Schweitzer, an Israeli terrorism expert. "I reject the notion that all female suicide bombers are 'damaged goods,'" he told me over coffee at the Tel Aviv University's Jaffee Center for Strategic Studies. Only a tiny minority, he said, is really coerced into committing suicide. "Most are true volunteers. Men and women alike clamor, to do this. I also reject the argument that women are more easily manipulated than men."

If anything, female suicide bombers, statistics show, tend to be better educated than their male counterparts. Between 30 percent and 40 percent of them have attended university. "They are the smarter of these smart weapons," says Anat Berko, an Israeli criminologist whose interviewed suicide bombers and those who sent them for her new book, The Path to Paradise (Praeger, 2007).

Now that suicide bombing has spread to some 32 groups in 28 countries, says Ami Pedahzur, an Israeli expert at the University of Texas, most counterterrorism experts have discarded the earlier "profiles" they assembled of the "average" suicide bomber. In the first wave of modern suicide bombing, which started against American and other western targets in Lebanon in the early 1980's, suicide bombers tended to be mostly young, male, and single. That is no longer the case.

The face of modern terrorism, and of suicide bombing in particular, is increasingly female. Though still a minority among suicide bombers in Israel and Iraq, the growing number of women willing to volunteer for such missions is especially evident in non-Palestinian and non-Islamic secular movements. Christoph

Reuter, the German author of My Life Is a Weapon: A Modern History of Suicide Bombing (Princeton University Press, 2004), notes that one-third of the estimated 10,000 Tamil Tiger cadres in Sri Lanka have been female. Among suicide commandos, female participation is close to 60 percent.

The same is true for the PKK, the Kurdistan Workers' Party, the largely secular Muslim militants who have been battling Turkey since the 1970s for Kurdish rights and autonomy. Eleven out of some 15 suicide bombings staged by the PKK since 1996 were conducted by women, as were three out of six foiled attacks. In Chechnya, women have conducted 43 percent of the attacks since suicide missions began there in 2000.

Even in Israel, where the total number of such attacks declined sharply in 2006, Reuven Ehrlich, who directs the Intelligence and Terrorist Information Center in Tel Aviv, reports in a recent study that a woman conducted one of the four suicide attacks.

Between 1985 and 2006, Schweitzer says, 220 women suicide bombers have accounted for 15 percent of the total number of successful or attempted attacks throughout the world. In 2006 alone, women were enlisted for suicide raids from Belgium, India, Iraq, Turkey, and the West Bank territories, he writes in Female Suicide Bombers: Dying for Equality (Jaffee Center for Strategic Studies, August 2006). Indeed, the phenomenon appears to be "contagious," especially among women, concludes Mia Bloom, an American expert.

Even in death, inequality endures: A family is usually paid far less for a woman's suicide than for a man's.

Bloom and Schweitzer caution that the increase in women suicide bombers reflects neither a progressive attitude towards women nor gender equality in the religious, revolutionary, and national liberation movements that promote such terror. Women continue to play a distinctly marginal role in most of these groups. Even in death, inequality endures: A Palestinian family, for instance, is usually paid far less for a woman's suicide death than for a man's. And despite efforts to honize their sacrifice and portray them as heroines, Schweitzer concludes, women serve mainly as "pawns and sacrificial lambs."

This perverse "feminization" of suicide attacks also undercuts the theory that women are more likely to choose peaceful mechanisms for conflict resolution than men. In her influential book, Dying to Kill (Columbia University Press, 2005). Bloom dismisses the notion that women are somehow inherently more inclined towards moderation. "But while male suicide bombers seem to be motivated by religious or nationalist fanaticism," she argues, female operatives, in Palestine and elsewhere, "appear more often motivated by very personal reasons." This was certainly the case for Shefa'a al-Qudsi, and even more dramatically for Wafa al-Biss, who seemed to have been driven by a "cocktail" of motives—personal distress and shame, a quest for revenge and enhanced social status for themselves and their families, nationalism, hatred of occupation, religious ideology, and political culture. Louise Richardson, a lecturer at Harvard, sums it up in what she calls the three "R'S"—"exacting revenge, attaining renown, and eliciting a reaction."

Although both al-Qudsi and al-Biss sprinkled their speech with references to Islam and what it permitted or banned, neither said she was particularly devout; nor did the allure of Islamic paradise seem to hold much appeal. Both appeared focused on how their families and friends would react to their deed rather than on the prospect of eternal pleasures, such as the proverbial 72 black-eyed virgins who are said to await their male counterparts if they succeed. Al-Biss scoffed at the very notion of paradise. "I knew I was not going to heaven," she told me, "and that all the other martyrs were not going there either."

Al-Qudsi's vision of her eternal reward was consistent with the empowerment she felt as the mistress of her own failed martyrdom mission. In paradise, she said, she would not only become the wife of a martyr, she would be able to choose which martyr she married.

In paradise, she said, she would not only become the wife of a martyr, she would choose which martyr she married.

The prospect of choice is especially seductive in a culture that offers women so few of them. In such rigid, unforgiving societies in which a single transgression, real or even rumored, particularly by a woman, can result in the loss of family honor, a chance to marry, and occasionally even death at the hands of outraged relatives, choosing to redeem one-self through a suicide mission does not seem so terrible, or irrational an alternative.

What also seems clear—based on my interviews with the two would-be bombers and a survey of the scholarly literature—is that no matter how desperate they may be, such vulnerable, disposable young women and men do not act in a vacuum. It takes a sophisticated organization to launch such missions and political, social, and religious approbation to sanction them. Someone must recruit, train, arm, finance, and dispatch a volunteer *jihadi*. Bombs and explosive vests must be made, safe houses established, reliable drivers and escorts found, media teams ordered to write and videotape the bomber's final statements. Friends and family, schools and mosques where they meet, must be complicit. It takes what journalist Anne Marie Oliver calls a "martyrdom machine" to produce people willing to sacrifice their lives in the numbers we have seen in Palestine and Iraq today. And it takes an entire society, not merely a cult, to promote the culture of death that has taken root in Palestine. Encouraged by the ostensibly secular Palestine Authority and the allegedly religious-inspired Hamas alike, soccer tournaments are named after "martyrs." Parents dress their babies up as suicide bombers and photograph them in fancy studios. Posters bearing the martyrs' faces are plastered on walls of stores and schools in every town and village. Saudi diplomats write poems in their honor while children exchange "martyr cards."

While scholars dispute what causes suicide attacks and how best to prevent them, they agree that the tactic itself—what Diego Gambetta of Oxford's Nuffield College calls the "defining act of political violence of our age"—has spread so far and so fast, among secular and religious groups alike, because it is effective. The 9/11 attacks led many Americans to equate suicide bombing with Islamic militants, but secular groups have used the tactic with equal tenacity.

Though still rare in the universe of armed conflicts, says Robert A. Pape of the University of Chicago, suicide bombing has been 12 times deadlier than any other form of terrorism. While such attacks constituted 3 percent of terrorist acts between 1980 to 2003, they caused 48 percent of terrorism deaths, excluding September 11 .

While the average shooting attack between 1980 and June 2005 killed 3.32 people and remote control bombs killed an average of 6.92 people per attack, suicide bombers wearing explosive belts claimed an average of 81.48 victims. If the bomber was driving an explosive-laden car, as are so many in Iraq, says Ami Pedahzur, the average soared to 97.81 victims.

The upward trend that began in 1999 has continued to grow exponentially in some places. Between 1981 and the end of 2003, there were 535 successful suicide missions. But in just two years—from January 2004 to December 2005—there were no less than 555 successful attacks, 84 percent of which took place in Iraq.

The experts, divided over what causes this pernicious form of terrorism, are even more at odds over how to prevent it. Pape argues that because suicide attacks are not a religious phenomenon but mainly "a response to foreign occupation," the most obvious solution is withdrawal from disputed territory. Suicide attacks in Lebanon virtually ended after Israel withdrew in 2000, he notes, and they also declined dramatically after Israel's unilateral withdrawal two years ago from Gaza two years ago. But the best evidence of his thesis, he claims, is Iraq. The country that had no suicide attacks before the U.S. invasion had 20 in 2003. And since American forces have been stationed there, Iraq's rate of suicide bombings has doubled each year. The only way to stop them, he argues, is to withdraw American forces there.

Though his analysis seems statistically compelling, few scholars agree with him. Assaf Moghadam, a German-Iranian scholar at Harvard's Olin Institute in Cambridge, and Mohammed Hafez, at the University of Missouri, argue that territorial struggle does not explain movements like al Qaeda or their increasing tendency to cross geographic boundaries and conduct missions along sectarian lines as in Iraq. These now "globalized" suicide attacks are truly transnational in nature and aspiration.

Nor would unilateral withdrawal from the West Bank—which few consider a politically viable option for Israel—be likely to satisfy Hamas or Islamic Jihad, since they claim all Israeli territory as their own. Yes, says Bruce Hoffman, a leading terrorism expert at Georgetown University, suicide missions dropped both in Lebanon and Gaza after Israel unilaterally withdrew. But in the absence of Israeli forces, Hezbollah in Lebanon and Hamas in Gaza imported, produced and used vast arsenals of rockets and missiles against Israel, built defensive tunnels and infrastructure to better counter Israeli strikes, and intensified the training of fighters and jihadis for future confrontations. "Militant Islamists switched tactics after Israel's withdrawal," Hoffman said. "It sent rockets rather than people to kill. It did not stop fighting."

Israeli security officials have, in fact, dramatically reduced the number of suicide attacks and casualties since their peak in 2002 by resorting to other controversial measures. Ehrlich notes that while 22 civilians were killed in 2005 (and 55 in 2004), 15 people were killed in such attacks and 104 wounded in 2006.

Israel's extension of its security fence— the much loathed "Wall" to Palestinians— has reduced suicide attacks.

Many Israeli and American terrorism experts assert that Israel's extension of its security fence and buffer zone—the much loathed "Wall" to Palestinians—to cover roughly half of the border between Israeli and Palestinian territory has not only reduced suicide attacks—at least temporarily—but all violent and property crime, an assertion heatedly challenged by Palestinians. Second, Israel has significantly increased the number of Palestinians it detains on suspicion of terrorist activities: whereas 4,532 Palestinians were arrested in 2005, 6,968 suspects were detained last year.

"It's the intel, stupid," says Hoffman. Israel has managed to reduce the rate of attacks by penetrating Palestinian bombing networks and stopping them before they occur. Withdrawing from territory absent a political solution, he fears, may make it harder for Israel to collect such vital information.

But scholars like Mia Bloom worry about the longer-term impact of such policies. Yes, harsh Israeli counterterror measures such as the use of targeted assassination, increasing detentions, and building a wall appear to have stemmed suicide terror in the short run. Yet over time, she argues, such heavy-handed tactics will only further humiliate and enrage Palestinians, providing ever more recruits for martyrdom missions. If the ultimate challenge is to make the Shefa'a al-Qudsi's and Wafa al-Biss's of Palestine forgo suicide terror and make their sacrifice unacceptable to Palestinian society, only a political compromise satisfactory to the key parties is likely to succeed. Between the Oslo peace accords of 1993 until the autumn of 2000, Palestinian support for suicide terror never exceeded one-third of the population, she notes. Today, that figure is well over 80 percent.

What lies ahead for the United States abroad and at home is even harder to project, and not surprisingly, equally divisive among scholars. Israeli-style "walls" in Iraq and Afghanistan will not keep out militants opposed to America's presence or policies there or contain Iraq's deadly sectarian violence that so far shows little sign of abating. A political compromise acceptable to the major factions, or neighbors who feed various

insurgents, has so far proven elusive. At home, Americans have yet to adopt a psychology of what one Israeli security official called "hardening your hearts as well as our targets" when terrorists strike. Israeli security takes pride in restoring "normal" life in Israel within hours after a suicide attack. Many Americans, by contrast, remain traumatized by the September 11 attacks.

On the other hand, many Israeli, Arab, and American scholars and security officials doubt that America is likely to endure domestically the waves of suicide terror that Israeli has weathered. Gil Kleiman, a former superintendent of the Israeli National Police who was partly raised in the U.S., says, "you need to control geographic and political territory to use the suicide weapon effectively. That space does not exist in America." Yes, non-Islamic fanatics, such as Timothy McVeigh, the right-wing militiaman whose 1995 Oklahoma bombing attack killed more Americans domestically than any other single terrorist strike prior to 9/11, have an infrastructure and friendly territory in which to work, build, and proselytize, Hoffman acknowledges. And McVeigh, in fact, contemplated a suicide strike against his target until he discovered how vulnerable it was.

Immunity to jihadist ideology, to the culture of death gripping Palestine and Iraq, is still our nation's most enviable defense.

Yet Hoffman argues that for all their faults, the counterterrorism measures adopted since 9/11 make it harder to conduct such an attack today than it was before. Al Qaeda still appears to lack an infrastructure in this country. Nor does the United States have the vast unassimilated foreign Muslim populations that have been radicalized in Europe and may be capable of launching sustained attacks.

Brian M. Jenkins of the Rand Corporation, notes that with a population of 350 million, Europe is home to between 30 and 50 million Muslims. By 2050, one-third of all children born there will Muslim. The U.S., by contrast, with 300 million people, has about 4.7 million Muslims, many of them native Americans. And of the 3.5 million Arab-Americans, fewer than 25 percent are Muslim. "Can we see individuals or a small cluster who self radicalize and carry out even a devastating attack in this country? Yes, clearly," he told me. "The small conspiracy likely to lead to one-off attacks is always possible, maybe even likely. But I see nothing so far that would support a campaign such as what we have seen in the occupied territories or Iraq."

Of course, even a "one-off" attack in the United States involving a weapon of mass destruction, which al Qaeda and like-minded militants have repeatedly sought to acquire and would not hesitate to use, would be psychologically devastating to Americans. And as I left Hasharon prison, it was hard not to be shaken by my meetings with al-Qudsi and al-Biss—by their despair-driven determination, their plight, and finally, the enormity of what they had tried to do. The fact that neither was a religious extremist nor obviously deranged suggested that the reservoir of potential suicide bombers might be larger than many Americans appreciate. But while complacency about such terrorism was a luxury Americans could ill-afford, a panicky overreaction might jeopardize the very immunity to jihadist

ideology, to the culture of death gripping Palestine and Iraq, that is still our nation's best, most enviable defense.

JUDITH MILLER is a journalist who writes about national security issues. She is the author of *God Has Ninety-Nine Names: Reporting From a Militant Middle East* (Simon and Schuster, 1996), among other books.

From *Policy Review,* June/July 2007, pp. 43–58. Copyright © 2007 by Judith Miller. Reprinted by permission of The Hoover Institution, Stanford University and Judith Miller. www.policyreview.org

Picked Last: Women and Terrorism

Alisa Stack-O'Connor

Scholars date the genesis of modern terrorism to the People's Will in Russia in the late 1800s.[1] If terrorism's Garden of Eden was indeed Russia, then Vera Zasulich was Eve. On January 24, 1878, Zasulich shot the Governor General of St. Petersburg. She was arrested and tried for attempted murder. Although this was not her first arrest—she had been in prison, banished, and under police supervision since 1869 for her political activities—two prosecutors refused to try her for the shooting.[2] She was ultimately acquitted and left Russia, but remained involved in the revolutionary movement, writing for two Marxist publications.

Although times have changed since Zasulich was active, in examining how and why terrorist groups employ women, many things remain the same. For example, in pre-revolutionary Russia, women were less likely to be arrested, and when they were, they were not taken seriously[3] or were forgiven, as was Zasulich. While her colleagues admired her act of violence, they had less respect for her intellect, reflecting a typical assumption that women act out of emotion rather than a rational political program.[4]

Women's roles in Russian revolutionary groups increased when the number of men available for political activism was reduced by the Russo-Japanese War and security measures.[5] These women had the reputation of personal, rather than ideological, dedication to the cause, leading to the belief that they were more willing to die than their male comrades.

These observations reflect a profound ambivalence about women and political violence. This article examines Chechen, Palestinian, and Tamil terrorist groups to discover how and why such groups employ women. Three themes about women's entry into and roles in these groups emerge:

- Terrorist attacks by women have unique propaganda value.
- Women have to fight for their right to fight.
- Groups overcome cultural resistance to women's involvement when tactics require it or they face a shortage of males.

There is little written about female terrorists. Most works on female violence look at women as victims, not perpetrators. Recent high-profile attacks involving female perpetrators—such as the 2004 Beslan hostage-taking and the April 2006 attack on Lieutenant General Sarath Fonseka, head of the Sri Lankan army—have sparked some academic and policy interest in the subject. The few works on female terrorism tend to focus on women's motivations for violence. This article, however, examines the groups' motivations for employing women.

Additionally, it offers proposals for policymakers to consider in combating terrorism.

> **Most works on female violence look at women as victims, not perpetrators.**

Female Terrorism as Propaganda

Terrorism has been called "propaganda of the deed."[6] When women do the deed, the story often becomes more about women than terrorism. This dynamic is particularly evident in the Russian-Chechen conflict. Until the hostage-taking at the Dubrovka theater in Moscow in October 2002, Chechen women were viewed primarily as victims of the Russian-Chechen wars. In the theater seizure, they emerged in the Russian and Western press as vicious, sympathetic, strong, fanatical, foolish, and weak, often in the same portrayal.

Two images come to the fore in media reporting on Chechen female terrorists. First, there is the "black widow," a suicide bomber who is driven to terrorism after the deaths of the men in her life. Second, there is the "zombie," who is forced or tricked into terrorism by Chechen men. Although the Chechen groups did not coin the terms *black widow* and *zombie* to describe their female members, their leaders, such as the recently killed Shamil Basayev, have played up the black widow image, emphasizing victimization. The zombie image is generally used by the Russian government and media to discredit the Chechen insurgent and terrorist groups.

The zombies tend to receive more sensational press coverage. The best example of a zombie is Zarema Muzhikhoeva. On July 9, 2003, Muzhikhoeva failed to set off her bomb at a Moscow cafe. She was arrested and has been in custody ever since. The Russian Federal Security Service released some of its interviews with her and also allowed a televised interview.[7] Some of Muzhikhoeva's statements contradict each other. However, her basic life story stays fairly constant: she was married in her teens and had a child. Her husband died fighting the Russians, and she and her child then became the responsibility of her husband's family. Desperate either to escape servitude to her in-laws or avoid marrying her brother-in-law, Muzhikhoeva ran away, leaving her child. When she could not find work, she borrowed money. When she could not repay her debt, she felt driven to become a suicide bomber. According to Muzhikhoeva's account, she went to a terrorist camp in the mountains of Chechnya in March 2003, where Arabs provided instruction on fighting and Islam. She reported being beaten for dressing inappropriately and having sex with the camp leader. She also reported that other women in the camp were raped, beaten, and drugged. After a month of training, she was sent to Moscow to conduct an attack. Zombie stories such as Muzhikhoeva's are attention-grabbing, benefiting Chechen objectives, and explain away women's violence, benefiting the Russian government.

Although the zombie depiction is less flattering to individual women than the black widow stereotype, both have similar effects on the public inside and outside of Russia. The Chechens gained much attention and some sympathy from terrorist attacks by women.[8] In a July 2003 survey, the Public Opinion Foundation of the All-Russia Center for the Study of Public Opinion found that 84 percent of Russians surveyed believed female suicide bombers were controlled by someone else (zombies); only 3 percent believed the women acted independently.[9] Similarly, Western authors have blamed Russian actions for forcing women into terrorism.[10] In contrast, there is little writing about the desperation of men who have lost wives, mothers, and sisters to excuse or explain the Chechen call to arms. Women terrorists serve a uniquely feminine role in propaganda by playing the victims even when they are the perpetrators.

Female Palestinian suicide bombers have been depicted in much the same way as the zombies and black widows. As in the Russian case, the Israeli government has not hesitated to use women's personal stories to discredit them and the movements they worked for. Palestinian groups, unlike their Chechen counterparts, have been more active in using women's stories for the group's benefit. Ayat Akhras, for example, an 18-year-old female, blew herself up outside a Jerusalem supermarket on March 3, 2002, in an attack claimed by Al Aqsa Martyr's Brigade. Her attack illustrates the propaganda value of female terrorists in shaming Arab men into action. In her martyr video, she states, "I am going to fight instead of the sleeping Arab armies who are watching Palestinian girls fighting alone; it is an *intefadeh* until victory."[11]

In both the Palestinian and Chechen cases, the propaganda effect of women's attacks does not appear to be a factor in group planning; rather, it is an externality provided by the media. The Liberation Tigers of Tamil Eelam (LTTE or Tamil Tigers), on the other hand, have been highly successful in employing women in propaganda. The LTTE allows active female fighters to meet with the press, publishes books about its female guerrillas (the Freedom Birds), makes films about them, and holds public events to commemorate them. It is also careful to separate the group's guerrilla and terrorist activities. Unlike the Chechen and Palestinian groups, the LTTE does not acknowledge suicide attacks. Instead, it promotes the Freedom Birds, showing them as equal to male fighters and liberated from cultural oppression through fighting for the organization.

In all three cases, the media coverage of terrorist events differs based on whether a male or female conducts the act. Media coverage of a female terrorist tends to focus on the woman's nonpolitical motivations (for example, death of a male family

member), her vulnerability to recruitment because of her personal life (for example, promiscuity), and her basically peaceful and nurturing character. The coverage of male terrorists, on the other hand, generally focuses on the act committed. As terrorists need media attention to spread their message, the unique portrayals of females are one of the important factors in women's employment in terrorist attacks.

With the exception of the LTTE, it seems male terrorists and insurgent leaders are unaware of the propaganda benefits of female attacks; however, whether they plan for it or not, the media create it for free. Because terrorist leaders may not recognize the propaganda value, it cannot by itself explain why terrorists would want to use women. For most groups, the sympathy or increased attention is an externality realized only after women are involved in the group and its violence.

Fighting to Fight

Like women entering legitimate militaries and the labor force in general, females have to demonstrate great determination in gaining access to terrorist groups. In the Palestinian, Chechen, and Tamil cases, they have asked for active roles in political violence before groups invite them to take part. This trend is most evident in the Palestinian case, particularly in Leila Khaled's story. Denied a fighter's role in the Arab Nationalist Movement and then Fatah, Khaled kept searching for a group that would allow her to fight until the Popular Front for the Liberation for Palestine (PFLP) put her into guerrilla training. She hijacked aircraft in 1969 and 1970 for the PFLP, eventually becoming active in the group's leadership. She garnered international media attention after her foiled 1970 hijacking landed her in jail in the United Kingdom. Like the attention to Chechen women more than 30 years later, the media focused on Khaled's beauty and youth, not her politics.

> **The propaganda effect of women's attacks does not appear to be a factor in group planning; rather, it is an externality provided by the media.**

Her fame and involvement in the political leadership and tactical operations of the PFLP are not typical of women participating in Palestinian militancy. Most were involved in support roles and on the fringe of groups. In addition to a male cultural aversion to bringing women into militant groups, social demands such as raising children have made participation difficult. Great individual effort has been required to overcome cultural barriers. The PFLP recognized Khaled's popular appeal and promoted her and her story to gain attention, legitimacy, and support, but it was her initiative that brought her to the organization.

In the years since Khaled's hijackings, women's involvement in Palestinian terrorism has been either inconsistent or invisible. Even after proving their success as hijackers, bombers, and cover for men, women have to remind terrorist leaders of their tactical usefulness. It has been especially difficult for them to find active fighting roles in Hamas and Palestinian Islamic Jihad (PIJ). Potential female suicide bombers have been turned down by Hamas but have kept searching until secular organizations accepted them. Despite the tactical and propaganda benefits demonstrated by secular female suicide bombers in 2002, Hamas and PIJ struggled to reconcile conservative beliefs with evolving terrorist tactics. By 2003, however, PIJ believed the operational gains outweighed the social costs and began actively recruiting women for suicide bombings.[12] Leader Ramadan Abdallah Shallah explained the ideological and organizational adjustments the group had to make to accommodate female suicide bombers:

> The Shari'ah or religious judgment also deems that if there are sufficient numbers of men to carry out jihad, it is not preferable for women to carry out the jihad. The reason is to keep the woman away from any kind of harm. . . . Every operation is scrutinized and if the female . . . might be taken prisoner or face harm . . . it would not be preferable for the woman to carry out the operation. But if the Mujahidin estimate that the operation would not be fit for or carried out except by a woman because of the circumstances of disguise and reaching the target necessitate it, then we would not object.[13]

Similarly, Sheikh Ahmed Ismail Yassin, founder of Hamas, stated that his organization did not need women in its jihad because "The woman is the second defense line in the resistance of the occupation."[14] Religiously based terrorists are often thought to be irrational and fanatical in their devotion to violence. Both Shallah's and Yassin's statements, however, show rational and practical approaches. Men are preferred if available. But if only a woman can get to a target, then a woman should be used.

Tamil women faced similar barriers in the LTTE. While the group credits its leader, Vellupillai Prabhakaran, for including females, both supporters and detractors acknowledge that women were asking to fight, and were fighting for other Tamil groups, before the LTTE began training them for combat in 1984. The Freedom Birds were organized as a result of group needs and women's initiative. Once in the organization, Freedom Birds say they must prove themselves continually. In most cases, there must be a practical reason for terrorist groups to decide to use women in political violence. Female demands for operational roles are insufficient to overcome cultural practices, even among groups such as the PFLP and LTTE that claim women's liberation as part of their cause.

If only a woman can get to a target, then a woman should be used.

Overcoming Cultural Resistance

One reason women must fight for involvement in politics and violence is that, in many societies, women's roles are limited to wife and mother. The LTTE is an example of this reality. It

took the group 12 years to admit women into fighting roles, and it had difficulty determining how to incorporate them. The group is one of the few terrorist/insurgent bodies in the world with explicit rules on cadres' romantic lives and when they can marry. It also experimented with how to train women and employ them in combat. The difficulty of deciding whether the Freedom Birds should cut their hair to help them fight is emblematic of the tension the group faces between the necessity of having women directly involved in political violence and preservation of the Tamil culture. At each turn, the LTTE had to weigh how using females in combat and terrorism would affect the group's discipline, ability to fight, and popular support. Its decisions were a result of trial and error.

Necessity appears to help terrorist leaders overcome biases about women. A shortage of male volunteers may have encouraged Palestinian, Chechen, and Tamil groups to involve women in attacks. Given the difficulty of obtaining reliable population statistics for the areas in conflict, it is hard to prove that one of the elements in an organization's decision is a shortage of men. However, in these cases, the number of men available for terrorist operations has been reduced by outward labor migration, a lack of male volunteers, and arrests, harassment, and investigations of men.

Women, on the other hand, can be left in conflict zones and can move between cities without generating suspicion from security services. For example, in the 1980s, the Sri Lankan government targeted Tamil males between the ages of 14 and 40 for interrogation and detention.[15] In 1986, when women began fighting in the Freedom Birds, the government detained about 3,000 Tamil men.[16] Additionally, males were targets for recruitment, interrogation, and detention by competing Tamil groups. Consequently, many males fled the country.[17]

Decisions not to employ women in attacks are shaped by culture, but cultural prohibitions can be overcome by practical requirements.

Target assessment may also have helped terrorist leaders overcome cultural biases. For instance, on January 14, 2004, Reem al-Reyashi detonated a suicide bomb at a border crossing in Jerusalem. After the attack, Sheikh Yassin stated that Hamas decided to use a female attacker due to the increasing operational difficulties of getting men to their targets.[18] Even in traditional societies, women's household duties place them in markets and other public places, allowing them to blend with daily life. They have more flexibility in their dress than men. These factors make them less noticeable and less threatening to security services.

In the Palestinian, Chechen, and Tamil cases, terrorist groups did not begin their activities with women in operational roles. Women became involved only when men were unavailable, in part because of states' security measures. The interaction and learning that occur between terrorist groups and states are important to understanding terrorist actions, particularly why groups would want women.

State Responses

Decisions not to employ women in attacks are shaped by culture, but cultural prohibitions can be overcome by practical requirements. The leaders of Hamas, PIJ, and the LTTE have been explicit in explaining that women are employed when the target necessitates it. As noted above, men tend to be the preferred option for these groups, and women are usually employed when there are not sufficient men for operations or males cannot reach the targets. These factors—manpower and access to targets—are influenced by state actions.

With all three groups, it is impossible with present data to show direct cause and effect between specific state actions and terrorists' decisions to use women. For example, in the 3 months prior to Wafa Idris' January 2002 suicide bombing in Jerusalem, there were at least 13 major terrorist attacks, including suicide bombings inside Israel by male Hamas, PIJ, and Fatah members. There was no change in Israeli security practices that prevented male terrorists from reaching targets and thus forcing Al Aqsa to employ women. Yet it is likely that state actions and policies to combat terrorism had an influence on groups' decisions to change their practices. Indeed, Hamas and PIJ are explicit about picking the right person based on assessment of targets.

Security services' expectations, and occasionally official "profiles" of terrorists, made it easy for governments to focus on men, which may have encouraged groups to employ women. Early in each conflict, states expected terrorists to be young and male. Women were not part of the profile despite evidence of their involvement in all three conflicts. *Mirror imaging* (assuming the adversary's behavior is the same as one's own) may be partly to blame for states' ignoring the possibility of female terrorists. When the terror campaigns began, these governments did not regularly include significant numbers of women in operational roles in the military, police, intelligence, and other government jobs. They may have assumed that terrorists would act similarly.

States also viewed the cultures from which their adversaries came as so repressive toward women that terrorists would not allow their involvement. The infrequency of female attacks and the invisibility of women in groups could have reinforced these assumptions.

At some point in each conflict, however, states' expectations and assumptions changed. In the Russian-Chechen conflict, Chechen men between the ages of 16 and 60 have been the targets of detention and interrogation. As in Sri Lanka, Russian forces took control of villages to "cleanse" them by removing the young men for interrogations, from which many did not return. Unlike Sri Lanka and Israel, Russia has taken steps aimed specifically at female terrorists, most notably expanding cleansing operations to include them. According to one estimate, about 100 women have disappeared in Chechnya since the 2002 Dubrovka hostage-taking.[19] In 2003, the Ministry of Internal Affairs issued a directive to search women in headscarves and other traditional Muslim clothing.[20]

Moscow has not been insensitive to the possibility that targeting women may produce more terrorists of both genders, and its response has taken into account the unique propaganda value of women. In statements explaining why females are targeted,

Russian officials emphasize that Chechen groups prey on women in mourning to make them "zombies." With this argument, detentions are meant to protect both Chechen women from becoming zombies and Russian society from the zombies. Federal Security Service officials also claimed that use of women in attacks indicated that the terrorist groups were defeated.[21]

Chechen terrorists' use of women may represent some success by Russian security services in decreasing the number of men available to the groups and their ability to reach targets. Furthermore, the government, through its influence over the media, has been able to take advantage of the unique propaganda tools that female terrorists offer in its strategy to defeat Chechen terrorism.

Israel has also taken advantage of women's particular propaganda value for counterterrorism. The Foreign Ministry has published reports on female suicide bombers, emphasizing the terrorists groups' desire to exploit vulnerable women. The government has published descriptions of both successful and unsuccessful suicide bombers to illustrate the women's personal problems and how male terrorists took advantage of them. Perhaps most important for this study, Israel stopped profiling individuals and started profiling circumstances—that is, looking for anomalies in behavior or situations as an indication of a terrorist attack rather than trying to identify a person or the type of person who could be a terrorist.

The lesson is not only to add women to an existing profile, but also to recognize the diversity of the threat.

The government has also tried to balance the need to conduct searches while not further inflaming Palestinian anger by touching Palestinian women. As a partial solution, Israel has included female soldiers and police officers at checkpoints and in interrogations. Because not every checkpoint can be covered, technologies such as X-ray wands have been used.

Sri Lanka has taken a similar approach in confronting female terrorists. As in Israel, it includes women in the police and military. Again, there are not enough women to cover all security checkpoints. Sri Lanka has been willing to negotiate with the Tamil Tigers and maintain ceasefire agreements. Unlike Israel, however, the government does not control all its territory. The LTTE effectively runs many communities in northern and eastern Sri Lanka, complicating counterinsurgency operations.

In all these cases, efforts by governments often increased tensions in the populations they sought to control. The states' actions reduced the number of men available through arrest, detention, and death, perhaps increasing women's motivations for political violence while making them attractive to terrorist groups. Additionally, the decision to search men but not women at checkpoints may have encouraged groups to employ women.

Policy Implications

The actions of the three states are important for understanding terrorists' decisions about the use of women in terrorism and for combating terrorism. First, as in studies of serial killers that drew only on male murderers, studies of individual terrorists have focused only on male terrorists. This emphasis, combined with assumptions about the female nature, created a popular and sometimes official profile of terrorists as young and male. Women's repeated involvement should be a signal that there is no standard terrorist. The first lesson Russia, Israel, and Sri Lanka learned from female terrorism was that women represented a threat. The lesson is not only to add women to an existing profile, as Russia has, but also to recognize the diversity of the threat. The Israeli approach of looking for anomalies in situations is time- and personnel-intensive but offers more promise than attempting to describe all possible individuals who could be terrorists.

Second, just as groups can gain from sympathetic media portrayals of women terrorists, governments can use groups' ambivalence about female members to state advantage. Israel and Russia use stories of socially marginal women being exploited by men to discredit terrorist groups and explain away female violence. By making the women anomalies in the public mind, states reinforce the idea that they are in control and the public need not fear. These stories could be further exploited to delegitimize and fracture terrorist groups. The LTTE's policies on members' sexual behavior show the difficulty some groups have integrating women. Using propaganda about the group's sexual practices, as in Russia, can both discredit the group and exacerbate mistrust between members.

Finally, the decision by a group to employ women may be a sign that the state's efforts to combat terrorism are having an effect. The LTTE as well as Palestinian and Chechen groups turned to women only when they had to. If that is true with other groups, evidence of the use of women by terrorists may open more policy choices to a government—such as negotiations or incentives to individuals to renounce terrorism—because the group is weakened.

Female participation offers both states and terrorist groups unique options. However, policymakers should be realistic; women remain the minority. While their roles may be limited, women are important elements of groups and should not be overlooked. Wives know where their husbands are and with whom they meet. Mothers teach their children violence. Sisters, girlfriends, and female comrades enable men to get to their targets. Female terrorists likely know and do more than some security forces or terrorist groups give them credit for.

After al Qaeda's attacks on the United States in 2001, much has been made of terrorists' ability to innovate. Just as states and publics must be wary of underestimating terrorists, they must be cautious of deifying them. The employment of women by terrorist groups in Chechnya, Israel and the Occupied Territories, and Sri Lanka is an example of the limits of terrorists' thinking. Like states, these groups are bound by cultural expectations, demographics, public support, and the international context. Their limited use of women illustrates their strengths and shortcomings. Further exploration of this topic may provide greater insights for governments in combating terrorism.

Notes

1. For example, see Walter Laqueur and Yonah Alexander, eds., *The Terrorism Reader* (New York: Nal Penguin, 1987), 48. David Rapoport, "The Four Waves of Modern Terrorism," in *Attacking Terrorism,* ed. Audrey Kurth Cronin and James M. Ludes (Washington, DC: Georgetown University Press, 2004), 47. For an alternate view of the origins of modern terrorism, see Lindsay Clutterbuck, "The Progenitors of Terrorism: Russian Revolutionaries or Extreme Irish Republicans?" *Terrorism and Political Violence* 16, no. 1 (Spring 2004), 155–156.

2. Samuel Kucherov, "The Case of Vera Zasulich," *Russian Review* 11, no. 2 (April 1952), 87.

3. Cathy Porter, *Women in Revolutionary Russia* (New York: Cambridge University Press, 1987), 13.

4. Jay Bergman, "The Political Thought of Vera Zasulich," *Slavic Review* 38, no. 2 (June 1979), 244.

5. Porter, 15–17.

6. See, for example, Walter Laqueur, *The New Terrorism* (New York: Oxford University Press, 1999), 43; and J.B.S. Hardman, "Terrorism: A Summing Up in the 1930s," *The Terrorism Reader,* 227.

7. "Russian TV Interview Jailed Would-Be Suicide Bomber," RenTV, June 24, 2004, FBIS CEP20040721000353.

8. Russian opinion surveys indicate positive attitudes toward Chechens. See Public Opinion Foundation Database, "Attitude to Chechens: Pity and Fear," January 30, 2003, available at <http:// bd.english.fom.ru/report/cat/societas/Chechnya/ chechenian/ed030429>.

9. Public Opinion Foundation Database, "The terrorist attack in Tushino—"they want to face us down," July 15, 2003, available at <http:// bd.english.fom.ru/report/map/ ed032826>.

10. See, for example, Genevieve Sheehan, "Rebel Republic," *Harvard International Review* 25, no. 3 (Fall 2003), 14.

11. Ibrahim Hazboun, "Eighteen-year-old woman is latest suicide bomber," The Associated Press, March 29, 2002.

12. Yoni Fighel, "Palestinian Islamic Jihad and Female Suicide Bombers," International Policy Institute for Counter-Terrorism, October 6, 2003, available at <www.ict.org.ll/articles/articledet .cfm?articleid=499>.

13. "Islamic Jihad Leader Views Israeli Raid on Syria, Suicide Operations," Al-Arabiyah Television, October 5, 2003, FBIS GMP20031006000207.

14. "Hamas Founder Opines on Participation of Palestinian Women in Suicide Bombings," *Al-Sharq al-Awsat,* February 2, 2002, 8, FBIS 20020202000123.

15. Rajan Hoole et al., *The Broken Palmyra* (Claremont, CA: The Sri Lankan Studies Institute, 1988), 308.

16. Edgar O'Ballance, *The Cyanide War: Tamil Insurrection in Sri Lanka, 1973–88* (London: Brassey's UK, 1990), 68.

17. By 2002, an estimated 500,000 people had fled Sri Lanka, and about 600,000 were internally displaced. Miranda Allison, "Cogs in the Wheel? Women in the Liberation Tigers of Tamil Eelam," *Civil Wars* 6, no. 4 (Winter 2003), 38.

18. "Hamas uses female suicide bomber and threatens escalation," Jane's Terrorism and Insurgency Center, January 14, 2004.

19. Mark Franchetti, "Russians hunt down potential 'black widows,'" *The Australian,* September 27, 2004, 14.

20. "Russia: MVD Confirms Nationwide Operation to Check Muslim Women," *Moscow Gazeta,* July 23, 2003, FBIS CEP20030724000198.

21. "Russia: FSB Says Desperate Militants Enlisting Female Suicide Bombers," *ITAR—TASS,* July 10, 2003, FBIS CEP20030710000164.

From *Joint Force Quarterly*, Issue 44, 1st Quarter 2007, pp. 95-100. Published in 2007 by National Defense University Press. www.ndu.edu

UNIT 9

Government Response

Unit Selections

Key Points to Consider

- What are the threats posed by fundamentalist Islam?

- What are the most successful ways to deter terrorism?

- Should torture be used in the war on terrorism?

- What can be done to improve airport security?

Student Website
www.mhcls.com

Internet References

Counter-Terrorism Page
 http://counterterrorism.com
ReliefWeb
 http://www.reliefweb.int
The South Asian Terrorism Portal
 http://www.satp.org/

Government response to terrorism is multifaceted and complex. Choices about domestic spending, the use of military force, and long-term foreign policy objectives are increasingly shaped by our commitment to a Global War on Terrorism.

While counterterrorism spending has increased significantly since 9/11, choices about how this money is to be used have become more difficult as various constituencies lobby to have their voices heard. As policymakers struggle to allay public concerns, choices between spending for security today and preparing for the threats of the future have become more difficult. The tragedy of September 11 and the subsequent anthrax attacks have fueled fears about catastrophic terrorism. This makes choices about public policy priorities even more difficult. Given limited resources, should governments focus their efforts on existing crises and the most likely threats, or should they focus their resources on countless potential vulnerabilities and catastrophic threats, which many experts agree may be possible but not likely? Ideally governments should do both. Realistically, even in a resource-rich environment, governments have to make choices.

Decisions about when or how to use military force are equally complex. Should governments adopt preemptive or defensive postures? Should governments focus their resources on state sponsors of terrorism, or should they focus their efforts on capturing or killing the leaders of existing terrorist groups? Does the long-term deployment of a military force to a foreign country increase or reduce the threat of terrorism? Should nonproliferation be a priority in the war on terrorism?

Finally, it is important to note that the U.S. commitment to a global war on terrorism has not only had an impact on long-term U.S. foreign policy objectives but also the foreign policies of others. There is an opportunity cost to foreign policy decisions. By prioritizing a particular set of objectives, governments inevitably sacrifice others. This impacts not only our policies but also the policies of others. By making terrorism a policy priority we influence and shape the policies of others, as states may act in support of U.S. policy or take advantage of the vacuums created by such policies.

This unit examines the methods and policies governments use to respond to the threat of international terrorism. In the first article, Ariel Cohen argues that "Western governments do not fully comprehend the multifaceted threats" posed by radical Islam. He draws upon the lessons of the "Israel-Hezbollah war" to argue for military reform. The second article discusses various efforts by public health agencies to prepare local communities for bioterrorism. In the article, Christopher Conte argues that preparations for bioterrorism are diverting resources from more pressing health issues. Next, CIA veteran James Olson

© Royalty-Free/Corbis

discusses the moral dilemma which faces the U.S. intelligence community as it pursues its war on terrorism. He offers ten case studies to test the moral acceptability of intelligence community activities, arguing that an "acceptable middle ground" must be found. The final selection in this unit takes a pragmatic look at air security. It argues that seven years after its creation, the TSA has failed to reach a number of critical performance benchmarks. According to the article, screening failures, questionable rules, insecure cockpits, and insufficient security forces have undermined air security.

Knowing the Enemy

Ariel Cohen

The conflicts in Iraq, Lebanon, and Afghanistan and the global Islamist insurgency have revealed that Western democracies and their political and military leaders do not fully comprehend the multifaceted threats represented by radical Muslim nonstate actors. In this, they violate the most famous dictum of Sun Tzu, the Chinese strategic genius of 2,500 years ago: "If you know yourself and understand your opponent you will never put your victory in jeopardy in any conflict."

The broad support that al Qaeda jihadis and radical Islamist militias such as Hamas and Hezbollah enjoy in the Muslim world and in the global Muslim diaspora, as well as among non-Muslim anti-American political forces around the world demonstrates that describing the global Islamic insurgency as a fringe or minority phenomenon is unrealistic and self-defeating. Since 9/11, democracies have fought three wars against nonstate Islamist actors. The West needs to draw important lessons from Iraq, Afghanistan, and the clash between Israel and Hezbollah to address these strategic deficits. Lack of clarity in defining the enemy and delays in formulating political and information strategy severely endanger U.S. national interests and the security of the West.

Fighting the Wrong Enemy

The bush administration lost valuable time before it finally defined radical Islam as the premier national security threat in October 2005. Initially in the post-9/11 period, the president targeted "evildoers" and "terrorism" as the enemy. Moreover, Islam was declared a "religion of peace" and Saudi Arabia, which has spent the last 30 years spreading its Wahhabi/Salafi gospel, was labeled as "our friend." Unsurprisingly, the nation and the military were somewhat disoriented.

The U.S. military quickly and successfully destroyed the Taliban regime in Afghanistan. After that, however, the menu of enemies became slim: Saudi Arabia, from which 15 out of 19 hijackers came, was considered too important an oil supplier and too pivotal a state in the Middle East to be engaged. Pakistan, both the parent and the nursemaid of the Taliban,

promised cooperation. Most important, the U.S. did not know (and still does not know) how to fight nonstate actors, be they sub-state terrorist organizations, militias, or supra-state religious/political movements.

The jury is still out as to all the reasons for the Soviet collapse, but it was defeated in part through an indirect strategy formulated by the Reagan administration, and in part because it disintegrated due to its own internal weaknesses. If we are to believe one who was "present at the destruction"—Russian Prime Minister Egor Gaidar—a key reason was the flooding of the world market with cheap Saudi oil. The Soviet Union was also bankrupted by its unsustainably expensive military-industrial complex. In addition, it was burdened with ideological fatigue and cynicism, torn by ethnic centrifugal forces, and being bled in Afghanistan by the U.S.-supported mujahedeen.[1]

For over a century, the U.S. military and other arms of the government have been designed, nurtured, and financed to fight nation states, from Spain in 1898, to Germany in the two world wars, to Japan in 1941–45. Working with insurgencies or counter-insurgencies hasn't been Washington's forte for a long time. The U.S. military did not succeed in defeating the North Vietnamese insurgency, nor did its Cold War guerilla allies prevail in Angola or Mozambique. Beside the Huk rebellion in the Philippines, and support of Afghan mujahedeen, U.S. insurgency and counterinsurgency successes have been limited and peripheral to war-fighting. The current conflict is fundamentally different.

The Wars That Went Awry

The U.S. entanglements in Iraq and Afghanistan are exactly where the jihadis want the United States to be. According to Ayman al Zawahiri, in a taped interview at the second anniversary of 9/11, "If they withdraw, they lose everything, and if they stay they will continue to bleed to death."[2] In other words, damned if you do and damned if you don't.

U.S. abandonment of Iraq would be seen as a major victory for anti-American and Islamist forces in the Middle East and throughout the Muslim world. After Iraq, jihadis may target Saudi Arabia, the Gulf States, and eventually Egypt and nuclear-armed Pakistan for takeover. It is the belief of al Qaeda leaders from Osama bin Laden all the way down that Iraq is going to do to America what Afghanistan did to Russia. And this would be a major accomplishment for a nonstate actor in a confrontation with the mightiest state on earth.

Meanwhile, the future of NATO operations in Afghanistan remains uncertain, with many European allies foretelling the Alliance's defeat there. A resurgent Taliban, supported by al Qaeda and by elements within Pakistan, is threatening to overwhelm the NATO effort. At the same time, many in the Middle East believe that Israel, which they see as America's proxy, was defeated in Lebanon by Hezbollah; and Iran remains defiant, bringing on line batteries of 3,000 centrifuges capable of enriching uranium for nuclear weapons as well as funding Shiite extremists in Iraq and Lebanon.

Islamist extremist/jihadi organizations, including movements and militias from Egypt to Afghanistan, represent clear and present dangers to American homeland security, our vital interests, and to our Arab and Israeli allies. If and when victorious, today's terrorist organizations, global Islamist movements such as Muslim Brotherhood or al Qaeda, and "civil militias" such as Hezbollah or the Mahdi Army, are likely to take over countries and acquire nuclear weapons and other weapons of mass destruction. With their implacable anti-American and anti-Western agendas, they will represent dangers comparable to, or greater than, those presented by the fully armed and mobilized nation states which topped the threat hierarchies of the twentieth century. Hezbollah's relative success against Israel in the summer of 2006 is an important case study, worth analyzing in greater detail.

The Hezbollah War as Jihadi War

The Israeli-Hezbollah front, which had been relatively dormant since the hasty Israeli withdrawal from Lebanon in 2000, erupted as world leaders gathered for the July 2006 G-8 Summit in St. Petersburg, Russia. Hezbollah's unprovoked killing of eight Israeli soldiers and kidnapping of two resulted in 34 days of fighting. The hostilities will have long-term repercussions for Israel and other states confronting terrorist organizations, militias outside of state controls, and other nonstate actors.

The main lesson of the Hezbollah war is that military responses are simply not enough. The jihadi threat needs to be defeated by a combination of political, ideological, media, military and intelligence measures. The good news is that the potential does exist for a broad coalition between Western, non-Western and Sunni Muslim and Arab nation-states to get the job done. The bad news is that these actors are still obsessed with weakening Israel and forcing its

withdrawal from the West Bank without the foundations for durable peace and have not fully realized the necessity of working together against radical forces. The process of attaining this realization itself is likely to be painfully slow and costly in blood and treasure.

The Hezbollah war is at least the third conflict in the Greater Middle East characterized by the involvement of an advanced Western democracy on the one hand and a sub-state actor on the other. The first two are the war against al Qaeda and the Taliban in Afghanistan and the fighting against the Sunni and Shiite anti-American insurgencies in Iraq. The three wars have important commonalities, as the guerilla forces are religiously motivated, demonstrate a willingness to fight to the end, possess superior knowledge of the local terrain; and rely on dispersal among the local population, often utilizing systems of underground bunkers and strongholds which they prepare in advance.

The Israel-Hezbollah conflict was hardly the first—or the last—jihadi war. Israel is already involved in a low-intensity conflict in Gaza, primarily against Hamas, Islamic Jihad, the Resistance Committees, the Al Aqsa Martyrs Brigades of the PLO, elements of al Qaeda, and a bevy of other jihadi organizations. The Gaza forces have used Qassam rockets, which are primitive compared with Hezbollah's Katyushas, the Zilzal 1, 2, and 3, and the Fajar low trajectory short-range ballistic rockets supplied by Syria and Iran, along with sophisticated anti-tank Russian-made missiles and SAMs.[3] Additionally, Hizb ut-Tahrir al-Islami (the global Islamic Party of Liberation founded by a Palestinian cleric in the early 1950s) called for the creation of a caliphate (an expansionist military-religious dictatorship operating under strict interpretations of Islamic religious law) in Gaza.[4] The declaration of a caliphate anywhere on the globe would allow jihadi movements everywhere to shift from a "defensive" jihad to an offensive one—the jihad to impose Islam on the non-Islamic world, something only a caliph is allowed to do.

At least two additional theaters are worth mentioning, as they are not yet attracting as much attention. The first is Somalia, until recently under the tenuous rule of the Islamic Courts. While the Ethiopian Army and the provisional government defeated the Courts in December 2006, the Islamists dispersed among the population and are in the process of making a comeback. The international links of the Islamic Courts are clear. Chechens, Arabs, and even British and Swedish Muslims were killed fighting in Somalia.

The second theater is Darfur, where the Arab Islamist militia Janjaweed, Hizb ut-Tahrir, and other jihadi organizations have promised to fight any U.N. peacekeeping contingent deployed there.[5] Somalia and Sudan's combined population is 44.4 million, thus the potential of these two impoverished countries to serve as a base of jihad in Africa and elsewhere can be vast—as long as the oil money from Islamist sponsors keeps flowing in to recruit, train, and deploy their populations as jihadi shock troops. Moreover, if Somalia reverts to Islamic rule despite the December defeat of the Islamic Courts, its location next to the Bab-el-Mandeb strait may put this strategic shipping lane at the mercy of suicide boat attackers operating from Somali coastal bases.

The Future of Deterrence

Even the most advanced militaries, such as the U.S. and Israeli, which relied on the deterrent capacity and reputation they gained in conventional, twentieth century warfare, will need to reaffirm or re-establish deterrence against sub-state actors by successfully destroying enemies in the future. This will not happen unless the nature of the new enemy is fully understood and new doctrines, approaches, tactics, and procedures are developed. Moreover, in the Israeli case, the reassertion of deterrence will not be complete before the appropriate reforms and training have been fully implemented in the Israel Defense Forces (IDF).

In the past, the U.S. relied on the power of its combined operations and technological and industrial superiority. Its aircraft and ships dominated the skies and the oceans during World War II. In addition, the two nuclear bombs dropped on Hiroshima and Nagasaki were a clear demonstration of overwhelming force by a weapon which, for a short time, remained exclusively in U.S. hands. The U.S. military performed majestically in Gulf One, in Afghanistan, and during the opening of the current conflict in Iraq. What happened after the last two campaigns is eroding U.S. power and the perception of that power around the world.

Israel has relied on the deterrence value of its military prowess, earned in the hard-won victory against five attacking Arab armies in 1948; the four-day defeat of the Soviet-equipped Egyptian army in the Suez campaign of 1956; and the victory over the Egyptian, Syrian, and Jordanian forces in 1967, in which Israel lost 779 soldiers while the combined Arab forces lost 21,000.

In the 1973 war, Israel was stunned by a Syrian-Egyptian surprise attack. Nevertheless, the Israeli Defense Forces (IDF) recovered in time to take back all of the Golan Heights, put Damascus within artillery range, and surround the Third Egyptian Army at Suez, with no effective fighting force between the Israeli troops on the African side of the Suez Canal and Cairo, within three weeks. In 1982, the IDF was at the gates of Beirut within a week, forcing the evacuation of Yassir Arafat's Palestine Liberation Organization (PLO) to Tunis, Iraq, and Yemen and destroying a third of the Syrian airforce (86 planes) in one day. While Israel lost 675 soldiers, close to 10,000 Syrian and PLO combatants were killed. Between 1982 and 2000 Israel lost over 1,200 soldiers in Lebanon. But the defeat handed to Syria and the PLO in Lebanon, despite the war having been strategically bungled and the occupation domestically unpopular, bought Israel a quarter of a century without a major war.

The deterrence value of Israeli military prowess, earned in hard-won victories, could not last forever.

The deterrence value of these victories could not last forever, however. The 1982–2000 South Lebanon conflict ended with Israel's poorly managed withdrawal and abandonment of the South Lebanon Army in May 2000. Prime Minister Ehud Barak and then-Chief of Staff Shaul Mofaz supervised the retreat, which was primarily triggered by internal Israeli protests and dismay over casualties being suffered by Israeli troops deployed in the self-styled "security zone" in South Lebanon. The fact and the form of the withdrawal generated a perception of Israeli weakness. Shortly thereafter, Yassir Arafat unleashed the Terror War (the Second Intifada) which lasted until 2004, in which over 1,100 Israelis were killed in bombings and shootings, 75 percent of them civilians. Many speculated that the hasty retreat from Lebanon contributed to Arafat's decision to launch the Second Intifada. However, if this was correct, the Israelis certainly failed to internalize the lesson. Their 2005 withdrawal from Gaza, including the abandonment of Jewish villages there, did nothing to stop the volleys of short-range Qassam rockets from Gaza into pre-1967 Israel. Many analysts now argue that Israeli withdrawal from Gaza, billed by the Sharon government as yet another "painful concession for peace," only contributed to the Hamas electoral victory in January 2006 and increased the Arab perception of Israeli weakness. In fact, in June 2006 Hamas conducted an assault and kidnapping operation similar to Hezbollah's subsequent attack, which triggered the latest war.

Systemic Failure

Many Israeli and foreign commentators are focusing, correctly, on the failures of the political leadership and top military to anticipate, evaluate, prepare for, and defeat the Hezbollah threat. They cast the net broadly, to include sociological, morale, bureaucratic and political issues—not only narrow military ones. All these categories of analysis are valid. They point out that the Tel Aviv-based secular leftist European elite of Israel, including many in the IDF high command, bought into the same approach to military transformation that had been promoted by former Secretary of Defense Donald Rumsfeld. The current generation of Israel's political and military leaders had dismissed the concept of overwhelming military victory in favor of a dysfunctional technocratic reliance on a "Revolution in Military Affairs," emphasizing high-tech systems and air power.[6] While high-tech gives an important advantage to developed countries and modern militaries, it cannot replace good old intelligence and boots on the ground.

There clearly was a misguided belief that Israel is so powerful, nothing bad could happen to it. The political, military, and strategic results of this, yet another failed Israeli "concept," are there for all to see.

The process of self-examination, investigation, and conclusions will be heart-wrenching. Israel went through a similar exercise after the perceived "earthquake" of 1973. However, the current war is viewed as a limited one but an even more decisive Israel failure than the Yom Kippur War was ever perceived to be. In 1973, the Israelis believed that the Arabs would not attack after the disaster of 1967—and paid for the misconception with 3,000 lives in a country of 3.6 million. Then, as now, the Israeli political class and the military became enamored of a concept which turned out to be a self-defeating construct rather than a valid reflection of reality.

In 2006, the political and military leadership suffered from a severe case of negligence and neglect. Israeli government and military institutions had been focused on "unilateral withdrawal"—first from Gaza and, with an eye toward the future, from the West Bank—to combat the perceived "drawbacks of occupation." The Olmert cabinet, and especially then-Defense Minister Amir Peretz, a former trade union leader, were busy championing social welfare issues instead of preparing the country for the forthcoming confrontation. At the same time, Syria and Iran were busily arming Hezbollah. The Israeli leadership also did nothing to prepare the country for the crucial realization that Hezbollah is not a conventional army, and that a repeat of the lightning victories of the past was highly unlikely.

During the period leading up to the war with Hezbollah, Israel under then-Prime Minister Ariel Sharon and then under Ehud Olmert failed to prepare ample bomb shelter space or to deploy the anti-missile defenses it claimed to have developed. It also failed to acquire vital intelligence (such as the location of Sheikh Sayyed Hassan Nasrallah, the Hezbollah leader, in the early days of hostilities; the scale of presence of Syrian short- and medium-range missiles in Lebanon; and the deployment of C-801/802 Iranian-made anti-ship missiles). Most important, the IDF did not implement existing plans to destroy Hezbollah through a ground operation and ad-libbed almost until the war's end.[7] Reports from the field of failures to plan and lead operations; disasters in supply and evacuation of the wounded; missing weapons, ammunition, fuel, and other supplies indicate that the country and the army, which had not been engaged in fighting a major war since 1982, needs a massive shake-up.[8]

The IDF did not implement existing plans to destroy Hezbollah and ad libbed almost until the war's end.

Losing in the Battlefield of Perceptions

Public diplomacy/strategic information is yet another area in which Israel utterly failed and which requires a major revamping. Throughout the world, Islamist insurgents masterfully use images and propaganda, relying on sympathetic elements among Western media and nongovernmental organizations to focus international attention on civilian collateral casualties (even to the point of staging them). They use these images to stir the outrage that increases recruitment for future rounds in the conflict.[9]

The Israelis have been particularly inadequate at perception management at least since the 1982 Lebanon war, when they were attacked for allegedly high civilian casualties. In the ensuing years, Israel was systematically smashed in the international media and by the NGO community for the "occupation" of Arab lands, the alleged incarceration of 10,000 Palestinian prisoners, and other much-publicized misdeeds. In the most recent fighting, many an NGO, such as Human Rights Watch, simply refused to recognize that Hezbollah and Hamas deliberately used civilians as human shields and practiced a consistent policy of locating rocket launchers in civilian dwellings, schools, mosques, and hospitals, despite ample reporting in the mainstream, including liberal left, English language media.[10]

With almost astounding ease, the media fell for every Hezbollah trick and deception, including doctoring Reuters photos;[11] publishing a picture of a non-existing Israeli frigate being hit by a Hezbollah rocket (it was an Australian demolition explosion);[12] falling for a sob story about an Israeli missile hitting a Lebanese ambulance right in the middle of its Red Cross;[13] or using the same ruins to claim Israeli missile hits on different dates and deploying rehearsed "city criers" to feed tear-jerking stories to Western correspondents. Most of these hoaxes were exposed by Western bloggers, not by Israeli information officials, whose job it should be to debunk enemy propaganda.

But, most important, in the war with Hezbollah—and in previous conflicts, as well—the media fail to comprehend, and the Israelis fail consistently and adequately to explain, that those who are and were fighting Israel (including the PLO's Yassir Arafat, Hezbollah's Sheikh Hassan Nasrallah, and his Iranian sponsors) seek genocide and the ultimate demise of the state of Israel in its totality. Similarly, the media often compartmentalize descriptions of jihadi atrocities and the overall strategic goal of jihadis to force the demise of Western civilization. Representatives of Western governments almost never explain these key points, or they explain them without sufficient facts. Western publics are rarely afforded coherent information through which to frame and understand events.

Stigmatized yet again by the conflict with Hezbollah, Israel lost what little support it enjoyed at the beginning of the conflict in Europe, among the American left, and in many developing countries, while the hatred of the Arab world was easily further inflamed by the daily stream of "atrocity news" being served up by Al Jazeera and Al Manar, the Hezbollah satellite TV network. However, Israeli efforts to engage in strategic information operations were and remain virtually nonexistent. The budget of Al Manar is greater than the entire Israeli foreign ministry public diplomacy (*hasbara*) budget. The architect of this failing public diplomacy/strategic information policy under former Prime Minister Ariel Sharon, Raanan Gissin, has admitted himself that Jerusalem was particularly lacking on this battlefield.[14]

The Israelis aren't facing this particular battle alone. The U.S. and the West faced similar difficulties after the liberation of Afghanistan and the "desecration of the Koran" allegations; and continue to encounter a media barrage over Guantanamo, Abu Ghraib, the Prophet Muhammad cartoons, and other perception crises, both real and media-generated. Winning hearts and minds is and will remain the greatest challenge for Israel—and the West—in the forthcoming wars against the jihadis.

Lessons Learned

Jihadi organizations, supported by anti-status quo powers such as Iran and Syria, do not threaten only individual states, but are bringing about instability and the destruction of regimes throughout entire regions (Iraq, the Levant, the Arabian Peninsula, the Gulf, the Indian subcontinent). At the same time, state support is a source of sub-state actors' vulnerability which is not sufficiently understood, let alone exploited. As nation-states have leaderships, assets, and interests, those need to be put under pressure to promote a cessation of support for sub-state or supra-state actors.

The Israel-Hezbollah war, as well as conflicts in Iraq and Afghanistan, yielded many important lessons vital for the success in the conflict against Islamist radicalism world wide. These include:

Do not underestimate the enemy. Not being a conventional army, Hezbollah elicited the contempt of Israeli political and military elites. The deputy chief of staff and Israeli Air Force intelligence commanders referred to Hezbollah as a "terrorist gang," discounting its lethality.[15] Hezbollah wasted no time, putting down roots in Gaza and attempting to penetrate the West Bank. The Pentagon leadership and the U.S. military top brass were slow to recognize the nature of the conflict in Iraq as an insurgency, not just a terrorist campaign.

Find sponsors and leaders. More intelligence penetration of Hezbollah and of Iraqi militias is necessary, both in terms of human intelligence and signal intelligence. More scrutiny needs to be focused on the location of Hezbollah's leadership; the Iran-Syria-Hezbollah link, including the identities of liaison officers; the type and volume of hardware supplied to Hezbollah; the nature and location of the joint Syrian-Iranian-Hezbollah command-and-control center in Syria; the identities of Iranian experts and trainers working with Hezbollah; the identities of Hezbollah personnel trained or training in Iran; and the doctrine and tactics, techniques, and procedures (TTP) that the Iranians are teaching Hezbollah and their allies in Iraq and elsewhere now or in the future.

Similarly, the leadership and connections to foreign states and funders of the Ba'ath underground and the Shiite militias need to be further mined for actionable intelligence of the kind collected in the January 2007 raid on the Iranian representative office in Mosul. Such information can assist in putting down the insurgency.

Hezbollah spied on Israel, recruited Israeli officers, and gained a deep understanding of Israeli doctrine and tactics.

Local knowledge, language skills, and understanding of political, historical, and religious dynamics of the theater of operations are weapons in themselves. Hezbollah spent a tremendous amount of resources spying on Israel, including recruiting Israeli military officers and gaining a deep understanding of Israeli doctrine and tactics. A similar effort is afoot in Iraq and Afghanistan. Every war is a war of intelligence, of strategic and operational deceit and subterfuge, but twenty-first-century wars will be outstanding for their heavy reliance on and integration with intelligence activities. Gathering and analysis of intelligence are impossible without linguistic and cultural knowledge.

Safe havens are crucial. These wars are not local. Just as Syria provided Hezbollah a safe haven, and Iran supplied money, weapons and training, the Taliban and other jihadi groups are using safe havens, such as in Pakistan, to train, equip, treat the wounded, and learn military and technological innovations. A task for the twenty-fist-century war against radical jihad will be to render safe havens unsafe, using diplomacy where possible and force where necessary.

The Hezbollah victory is empowering Iran and threatening to destabilize the whole Middle East. Iranian leaders from Ayatollah Ali Khameini to President Mahmoud Ahmadinejad have called the outcome "the divine victory." Arab commentators have already opined that the Hezbollah success will boost jihadis (both Sunni and Shiite) from Iraq to Jordan to Egypt.[16]

Riyadh, Amman, and Cairo were deeply uncomfortable about the Iranian involvement with Iraqi Shiites and support of Hezbollah. Sunni radicals, however, sided with

Iran. Ayman al Zawahiri, Osama bin Laden's top lieuten-ant, welcomed Hezbollah's resilience, opening the way to expanded cooperation between extremist Sunnis and extremist Shiites in toppling pro-Western regimes. Cooper-ation between the United States, European powers, out-of-area actors, and the moderate/pragmatic Arab nation-states, as well as Israel, needs to be boosted to stem the Iranian expansion and a possible anti-American Sunni-Shiite jihadi alliance.

Information warfare and perception management is paramount. Without effective hearts-and-minds strate-gies that are an integral part of the overall war strategy, the West and its allies in the area have very little in terms of soft power to counter Iran and the jihadis. This infor-mation strategy has to affect not just the Western and Muslim media, but also the mosques and the education systems. Modern states and militaries have repeatedly failed to clearly recognize, much less effectively counter, the deliberate campaign of manipulation and propaganda being carried out by militant Islamists/jihadis through the mass media, especially the Internet. The largely paci-fist Western nongovernmental organization (NGO) sec-tor is often a target of Islamist propaganda that vilifies the U.S. and its allies. Islamists consistently score points through the media, academia, and the NGO community in the court of the public opinion. A case in point for an information warfare offensive would be pressuring the Gulf states, including Saudi Arabia, to further cut sup-port not just to al Qaeda and other jihadi organizations, but also to radical Islamic charities and madrassahs, and to deleigitimize jihadi-supporting preachers and imams. More efforts are needed to boost the profile of those cler-ics who promote a message of tolerance and to facilitate the launch of satellite TV channels and websites with agendas aimed at reconciliation and peace. This should be the highest priority in the war of ideas—information warfare that so far the U.S. has been fighting only half-heartedly, and unquestionably losing.

The U.N. is an unreliable agency for peace. Former UN Secretary General Kofi Annan and the permanent mem-bers of the Security Council, especially France and Russia, did precious little to fight terror in Lebanon or Iraq. As far as France is concerned, things are improving under the new administration of President Nicolas Sarkozy. The UN peacekeeping force, UNIFIL, has collected and published detailed data about Israeli force movements in wartime, endangering the lives of Israeli servicemen and women, and violating its own neutrality mandate.[17] Just as the UNSC sat on its hands when Lebanon and Hezbollah failed to implement UNSC Resolution 1559, which stipu-lated the disarmament of Hezbollah and deployment of the Lebanese Armed Forces to the South, the violation of UNSC Resolution 1701, which demanded the same and more, began the day it was signed. Specifically, Hezbollah

announced that it refused to consider procedures to disarm, and it refuses to stop the resupply of weapons from Syria; it considers Israeli troops legitimate targets—with no repercussions from the UN. Syria and Iran are openly defying the UN and furnishing arms supplies to Hezbollah, with no sanctions and no calls for sanctions against these terror-sponsoring states. Those U.S. and Israeli decision-makers who actively lobbied for Resolution 1701 as the solution for the conflict now look naïve at best, and possi-bly worse than that. All this is hardly surprising in view of previous UN failures in the Middle East (such as the hasty evacuation from Sinai of the UNEF by Secretary General U Thant in 1967) and the UN "peacekeeping" disasters in Bosnia, Somalia, and Rwanda.

The Israelis managed to snatch a public perception of failure from the jaws of potential victory.

Under-promise and over-deliver. The best strategy is not to advise the enemy of your strategic goals. Policy-makers should not have promised "a new Middle East" safe for democracy; they should not have proclaimed that Hezbollah would be destroyed, disarmed, or denied the ability to fire rockets into Israel. All Israeli leaders needed to say was "Hezbollah will pay the price"—and strike at a time and place of their choosing. Instead, they fought when and where Hezbollah wanted them to. Rather than under-promising and over-delivering, the Israelis inflated expec-tations, articulated maximum goals, and managed to snatch a public perception of failure from the jaws of potential victory. Similarly, the U.S. over-promised in Iraq by talking about turning the country into a model of democracy for the New Middle East. Now Washington needs to find ways to exercise the art of the possible and achieve pacification with the least number of American and Iraqi casualties. Whether this is in fact possible remains to be seen.

The Time Is Now

When facing sub-state actors, conventional, twentieth-century military doctrines aimed at wars against nation-states and industrial-era mass armies are effectively dead. Even the best traditional militaries, such as the U.S. and Israeli armies, face formidable difficulties when con-fronted with irregular, well-motivated, and foreign-sup-ported forces, which enjoy media battlefield advantages. The Israel-Hezbollah conflict was not so much a defeat of Israel as it was a defeat of the old-style warfare by the new. The same can be said about the U.S. military in Iraq. The best nineteenth-century cavalry army would be impotent against small and well-trained tank and mechanized infantry divisions. And with modern warfare becoming increasingly political, intelligence-based, and waged on the information battlefield, it is time to restructure the military to answer these challenges. The time to wake up and rethink the paradigms is now. Tomorrow may be too late.

Notes

1. Ariel Cohen, *Russian Imperialism: Development and Crisis* (Greenwood Publishers, 1998).

2. Ayman Al Zawahiri, quoted in Bruce Hoffman, "Combating Al Qaeda and the Militant Islamic Threat," Testimony presented to the House Armed Services Committee, Subcommittee on Terrorism Unconventional Threats and Capabilities, RAND Corporation CT-255 (February 2006).

3. Anthony Cordesman, "Preliminary Lessons of the Israeli-Hezbollah War," Center for Strategic and International Studies (August 27, 2006).

4. Julie Stahl, "Radical Group May Declare Islamic Caliphate in Gaza," CNSNews.com (August 24, 2006).

5. Opheera McDoom, "Islamist Threaten to Fight U.N. Darfur Force," Reuters (August 25, 2006). See also, Ariel Cohen, "Hizb ut-Tahrir: An Emerging Threat to U.S. Interests in Central Asia," Heritage Foundation, Backgrounder 1656 (May 30, 2003).

6. Ari Shavit, "Systemic Failure," *Haaretz* (August 4, 2006); Yuval Steinitz (the former chairman of the Knesset foreign affairs and defense committee), "The War That Was Led Astray," *Haaretz* (August 17, 2006).

7. Interview with the author, retired general, Israeli general staff (August 8, 2006).

8. Ralph Peters, "Hezbollah 3, Israel 0," *New York Post* (August 17, 2006).

9. Anthony Cordesman, "Qana and the Lessons for Modern War," Center for Strategic and International Studies (July 31, 2006).

10. Alan Dershowitz, "What are they Watching," *New York Sun* (August 23, 2007).

11. "Reuters Drops Beirut Photographer," BBC, (August 8, 2006).

12. "Hezbollah sinks Australian War Ship," *Herald Sun,* Andrew Bolt's Blog (August 22, 2006).

13. "The Red Cross Ambulance Incident. How the Media Legitimized an Anti-Israel Hoax and Changed the Course of a War" http: //www.zombietime.com/fraud/ambulance/.

14. Raanan Gissin, "The Critical Importance of Israeli Public Diplomacy in the War Against the Iran-Hizballah Axis of Terror," Jerusalem Issue Brief, Institute for Contemporary Affairs 6:9 (August 23, 2006).

15. Gissin, "The Critical Importance of Israeli Public Diplomacy."

16. Tamim Al-Barghouti, "Two souths, one war," *Al Ahram Weekly Online* (August 3–9 2006).

17. Lori Lowenthal Marcus, "What did you do in the war, UNIFIL?" *Weekly Standard* (September 4, 2006).

ARIEL COHEN is senior research fellow at the Heritage Foundation. He is the editor and co-author of *Eurasia in Balance* (Ashgate, 2006.)

From *Policy Review,* 145, October/November 2007, pp. 41–53. Copyright © 2007 by Ariel Cohen. Reprinted by permission of The Hoover Institution, Stanford University and Ariel Cohen. www.policyreview.org

Are We Ready Yet?

We're building our defenses against bioterrorism, but we face growing questions about costs and priorities.

CHRISTOPHER CONTE

Patrick Libbey likes to be positive. When the executive director of the National Association of County and City Health Officials is asked about how ready state and local governments are to respond to bioterrorism—it's a question he hears frequently—he'll tell you, "Significant progress has been made."

It's true. As the nation moves into its fifth year of a crash effort to build defenses against a possible bioterrorist attack, states have developed a wide range of emergency plans, conducted numerous exercises, and modernized their information and communications systems. But Libbey is not really satisfied with his answer. That's because there is no "consistent measure of where we are or where we need to be," he says. "That is probably our largest failing since the whole push began."

Libbey is not alone. George Hardy, executive director of the Association of State and Territorial Health Officers, sings a similar refrain. "It is absolutely critical that we develop some metrics," Hardy says. "We need accountability indicators for federal funds that are going out, and we need indicators for the overall level of community preparedness."

The two men, who together represent public health agencies serving the majority of Americans, no doubt have complex motives in pressing for standards to gauge preparedness efforts. On one hand, they are eager to keep federal bioterrorism funds—the first significant influx of new money into the public health system in decades—flowing. Many state and local public health agencies have launched ambitious infrastructure-building efforts on the expectation that bioterrorism readiness will continue to be a federal priority, and they clearly would like more support. Although the federal government has been sinking $1 billion annually into public health readiness, researchers at the RAND Corp. recently concluded from an assessment of California public health agencies that spending is only one-third to one-half of what local officials believe is needed.

At the same time, Libbey and Hardy also may be eager to draw some boundaries around bioterrorism-preparedness activities. The emphasis on preparing for mass-casualty incidents is diverting attention from other mounting public health problems—such as diabetes, tuberculosis and sexually-transmitted diseases—that may be relegated to the back burner for some time to come. "Our initial response to building emergency capacity was to treat the problem as if it were an emergency," Libbey says. "We thought we would drop everything we were doing, tend to the problem, and then everything would go back to normal. But there isn't the old 'normal' to go back to. Emergency preparedness is now part of our ongoing work."

All of this suggests that Americans are due for some serious soul-searching about what to expect from their public health system. What does it mean to be prepared? How do we balance the goal of making people safer with keeping them healthier? And what are the long-term implications of the growing role Washington is assuming in shaping a public health system that traditionally has been local in nature?

Mixed Results

Until recently, most health departments have been too busy trying to get a seat at the emergency-planning table to spend much time on such big-picture questions. "We spent the first year or more just building relationships," notes Darren Collins, director for the DeKalb County, Georgia, Board of Health's Center for Public Health Preparedness. That effort, at least, has paid off. Before 2001, public health departments rarely played a role in disaster planning. But now, they are integral players in most local emergency planning teams, serving on—and in some cases leading—unified incident command systems that can be activated any time there is an emergency. "We have much greater visibility in the community now," says Martin Fenstersheib, the health officer for Santa Clara County, just south of San Francisco. "With the advent of biological issues, we are now in at the top among first responders."

Along the way, public health agencies have acquired many new tools. Public health workers in Santa Clara County, for instance, now have "go-kits"—duffle bags containing personal protective gear, cameras, computers, specimen-gathering equipment and other tools to help them diagnose health problems in the field. The county also issues packs of laminated cards and reference materials so doctors can quickly recognize outbreaks of anthrax, smallpox, plague or Ricin toxin.

North Carolina's Health Department uses the Internet to review hospital admission records and check on the availability of hospital beds in real time—capabilities that could help it detect disease outbreaks more quickly and respond more effectively to mass-casualty situations. The state also has seven Public Health Regional Surveillance Teams, each consisting of a physician, an epidemiologist, an industrial hygienist and a field veterinary officer. A team can be deployed anywhere in the state in an emergency.

Montgomery County, Maryland, has been training public works and other county employees, as well as lay educators, parish nurses and other medical professionals, to serve as volunteers in emergencies, and it is helping schools, nursing homes and group homes make their own preparations to respond to emergencies. "In a crisis, we won't be able to get to people right away," says Kay Aaby, project coordinator at the county's Department of Health and Human Services. "They have to know how to shelter in place."

Should a pandemic of influenza hit, the Seattle-King County public health department has procedures for imposing a large-scale quarantine. It has identified a facility where sick people could be isolated from the general population. The department also is working with area governments and businesses to plan how they will keep operating during a pandemic, in which absenteeism could run as high as 30 percent.

Despite such progress, however, most public health officials concede the country still is not ready for a public health calamity. One reason for the gap is the sheer magnitude of the job and the dearth of trained personnel to do it. While public health laboratories have acquired a lot of new equipment in the past four years, more than half say they don't have enough scientists to run tests for anthrax or plague, and a majority lack sufficient capabilities to test for chemical terrorism, according to a report issued last year by Trust for America's Health, a public health advocacy group.

Similarly, two-thirds of the states still don't use the Internet to contribute to a national database on disease outbreaks—a capacity the federal Centers for Disease Control and Prevention believes would greatly increase the public health system's ability to identify and stamp out harmful biological agents. "A lot of gears are moving, but they aren't meshing together," says Shelley Hearne, TFAH's executive director. "The jalopy has gotten better oil and faster wheels, but it is not a race car that can get you from zero to 60 when you give it a good push on the gas."

Meanwhile, low pay and an aging workforce are complicating efforts to bolster public health staffs. Some 30 of 37 states that responded to a 2003 survey conducted by the Association of State and Territorial Health Officers reported shortages of public health nurses, 15 lacked enough epidemiologists, 11 didn't have as many laboratory workers as they need, and 11 others said they are shy of environmental specialists. And it may become difficult to stay even, let alone get ahead. The average age of public health workers is 46, compared with 40 for the overall U.S. workforce, and retirement rates are projected to run as high as 45 percent over the next five years.

Low pay and an aging work force are complicating much-needed efforts to bolster the public health system.

Perhaps most important, there is growing concern among some public health officials about the impact preparedness efforts have had on our ability to deal with our chronic health problems. RAND researchers have noted that the increased emphasis on bioterrorism has led to retrenchments in programs to control sexually-transmitted diseases and tuberculosis, as well as teen pregnancy-prevention programs. In Madison County, North Carolina, public health nurse Jan Lounsbury had to drop work on programs to discourage smoking and promote exercise and better nutrition when she became bioterrorism planner for the county, in the state's western mountains. "Health promotion has been put on the back burner," says Lounsbury. And Russell Jones, a state epidemiologist based in Temple, Texas, warns that budget cuts have left the Lone Star State seriously vulnerable to an outbreak of pertussis (it had one several years ago). "In bioterrorism, we're adequate," Jones says. But otherwise, "if something bad happens, we are not prepared."

The New York-based Century Foundation, meanwhile, has questioned the cost-effectiveness of syndromic surveillance, a glitzy new technology that has gotten a big boost thanks to bioterrorism funding. It involves amassing a wide range of information, such as hospital admission forms, 911 calls, over-the-counter drug sales, school absenteeism figures and more, into a single database that allows analysts to look for clusters of symptoms that might indicate the beginning of a new disease outbreak. But it's expensive—New York City's system, widely considered the state of the art, costs $1.5 million annually, or about $4,000 a day—and so far largely unproven. "If it is sensitive enough to catch the few additional cases that may be the harbinger of a bioterrorist attack, it is likely to generate many false alarms as well and to command scarce resources," the foundation warns.

Defining Moments

One of the most glaring deficiencies in the public health system today is a serious gap between many health departments and the communities they serve. When RAND researchers assessed California public health departments, for instance, they noted that many local health departments have shockingly little information about their own communities. "In some jurisdictions," the analysts wrote, "representatives from police and fire departments appeared to have better knowledge of vulnerable populations than the health departments had."

Although this problem didn't begin with the national push for bioterrorism readiness, it hasn't been helped by it either. Some public health officials believe it may be a major reason why we are less safe than we need to be. That is the view of leaders of the Alameda County Public Health Department in California (it's unknown whether the department was part of the RAND study, which was conducted under a pledge of confidentiality). The department has devoted considerable time and effort to reaching out to neighborhoods. Most of its public health nurses work out of satellite offices in various communities, not out of the department's office in downtown Oakland. In some low-income communities, public health workers have gone door-to-door to survey residents, organize community meetings and otherwise help neighbors learn how to address common concerns. Public Health Director Arnold Perkins believes such "capacity building" will improve health in the targeted communities by reducing the myriad tensions and sense of isolation that significantly contribute to problems ranging from high infant mortality to heart disease, hypertension and asthma.

When federal bioterrorism funds began flowing to Alameda County, the department worked hard to integrate them into its ongoing activities, rather than let them be a diversion. One solution was to provide special "survival kits"—first aid items, food bars, water boxes, thermal blankets, ponchos, water purification tablets, dust masks, vinyl gloves and a combination radio-siren-flashlight—to people in the troubled communities in return for their participation in the capacity-building effort.

Are the kits just a clever subversion of a federal program? Not according to Anthony Iton, the county health officer. People in low-income neighborhoods have too many daily concerns—many lack health insurance or have high blood pressure; the local food stores sell liquor and junk food rather than fresh fruit and vegetables; and the neighborhood park has been taken over by drug dealers—to spend much time worrying about bioterrorism. By lacing information and self-help tools about bioterrorism into a broader effort to address residents' concerns, the department believes it has a better chance of getting its message across than if it tried to deal with preparedness separately. Moreover, by showing people that it is working to make their daily lives better, the health department is increasing the chances they will cooperate with it in an emergency—by staying home to slow the spread of a new virus or by coming to a mass inoculation site, for instance. "It's all about trust," says Iton. "If people don't trust us, they won't follow our instructions in emergencies."

Iton contends that the health department's work with poor neighborhoods effectively addresses one of the weakest links in current bioterrorism defenses. Most epidemics take root first in poor communities and then spread from there. In affluent communities, people are quick to see doctors if they get sick, increasing the chances that any new epidemic will be quickly detected. But in poor communities, people avoid going to doctors because they lack health insurance, can't afford to pay for health care or distrust mainstream institutions. That gives germs a better chance to incubate and spread. And because low-income people often commute from their homes to places such as airport concession stands, where diverse people commingle, these bugs have abundant opportunities to leap to the population at large. "Lack of health insurance, unfamiliarity with diseases and what to do about them, and the fact that the health care system turns poor people away—those are our greatest causes of vulnerability to bioterrorism in Alameda County," Iton argues.

Federal agencies aren't likely to accept as expansive a definition of emergency preparedness as Iton's views imply are necessary. To be sure, the Bush administration does view preparedness in broader terms today than it did a few years ago. When the U.S. Department of Homeland Security recently issued a "target capabilities list" for emergency planning, for instance, it identified 15 possible health calamities that would have "national significance"—including some, such as pandemic flu and major earthquakes and hurricanes, that aren't terrorism-related. But the list doesn't include lack of health insurance or community cohesion.

Nor does a list of 62 "critical tasks" and 34 performance measures recently issued by the CDC in response to calls for clearer standards to govern emergency public health preparations. Some of the proposed performance measures are highly specific (one says, for instance, that health departments should be able to bring the "initial wave" of personnel on board to conduct emergency operations within 90 minutes). Others deal with preparedness quite broadly (a knowledgeable public health professional should be available to answer a call reporting a suspicious disease within 15 minutes). But the CDC rules don't go so far as to tackle community capacity-building or require public health departments to spend more time meeting constituents in their own neighborhoods.

The current federal rules won't be the final world on preparedness; the CDC has pledged to meet with major players in the bioterrorism-preparedness arena to discuss them in detail. But the rules nevertheless represent a significant assertion of federal influence in a field that has generally been a state and local responsibility—one that nudges local health departments more in the direction of emergency preparedness. Given the absence of similar pressures to address other long-standing public health concerns, it's easy to imagine that local health departments' ability to deal with non-emergency health problems will become even more attenuated. So here's a word of advice to NACCHO's Libbey, ASTHO's Hardy and other state and local representatives who will be discussing the issues with Washington in the months ahead: Be careful what you ask for.

CHRISTOPHER CONTE can be reached at crconte@earthlink.net

Intelligence and the War on Terror
How Dirty Are We Willing to Get Our Hands?

The nature of intelligence work requires spies to maintain steadfast dedication to the best interests of their country, while carrying out acts of profound deceit and betrayal. In this article, CIA veteran James Olson explores this moral paradox by reviewing the history of intelligence in the United States, and posing a series of realistic scenarios capturing the brutal nature of the war on terror. He concludes by calling for a national dialogue to determine a set of moral guidelines to guide intelligence work.

JAMES M. OLSON

Let me pose the following paradox:

Point 1: The most important things in my life, along with my country and my family, are my honor and my faith.

Point 2: I spent my entire CIA career lying, cheating, stealing, manipulating, and deceiving.

How can these two points be reconciled? Can a person of good faith and conscience engage in espionage and covert action on behalf of the United States, and not compromise his or her moral values? As a country, what kinds of intelligence activities are we prepared to condone in the fight against international terrorists? This article addresses the timely topic of whether the CIA and other U.S. intelligence agencies should be unleashed in the war on terror. How far should they be allowed to go? What kind of country are we going to be? In short, how dirty are we willing to get our hands, if we are willing to get them dirty at all?

Most Americans will agree in principle that intelligence is vital to our war on terror. But the tricky question is what kind of intelligence? Which intelligence techniques, specifically, do the president, the Congress, and the American people want the U.S. Intelligence Community to use against terrorists? In the face of this new threat, are they prepared to remove some or all of the restrictions that have been placed on our spies? Are they prepared to redefine or stretch the ethical limits of behavior? Perhaps, most importantly, are they willing to relinquish some of their individual rights in the interest of greater safety for all U.S. citizens?

A Historical Aversion

For most of our country's history, spying has been considered immoral, dishonorable, and inconsistent with a free and democratic society. We can find an early example of this attitude during the Revolutionary War. The situation for the colonials looked bleak after British General William Howe defeated George Washington on Long Island in 1776 and prepared to attack across the East River into Manhattan. Washington desperately needed intelligence on the size of the British force, its armaments, and its intentions. He called upon his officers to volunteer to go behind enemy lines and spy. No one stepped forward. It would be a very dangerous mission, and fear was undoubtedly a factor. Other causes of reluctance were the lack of training, poor cover, and weak communications. But the real reason no one volunteered was that spying was considered disreputable and ungentlemanly.

[S]pying has been considered immoral, dishonorable, and inconsistent with a free and democratic society.

It was only 21 year-old Captain Nathan Hale of Connecticut who, after an agonizing night of indecision, told a fellow officer that he would volunteer for the spying mission because, as he put it, "any kind of service necessary to the public good becomes honorable by being necessary." A statue of Nathan Hale stands outside the main entrance of the CIA headquarters, and his statement is often cited by U.S. intelligence professionals as one of the moral justifications for spying. But what kind of standard did Nathan Hale actually give us? Do we accept the ancient Latin maxim of "necessity has no law"?[1] Is *any* kind of service permissible if it serves the public interest, and who determines what is necessary?

George Washington was remarkably sophisticated in his understanding of intelligence and his support for intelligence activities—but most of his successors were not. A strong negative bias toward intelligence persisted throughout the nineteenth and into the twentieth century. As a result, there was no real professional intelligence service in the U.S. until the creation of the Office of Strategic Services (OSS) in World War II. German and Japanese attacks and atrocities appeared to banish the traditional American squeamishness about the dirty business of spying. Still, President Harry S. Truman disbanded the OSS shortly after the war, and resisted efforts by General William Donovan and others to establish a post-war version of the OSS. Truman declared that he did not want to create an "American Gestapo."

The Cold War changed Truman's mind, and the CIA was established in 1947 to counter the growing Soviet threat. By the time Dwight Eisenhower was president, the country's attitude toward spying had clearly evolved. The Doolittle Report,[2] commissioned by President Eisenhower and released in 1954, probably reflected not only the current government position, but also that of the American people:

> It is now clear that we face an implacable enemy whose avowed objective is world domination by whatever means and at whatever cost. There are no rules in such a game. Hitherto acceptable norms of conduct do not apply. If the United States is to survive, long-standing American concepts of fair play must be reconsidered. We must develop effective espionage and counter-espionage services and must learn to subvert, sabotage and destroy our enemies by more clever, more sophisticated and more effective methods than those used against us.

The parallels between 1954 and 2007 are striking. Terrorists have become the new Soviets. Concern regarding the spread of Soviet communism preoccupied our security thinking then, just as the global war on terrorism does today. Throughout our history, we have tended to be more open to the "dirty tricks" side of the intelligence business when the country has faced a looming external threat. Conversely, when the country seems safe and secure, Americans typically fall back on traditional scruples and rein in intelligence activities. There have been several such cycles throughout our history. The enemy we confront today has no rules, so it is tempting to assume that

we should fight back in the same manner. But if we fight without principles, at what point do we betray the values we are fighting so hard to defend? At what point do we become them? It is an untenable position today, as Doolittle put it back then, to say that "there are no rules in such a game." But what should the rules be, and who should set them? We cannot lose the war on terror—our way of life would never be the same again—but what will be the moral costs of our victory?

Terrorists have become the new Soviets.

New Rules for a New Game?

A key factor in determining a new set of rules is assessing the influence of the September 11, 2001 terrorist attacks. Cofer Black, the former chief of the CIA's Counterterrorism Center, put it bluntly in his testimony before Congress in 2002, when he declared that, "All I want to say is that there was 'before' 9/11 and 'after' 9/11. After 9/11 the gloves came off."[3] Vice President Richard Cheney shared this sentiment when speaking on *Meet the Press* on September 26, 2001:

> We also have to work, though, sort of the dark side, if you will. We've got to spend time in the shadows in the intelligence world. A lot of what needs to be done here will have to be done quietly, without any discussion, using sources and methods that are available to our intelligence agencies, if we're going to be successful. That's the world these folks operate in, and so it's going to be vital for us to use any means at our disposal, basically, to achieve our objective.

Vice President Cheney was likely engaging in wishful thinking when he said we could use "any means at our disposal" and could do it "quietly, without any discussion." That sort of conduct is simply not possible in the current era. The U.S. intelligence community has been under a magnifying glass: second-guessed at every turn, criticized in Congress, and lambasted in the press. Long gone are the days when American spies could do whatever they needed to do "quietly, without any discussion."

The manner in which the U.S. intelligence community fights the war on terror *is* open to public discussion, and in our democratic society, it should be. While there should not be a direct public role in operational decision-making—the public has no need to know about specific operations or sensitive sources and methods—they should know what our moral parameters are. How and what we decide upon will go a long way toward defining who we are as a people, what kind of moral authority we have, and how we are perceived around the world. We need to get it right.

Our starting point is not encouraging. First, very few Americans have any real understanding of what the world of spying is like. Their views are shaped and distorted by the media and Hollywood. Recent movies like *The Good Shepherd* and popular spy novelists like Robert Ludlum give a grossly inaccurate picture of how espionage and covert action are done. This is unfortunate, because we cannot have an informed and serious debate on the morality of spying when there are so many misconceptions to overcome. Second, spying has become increasingly politicized. Many Americans look at intelligence through a partisan optic and have adopted obdurately ideological views of what should and should not be allowed. Their minds are made up before the discussion can even begin. This is true of people on both ends of the political spectrum. On one side, we have the "Rambo-types," for whom anything goes. They've rarely seen a covert action operation they didn't like. On the other side, we have the hardcore civil libertarians and human rights advocates who fundamentally object to any use of deceit, manipulation, or coercion in our intelligence operations. One university professor, upon reading some of the scenarios from my book on ethics in intelligence, told me I was making a basic and fatal error by even examining the topic. He said, "by posing these questions, you are making the erroneous assumption that *anything* the CIA could *ever* do could ever be moral." He continued by noting "that's wrong, because the CIA is a fundamentally immoral institution supporting a fundamentally immoral government." That is one point of view—and he's entitled to it. But it does not speak to a clear or sophisticated understanding of the nature of intelligence work.

The vast majority of the U.S. public seems to be somewhere in the middle, but it is unclear where their judgments lie. Where should we draw that elusive line between permissible and prohibited intelligence activities? And who should draw it? I trust the U.S. intelligence community, but it should not be tasked with drawing this line. No organization should police itself, particularly organizations like the CIA that can hide behind a veil of secrecy. That, unfortunately, has too often been a recipe for abuses, violations of the law, and cover-ups. No one wants another Watergate, Iran-Contra, MHCHAOS,[4] or MKULTRA.[5] We simply cannot operate that way.

If our spies should not set the rules themselves, who should? For me, the answer is clear and unavoidable: Congress and the executive branch—elected officials who are answerable to the U.S. electorate. We urgently need clearer rules from Congress and the White House, but few politicians have been willing to put their names on any document, law, or order that could later be construed by their political opponents as stretching moral limits. The mere appearance of possibly compromising ethics in intelligence has been unacceptable to politicians. All too often our intelligence personnel have been left with ambiguity, uncertainty, and even potential criminal liability.

This is not only unfair to our intelligence professionals, but it is also an extremely poor way to fight the war on terror. Without clear rules of engagement, our intelligence personnel overseas become risk averse and self-restrained. That is not the way to defeat terrorists—our spies need to be as aggressive as possible. They should not cross the line, but they must come right up to it. They cannot do that unless they know where the line is. The U.S. public must bear the responsibility of informing itself about intelligence work, getting involved in the debate, and making its voice heard. It will then be up to our policymakers to listen, to recognize the urgency of the situation, and to have the political courage to start drawing lines.

Case Studies: Presenting the Moral Dilemma

An important tool for framing the debate on intelligence ethics is assessing probable scenarios involving tough decisions. In teaching my classes on intelligence at the Bush School of Government and Public Service, I was amazed by how little our students knew about spying—and what they thought they knew was often badly skewed by the old stereotypes and distortions in the media. I also noted how fixated these students were on the moral aspects of spying. Many of them were considering careers in intelligence but had serious reservations about the kind of work spies do.

To address their interests and concerns, I presented my students with true-to-life operational scenarios to make the moral issues as clear and relevant as possible. These scenarios were thinly fictionalized, and designed to accurately pose the ethical dilemmas our spies in the field actually face, or could face in the future. The students became deeply engaged in the scenarios, and our classroom discussions included the obvious controversial issues of the day, assassination, torture, rendition and electronic eavesdropping, but also included some subtler moral issues.

Some students were looking for black and white answers, but in most cases they had to settle for gray. It was hard for them to find moral absolutes. The scenarios were not to provide answers, because I do not pretend to know what they are or should be, but instead to raise the issues and encourage debate. With a well-informed and thoughtful debate on intelligence ethics, my hope is that we can arrive at some form of national consensus. The time has come for America to make up its mind on how dirty it is willing to get its hands.

The following scenarios are shortened versions of fictionalized case studies I developed for classroom use and then adapted for inclusion in my book on intelligence ethics. Read the following case studies and decide whether the given course of action in each of the ten case studies below is morally acceptable or not. Exclude practical, legal, or operational considerations from your decision, and focus on whether you are comfortable with U.S. intelligence agencies engaging in the indicated activities.

Case study #1. A senior al-Qaida operative, known to have masterminded a major terrorist attack in the United States (killing 700 U.S. citizens), is in hiding in Sudan. The CIA learns from intelligence sources exactly where he is, and has the capability of inserting an assassination team into Sudan. Other options, such as kidnapping or extraditing him, are excluded for operational and political reasons. Would it be morally acceptable for the CIA to assassinate this terrorist inside Sudan?

Case study #2. U.S. forces capture a high-level terrorist leader in the Tora Bora region of eastern Afghanistan. There is no doubt that he has extensive information on the identities and locations of other terrorists, their communications, finances, and future attacks. He is not talking. Would it be morally acceptable for the CIA to use full-fledged torture, including beatings and electric shock, to extract his information?

Case study #3. An Albanian member of the terrorist group Egyptian Jihad is running a large cell of this organization in Sofia, Bulgaria. Would it be morally acceptable for the CIA, in collaboration with its official liaison within Bulgarian security, to kidnap this terrorist on the streets of Sofia, send him secretly to Cairo, and turn him over to Egyptian authorities for interrogation that will likely include beatings and torture?

Case study #4. A CIA officer under business cover in Tehran becomes friends with a young Iranian official working for the Iranian Ministry of Defense. The young Iranian reveals that he is secretly opposed to the Iranian regime. The CIA's assessment is that he would never

knowingly work for the CIA, but he might be enticed to cooperate with a reputable international organization. Would it be morally acceptable for the CIA officer to tell the Iranian (falsely) that he works for Amnesty International in order to recruit him as a reporting source from inside Iran?

Case study #5. A Cuban intelligence officer is working undercover as a second secretary at the Cuban mission to the United Nations in New York. FBI surveillance of him in New York indicates that he frequents gay bars and engages in promiscuous homosexual sex. Homosexuality is grounds for dismissal from the Cuban intelligence service, and the Cuban has concealed his sexual orientation from his family, friends, and colleagues. Would it be morally acceptable for the FBI to attempt to recruit this Cuban as a source on Cuban intelligence operations by blackmailing him on the basis of his homosexuality?

Case study #6. The CIA has an extremely productive clandestine relationship with a Chinese official who announces that he will soon be reassigned to a high-ranking position with the Chinese Communist Party in the city of Kunming. The CIA wishes to continue its secret meetings with him in Kunming but has very limited cover options for inserting an officer there. Only one option presents itself: Christian missionary cover. Would it be morally acceptable for the CIA to place an officer undercover with the U.S.-based Divine Word Outreach (which has a presence in Kunming) to maintain clandestine contact with the Chinese source?

Case study #7. A female CIA officer is operating undercover in Rome. To expand her spotting opportunities for potential recruits, she joins a local tennis club. She strikes up a friendship with the Deputy Chief of Mission of the Iranian Embassy, who is an avid tennis player. Over time, it is clear to the CIA officer that the Iranian is infatuated with her and can be easily manipulated. Would it be morally acceptable for the CIA officer to seduce the Iranian (she is willing to do so) as a means of drawing him into espionage on behalf of the United States?

Case study #8. The FBI is interested in recruiting Chinese graduate students at U.S. universities who will return to China in sensitive defense jobs. If these students are recruited in the U.S., they will be turned over to the CIA for clandestine handling inside China. Would it be morally acceptable for the FBI to recruit a Chinese-American professor at a major university (who agrees to assist without payment) and to task him/her to befriend

Chinese students and to report to the FBI on their person-alities, potential vulnerabilities, and activities?

Case study #9. A Middle Eastern graduate student at a U.S. university walks into the local FBI office, and volunteers his services as a penetration of an Islamic terrorist cell of which he is a secret member. In exchange, he wants the FBI to assist him in completing his Ph.D. dissertation, with which he says he is hopelessly bogged down. Would it be morally acceptable for the FBI to assist the student in plagiarizing his dissertation in return for his cooperation against the terrorist cell?

Case study #10. The CIA has recruited a penetration of an important al-Qaida cell in Hamburg, Germany. He is providing valuable intelligence on terrorist activities and personnel, not only in Germany but throughout Europe. At a secret meeting at a safehouse in Hamburg, the terrorist asks his CIA handler to provide him with a prostitute. He says it would be dangerous for him to frequent red-light districts in Hamburg because he knows the German police patrol there heavily, and he fears disease. He adds that if the CIA does not comply with his request, he will break off contact and the CIA will lose him as a source. Would it be morally acceptable for the CIA to procure a medically-cleared prostitute for this terrorist?

If you found nine or ten of these case studies morally acceptable, you probably subscribe to the Doolittle principle that "long-standing American concepts of fair play must be reconsidered" in the face of today's terrorism threat. If you were comfortable with seven or eight of them, you are aggressive and forward-leaning, but draw the line at certain activities. You want to play hardball, mostly by the rules, but are willing to cut a few corners if necessary. If you found three to six of the case studies acceptable, you are not willing to abandon the moral high ground, but understand that the moral terrain has shifted since September 11, 2001. This is likely the mainstream opinion in the U.S. If you found two or fewer of the case studies acceptable, you probably do not fully understand the magnitude of the threat the U.S. faces and the means that must be employed to defeat it. An important lesson from this exercise is recognizing that good, thoughtful, decent, and patriotic Americans can and do disagree on these difficult moral issues. But there is no excuse for inaction.

Where Do We Go from Here?

The global war on terror will be long and deadly. It will be the defining reality of this generation and quite possibly beyond. Most U.S. citizens accept the importance of combating terrorism at its source by addressing the scourges of poverty, discrimination, and disenfranchisement. The challenges and opportunities for U.S. diplomacy and aid may never have been greater, and many of us are reminded of the darkest days of the Cold War. We can and will make a difference; we can and will reduce injustice, hatreds, and violence. But this cannot be accomplished overnight. Meaningful changes in attitudes toward the U.S. may take years, perhaps even generations. Until these changes occur, we will remain in the bull's eye of the terrorists' target. Like it or not, the U.S. has a war to fight—and we cannot wait until we have won over the hearts and minds of our adversaries.

Terrorism is nothing new. The U.S. has been the target of systematic terrorism for years, particularly since the 1970s. But terrorism is now a serious threat inside our own borders, and the potential death and destruction have been increased to nightmarish proportions with terrorists' access to weapons of mass destruction. The imperative of stopping terrorism has never been greater. We cannot turn inward and allow another attack akin to those on September 11, 2001.

Our intelligence services have thwarted many terrorist attacks since 2001, some of which have been publicized, others which have not. Our spies are on the front lines collecting the intelligence critical to protecting our country. The job they are doing is difficult and dangerous, and they deserve clearer guidelines. Unlike their military colleagues, they lack detailed rules of engagement, standing orders, and international conventions to define limits of behavior. In some areas, there are laws and executive orders that apply, but these have been slow in coming and do not cover the wide range of moral issues our intelligence personnel encounter. We must do better. With our national security at stake, it is essential to have a serious non-partisan debate, find an acceptable middle ground, and give our spies the unambiguous guidelines they so urgently need.

Notes

1. *Necessitas legem non habet.* This legal principle was not known to Roman jurisprudence, but was referred to extensively during the Middle Ages and later to justify state actions that went beyond legal authority.

2. Report of the *Special Study Group on the Covert Activities of the Central Intelligence Agency,* September 30, 1954. Eisenhower, on the heels of successful CIA covert action operations in Iran and Guatemala, established an ad hoc committee under the leadership of General James Doolittle to determine how far U.S. intelligence should be allowed to go in fighting Soviet communism.

3. Hearing before the Joint House and Senate Intelligence Committee, September 26, 2002.

4. The CIA's illegal surveillance of anti-war activists in the United States during the 1960s and 1970s was codenamed MHCHAOS.

5. MKULTRA was the CIA codename for illegal drug experiments conducted on Americans in the 1950s and 1960s.

JAMES M. OLSON served in the Directorate of Operations of the Central Intelligence Agency. He teaches courses on intelligence and national security at the George Bush School of Government and Public Service at Texas A&M University. He is the author of *Fair Play: The Moral Dilemmas of Spying,* Potomac Books, 2006. This article is adapted from speeches delivered by the author at the Association for Intelligence Officers in Washington, D.C., on January 21, 2007, and at the Pritzker Military Library in Chicago, on May 24, 2007.

From *SAIS Review*, Vol. 28, No. 1, Winter/Spring 2008, pp. 37-45. Copyright © 2008 by Johns Hopkins University Press. Reprinted by permission.

Air Security

Why You're Not as Safe as You Think

One Sunday evening last March, a baggage handler was loading up an Airbus jet when he noticed that a passenger's bag was burning.

Officials halted the flight, found the passenger, and told him they were taking all of his baggage off the plane for re-screening before the flight could continue, the captain said in a report to federal aviation officials.

In the burnt bag, authorities discovered a suspicious bundle of wires and a video game battery pack. The captain, meanwhile, thought the passenger's behavior was suspect. He had a one-way ticket, volunteered to be removed from the flight without being asked, and said he would fly another day.

"Had we left the gate on time, we would have been airborne when this bag ignited," the report noted.

The captain complained in his filing with the federal Aviation Safety Reporting System that there was no security follow-up although many questions remained: "Who was this individual? Were his actions intentional? Why was his behavior so abnormal?"

Despite an extensive security effort since the 2001 terrorist attacks, those kinds of questions are still being asked with alarming frequency at U.S. airports.

Many steps have indeed been taken, including creation of the Transportation Security Administration (TSA), to improve security at the nation's 400 commercial airports and at all airlines.

But six years later, the TSA still falls short in 7 of 24, or almost one-third, of critical performance benchmarks set for the agency, an August 2007 federal report says. The shortfalls included securing areas of airports that are supposed to be restricted and adequate screening of air cargo, according to the Government Accountability Office (GAO), the federal government's audit agency.

Some of those problems were cited in a March 2007 CONSUMER REPORTS investigation, "An Accident Waiting to Happen?," which found that increased outsourcing by airlines had created safety and security loopholes. Now, even for some areas in which the TSA has supposedly met its goals, CONSUMER REPORTS has found major security lapses, including the following:

Screening failures. The TSA has an erratic record at checkpoint screening, including failures during undercover tests to identify weapons and explosives. A November 2007 GAO report found that agents smuggled bomb-making material past checkpoints in several instances.

Questionable rules. The TSA has issued 25 versions of screening procedures over the years, and there's still confusion about bringing liquids and gels aboard. It also allows items such as lighters, tools, corkscrews, and pointed scissors that could be used as weapons, just as box cutters were used in some of the Sept. 11 attacks.

Insecure cockpits. In easing the rules, the TSA pointed to other security measures, such as strengthening cockpit doors to deter hijackings. But CONSUMER REPORTS documented dozens of problems with those barriers, including doors popping open in flight, pilots being locked out, and flight attendants breaking the doors by slamming them shut.

Thin security forces. The government has tried to plug security holes in part by authorizing more flight crew members to carry guns. But the effort has lagged because of cumbersome training arrangements. And deployment of armed air marshals is hurt by staffing and morale problems, say several current and former marshals. Air marshals also complain that their reports of suspicious activity often seem to be ignored.

Although there has not been a successful terrorist attack in the U.S. since 9/11, dozens of security officials and others on the front lines say the security lapses make it easier for one to take place.

"The clock is ticking," says David Mackett, president of the Airline Pilots Security Alliance. "There's a term we are using in the airline industry: We are being ridden," he says of terrorists or their supporters whom he believes are continually riding planes and testing the system. "They're not wannabes. In some way, they're assisting Al Qaeda. People ask me, 'Will there be another 9/11?' I think there will be more 9/11s."

Clark Kent Ervin, inspector general for the U.S. Department of Homeland Security (DHS) from 2003 through 2004, says: "Al Qaeda is back in business. They're intent and they have this fixation on aviation."

Ervin's office criticized the TSA's oversight of security and its spending. He says it would be "very, very hard" for terrorists to commit an act similar to 9/11, but also says: "We Americans tend to fight the last war. I don't think we're much farther along, to tell you the truth."

Not everyone is so pessimistic. "We are significantly safer now than on Sept. 10, 2001," says Bob Hesselbein, chair of the National Security Committee for the Air Line Pilots Association, the nation's largest pilots' union. "Does that mean we're content? No. But we're in a much better place."

TSA spokesman Darrin Kayser says, "TSA has made significant strides in testing and deploying the latest technologies to better detect explosives and other potential threat items."

If outer defenses falter, federal auditors note, the authorities are counting on "able-bodied passengers" to engage in "self-defense actions should an incident occur onboard commercial aircraft."

A 'Facade of Security'

Before 9/11, airline security was largely delegated to airlines and airports, which hired private firms.

Congress created the TSA in November 2001 to secure all modes of transportation, starting with aviation. The agency hired more than 50,000 people to screen passengers and luggage. But Kimberly Kraynak, a lead TSA officer in Pittsburgh and women's coordinator for TSA Local 1 of the American Federation of Government Employees, which represents officers, says employees do not receive proper training at some airports. "We've been short-staffed since the beginning," she says.

Larry Tortorich, a TSA training officer and former representative to the Joint Terrorism Task Force who retired in 2006, also says he saw problems from the inside. "There was a facade of security. There were numerous security flaws and vulnerabilities that I identified. The response was, it wasn't apparent to the public, so there would not be any corrective action."

An internal e-mail obtained by CONSUMER REPORTS suggests that the TSA might be stacking the deck to try to perform better on covert tests. In April 2006 the TSA's Office of Security Operations sent a memo to numerous security personnel titled "Notice of Possible Security Test." It warned that airport security was being tested by the Department of Transportation in several airports and even gave some clues: The testing couple included a woman who had "an ID with an Oriental woman's picture, even though she is Caucasian. We are getting the word out."

"I continue to be concerned at how poorly screeners are doing on under-cover testing," says Ervin, the former inspector general. "The results continue to be dismal."

The TSA has also been the subject of reports of mismanagement. For example, a federal report in 2005 found that a private firm used to hire screeners for the TSA had estimated its fee at $104 million but was paid $741 million, including $1.7 million for the use of a Telluride, Colo., ski resort for recruiting.

Screeners also report that equipment that could help security remains locked up at some airports. "We've wasted millions on machines we're not using," says Don Thomas, a TSA officer in Orlando, Fla., and president of TSA Local 1.

In its annual report card for the TSA last April, the House Committee on Homeland Security gave the agency a C for aviation security and an F for employee morale, a factor contributing to high staff turnover.

Responding to the criticism, Kip Hawley, the TSA's administrator, told Congress in November, "Our workforce is fully engaged." He said that reforms in the agency's personnel system have been aimed at improving staffing issues.

Questionable Carry-Ons

After an alleged terrorist plot that aimed to use liquid and gel explosives on London-to-U.S. flights was disrupted in 2006, the TSA issued conflicting bans on carrying those items aboard.

In short order, rules changed from a ban on liquids and gels to allowing small containers in clear plastic quart-sized bags. Then came approval for larger items bought in shops past checkpoints.

Ervin says airport vendors applied pressure to have the liquids ban modified. "Are the amounts of liquids dangerous? Either it's true or it's not," he says. "Why is it OK to buy them past the checkpoint now?"

Bogdan Dzakovic, a TSA officer and former Federal Aviation Administration undercover leader, says the emergence of liquid explosives was inevitable because of the TSA's focus on detecting powdered nitrate-based bombs. He says the TSA had been public about its trace-detection and checked-baggage machines, so terror groups "turned to gel-based explosives."

Exploiting loopholes in the liquid/gel rules, undercover investigators smuggled components for several explosive devices and an incendiary device through TSA checkpoints and onto airline flights without being challenged, according to the November 2007 federal audit report. One agent even deliberately provoked a second screening but was able to smuggle the items through anyway.

In another symptom of confusion, an April 2007 GAO report says the TSA allowed pointed scissors with blades 4 inches long and tools as long as 7 inches back on planes in December 2005 without having any justification for doing so. Cigarette lighters were allowed back onboard in August 2007, with the TSA saying that they no longer pose a significant threat.

While the TSA said that would free up time for other screening, some aviation experts consulted by the GAO for the report said, "Permitting scissors increases the risk of violence against passengers and flight crew."

'Secured' Doors Broken

One of the most visible elements of the new security effort was the requirement that reinforced doors be installed. By March 2002, the FAA reported that all major U.S. airlines had complied. Critics, however, say a stronger door is only half the solution. "People have this illusion hardened cockpit doors work, and they don't," Dzakovic says. "If you want to have a secure door, you need to have a double-hulled door."

CONSUMER REPORTS searched NASA's Aviation Safety Reporting System and found 51 incidents since April 2002 in which flight crews reported problems with the hardened doors.

In many instances, the door unexpectedly opened in flight or the locking mechanisms failed. In one case, the door spontaneously opened twice on a Bombardier CRJ200 regional jet, interrupting a takeoff. And a captain said the doors on two DC9s were broken after flight attendants slammed them.

A 2006 study of aviation security by DFI International, a Washington, D.C., security consultancy, found that a drunken passenger kicked a hole in a door panel and that aircraft cleaners "broke a fortified door off its hinges by running a heavy snack cart into it on a bet."

In October 2007, Rep. Steve Israel, D-N.Y., introduced a bill that would require the FAA to order the installation of secondary barriers on commercial airliners, at a cost he estimates at $5,000 to $10,000 per aircraft. "Without secondary cockpit barriers, the door is literally wide open to terrorists," he stated in proposing the measure.

Hesselbein, of the Air Line Pilots Association, agrees, saying "We believe it's the No. 1 thing that can be done for security."

Armed and Worried

As part of the response to the terror threat, the federal air marshal service expanded from 33 to thousands of marshals and was transferred from the FAA to the TSA. But the transition did not go smoothly, according to a 2005 GAO report. Over the next two years the marshal service was transferred two more times, then was sent back again to the TSA.

The service also tried unsuccessfully to develop a "surge" capability with customs and immigration agents trained to work as air marshals when needed. The auditors warn that without changes in career development and advancement, the force could face "a decline in employee morale and an increase in attrition rates."

That has happened, experts say. While the exact number of marshals is classified, a report on the Airline Pilots Security Alliance website says, "The current air marshal force, 2,200 officers working in teams, protects only 5 to 10 percent of daily flights, if that." The alliance says that's down from a peak of 4,000.

"Everyone thinks there are enough air marshals on the planes, and there are not," says P. Jeffrey Black, an air marshal and whistle-blower who testified before the House Judiciary Committee in 2004.

An incident onboard a Northwest Airlines flight in June 2004 in which 13 Middle Eastern men in a musical group acted suspiciously prompted an inspector general's probe. The full report, not made public, provides these details: "During the flight, the men again acted suspiciously. Several of the men changed seats, congregated in the aisles, and arose when

---

Closeup Security Cards for the Fast Lane

If you've recently heard ads touting ways to get through airport security more quickly, you might wonder how it works. The Transportation Security Administration has set up a Registered Traveler program, under which private firms run a thorough background check and use biometrics such as fingerprints and iris scans. There are six approved programs, with one being Verified Identity Pass, offering the Clear card for $100 a year. But the fast lanes are only at 13 airports, sometimes only at certain checkpoints and for certain airlines. The overall Registered Traveler program has drawn criticism for privacy and security reasons. The American Civil Liberties Union says it is "based on intrusive but ultimately ineffective probes into travelers' lives." Some say it could aid terrorists, who could get recruits with clean records so that they can speed through security checkpoints more easily.

---

the fasten seat belt sign was turned on; one passenger moved quickly up the aisle toward the cockpit and, at the last moment, entered the first class lavatory. The passenger remained in the lavatory for about 20 minutes." Another man carried a large McDonald's restaurant bag into a lavatory and made a thumbs-up signal to another man upon returning to his seat.

An FBI check indicated that the musical group's promoter had been involved in a similar incident in January 2004. "No other derogatory information was received, and all 13 of the men were released," the report says, although visas for 12 of the passengers expired weeks before the flight. Twelve of the men had left the country by mid-July; the FBI started its investigation later that month, after another passenger wrote an article about her experience on the flight and appeared on television.

The federal report cited marshals' problems in communicating with the cockpit and confusion over which federal agency had authority.

To complement the air marshals, the government allows crew members to become Federal Flight Deck Officers and to carry guns in the cockpit. But an inspector general's report in 2006 stated "more needs to be accomplished to maximize the use of FFDOs on international and domestic flights." The ranks are thin: Only an estimated 8 to 10 percent of domestic flights have an armed crew member in the cockpit.

Mackett, of the Airline Pilots Security Alliance, sees arming pilots as an unobtrusive system that uses current resources. But he says that the TSA is "grudgingly tolerating" the program. He says airlines aren't required to pay for the voluntary training, and some won't provide time off.

Kayser, the TSA spokesman, says "procedures must be followed to maintain the high standards of any law enforcement professional."

While the U.S. has made significant efforts in aviation security since 2001, many experts cite El Al Israel Airlines as the benchmark for aviation security, with double cockpit doors and more extensive passenger and baggage screening.

Consumers Union, the nonprofit publisher of CONSUMER REPORTS, believes the government should close the gaps in security by instituting more effective screening measures, creating a second cockpit barrier, and improving training of TSA officers, and providing more help for federal air marshals and flight crew members.

"It is clear that the TSA continues to struggle with the implementation of fundamental security measures," says Rep. Edward J. Markey, D-Mass., of the House Homeland Security Committee. "Congress will need to keep shining a spotlight on TSA operations and provide the resources and training needed for TSA employees to perform their difficult jobs."

UNIT 10
Future Threats

Unit Selections

Key Points to Consider

- What challenges will terrorists pose in the future?

- What role will Al Qaeda play in the future of terrorism?

- Why is Al Qaeda not likely to attack the United States in the next five years?

Student Website
www.mhcls.com

Internet References

Centers for Disease Control and Prevention—Bioterrorism
   http://www.bt.cdc.gov

Terrorism will, undoubtedly, remain a major policy issue for the United States well into this 21st century. Opinions as to what future perpetrators will look like and what methods they will pursue continue to vary. While some argue that the traditional methods of terrorism, such as bombing, kidnapping, and hostage taking will continue to dominate this millennium, others warn that weapons of mass destruction or weapons of mass disruption, such as biological and chemical weapons, or even nuclear or radiological weapons, will be the weapons of choice for terrorists in the future.

Experts believe that there are certain trends that will characterize international terrorism in the coming years. Some scholars predict that the continuing rise of Islamic extremists will give rise to a new generation of violent, anti-American terrorists. Others warn of a rejuvenation of left-wing terrorism in Europe. Most believe that the tactics employed by terrorists will be more complex. Future terrorism will likely cause more casualties and may involve the use of weapons of mass destruction.

The first article provides a broad overview of the challenges posed by the changing face of violence. It argues that states need "integrated strategies that address conflict prevention, conflict management, conflict resolution, and post-conflict reconstruction." Next, Marc Sageman argues that a new generation of terrorists, "even more frightening and unpredictable than its predecessors," is on the rise. He believes that in order to accelerate their eventual demise "terrorist acts must be stripped of glory." Finally Peter Bergen predicts that al Qaeda is unlikely to attack the United States in the next five years and that while al Qaeda's media war for the hearts and minds continues, "Muslims around the world are increasingly taking a dim view of this group."

© U.S. Air Force photo by Mr. Gerald Sonnenberg

The Shifting Face of Violence

THEODOR H. WINKLER

One can argue that we live today in relatively peaceful times. Organized violence was throughout most of history, both in absolute and relative terms, a much more prevalent part of mankind's daily life than today—from antiquity to the twentieth century. European integration has pacified the old continent. The creation of the United Nations has provided us with an instrument of collective security that can, if permitted, work. The threat of an all-out nuclear exchange has receded.

Still, conflict, in its traditional form of organized violence between two states or coalitions of states, continues to exist. Examples include the Iraqi invasion of Kuwait, the U.S. campaigns against Saddam Hussein's Iraq, and the possibility of a U.S.-Israeli attack against Iran's emerging nuclear capabilities. A significant amount of the world's military power and arms procurement is still invested in coping with such contingencies. It cannot be excluded that the risk of traditional conflict might grow again in the years to come. Should the United States—in many respects the world's de facto hegemon—be perceived as being increasingly tied down in Iraq, Afghanistan, and possibly other critical hot spots, and thus be seen as unable (or unwilling) to react to new challenges, then the temptation would develop for many to seize the initiative and create military *faits accomplis*. One may argue that the Iranian nuclear program is just such an attempt.

Most conflicts in the twenty-first century, however, are no longer of a traditional nature. They are no longer fought between states, but between a government and such forces as politically or ethnically based militias and armed bands, guerrilla or terrorist organizations, clans, warlords, organized communal groups, or simply criminal gangs. An increasing number of conflicts are even being conducted between such groups themselves—with little, or only indirect, government involvement. The phenomenon of disintegrating, failed, or faltering states—from the Western Balkans and Somalia to West Africa and Darfur—has led, particularly in the second half of the 1990s, to violence at a level unheard of for quite some time. We are confronted by a multiplication of actors, issues, and means, leading to new conflict patterns and an increase of conflicting matters at stake. The trend will continue to build in the next 25 years.

Such non-traditional conflicts, moreover, prove difficult to extinguish. The most striking example is clearly the ongoing strife between Israel and the Palestinians. Other examples include Kashmir; the Horn of Africa and the Great Lakes region extending from Burundi and Rwanda across Congo, Uganda, northwestern Kenya, and Tanzania; parts of Southeast Asia; and Colombia. Historical data show that roughly half of the conflicts stopped as a result of national reconciliation efforts or a United Nations or other

international crisis management mechanism erupt again within the next five years. Peace is indeed a fragile commodity.

The reasons are multiple and specific to each locale. However, there is a common denominator: the ability to conclude lasting peace is seriously handicapped if the state monopoly of legitimate force is lost and when non-state actors become involved. Such groups have, as a rule, a highly specific agenda, a restricted political base, are often involved in sharp competition with each other (for example, the various Palestinian groupings), and are ill-prepared to establish stable governmental structures capable of exercising effective control over all armed elements and thus to offer security to the entire population. This last inability encourages, in turn, the creation of rival militias drawn from those segments of the population that feel particularly threatened (for example, in Iraq). They can, and most often do, provide the sparks for new and even more violent conflagrations.

There is also the phenomenon that many non-traditional conflicts have a regional—some even a global—dimension. The multiple conflicts in Sierra Leone and Liberia, which, at the turn of the twenty-first century shook West Africa, were interlinked. The fact that ethnicities, tribes, and clans often live on both sides of a border contributes to the emergence of what can best be described as regional civil wars. On an even larger scale, Afghan *mujahedin* have fought not only in Afghanistan itself, but in places as disparate and widely dispersed as Bosnia and Herzegovina, Chechnya, and Iraq. If a peace agreement cannot be extended into a regional settlement, the risk that non-traditional conflicts will both proliferate and rekindle is substantial.

There is another fact that augurs badly for the future: non-traditional conflicts are cheap. They do not require highly sophisticated weaponry. Though some advanced equipment—such as modern explosive devices or shoulder-fired, surface-to-air missiles—may be involved, for the most part, small arms and light weapons (as well as some Toyota 4 × 4s) will suffice. Conservative estimates place the number of guns in the world at a staggering 500 million, including 55 million to 72 million automatic rifles. As for manpower, extensive use has been made of child soldiers, particularly in Africa. And what of the cost of perpetuating these conflicts? More often than not, funds are raised by warlords through trafficking in drugs, human beings, and contraband. It is not by chance that Afghanistan has emerged, after the U.S.-led intervention, as the world's largest drug supplier (providing up to 92 percent of the world's heroin production).

Though not new itself, the most disturbing form of this coming era of conflict is terrorism. The United States is now confronted in its "War on Terror" not only with asymmetric warfare, but with a set of adversaries that pursue asymmetric objectives. Al Qaeda does not want to *win* the war, but wants the United States to *lose* it. That is by no means the same thing. The ultimate target group of Islamic fundamentalist terrorist groups is not the United States or the West as such. Their real target is the minds of the Muslim communities. They fear that the Islamic world might gradually become Westernized, that multicultural societies might emerge that stray from a rigid and medieval interpretation of the Koran. Terrorists do not kill for the sake of killing, but for the sake of political impact. They seek large numbers of victims in order to outrage. The stiffer the reaction to such crimes, the more likely it is, they hope, that inter-communal hatred will replace common values and multicultural cooperation and integration. Terrorism is not rugby, but a complex game of pocket billiards. Thus, it is all the more difficult to fight effectively. It is to be expected that terrorism, indeed non-traditional conflict in general, will remain a determining feature of organized violence in the years to come.

Terrorism is not rugby, but a complex game of pocket billiards . . . all the more difficult to fight effectively.

That perspective gains a particularly ghastly dimension when combined with the threat of weapons of mass destruction. The question is indeed not whether, but when terrorists will use weapons of mass destruction. Since the stealing or building of nuclear weapons is—and will in all likelihood remain—difficult, crude radiological weapons and (not so crude) biological weapons appear today as the most likely weapons to be used. And, as delivery systems for these arms are costly and difficult to acquire, another nightmare option could be an unsophisticated and unwieldy nuclear device assembled right in the middle of a target city.

The slow crumbling of the non-proliferation regime (and the simultaneous proliferation of ballistic missiles) provides an unsettling background to this perspective. Moreover, there are the equally catastrophic possibilities of nuclear material being stolen, risks of regional nuclear war, and the consequences of potential coups and civil strife in some of the new countries in possession of nuclear weapons. A nuclear-armed Pakistan under a Taliban-type government would be a nightmare. The picture is further darkened by the erosion of arms control in the North and its virtual absence in the South.

Finally, in the next 25 years there will be new forms of nontraditional warfare given the increasing vulnerability of modern societies. In 2007, Estonia became the first victim of a large-scale, well-organized cyber-attack that threatened to bring about the immediate collapse of the country's entire social, economic, and political fabric—from emergency services to banking, insurance to government. The ability to launch such attacks for the moment, at least, remains largely restricted to governments, but may proliferate to well-organized non-state actors and criminal gangs.

From Raw Materials to Migration

Access to raw materials has historically been a strong driving force for conflict. It was one of the motors of colonialism. In an age of globalization, the need for freer access to raw materials

and their production would seem self-evident. Yet this is not the case. What we are witnessing is a return to a new sort of "Great Game."

From late 2007 onwards, world oil prices have started to explode. There is a host of reasons: a growing demand from India and China, inefficient use of scarce oil resources in the Western world, and the fact (or fear) that world oil production is about to peak—or has already. All these factors encourage speculation in global markets, which has contributed to the price spike. The rise in oil prices has spilled over, causing serious disturbances in other commodity markets as well. Most notably, the use of significant amounts of agricultural products, especially corn, for the production of biofuels has triggered a global increase in the price of some commodities—which in turn has led to dire food crises in developing countries.

The geopolitical result is a silent, though increasingly bitter, contest among the world's great and rising powers over access to, and transit rights for, key raw materials. Thus, China has multiplied its diplomatic missions to, and agreements with, African states and other countries in resource-rich regions. Russia has begun showing its muscles by cutting down or increasing the price of its gas and oil deliveries to neighboring states in order to bring them into line politically. And the United States has always been an active player in this game, maintaining strategic alliances and negotiating preferential agreements with states with oil and natural resources. Even neutral Switzerland has sent out high-ranking delegations to negotiate energy deals.

The race to gain control over natural resources is only likely to intensify in the coming decades. From today's perspective, it is quite unlikely that raw materials will become the trigger of major military conflicts such as a war between China and the United States. Some direct military action is possible, for instance, in the contested continental shelves of Asia. What seems more likely is a return to proxy wars (often at a low-intensity level) of the Cold War type, waged this time over the control of natural resources and trading arteries. The conflicts in Darfur and southern Sudan, in the Caucasus and in parts of Africa, already have defined this dimension. More is likely to come—particularly when the list of scarce resources will soon include access to fresh water and arable land. Yet it is not only the access to fossil fuels, but even more important their consumption, that is likely to bolster the potential for conflict in the decades to come.

The impact that global warming will have on our planet will be severe at best, catastrophic at worst. The UN Intergovernmental Panel on Climate Change predicts that, depending on the scenario, the atmosphere will heat up by 1 to 4 degrees Celsius by the end of this century. This will cause substantial problems for the industrialized world—from the melting of glaciers in Europe's Alps to desertification in parts of the American plains. But consequences will be disastrous for other parts of the world as well. Regions that already suffer from hunger and scarcity of water will be most severely hit—notably Sub-Saharan Africa. Other regions will experience ever more severe storms and rising sea levels that will inundate precious arable land and living space—from the United States to Bangladesh. Forecasters even predict that by the turn of the next century, 22 of the 50 largest cities of the world (including New York) will be threatened by coastal flooding. Other horrific impacts of global warming include desertification, droughts, bush and forest fires, and the accelerated spread of insect-transmitted tropical diseases. And changing weather patterns will put in jeopardy our ability to grow agricultural produce and get regular access to fresh water.

In the short and medium term, climate change will force millions of people—and in the longer term hundreds of millions of people—to decide whether to stay where they are (and eventually die) or migrate. The answer is obvious: global warming will significantly accentuate the trend towards large-scale migration.

Indeed, that trend is already in full swing, not only because of hunger and the search for better living standards, but more profoundly because of strong demographic imbalances that will continue to widen in the decades to come. In Western Europe, China, and other parts of the world, the growth of the elderly will dramatically outpace the general population. The reverse holds true for large parts of the developing world, where on average 37 percent (and, in the least developed countries, a staggering 47 percent) of the population is 18 years old or less. This is alarming: studies have shown that societies in which 15-to-30 year olds comprise more than 20 percent of the total population are prone to violence and conflict, for they are no longer able to offer to third-and fourth-born males viable economic and social opportunities. The result is a building migratory pressure—from the South to the North and from the countryside towards the great cities.

Migration poses multiple problems: it is often illegal and an increasingly lucrative activity for organized crime. First, the uprooting of people in their nations of origin puts additional strain on already fragile local societies. Second, the migratory flows tend to create temporary basins where people collect when they encounter obstacles on their road to opportunity: for example, Mali and Mauritania on the way to Spain and the Canary Islands; Morocco before the crossing of the Straits of Gibraltar; Tunisia and Libya before the attempt to cross over to Pantelleria and Lampedusa in Sicily, or mainland Italy; Egypt, into which an ever increasing number of migrants from Sudan and the Great Lakes area migrate; Turkey, the springboard for the Balkan road into Europe; and Mexico, the gateway to the United States.

Many of these temporary host nations find themselves in a precarious demographic and economic situation. The migratory pressure is difficult to absorb, reducing further the already meager opportunities of the local youth (54 percent of the population of Morocco is less than 20 years old), thus creating in turn additional impetus to go abroad in search of work. In the Mediterranean context, the lack of expectation for and hope of economic or social advancement, intensified by migratory pressure, has already begun laying the foundation for a growing religious radicalization of young people—and hence for extremism and conflict. Today's Moroccan youths, for instance, are significantly more religious than were their parents. The same is true in other North African states.

Yet even if the migrants succeed and reach the *banlieus* of Paris or Marseille, they often face insecurity, youth gangs, drugs, violence, and fundamentalist Islam. As recent terror attacks in Europe have shown, these young immigrants risk becoming the easy prey of radical preachers—thereby accelerating a vicious cycle of intercultural tension amid their own isolation.

Those who are attracted by the sprawling cities in the developing world hardly fare much better. In 1800, only 2 percent of the world's population lived in cities. By 1950, it was 30 percent, in 2003 49 percent, and in 2030 an estimated 60 percent of the world's population will reside in urban centers. While this migration is most dramatic in the developing world, the cities offer only meager prospects. Today, one in six people live in an urban slum. And their numbers will likely explode, doubling from some 720 million in 1990 to 1.4 billion by 2020. Moreover, the lack of a hopeful future will lead to a dangerous increase in urban violence. The situation is most dramatic in, but not unique to, Rio de Janeiro, where criminal gangs already control entire sectors of the city that police can only penetrate with military type operations involving armored units, heavy weapons, and helicopters. Indeed, between 1979 and 2003, some 500,000 Brazilians lost their lives to guns.

A New Dimension: Globalization

After the end of the Cold War, there was hesitation for quite some time over what to call this new era in which we found ourselves living. The "post-Cold War world" was for years the best anyone could come up with. Today, however, globalization is the key word. The original uncertainty over what to call the new age mirrored the absence of any clear concept of what lay ahead and, above all, what to do about it. The often bitter learning process is by no means over.

The first to recognize the new global situation, and the opportunities it offered, was organized international crime. It has evolved into, and will remain, a threat of strategic proportions. Never before have so many drugs been produced and sold in the streets. Never before were so many human beings bought and sold, so much contraband smuggled. The enormous profits from criminal enterprise (estimated at \$1 trillion to \$1.5 trillion per year) provide the means for organized crime to outclass and outspend many, if not most, of the world's police forces. At the same time, the problem of corruption has grown dramatically in importance. The multiplication of armed nonstate actors and the emergence of failed states dominated by rival warlords have accentuated the problem. Many of these armed non-state actors are closely linked to or funded by organized international crime. Even piracy—that hoary business—has seen resurgence in the waters around the Horn of Africa and Asia.

The first to recognize the new global situation, and the opportunities it offered, was organized international crime.

More important, globalization has also profoundly altered the world economy and the financial markets. The latest financial crisis, triggered by the collapsing United States credit market, has unveiled an ever more bewildering array of financial products and derivatives in ever more opaque packaging—all offered today on freely traded international markets. The ability of states, central banks, and other regulatory mechanisms to oversee effectively such a market is dwindling. National authority is no longer enough, while international tools are still insufficiently developed.

A closely related problem is the emergence of companies that are genuinely international in nature and thus no longer firmly linked to any specific country. These companies have become significant international players in their own right—for their interests may not always coincide with the country where they have their headquarters or where they are, ostensibly, regulated.

And there are other reasons to worry about the pace and breadth of our global economic interconnectedness. Driven by a revolution in information technologies, money can now be transferred, earned, and lost in split seconds. Earnings are measured in quarters, not growth over decades. This is a powerful motive for bankers and traders striving for short-term gains to meet financial targets and secure bonuses. Such targets have led not only to an explosion in the salaries of top executives (who all too often have lost touch with reality), but to dangerous forms of ever more short-sighted speculation. The 2008 rise in oil prices was significantly accelerated by speculation, likewise the spike in prices of agricultural produce. A financial market that lacks a longer term perspective may become a genuine threat to the stability and prosperity of the world. Can violence be far behind? And, if no remedy is found, capitalism risks becoming its own worst enemy.

Perhaps the most profound effect of globalization in the years to come will be the speed of change it introduces into our world. That speed is far greater than the ability of human beings to adapt emotionally. The growing attraction of religious fundamentalism is the most obvious expression of this reality, and equally, the rise of nationalism. The assumption that the success of a market economy must automatically lead also to the victory of democracy and hence peace (according to the widely held theory that democracies are less likely to go to war) may be simply wrong. Russia, China, the Gulf states, and Singapore are just a few examples to illustrate that a flourishing economy may well be married to different political approaches.

Filling the Strategic Void

Not only human beings, but states as well, have shown great difficulties adapting to the challenges and requirements of a globalizing world. States are by definition slow-moving animals: new laws and regulations take time, established bureaucratic structures instinctively oppose change, force structures are difficult to reorganize quickly. And, in the security sector, cooperation between different components (*e.g.,* police, army, intelligence) is often handicapped by singular institutional cultures and approaches. International organizations and multilateral actors can be even more sclerotic. The difficulties of the European Union on its road towards a constitutional treaty or the unwieldiness of much of the United Nations bureaucracy are telling illustrations.

The early years of globalization were thus marked by the absence of what would have been most needed: a *gesamtschau,* i.e., a comprehensive understanding of what is going on that forms the basis for an integrated and multifaceted strategy for coping with the negative aspects of change. But the West's reaction to globalization was marked by a strategic void: too many issues are still being approached piecemeal, with each individual problem taken in isolation. What has been lacking is the understanding that issues are now more than ever interlinked, forming a dynamic and fluid reality.

This has been particularly evident in the military field. Concepts and buzzwords such as the "Revolution in Military Affairs," "Net-Centric Warfare," or "Transition" have ignored the lessons of Clausewitz. The ability to dominate the battlefield has been confused with the ability to secure peace. Military power of late is not so much a continuation of politics through other means, but a substitute for it. Particularly with regard to the United States in Iraq, the ability to conduct joint and combined operations was seen as sufficient to ensure success. But what truly counts is the ability to plan, prepare, and conduct integrated missions that link all aspects of the security sector (from armed forces to police and border guards) and that, above all, combine soft and hard security components into a coherent, integrated, and long-term strategic and operational plan. However, timing is critical. The integration of the multiple aspects necessary for success cannot take place in the field, but must be built into all training, planning, and force structuring processes. Particularly after Iraq, such integration is increasingly—if somewhat belatedly—being recognized. Thus, in Afghanistan much emphasis is laid on a mix of soft and hard components, notably through the Provincial Reconstruction Teams.

To deal with violence will require the ability to address root causes, not only symptoms. This includes the whole spectrum of issues described above—from global warming to hunger, from demographic trends and migration to organized crime and corruption. So it must be understood that, for instance, the Kyoto Protocol is not only an ecological question but a concrete security issue.

Already there has been some movement in that direction. Former UN Secretary-General Kofi Annan's 2005 report, *In Larger Freedom,* recognized for the first time that development, security, and human rights form a triangle whose components are intimately interlinked. There cannot be development without security: nobody invests in a war zone. On the other hand, without security there cannot be development either: people with empty stomachs will eventually turn to their Kalashnikovs. Finally, development and security can only be ensured in the long run if human rights are respected. But if security is the precondition for development and the rule of law, then good governance and reform of the security sector become of paramount importance—as do the entirety of governmental approaches that coordinate the three "D's" (Defense, Development, and Diplomacy).

We need integrated strategies that address conflict prevention, conflict management, conflict resolution, and post-conflict reconstruction, and thus respond to the challenge of a shifting face of violence. It will be necessary both to broaden and deepen the integrated government approach. Strategies cannot only sit on drawing boards and in government reports; they need to be made operational through implementation mechanisms. Moreover, the various initiatives need to be coordinated by the United States, the United Nations, and the European Union—the three most important international players in this area—to pursue strategies that are mutually compatible.

We have asked, at the outset, three questions: Is the potential for violence growing? Are we doing the right thing? And, is time on our side? The answers are evident: yes, the potential for violence is growing in the years to come—for many reasons and with ever-increasing speed. Yes, we are doing some things right, but not enough of them—more holistic and imaginative approaches are needed. And no, time is not yet on our side. We must do better.

THEODOR H. WINKLER is the director of the Centre for Democratic Control of Armed Forces in Geneva with the rank of ambassador and previously served as head of the Division for International Security Policy of the Swiss Department of Defence.

From *World Policy Journal,* vol. 25, No. 3, Fall 2008, pp. 29–36. Copyright © 2008 by The World Policy Institute. Reprinted by permission of MIT Press Journals.

The Next Generation of Terror

The world's most dangerous jihadists no longer answer to al Qaeda. The terrorists we should fear most are self-recruited wannabes who find purpose in terror and comrades on the Web. This new generation is even more frightening and unpredictable than its predecessors, but its evolution just may reveal the key to its demise.

MARC SAGEMAN

When British police broke down Younis Tsouli's door in October 2005 in a leafy west London neighborhood, they suspected the 22-year-old college student, the son of a Moroccan diplomat, of little more than having traded e-mails with men planning a bombing in Bosnia. It was only after they began examining the hard drive on Tsouli's computer that they realized they had stumbled upon one of the most infamous—and unlikely—cyberjihadists in the world.

Tsouli's online username, as they discovered, was Irhabi007 ("Terrorist007" in Arabic). It was a moniker well known to international counterterrorism officials. Since 2004, this young man, with no history of radical activity, had become one of the world's most influential propagandists in jihadi chatrooms. It had been the online images of the war in Iraq that first radicalized him. He began spending his days creating and hacking dozens of websites in order to upload videos of beheadings and suicide bombings in Iraq and post links to the texts of bomb-making manuals. From his bedroom in London, he eventually became a crucial global organizer of online terrorist networks, guiding others to jihadist sites where they could learn their deadly craft. Ultimately, he attracted the attention of the late leader of al Qaeda in Iraq, Abu Musab al-Zarqawi. When British police discovered this young IT student in his London flat, he was serving as Zarqawi's public relations mouthpiece on the Web.

Tsouli's journey from computer geek to radical jihadist is representative of the wider evolution of Islamist terrorist networks today. Since Sept. 11, 2001, the threat confronting the West has changed dramatically, but most governments still imagine their foe in the mold of the old al Qaeda. The enemy today is not a product of poverty, ignorance, or religious brainwashing. The individuals we should fear most haven't been trained in terrorist camps, and they don't answer to Osama bin Laden or Ayman al-Zawahiri. They often do not even adhere to the most austere and dogmatic tenets of radical Islam. Instead, the new generation of terrorists consists of home-grown wannabes—self-recruited, without leadership, and globally connected through the Internet. They are young people seeking thrills and a sense of significance and belonging in their lives. And their lack of structure and organizing principles makes them even more terrifying and volatile than their terrorist forebears.

The New Face of Terror

The five years between Osama bin Laden's 1996 declaration of war against the United States from his safe haven in Afghanistan to the attacks of 9/11 were the "golden age" of what could be called al Qaeda Central. Those days are long over, but the social movement they inspired is as strong and dangerous as ever. The structure has simply evolved over time.

Today's new generation of terrorists constitutes the third wave of radicals stirred to battle by the ideology of global jihad. The first wave to join al-Qaeda was Afghan Arabs who came to Pakistan and Afghanistan to fight the Soviets in the 1980s. They were, contrary to popular belief, largely well educated and from solidly middle-class backgrounds. They were also mature, often about 30 years old when they took up arms. Their remnants still form the backbone of al Qaeda's leadership today, but there are at most a few dozen of them left, hiding in the frontier territories of northwest Pakistan.

The second wave that followed consisted mostly of elite expatriates from the Middle East who went to the West to attend universities. The separation from family, friends, and culture led many to feel homesick and marginalized, sentiments that hardened into the seeds of their radicalization. It was this generation of young men who traveled to al Qaeda's training camps in Afghanistan in the 1990s. They were incorporated into al Qaeda Central, and today there are at most about 100 of them left, also in hiding in northwest Pakistan.

The new, third wave is unlike its predecessors. It consists mostly of would-be terrorists, who, angered by the invasion of Iraq, aspire to join the movement and the men they hail as heroes. But it is nearly impossible for them to link up with al Qaeda Central, which was forced underground after 9/11. Instead, they form fluid, informal networks that are self-financed and self-trained. They have no physical headquarters or sanctuary, but the tolerant, virtual environment of the Internet offers them a semblance of unity and purpose. Theirs is a scattered, decentralized social structure—a leaderless jihad.

Take the case of Mohammed Bouyeri, perhaps the most infamous member of a network of aspiring jihadists that Dutch authorities dubbed the "Hofstad Netwerk," in 2004. Bouyeri, then a 26-year-old formerly secular social worker born to Moroccan immigrants in Amsterdam, could also trace his radicalization to outrage over the Iraq war. He became influential among a loosely connected group of about 100 young Dutch Muslims, most of whom were in their late teens and born in the Netherlands. The network informally coalesced around three or four active participants, some of whom had acquired a local reputation for trying (and failing) to fight the jihad abroad. Some of the initial meetings were at demonstrations for international Muslim causes, others at radical mosques, but mostly they met in Internet chatrooms. Other popular meeting spots included Internet cafes or the few apartments of the older members, as most of the network still lived with their parents. The group had no clear leader and no connection to established terrorist networks abroad.

On Nov. 2, 2004, Mohammed Bouyeri brutally murdered Dutch filmmaker Theo van Gogh on an Amsterdam street, nearly sawing off van Gogh's head and pinning a five-page note threatening the enemies of Islam to his victim's chest. Bouyeri had been enraged by van Gogh's short film, *Submission,* about Islam's treatment of women and domestic violence, and written by former Dutch parliamentarian Ayaan Hirsi Ali. After killing van Gogh, Bouyeri calmly waited for the police in the hope that he would die in the gunfight that he expected would follow. He was only wounded and, less than a year later, sentenced to life in prison. A series of raids against other members of the network uncovered evidence of plans to bomb the Dutch parliament, a nuclear power plant, and Amsterdam's airport, as well as assassination plots against prominent Dutch politicians.

The fluidity of the Hofstad Netwerk has created problems for Dutch prosecutors. The first few trials succeeded in convicting some members as belonging to a terrorist organization because they met regularly. But at later trials, when defendants faced more serious charges, the prosecutors' cases began to break down. Some guilty verdicts have even been subsequently overturned. In January, a Dutch appeals court threw out the convictions of seven men accused of belonging to the Hofstad Netwerk because "no structured cooperation [had] been established." It is difficult to convict suspects who rarely meet face to face and whose cause has no formal organization.

The perpetrators of the Madrid bombings in March 2004 are another example of the self-recruited leaderless jihad. They were an unlikely network of young immigrants who came together in haphazard ways. Some had been lifelong friends from their barrio in Tetouan, Morocco, and eventually came to run one of the most successful drug networks in Madrid, selling hashish and ecstasy. Their informal leader, Jamal Ahmidan, a 33-year-old high school dropout who liked to chase women, wavered between pointless criminality and redemptive religion. When he was released from a Moroccan jail in 2003 after serving three years for an alleged homicide, he became increasingly obsessed with the war in Iraq. He linked up with Tunisian-born Sarhane Ben Abdelmajid Fakhet, who had moved to Madrid to get his doctorate in economics. They were part of a loose network of foreign Muslims in Spain who spent time together after soccer games and mosque prayers. They later masterminded the Madrid bombings, the deadliest Islamist terror attack on European soil. As Spanish authorities closed in on their hideout several weeks after the bombings, Fakhet, Ahmidan, and several accomplices blew themselves up as the police moved in.

The tolerant, virtual environment of the Web offers these wannabes a semblance of unity and purpose.

Try as they may, Spanish authorities have never found any direct connection between the Madrid bombers and international al Qaeda networks. The 2007 trials of collaborators concluded that the bombings were inspired by al Qaeda, but not directed by it.

Evidence of hopeful young jihadists is not limited to Western Europe. In June 2006, Canadian security forces conducted a series of raids against two clusters of young people in and around Toronto. The youths they apprehended were mostly second-generation Canadians in their late teens or early 20s and from secular, middle-class households. They were accused of planning large-scale terrorist attacks in Toronto and Ottawa, and when they were arrested, they had already purchased vast quantities of bomb-making materials. The core members of the group were close friends from their early high school years, when they had formed a "Religious Awareness Club," which met during lunch hours at school. They also created an online forum where they could share their views on life, religion, and politics. Eventually, a number of the young men and women intermarried while still in their teens.

The group expanded their network when they moved to other parts of the greater Toronto area, attending radical mosques and meeting like-minded young people. They also reached out in international chatrooms, eventually linking up with Irhabi007 prior to his arrest. Through his forum, they were directed to websites providing them with information on how to build bombs. Other militants in Bosnia, Britain, Denmark, Sweden, and even Atlanta, Georgia, also virtually connected through this forum and actively planned attacks. Again, there is no evidence that any of the core Toronto plotters were ever in contact with al Qaeda; the plot was completely homegrown.

What makes these examples of the next generation of terrorists so frightening is the ease with which marginalized youths are able to translate their frustrations into acts of terrorism, often on the back of professed solidarity with terrorists halfway around the world whom they have never met. They seek to belong to a movement larger than themselves, and their violent actions and plans are hatched locally, with advice from others on the Web. Their mode of communication also suggests that they will increasingly evade detection. Without links to known terrorists, this new generation is more difficult to discover through traditional intelligence gathering. Of course, their lack of training and experience could limit their effectiveness. But that's cold comfort for their victims.

Why They Fight

Any strategy to fight these terrorists must be based on an understanding of why they believe what they believe. In other words, what transforms ordinary people into fanatics who use violence for political ends? What leads them to consider themselves special, part of a small vanguard trying to build their version of an Islamist utopia?

The explanation for their behavior is found not in how they think, but rather in how they feel. One of the most common refrains among Islamist radicals is their sense of moral outrage. Before 2003, the most significant source of these feelings were the killings of Muslims in Afghanistan in the 1980s. In the 1990s, it was the fighting in Bosnia, Chechnya, and Kashmir. Then came the second Palestinian intifada beginning in 2000. And since 2003, it has been all about the war in Iraq, which has become the focal point of global moral outrage for Muslims all over the world. Along with the humiliations of Abu Ghraib and Guantánamo, Iraq is monopolizing today's conversations about Islam and the West. On a more local level, governments that appear overly pro-American cause radicals to feel they are the victims of a larger anti-Muslim conspiracy, bridging the perceived local and global attacks against them.

In order for this moral outrage to translate into extremism, the frustrations must be interpreted in a particular way: The violations are deemed part of a unified Western strategy, namely a "war against Islam." That deliberately vague worldview, however, is just a sound bite. The new terrorists are not Islamic scholars. Jihadists volunteering for Iraq are interested not in theological debates but in living out their heroic fantasies.

How various individuals interpret this vision of a "war against Islam" differs from country to country, and it is a major reason why homegrown terrorism within the United States is far less likely than it is in Europe. To a degree, the belief that the United States is a melting pot protects the country from homegrown attacks. Whether or not the United States is a land of opportunity, the important point is that people believe it to be. A recent poll found that 71 percent of Muslim Americans believe in the "American Dream," more than the American public as a whole (64 percent). This is not the case in Europe, where national myths are based on degrees of "Britishness," "Frenchness," or "Germanness." This excludes non-European Muslim immigrants from truly feeling as if they belong.

Feeling marginalized is, of course, no simple springboard to violence. Many people feel they don't belong but don't aspire

to wage violent jihad. What transforms a very small number to become terrorists is mobilization by networks. Until a few years ago, these networks were face-to-face groups. They included local gangs of young immigrants, members of student associations, and study groups at radical mosques. These cliques of friends became radicalized together. The group acted as an echo chamber, amplifying grievances, intensifying bonds to each other, and breeding values that rejected those of their host societies. These natural group dynamics resulted in a spiral of mutual encouragement and escalation, transforming a few young Muslims into dedicated terrorists willing to follow the model of their heroes and sacrifice themselves for comrades and cause. Their turn to violence was a collective decision, rather than an individual one.

During the past two or three years, however, face-to-face radicalization has been replaced by online radicalization. The same support and validation that young people used to derive from their offline peer groups are now found in online forums, which promote the image of the terrorist hero, link users to the online social movement, give them guidance, and instruct them in tactics. These forums, virtual marketplaces for extremist ideas, have become the "invisible hand" that organizes terrorist activities worldwide. The true leader of this violent social movement is the collective discourse on half a dozen influential forums. They are transforming the terrorist movement, attracting ever younger members and now women, who can participate in the discussions.

At present, al Qaeda Central cannot impose discipline on these third-wave wannabes, mostly because it does not know who they are. Without this command and control, each disconnected network acts according to its own understanding and capability, but their collective actions do not amount to any unified long-term goal or strategy. These separate groups cannot coalesce into a physical movement, leaving them condemned to remain leaderless, an online aspiration. Such traits make them particularly volatile and difficult to detect, but they also offer a tantalizing strategy for those who wish to defeat these dangerous individuals: The very seeds of the movement's demise are within the movement itself.

Islamist terrorism will likely disappear for internal reasons—if America has the sense to allow it.

The Beginning of the End?

There has been talk of an al Qaeda resurgence, but the truth is that most of the hard-core members of the first and second waves have been killed or captured. The survival of the social movement they inspired relies on the continued inflow of new members. But this movement is vulnerable to whatever may diminish its appeal among the young. Its allure thrives only at the abstract fantasy level. The few times its aspirations have been translated into reality—the Taliban in Afghanistan, parts of Algeria during its civil war, and more recently in Iraq's Anbar Province—were particularly repulsive to most Muslims.

What's more, a leaderless social movement is permanently at the mercy of its participants. As each generation attempts to define itself in contrast to its predecessor, what appeals to the present generation of young would-be radicals may not appeal to the next. A major source of the present appeal is the anger and moral outrage provoked by the invasion of Iraq. As the Western footprint there fades, so will the appeal of fighting it. And new hotheads in the movement will always push the envelope to make a name for themselves and cause ever escalating atrocities. The magnitude of these horrors will, in turn, likely alienate potential recruits.

The U.S. strategy to counter this terrorist threat continues to be frozen by the horrors of 9/11. It relies more on wishful thinking than on a deep understanding of the enemy. The pursuit of "high-value targets" who were directly involved in the 9/11 operation more than six years ago was an appropriate first step to bring the perpetrators to justice. And the United States has been largely successful in degrading the capability of al Qaeda Central.

But this strategy is not only useless against the leaderless jihad; it is precisely what will help the movement flourish. Radical Islamist terrorism will never disappear because the West defeats it. Instead, it will most likely disappear for internal reasons—if the United States has the sense to allow it to continue on its course and fade away. The main threat to radical Islamist terrorism is the fact that its appeal is self-limiting. The key is to accelerate this process of internal decay. This need not be a long war, unless American policy makes it so.

Terrorist acts must be stripped of glory and reduced to common criminality. Most aspiring terrorists want nothing more than to be elevated to the status of an FBI Most Wanted poster. "[I am] one of the most wanted terrorists on the Internet," Younis Tsouli boasted online a few months before his arrest in 2005. "I have the Feds and the CIA, both would love to catch me. I have MI6 on my back." His ego fed off the respect such bragging brought him in the eyes of other chatroom participants.

Any policy or recognition that puts such people on a pedestal only makes them heroes in each other's eyes—and encourages others to follow their example. These young men aspire to nothing more glorious than to fight uniformed soldiers of the sole remaining superpower. That is why the struggle against these terrorists must be demilitarized and turned over to collaborative law enforcement. The military role should be limited to denying terrorists a sanctuary.

It is equally crucial not to place terrorists who are arrested or killed in the limelight. The temptation to hold press conferences to publicize another "major victory" in the war on terror must be resisted, for it only transforms terrorist criminals into jihadist heroes. The United States underestimates the value of prosecutions, which often can be enormously demoralizing to radical groups. There is no glory in being taken to prison in handcuffs. No jihadi website publishes such pictures. Arrested terrorists fade into oblivion; martyrs live on in popular memory.

This is very much a battle for young Muslims' hearts and minds. Any appearance of persecution for short-term tactical gains will be a strategic defeat on this battlefield. The point is to regain the international moral high ground, which served the United States and its allies so well during the Cold War. With the advent of the Internet, there has been a gradual shift to online networks, where young Muslims share their hopes, dreams, and grievances. That offers an opportunity to encourage voices that reject violence.

It is necessary to reframe the entire debate, from imagined glory to very real horror. Young people must learn that terrorism is about death and destruction, not fame. The voices of the victims must be heard over the bragging and posturing that go on in the online jihadist forums. Only then will the leaderless jihad expire, poisoned by its own toxic message.

Marc Sageman, a forensic psychiatrist and former CIA case officer, is author of *Leaderless Jihad: Terror Networks in the Twenty-First Century* (Philadelphia: University of Pennsylvania Press, 2008).

Al Qaeda at 20 Dead or Alive?

PETER BERGEN

Two decades after al-Qaeda was founded in the Pakistani border city of Peshawar by Osama bin Laden and a handful of veterans of the war against the Soviets in Afghanistan, the group is more famous and feared than ever. But its grand project—to transform the Muslim world into a militant Islamist caliphate—has been, by any measure, a resounding failure.

In large part, that's because Osama bin Laden's strategy for arriving at this Promised Land is a fantasy. Al-Qaeda's leader prides himself on being a big-think strategist, but for all his brains, leadership skills and charisma, he has fastened on an overall strategy that is self-defeating.

Bin Laden's main goal is to bring about regime change in the Middle East and to replace the governments in Cairo and Riyadh with Taliban-style theocracies. He believes that the way to accomplish this is to attack the "far enemy" (the United States), then watch as the supposedly impious, U.S.-backed Muslim regimes he calls the "near enemy" crumble.

This might have worked if the United States had turned out to be a paper tiger that could sustain only a few blows from al-Qaeda. But it didn't. Bin Laden's analysis showed no understanding of the vital interests—oil, Israel and regional stability—that undergird U.S. engagement in the Middle East, let alone the intensity of American outrage that would follow the first direct attack on the continental United States since the British burned the White House in 1814.

In fact, bin Laden's plan resulted in the direct opposite of a U.S. withdrawal from the Middle East. The United States now occupies Iraq, and NATO soldiers patrol the streets of Kandahar, the old de facto capital of bin Laden's Taliban allies. Relations between the United States and most authoritarian Arab regimes, meanwhile, are stronger than ever, based on their shared goal of defeating violent Islamists out for American blood and the regimes' power.

For most leaders, such a complete strategic failure would require a rethinking. Not for bin Laden. He could have formulated a new policy after U.S. forces toppled the Taliban in the winter of 2001, having al-Qaeda and its allies directly attack the sclerotic near-enemy regimes; he could have told his followers that, in strictly practical terms, provoking the world's only superpower would clearly interfere with al-Qaeda's goal of establishing Taliban-style rule from Indonesia to Morocco.

Instead, bin Laden continues to conceive of the United States as his main foe, as he has explained in audio- and videotapes that he has released since 2001. At the same time, al-Qaeda has fatally undermined its claim to be the true representative of all Muslims by killing thousands of them since Sept. 11, 2001. These two strategic blunders are the key reasons why bin Laden and his group will ultimately lose. But don't expect that defeat anytime soon. For now, al-Qaeda continues to gather strength, both as a terrorist/insurgent organization based along the Afghan-Pakistani border and as an ongoing model for violent Islamists around the globe.

So how strong—or weak—is al-Qaeda at 20? Earlier this year, a furious debate erupted in Washington between two influential counterterrorism analysts. On one side is a former CIA case officer, Marc Sageman, who says that the threat from al-Qaeda's core organization is largely over and warns that future attacks will come from the foot soldiers of a "leaderless jihad"—self-starting, homegrown radicals with no formal connection to bin Laden's cadre. On the other side of the debate stands Georgetown University professor Bruce Hoffman, who warns that al-Qaeda is on the march, not on the run.

This debate is hardly academic. If the global jihad has in fact become a leaderless one, terrorism will cease to be a top-tier U.S. national security problem and become a manageable, second-order threat, as it was for most of the 20th century. Leaderless organizations can't mount spectacular operations such as 9/11, which required years of planning and training. On the other hand, if al-Qaeda Central is as strong as Hoffman thinks it is, the United States will have to organize its policies in the Middle East, South Asia and at home around that threat for decades.

Sageman's view of the jihadist threat as local and leaderless is largely shared by key counterterrorism officials in Europe, who told me that they can't find any evidence of al-Qaeda operations in their countries. Baltasar Garzon, a judge who has investigated terrorist groups in Spain for the past decade, says that while bin Laden remains "a fundamental reference point for the al-Qaeda movement," he doesn't see any of the organization's fingerprints in his recent inquiries.

But this view is not shared by top counterterrorism officials in the United Kingdom and the United States. A 2007 U.S. National Intelligence Estimate concluded that al-Qaeda was growing more dangerous, not less.

Why the starkly differing views? Largely because U.S. and British officials are contending with an alarming new phenomenon, the deadly nexus developing between some militant British Muslims and al-Qaeda's new headquarters in Pakistan's lawless borderlands. The lesson of the July 2005 London subway bombings, the foiled 2006 scheme to bring down transatlantic jetliners and several other unnerving plots uncovered in the

United Kingdom is that the bottom-up radicalization described by Sageman becomes really lethal only when the homegrown wannabes manage to make contact with the group that so worries Hoffman, al-Qaeda Central in Pakistan.

"Hotheads in a coffeehouse are a dime a dozen," said Michael Sheehan, who until 2006 was the deputy New York police commissioner responsible for counterterrorism. "Al-Qaeda Central is often the critical element in turning the hotheads into an actual capable cell." Which is why it's so worrisome that counterterrorism officials have noticed dozens of Europeans making their way to the tribal areas of Pakistan in the past couple of years.

That's a major shift. Until 2006, hardcore European jihadists would have traveled to Iraq. But the numbers doing so now have dwindled to almost zero, according to several European counterterrorism officials. That's because al-Qaeda's affiliate in Iraq has committed something tantamount to suicide.

Al-Qaeda in Iraq once held vast swaths of Sunni-dominated turf and helped spark a civil war by targeting Iraqi Shiites. But when the group imposed Taliban-style measures, such as banning smoking and shaving, on Iraq's Sunni population and started killing other insurgents who didn't share its ultra-fundamentalist views, other Sunnis turned against it. Today al-Qaeda in Iraq is dead, at least as an insurgent organization capable of imposing its will on the wider population. It can still perpetrate large-scale atrocities, of course, and could yet spoil Iraq's fragile truce by again attacking Iraqi Shiites. But for the moment, al-Qaeda in Iraq is on the run, demoralized and surrounded by enemies.

While that's good news for Iraq, there are alarming signs elsewhere. The border region of Pakistan and Afghanistan, an area where jihadists operate with something close to impunity, has become a magnet for foreign fighters. One particularly unwelcome development here: Al-Qaeda Central now exerts a great deal of ideological sway over Baitullah Mehsud, the new leader of the Taliban movement inside Pakistan, who has vowed to attack New York and London.

Next door in Afghanistan, the Taliban have also increasingly adopted bin Laden's worldview and tactics, which has helped them launch a dangerously effective insurgency based on sustained suicide attacks and the deft use of IEDs. And bin Laden's influence extends well beyond the Afghanistan-Pakistan theater. The same mainland European counterterrorism officials who are relieved not to be finding al-Qaeda Central cells in their own countries now worry that bin Laden's North African ally, al-Qaeda in the Islamic Maghreb, may be finding recruits among poorly integrated North African immigrants living in France, Belgium, Spain and Italy.

Al-Qaeda's war for hearts and minds goes on, too. Bin Laden once observed that 90 percent of his battle is waged in the media—and here, above all, he remains both relevant and cutting-edge. The most reliable guide to what al-Qaeda and the wider jihadist movement will do have long been bin Laden's public statements.

Since 9/11, bin Laden has issued more than two dozen video- and audiotapes, according to IntelCenter, a government contractor that tracks al-Qaeda's propaganda activities. Those messages have reached untold millions worldwide via TV, the Internet and newspapers. The tapes exhort al-Qaeda's followers to continue to kill Westerners and Jews, and some have also carried specific instructions for militant cells. In the past year, for instance, bin Laden has called for attacks on the Pakistani state—one of the reasons Pakistan saw more suicide attacks in 2007 than at any other time in its history.

Despite al-Qaeda's recent resurgence, I think it highly unlikely that the group will be able to attack inside the United States in the next five years. In the past, al-Qaeda terrorists trying to strike the U.S. homeland have had to slip inside from elsewhere, as the 9/11 hijackers did. No successful past plot has relied on al-Qaeda "sleeper cells" here, and there is little evidence that such cells exist today. Moreover, the United States is a much harder target than it was before 9/11. The U.S. government is on alert, as are ordinary citizens. (Just ask the would-be shoe-bomber, Richard Reid.)

Of course, homegrown terrorists inspired by al-Qaeda might carry out a small-bore attack inside the United States, although the U.S. Muslim community, which is far better integrated than its European counterparts, has produced few violent radicals. And al-Qaeda itself remains quite capable of attacking a wide range of U.S. interests overseas, killing U.S. soldiers in Iraq and Afghanistan and targeting U.S. embassies. But on balance, we have less to fear from al-Qaeda now than we did in 2001.

We would also be far better off if we managed to kill or capture al-Qaeda's innovative chief. So what is the U.S.-led hunt for bin Laden turning up? The short answer is nothing. Washington hasn't had a solid lead on him since radio intercepts placed him at the battle of Tora Bora in eastern Afghanistan in December 2001. U.S. intelligence officials widely assume that he is now in or near Pakistan's tribal areas—a particularly shrewd hiding place, according to Arthur Keller, a former CIA officer who ran a spy network there in 2006.

Keller told me that al-Qaeda's leaders have excellent operational security. "They have had a Darwinian education in what can give them away, and their tradecraft has improved as we have eliminated some of the less careful members of their organization," he noted. "They're hiding in a sea of people who are very xenophobic of outsiders, so it's a very, very tough nut to crack."

No matter what bin Laden's fate, Muslims around the world are increasingly taking a dim view of his group and its suicide operations. In the late 1990s, bin Laden was a folk hero to many Muslims. But since 2003, as al-Qaeda and its affiliates have killed Muslim civilians by the thousands from Casablanca to Kabul, support for bin Laden has nose-dived, according to Pew polls taken in key Muslim countries such as Indonesia and Pakistan.

At 20, al-Qaeda is losing its war, but its influence will live on. As Michael Scheuer, who founded the CIA's bin Laden unit in 1996, points out, "Their mission is accomplished: worldwide instigation and inspiration." To our grief, that legacy will endure, even after al-Qaeda is defeated.

PETER BERGEN is a fellow at both the New America Foundation and New York University's Center on Law and Security. He is the author of *The Osama bin Laden I Know*.

Test-Your-Knowledge Form

We encourage you to photocopy and use this page as a tool to assess how the articles in *Annual Editions* expand on the information in your textbook. By reflecting on the articles you will gain enhanced text information. You can also access this useful form on a product's book support website at *http://www.mhcls.com*.

NAME: DATE:

_____

TITLE AND NUMBER OF ARTICLE:

_____

BRIEFLY STATE THE MAIN IDEA OF THIS ARTICLE:

_____

LIST THREE IMPORTANT FACTS THAT THE AUTHOR USES TO SUPPORT THE MAIN IDEA:

_____

WHAT INFORMATION OR IDEAS DISCUSSED IN THIS ARTICLE ARE ALSO DISCUSSED IN YOUR TEXTBOOK OR OTHER READINGS THAT YOU HAVE DONE? LIST THE TEXTBOOK CHAPTERS AND PAGE NUMBERS:

_____

LIST ANY EXAMPLES OF BIAS OR FAULTY REASONING THAT YOU FOUND IN THE ARTICLE:

_____

LIST ANY NEW TERMS/CONCEPTS THAT WERE DISCUSSED IN THE ARTICLE, AND WRITE A SHORT DEFINITION:

We Want Your Advice

ANNUAL EDITIONS revisions depend on two major opinion sources: one is our Advisory Board, listed in the front of this volume, which works with us in scanning the thousands of articles published in the public press each year; the other is you—the person actually using the book. Please help us and the users of the next edition by completing the prepaid article rating form on this page and returning it to us. Thank you for your help!

ANNUAL EDITIONS: Violence and Terrorism 10/11

ARTICLE RATING FORM

Here is an opportunity for you to have direct input into the next revision of this volume.
We would like you to rate each of the articles listed below, using the following scale:

1. **Excellent: should definitely be retained**
2. **Above average: should probably be retained**
3. **Below average: should probably be deleted**
4. **Poor: should definitely be deleted**

Your ratings will play a vital part in the next revision.
Please mail this prepaid form to us as soon as possible.
Thanks for your help!

RATING	ARTICLE	RATING	ARTICLE
	1. How to Define Terrorism		20. White-Pride Mom
	2. What Makes a Terrorist?		21. The Al-Qaeda Media Machine
	3. The Myth of the Invincible Terrorist		22. Nets of Terror: Terrorist Activity on the Internet
	4. From the H-Bomb to the Human Bomb		23. Jihad with a Hip-Hop Pose Is an Easier Sell with Youth
	5. The Al Qaeda Weapons Race Continues		24. The Globe of Villages: Digital Media and the Rise of Homegrown Terrorism
	6. Terrorism and Extortion		
	7. Toy Soldiers: The Youth Factor in the War on Terror		25. Congress and the "YouTube War"
	8. Rogue Operators		26. Qutbism: An Ideology of Islamic-Fascism
	9. Iran's Suicide Brigades: Terrorism Resurgent		27. In Search of Moderate Muslims
	10. The Growing Syrian Missile Threat: Syria after Lebanon		28. The Madrassa Scapegoat
			29. Female Suicide Bombers: A Global Trend
	11. Chávez Bides His Time		30. The Bomb under the Abaya
	12. Trail of Terror		31. Picked Last: Women and Terrorism
	13. Peace at Last?		32. Knowing the Enemy
	14. Tamil Tiger Trap		33. Are We Ready Yet?
	15. In Europe, Where's the Hate?		34. Intelligence and the War on Terror: How Dirty Are We Willing to Get Our Hands?
	16. Incidents of Terrorism in the United States, 1997–2005		
			35. Air Security: Why You're Not as Safe as You Think
	17. The Year in Hate: Number of Hate Groups Tops 900		36. The Shifting Face of Violence
	18. Green Rage		37. The Next Generation of Terror
	19. When Activists Attack: Companies Square Off against Animal Rights Groups		38. Al Qaeda at 20 Dead or Alive?

ABOUT YOU

Name   Date

Are you a teacher? ☐ A student? ☐
Your school's name

Department

Address   City   State   Zip

School telephone #

YOUR COMMENTS ARE IMPORTANT TO US!

Please fill in the following information:
For which course did you use this book?

Did you use a text with this ANNUAL EDITION? ☐ yes ☐ no
What was the title of the text?

What are your general reactions to the Annual Editions concept?

Have you read any pertinent articles recently that you think should be included in the next edition? Explain.

Are there any articles that you feel should be replaced in the next edition? Why?

Are there any World Wide Websites that you feel should be included in the next edition? Please annotate.

May we contact you for editorial input? ☐ yes ☐ no
May we quote your comments? ☐ yes ☐ no

NOTES

NOTES

NOTES

NOTES

NOTES

NOTES

NOTES

NOTES